ERGONOMICS AT WORK

2ND EDITION

David J. Oborne
University College of Swansea

JOHN WILEY & SONS

Chichester · New York · Brisbane · Toronto · Singapore

Copyright © 1987 by John Wiley & Sons Ltd.

Reprinted November 1988 (pbk)
Reprinted August 1989
Reprinted March 1991
Reprinted June 1992

Library of Congress Cataloging-in-Publication Data:

Oborne, David J.,
  Ergonomics at work.   .

  Includes indexes.
  1. Human engineering. I. Title.
TA166.025 1987   620.8′2   86-24567

ISBN 0 471 90943 2
ISBN 0 471 90942 4 (pbk.)

British Library of Congress Cataloguing in Publication Data:

Oborne, David J.,
  Ergonomics at work.—2nd ed.
  1. Human engineering
  I. Title
  620.8′2   TA166

ISBN 0 471 90943 2
ISBN 0 471 90942 4 (pbk)

Typeset by Witwell Ltd., Liverpool
Printed and bound in Great Britain by Courier International Ltd., East Kilbride

CONTENTS

ACKNOWLEDGEMENT

I should like to acknowledge the help given to me by Mr Paul Wood of the Swansea Psychology Department, in preparing the figures for this book.

PREFACE TO THE SECOND EDITION

The first Edition of *Ergonomics at Work* took an unashamedly evangelical stance. Through explanation and description of the available literature, its aim was to provide the reader with a reasonable grounding in the bases of ergonomics, and to illustrate the fundamental role that ergonomics (and its American sister discipline human factors) takes in the modern, industrialized society in which we live. Without doubt, space would not have been conquered, computers would not have been used effectively, working practices would not be as safe as they are without the rise and continued discipline of ergonomics. The first edition of this volume illustrated this fact.

But in only a short passage of time, an emerging and important discipline such as ergonomics produces considerable additional information as its disciples push back the frontiers of its knowledge. Over only the past four years, increases in our knowledge concerning a number of different human activities with work have meant that an update and expansion of *Ergonomics at Work* has become necessary.

In this edition, a number of specific areas included within the first edition have been expanded: more details are provided relating to our body capacities in lifting and transporting loads, in our use of displayed material — particularly with the recent 'explosion' of electronic information systems — and of controlling the system. Further material has been included relating to the environment: lighting, noise and vibration, for example. Indeed, although throughout the book the chapters' structures remain essentially the same, considerable additional material will be obvious in a number of chapters.

However, the basic crusading approach remains. This second edition still aims to convert people to the ergonomics view of the world. That is that people are at the centre of events; that systems will not be operated efficiently, comfortably or safely without understanding the basic behaviour of the operator within the system — what he or she can do and wants to do. Any working system, in the office, shop-floor, or organization, that includes people interacting either with other people or with their physical environment needs ergonomics. This book explains why, how and where.

David J. Oborne
Swansea, 1986

PREFACE TO THE FIRST EDITION

Ergonomics experienced its birth during the Second World War and it is perhaps fitting that during this period the cry was continuously heard 'Give us the tools, and we will finish the job'. The 'job' then was particularly straightforward: victory over a fearsome aggressor. The present day 'job' is perhaps more diverse: victory over the oppressive forces which continue to make work less productive, less pleasant, less comfortable and less safe.

Today, Churchill's plea is as real as it was during the dark days of the Second World War. Modern work would be almost impossible without adequate tools: a screwdriver to turn a screw, or a hammer to force home a nail. Microscopes allow otherwise invisible objects to become visible; and computers supplement people's cognitive capacities to enable them to perform operations unthinkable a decade or so ago.

Unfortunately, however, machines suffer at least one major drawback, they have to be operated: the screwdriver must be turned, the hammer wielded, the microscope adjusted, and the computer programmed. The tools are useless without the energy and decision-making abilities of the human operator. Until the era arrives of machines which are able to carry out intelligent thought, make and take decisions and perform complex actions, the working system needs the help of 'man'. This symbiotic relationship between the human operator and the environment must remain.

This book is concerned with the ways in which the working relationship can be adapted to perform at its most efficient. It will consider how the behaviour of both the operator in the system and the system itself can either enhance or reduce the system's effectiveness. In short it will examine the various ways in which the two major components in the system — 'man' and 'environment' — interact and communicate with each other.

In some senses the book is intended to be evangelical in its approach. It does not set out to provide the reader with a comprehensive databank with which he can design an environment. Rather it intends to present the fundamental aspects of man–machine interactions, and to explain ergonomics (and its American sister discipline human factors) and its role within the context of modern day work. It will emphasize aspects of the working situation which need to be considered, and explain the reasons why various solutions are proposed. It then hopes to motivate and to point the reader in the right direction to discover more about the various facets of the man–environment interaction within his own working system.

'Information' and 'communication' are the two keywords to this interactive process; one is transferred by the other. As the reader progresses through this book he should become aware of their importance. Without them no interaction can take place. More importantly if they are of poor quality, then very poor interaction will occur. Either of these lead to inefficient, uncomfortable or unsafe situations which are good for neither the operator nor the employer.

After the first chapter which considers ergonomics in its widest context (its basis and history, its position amongst the disciplines, and its financial value), the following two chapters examine the way in which the human body allows the communicative processes to occur. Chapter 2 considers the communication channels from the environment into the operator, through the senses, while Chapter 3 examines the flow in the opposite direction, through the operator's limbs to the environment.

In the following three chapters, the behavioural aspects of these communication channels will be discussed. First communication between operators (primarily sensory); second communication between the environment and the operators (again primarily sensory) and finally communication between the operators and the environment (mainly using the limbs, but also sensory aspects).

Having considered these communication requirements in fine detail, Chapters 7, 8 and 9 discusses the ways of arranging the environment to the operator's benefit — again to enhance the communication channels. In Chapter 7 the operator's immediate work area — perhaps the machine, the console or even the writing pad — is investigated. Chapter 8 then discusses the most appropriate ways of building up the workplace — which consists of many machines and men — again to enhance the communication. Finally, and possibly as an extension of Chapter 8, Chapter 9 considers the function and value of appropriate seating and posture at work.

At this point, then, the communication channels are open and are efficient. However, they do not operate *in vacuo*. Their efficiency can be affected, sometimes radically, by the environment in which the operator is expected to perform. Four environmental aspects are considered in Chapters 10 and 11: the vibration, the noise, the temperature, and the illumination. Although it is stressed that these are by no means the only environments at work, they are, perhaps, the most relevant for most operators.

The purpose of Chapters 12 and 13 is to demonstrate the importance of applying the ergonomic principles discussed and described earlier. Chapter 12 deals specifically with safety, and illustrates the cost to the individual, to the organization, and to the nation, of unsafe behaviour and environments. It demonstrates how the disruption of efficient communication channels and the establishment of alternative and less optimal channels can reduce safety and lead to accidents.

Death, injury and substandard work, however, are not the only result of a lack of ergonomic considerations, as Chapter 13 illustrates. In many situations it can lead to reduced efficiency caused by poor feedback to the operator. In this way the maintenance of system effectiveness and the inspection process can suffer

Having roused the reader to consider his sytem more fully, Chapter 14 illustrates many of the pitfalls ready to trap the unwary investigator who has to deal with the behaviour of human beings as subject-matter in an experimental design. Armed with such information, however, it is hoped that the reader will be in a fit position to progress further in implementing ergonomic solutions to the man–environment interaction problems.

To paraphrase Churchill, after having read this book it is hoped that the reader will cry 'Give us the ergonomic tools, tools that have been designed so that we can interact efficiently with them, and we will finish the job more effectively'.

David J. Oborne

CHAPTER 1

ERGONOMICS: PAST AND PRESENT

Over recent years the word 'ergonomics' has become widely used in many different situations: in conversations at work, in advertisements, in the media, by people both in and out of the 'know'. Gradually, the message is emerging that ergonomics has value; that it eases our interactions with the man-made environment. But what really is ergonomics? What is its central theme? What use is it and why should it be considered at all? This book will address many of these questions.

ERGONOMICS AND PROCRUSTES

In many respects, ergonomics is a concept; an idea. It is a way of looking at the world, of thinking about people at work (any type of work) and how they cope with it — their environment, their machines and their working equipment. As this book will demonstrate, ergonomics takes the central argument that since 'man' inhabited this world well before machines (indeed, 'man' invented the machines) it is only appropriate that 'man' remains in full operating control of them. The 'machines' and the working environment, then, should be adapted to fit 'man's' thoughts, wishes and abilities.

This is the way in which ergonomists view working situations. By understanding how people behave at work, how they interact with their environment and their machines at a physical and an emotional level, it is possible to create working environments that do not require more than the operator is able to give. When this happens, when 'man' and machine are in perfect harmony, productive output is likely to be increased.

Having painted a broad picture of an ergonomist's view of the world it is interesting to consider an equally prevalent, but opposite, view: that people are more adaptable than their machines and environments and so it is easier to make *them* 'fit' their surroundings. This is often called the 'Proscrustean approach', a term which is borrowed from Greek mythology.

Once upon a time there was a Greek robber called Procrustes who had devised an exceedingly cunning way of extorting money from weary travellers unfortunate enough to pass his door. He simply offered them lavish hospitality on the strict understanding that they would either sleep in one of his spare beds or pay for the food and drink they had consumed. If the offer of a bed was accepted, as most frequently it was, then Procrustes made an additional stipulation: that the traveller should fit the bed exactly. After being wined and dined the unsuspecting victim would be shown to the bedchamber in which there were two beds; one was very long, the other very short but neither was the correct size to accommodate the unfortunate person. Now Procrustes' trick became apparent even to the least intelligent. Unless the exorbitant fees were paid, Procrustes would threaten to *make* his victims fit one or other of the beds — either by putting them on the short bed and cutting off their legs, or by stretching their bodies enough to fit the long bed. Needless to say, most tired travellers took the easy way out and paid up.

There is, of course, a moral to this tale.

Ever since man first began to interact with the environment in any complex way, this form of Procrustean approach has been widespread. Industrial man in particular has constantly been 'tailored' to 'fit' the demands of the physical world, and most victims accept a fair degree of discomfort and disability without too much fuss. In metaphorical terms, arms have been elongated to reach inaccessible controls and perceptual abilities stretched to hear or to see virtually inaudible or invisible signals. At the other end of the Procrustean scale, legs have frequently been cut to fit cramped workplaces and cognitive capacities shrunk to cope with boring tasks.

Industrial expansion and increased complexity of both work and machines have compounded such problems. Because of a poor 'fit' between the human operator and the environment, lives have been lost, productivity reduced, and errors incurred in countless thousands of cases. Until relatively recently the demands of the environment have been paramount, with the needs and abilities of the person in the environment taking only secondary importance.

Over the years, then, there has been a prevailing view that people should be adapted in a Procrustean way to the needs of the working conditions — albeit using rather more humane methods than stretching or amputation, such as training them to work in less than ideal situations. Unfortunately for this view, however, considerable evidence exists to demonstrate that training alone is not a useful solution to ensure high productivity. There are three reasons for this: first, the cost of making the operator fit the environment; second, the effectiveness of this approach; and third, the possible disruption of performance which can occur when a person is placed under stress.

In financial terms, training people to perform either difficult tasks or tasks that are not designed with the operator in mind is often very expensive. Both errors and training time are likely to increase, and some examples of this will be given later. It is accepted, of course, that training schedules cannot be dispensed with altogether but, as will be shown throughout this book, in the majority of cases training and production times can be reduced considerably if the environment is designed to reflect the operator's abilities.

A Procrustean type of training approach is also highly suspect from the viewpoint of effectiveness. Although operators can be trained to fair levels of competence, training alone will not solve their problems and expand their output. With increasingly complex industrial plant and machinery the trained working behaviour may still not be effective enough if the operator's total environment is not suitably considered. Further help is often needed in the form of appropriately designed and positioned controls, perceptible displays and other important features before the effects of any training can be maximized. An example of this point is provided in a study by Chaney and Teel (1967), who compared the detection efficiency of experienced machine parts inspectors after either a four-hour training programme or after being given a set of specially designed visual aids and displays. Whereas the training programme increased defect detection by 32 per cent, using appropriate visual aids resulted in a 42 per cent increase. Although training was useful, therefore, providing an appropriately designed environment was even more so.

Training effectiveness can also be considered in terms of the degree to which the trained behaviour is maintained without practice. In this respect Ellis and Hill (1978) showed that with short viewing times numbers produced by the now common seven-segment liquid crystal displays (see Chapter 5) are more difficult to read (they lead to more reading errors) than are conventional numbers. Although training helped to overcome these difficulties, performance decreased significantly over a month without the opportunity for practice. When having to use poor equipment, then, skills learned through training are difficult to sustain.

The final limitation of the Procrustean approach is one of the most important and, perhaps, the most insidious. As Taylor and Garvey (1966) point out, no matter how well an operator has been trained, if the behaviours learned are inappropriate to the task they can easily become disrupted under stress so that the wrong responses may be made. For example, Murrell (1971) cites the case of an hydraulic press which was damaged during a stress-inducing emergency. To raise the press a lever needed to be pushed down, an action which is contrary to normal expectations (as will be seen in Chapter 7 it is usually expected that a control should be *raised* to make an associated part move upwards). Although the operator had been trained to carry out this action very efficiently under ordinary conditions, when the emergency occurred and the press needed to be raised in a hurry he forgot his training and 'did what came naturally' — he quickly pulled the lever up. This caused the platen to fall and the press was wrecked. In the majority of cases (and using normally accepted training regimes) no amount of training will overcome the tendency of an operator to 'do what comes naturally' under stress. Reasons why this may occur will be given later, but they relate primarily to the amount of 'attention' that the operator is able to give to any one part of the task.

It is clear from these examples that training alone will not use the human operator's full potential. Only when training schedules are linked to a full understanding of the task being carried out, so that the work is designed to be in harmony with the operator's physical, cognitive and emotional capacities will performance be optimal under a range of conditions. Ergonomics' role is to highlight this concordance between the environment and the operator.

The role of ergonomics, then, is to help redress the balance which has previously been biased towards a predominantly Procrustean approach. It does this by understanding and measuring the human operator's capabilities and then arranging the environment to fit them. As Rodger and Cavanagh (1962) describe it, ergonomics attempts to 'fit the job to the man' rather than to 'fit the man to the job'.

THE RISE OF ERGONOMICS

Any new being has a date on which it was introduced to the world, and ergonomics' birth date can be pinpointed fairly accurately to 12 July 1949. On this day a meeting was held at the British Admiralty at which an interdisciplinary group was formed (the Human Research Group) for those interested in human work problems (see Murrell, 1980; Edholm and Murrell, 1973). Later, at a meeting on 16 February 1950, the term *ergonomics* (from the Greek; *ergon* — work; *nomos* — natural laws) was adopted and the discipline could finally be said to be born. (It should be pointed out, however, that the name *ergonomics* is not new. Seminara (1979) points out that it was first used in Poland by Professor Wojciech Jastrzebowski in an article published in 1857.)

Of course, as with a human being, the fact that a birth has occurred implies that a great deal of thought and effort has been expanded prior to the big event. Like any other living creature, an idea has to be conceived, nurtured and developed properly before it is born. Ergonomics (and its American sister discipline, human factors) received considerable prenatal care over many decades.

Although the birth date of ergonomics can be fairly well defined, the gestation period of this new discipline was long and tortuous, and certainly no precise date can be given for its conception. However, the initial rise of interest in the relationship between man and the working environment could be said to have commenced at about the time of the First World War. Workers in munition factories were essential in maintaining the war effort, but the drive for higher arms output created a number of unforseen complications in Great Britain. The attempt to resolve these problems led, in 1915, to the establishment of the Health of Munitions Workers' Committee which included some individuals who were trained in physiology and psychology among its investigators. At the end of the war, this Committee was reconstituted as the Industrial Fatigue Research Board (IFRB), chiefly to carry out research into fatigue problems in industry.

In 1929 the IFRB was renamed the Industrial Health Research Board and its scope broadened to investigate general conditions of industrial employment, 'particularly with regard to the preservation of health among the workers and to industrial efficiency'. It employed people who were trained as psychologists, physiologists, physicians and engineers and who worked, both separately and together, on problems covering a wide area. These included posture, carrying loads, the physique of working men and women, rest pauses, inspection, lighting, heating, ventilation and 'music-while-you-work' — as well as selection and training. Two features of the work carried out between the wars are important. First, it was at times interdisciplinary. Second, it was largely 'exploratory in character being in the nature of a probing of the "natural history" of industry'. Already, then, working behaviour and its role in productive outcomes was being explored.

The outbreak of the Second World War saw a rapid development in the military field. As if the stresses of battle were not enough, however, the military equipment developed in response to the need to fight in different environments, with different people and in different ways soon became extremely complex and very difficult to use. The operating speeds demanded, for example, were often so high that the additional stresses caused personnel either to fail to get the best out of their equipment or to suffer operational breakdown. It became essential, therefore, for more to be known about people's performance capabilities and limitations. Naturally this produced extensive research programmes in many diverse fields and it was as reaction to the desire to draw together this new-found knowledge that the Admiralty meeting took place. With this meeting the modern discipline of *ergonomics* was finally born.

As this book will illustrate, from its birth ergonomics has grown into a mature adult, without whose help many of the industrial and manufacturing steps taken since the Second World War could not have been made so efficiently: safely harnessing natural energy supplies often in adverse environments; effectively exploiting communications technology; radically improving domestic design and, of course, dramatically travelling beyond the confines of our world to conquer space itself. All of these activities and more would have been impossible without considering the ergonomic implications. Quite simply they all need people, and people would be unable to do them if considerable thought had not gone into designing systems to fit their cognitive and physical capacities.

THE SCOPE OF ERGONOMICS

Ergonomics, then, developed via the interests of a number of different professions and it still remains a multidisciplinary field of study. To provide information about working behaviour and what people can and cannot do, it crosses the boundaries between scientific and professional disciplines and draws on the data, findings, principles and concepts of each. Present-day ergonomics is an amalgam of physiology, anatomy and medicine as one branch; physiological and experimental psychology as another; and physics and engineering as a third. The biological sciences provide information about the body's structure: the operator's physical capabilities and limitations; body dimensions; how much can be lifted; the physical pressures that can be endured, etc. Physiological psychology deals with ways in which the brain and nervous system function and determine behaviour; while experimental psychologists study the basic ways in which individuals use their body to behave, to perceive, to learn, to remember, to control movements, etc. Finally physics and engineering provide similar information about the machine and the physical environment with which the operator has to contend. In many respects the chapters in this book will follow these influences.

From these areas an ergonomist takes and integrates information to maximize the operator's safety, efficiency and performance reliability, to make the task easier to learn and to increase feelings of comfort.

These criteria, however, are by no means independent. For example, efficiency depends on accuracy, but accuracy is not its only component — others include reliability, speed, effort and fatigue. Arguing in the same vein, ergonomics seeks to increase safety. In turn this should result in reduced time lost through accidents and (perhaps) a corresponding increase in (worker) efficiency. By the same token, however, safety will itself depend on efficiency. Indeed, this book will give many examples which show that the margin of safety left in an operation is largely a function of the operator's speed or reliability.

A further aim of ergonomics is to reduce operator unpredictability, in other words to increase reliability. Thus the human operator should not only be fast and efficient but reliably so. Again, although reliability is related to accuracy they may also act independently. An operator may perform a task accurately most of the time but, because of some intermittent action of the work situation, this accuracy may be unreliable.

The question of ease of learning has already been discussed. Thus a system which has been designed so that the individual tasks are easier to learn will reduce training time and costs, and may produce fewer errors under stress.

The final aspect, comfort, is a subjective criterion that is becoming increasingly important in present-day situations and refers to a sense of wellbeing and ease induced by the system. The concept of comfort, and the controversies surrounding its definition will be discussed in later chapters, but it is sufficient to point out here that an uncomfortable operator will be prone to errors and is likely to perform less efficiently.

In summary, therefore, the ergonomist's task is first to determine the capabilities of the operator and then to attempt to build a workable system around these capabilities. Only when this approach has been fully accepted can the spirit of Procrustes finally be said to be exorcised.

MAN-MACHINE SYSTEMS

Ergonomics seeks to maximize safety, efficiency and comfort by shaping the 'machine' (or indeed any aspect of the workplace that has to be used) to the operator's capabilities. By linking the machine to the person in this way (*and in this direction*) a relationship is established between the two components, so that the machine presents information to the operator via the operator's sensory apparatus to which a response may be made in some way — perhaps to alter the machine's state via various controls. For example, to drive a car safely and efficiently along a road, a relationship needs to be built up between the driver and the vehicle such that any deviation of the car from a prescribed path (which is determined by both the driver and the road's shape and conditions) will be displayed back to the driver via the visual (and perhaps auditory) senses. These deviations can then be corrected by limb movements via the steering-wheel and perhaps the brake or accelerator pedal. In their turn, the corrections will be perceived as displayed information and the sequence continued until the journey's end. In this way information passes from the machine to the person and back to the machine in a closed, information-control, loop (see Figure 1.1).

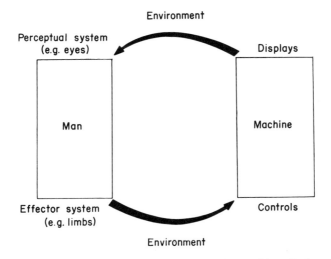

Figure 1.1 The 'man-machine' loop. The machine displays information to the operator who uses controls to affect the machine. The environment can interfere with the efficiency of this loop

Many examples of single man-machine loops can be seen in a range of different work situations. However, in modern-day working environments these single loops are often combined to produce more complex behavioural systems which, being composed of groups of different components (both people and machines, and parts of people and parts of machines) have to be designed to work together.

It is the ergonomist's task to preserve and to enhance the operation of complex loops of this nature. For example, the speed of information transmission to the car driver may be increased (perhaps by a cleaner windscreen or by more understandable road signs) or the operation of a control may be made more efficient (perhaps by servo-assisted steering or by altering the control type, position or dimensions). Similarly, knowing something about the antecedents and effects of, say, boredom might help to improve the driver's reactions to displayed signals; while understanding something of the behaviour of pedestrians might help in the design of vehicles, roads and footpaths that will contribute to road safety and reduce the frequency and severity of pedestrian-vehicle contacts.

The car driver analogy illustrates some of the problems that face ergonomists when attempting to design environments to fit the human operator: for a number of reasons the simple single man-machine loop does not exist in the 'real-world'. Things are far more complex and in working situations many loops are often combined to produce more complex systems. Being composed of groups of different components (both operators and 'machines'), these must be designed to work together. From an ergonomics viewpoint such combinations can create many problems: two loops may act efficiently when considered separately, but when combined into a simple system they might work antagonistically owing to unexpected interactions. For example, one loop may involve an operator pushing a lever in response to a deflection on a display. A second loop might require a button to be pushed in response to a warning sound. Taken separately the two loops may work extremely efficiently: the display is well designed, the lever compatible with the operator's force capabilities, the warning sound audible and attention getting and the push-button easy to use. When operating together, however, the two loops might interact to cause the operator's normally efficient behaviour to break down. For example, if put in the 'wrong' place, the operator's natural response may be to operate (incorrectly) the lever in response to the warning sound and attempt to change (unsuccessfully) the machine state by pushing the button. It is not too difficult to conceive how problems of this nature can be increased in proportion to the number of extra loops which are added to the system.

A second problem concerns the effect of the environment in which these information-control loops operate. As Figure 1.1 illustrates, the environment's physical and social aspects can affect the efficient operation of these loops. For example, an operator's ability to see a message on a computer screen can be interrupted simply by the sun appearing from behind a cloud and producing glare on the screen; noise can interfere with an otherwise audible auditory message; the presence of other people walking or talking nearby can disrupt concentration. Many hundreds of examples could be given to illustrate the fact that the quality of information transmitted from the operator to the system and back again is mediated by the environment.

For this reason, the emphasis of modern ergonomics has been to investigate the operator and the environment as equal partners within the total working system, rather than to examine in minute detail the components which constitute any one man–machine loop. Ergonomics, therefore, seeks to consider aspects of the job beyond a 'knobs and dials' approach, 'beyond the panel' (Murrell, 1969), to the man–machine system — to the *total* interaction between the operator and the environment.

Work and Performance

With all of the important control loops having to be taken into account, it is clear that the interaction between an operator and the environment is a very complex event. It is now important to question how this complexity can interfere with work performance — and the converse: how reducing the task complexity and creating a working environment that 'fits' the capacities of the operator can increase performance.

The relationship between the task's demands and the operator's performance can be described fairly simply by an inverted-U relationship as shown in Figure 1.2. As can be seen only when the task (environmental) demands are within a narrow, middle range will performance be highest. The continuum which underlies the task demands feature of the relationship is actually operator arousal which is a concept that refers, essentially, to the amount of brain activity (indeed, it is often measured using electroencephalography (EEG)). Thus, when a person is asleep or drowsy then brain activity or arousal is low; when under stress arousal is high (this is often accompanied by such physiological reactions as sweating.)

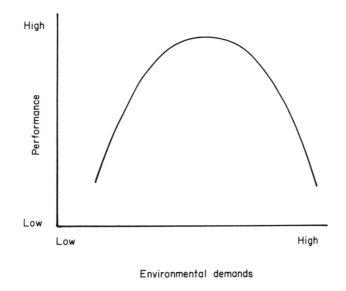

Figure 1.2 The hypothetical inverted-U relationship of environmental demands versus performance

The importance of this relationship lies in the fact that an individual's arousal level is related to the amount of external and internal stimulation received. In this respect the nature of the task and the environment is clearly a varying source of stimulation, as, too, is the operator' own emotional state. So, during periods of low stimulation — perhaps from a boring job, or when signals are infrequent — because arousal is low so will be performance. Similarly, cases in which the stimulation is too high can cause reduced performance levels. Too much noise, for example, or performing tasks that are difficult or stressful, or have been designed without considering the operator's needs can help to increase arousal levels and reduce performance ability.

Unfortunately the inverted-U arousal/performance curve is only a general relationship. Both the shape of the curve and the level of arousal at which performance is optimum depend on characteristics of the operator and the type of stimulation. Personality and intelligence are just two individual characteristics that can alter the relationship. For this reason it is not possible to provide 'tables' of the optimum arousal/stimulation levels. All that can be done is to recognize the existence of the relationship and ensure that the working system neither over nor under stimulates the individuals concerned. If the environment is found to be less than optimum, then appropriate steps can be taken either to increase or reduce the levels of stimulation. For example, Fox (1983) discusses the value of industrial music as a means of increasing arousal levels for boring, repetitive tasks.

Before leaving the discussion of the arousal/performance relationship, it should be emphasized that an operator obtains stimulation from a number of features at work: physical, physiological, social, personal, etc. Each can operate to raise or to lower the overall arousal level. The implication of this is that the value of an otherwise 'ideal' physical environment may be reduced if the operator's arousal is increased or lowered by say, bad social relationships with colleagues or worries at home. Of course, such stressors may act detrimentally on one occasion and not on another.

As well as describing this task/performance relationship in terms of an arousal model, attempts have also been made to model the effects in terms of 'mental capacity' (for example, Brown and Poulton, 1961; Brown, 1965; Ogden, Levine and Eisner, 1979). In essence this descriptive model suggests that an operator brings to a task a limited capacity to perform that task. Provided the capacity is not exceeded, the task will be executed efficiently. Performance is reduced, however, if the task demands more than the operator is able to give — often because other, secondary, features of the task to be performed intrude. Wetherall (1981) provides a review of the extent to which different types of secondary task can detrimentally affect various types of activity.

The essential value of this model lies in the fact that it suggests that when performing a task some sort of trade-off often takes place between the demands of the task and environment on the one hand, and the operator's own abilities on the other. The spare mental capacity model, therefore, suggests that any increased requirements made by less-than-optimum working situations can be compensated by additional operator effort. For example, when working a lathe an operator may normally be able to accommodate poor environmental conditions without any outward adverse effects simply because more of the limited spare mental capacity is used — the operator 'works' hard or 'concentrates' more. If the task and environment demand too much, however (perhaps other machines start up causing increased noise levels, and so increased stimulation) the spare mental capacity that was otherwise used by the task will be exhausted with resultant reductions in performance. The additional work required, therefore, was the 'straw that broke the camel's back'. In terms of ergonomics' philosophy, it is likely that a difficult task or one which is not designed to 'fit' the operator will leave less spare mental capacity and will be affected quicker and to a greater extent than would an easier or more sensibly designed task.

The implications of these two models, therefore, are clear. Operators are able to adapt to work in less than optimum conditions but only at a cost. Provided the environment does not demand more spare mental capacity than is available, performance will be maintained although at a level which is related in some way to the arousing qualities of the task. Too much demand will reduce efficiency because of increased arousal and reduced spare mental capacity.

Allocating Functions between Man and Machine

It has been argued that one of the first and most important problems in man–machine system design concerns allocating functions between the operator and the machine. What functions of the system should be assigned to people and what to machines? Or, what kind of things can and should human operators be doing in a man–machine system?

In response to questions such as these, a number of authors have attempted to compile lists of operations which are carried out most efficiently by people and by machines (for example, Chapanis, 1960; Murrell, 1971). Taken together these lists suggest that man is a better decision-maker, particularly in cases in which flexibility is required and unexpected events may occur; is able to improvise; has a fund of past experience; and is able to perceive and to interpret complex forms involving depth, space and pattern. Machines, on the other hand, are highly efficient computing, integration and differentiation devices; are able to deal with predictable events in a reliable fashion; and are useful in hazardous environments. Even with modern computing equipment, many of these distinctions still hold true. Price (1985), for example, has described a number of such lists and has evaluated their potential.

Although such lists are helpful in directing an ergonomist's thinking towards man–machine problems, and providing reminders of some of the characteristics that people and machines have as systems components, they do tend to lose sight of the basic nature of a system containing humans and machines, and the ways in which these components may interact. For example, before deciding on the respective advantages and disadvantages of 'man' and machine one also needs to know something about the operator's preferences. A person who does not accept willingly some of the necessary tasks may cause undesirable behaviours such as absenteeism, strikes, and reduced productivity.

In addition, Chapanis (1965a) suggests three further problems: First, general man–machine comparisons can be wrong or misleading. In many cases the system itself determines the adequacy of its individual components. For example, the general statement that 'man' is superior to a machine for decision-making tasks is just that — a general statement. It cannot be true for all people or for all machines.

The second argument that Chapanis raises is that it is not always important to decide which component can do a particular job better. In many cases the question should be 'is the component good enough for the job?' Fitts (1962) rephrases this question to ask 'which component will do an adequate job for less money, weight or power, or with a smaller probability of failure and less need for maintenance?'

This leads to Chapanis' final criticism — that general comparisons between people and machines give no considerations to trade-offs. When choosing between the two components to perform a particular function many additional considerations need to be taken into account, for example, weight, cost, size or availability. Variables such as these have to be traded off, one against the other, before the ideal system can be designed. The type of question which may need to be asked, therefore, could be 'is it better to design a system which, because of size limitation, includes a human operator and less equipment, or would it be better to reject the human operator and so lose some flexibility but include more equipment'. Simple lists which compare the values of 'men' and machines separately do not help to solve this type of trade-off problem.

ERGONOMICS COSTS AND REWARDS

Deciding on the relative values of 'men' and machines is a difficult task which is made more complex when the question of their respective costs is included. It is germane at this point, therefore, to consider how ergonomics fares when it is subjected to some sort of cost–benefit analysis. Any manager who contemplates either implementing an ergonomics investigation of part of a plant or introducing a system designed to ergonomic principles must be able to justify the cost in relation to the rewards.

Chapanis (1976) points out that a full cost–benefit equation is extremely difficult to devise since many factors, some of them 'invisible', are involved when assessing the value of a system. Those which he considers important include, on the benefit side, the value of all goods and services produced by the system and the values which accrue from any incidental or 'spin-off' products. On the negative side of the equation Chapanis includes equipment costs, replacement or maintenance costs, operating costs, the cost of job aids, auxiliary equipment and manuals, of personnel selection, of training, of salaries and wages, of accidents, errors and breakages or wastage, and the social costs of implementing the system (for example, the long-term costs of pollution).

Many of these factors can be expressed in tangible, monetary terms. Others, however (for example, the cost of pollution, selection, accidents, etc.), are less quantifiable (see Chapter 12). Nevertheless they make important contributions to reducing the efficiency and productivity of a system and must be taken into account.

In addition to these factors Corlett and Parsons (1978) describe other criteria which ought to be included in the assessment. These include reduced stress, turnover costs and increased work interest and satisfaction.

A further problem when considering how ergonomics relates to the cost–benefit equation is that few well-controlled studies are available. From an economic viewpoint this is understandable — a redesigned piece of equipment, for example, which is thought to be better than its existing counterpart will naturally be used throughout the plant as soon as possible. However, it does mean that comparative measurements of the system effectiveness with and without the new equipment and under otherwise similar conditions (pay, time of year, type of operator, etc.) are extremely difficult to obtain.

Despite these problems some studies are available which illlustrate the cost effectiveness of ergonomics.

Sell (1977) describes detailed work which was carried out in the early 1960s at the British Iron and Steel Association to design overhead crane cabs. One problem which had occurred involved damage to railway wagons caused by drivers of some cranes swinging the magnetic hooks against the side of the railway truck. It was estimated that this damage was costing the company around £60 per week in wagon repairs. Simple observations showed that a factor which contributed to the lack of operator's control over the hook was that he was unable to reach all of his controls, and at the same time look out of the crane to see the position of the magnet. By redesigning the position of both the magnet and the other controls so that the operators could see the hook and reach the controls, the design fault was eliminated. Beevis and Slade (1970) have suggested that the modifications cost £270, which meant that the costs were repaid within about six weeks.

Along the same theme, Teel (1971) describes the costs and rewards accruing from two separate ergonomics studies. The first evaluated the effectiveness of specially prepared visual aids in improving the performance of machine parts inspectors. (These inspectors examined precision parts for defects which might make then unsuitable for use.) The cost of the study, in other words, of preparing the aids, was calculated to be $7200. The savings in the first year alone, however, were over $10000. Since the production was to continue for three years, Teel argues that the total savings accounted for more than four times the cost of the study.

In his second study Teel considered, the workplace of electronic assemblers according to ergonomic principles. Using a redesigned console, for example, the time taken by each operator to complete a task was reduced by 64 per cent with 75 per cent fewer errors. The cost of the study amounted to $4200, while the savings per year were calculated to be in excess of $28000.

These are merely two examples of the benefits to be obtained from considering the work from the point of view of the operator. However, as Chapanis' (1965a) list discussed earlier indicates, productivity benefits to a company may not always be measurable simply in terms of the number of units produced. For example, in some cases productivity may rise simply because all of the workers remain at their jobs. In these terms sickness and accidents may diminish the workforce. Even if a worker is only temporarily hurt by an accident, and takes perhaps half an hour off work to visit the sick bay or doctor, the productive time is reduced by at least that hour and probably more.

As an example of this problem, Drury et al. (1983) describe the design of a palletizing aid to help in the manual stacking of boxes on a shipping pallet. The new aid reduced the amount of spinal compression due to lifting from about 250 kg to about 150 kg. Taking account of the number of spinal injuries that occur each year from lifting inappropriate weights and weight distributions, the authors calculated that the specifically designed aid would reduce spinal injuries by a factor of four. Relating this to actual costs per operator, they calculate that the *expected cost* of back injuries could be reduced from $503 per man year to $129 per man year — a saving of $374 per man year. They also computed the saving that their new design would make in terms of reduced cardiovascular strain: between $3000 and $4000 in eliminating relief (resting) time.

Finally, it should be remembered that in a number of circumstances appropriate ergonomics consideration is not merely desirable — it is sometimes critical and is embodied in legal statutes. For example, Wilson (1983) discusses the concept of a manufacturer's liability for the production of safe consumer products and describes some of the costs incurred by manufacturers found to be contravening design safety standards. Consumer pressure groups in many countries are constantly creating critical climates against which products are evaluated for both legal and commercial viability. Ease, safety and efficiency of use, and the extent to which the user has been considered in the product design are assessment criteria that are frequently employed.

Ergonomics, therefore, is not only desirable it can be financially beneficial.

SUMMARY

This chapter has discussed how ergonomics, and its American sister disicpline human factors, arose as a response to the need to consider how the human operator manages to cope with the environment. The important concept is that discrepancies between what the environment requires and what the operator is able to give should be resolved by adapting the environment to the operator, rather than the normal approach of making the operator suit the environment. If such a basic change is made, it is argued, then the efficiency, safety, comfort and productivity of the total man–machine system will be enhanced. The remainder of this book considers the various aspects of the system and the nature of improvements.

CHAPTER 2

THE STRUCTURE OF THE BODY

I   The Sensory Nervous System

At a structural level the human operator can be said to be little more than a rather complex system of bones, joints, muscles, tissues, nerves and fluids. Such a statement, however, presents a rather simplistic view of a living human being. The rich complexity of human life is made up of the infinite variations which can occur in the arrangement of the body structures and in the individual ways in which they are used. Since it is impossible to understand fully how a proper relationship between the human operator and the mechanical environment can be created without some idea of the body structure, the purpose of this and the following chapter is to take this simplistic approach to look at the manner in which the bones, joints, tissues and nerves are arranged to make up the human body. The limitations of these structures define the most basic concept of ergonomics: literally that of fitting the environment to the person.

As should have become apparent already, the relationship between people and their environment hinges, primarily, on a complex closed-loop system. At its simplest level, this involves firstly the display of information from the machine to the operator: a light flashes, a colour appears, a sound is made, a lever changes position, etc. On the basis of this information, the operator may have to carry out some action — pull a lever, push a switch, adjust a rudder, etc. This transmits commands to the machine which alters the display and, with the display of information back to the operator, the loop is completed.

The efficient operation of this closed-loop system requires a number of body structures to be brought into play. First, there are the receptor agencies of the human body, the sense organs; through these the information is initially passed to the operator and they represent the first possible area in which errors can occur. Second, the nerves carry information from the sense organs to the interpretation and decision-making areas of the brain, and from the brain to the muscles. Although their speed of conduction is very fast, nerves have their limitations. Third are the body structures which carry out various actions — the effector processes. Once a decision to act has been made, the information is transmitted to the muscles which control the action of the bones, joints and tendons. In addition to the decision-making capacities, these effector processes represent possibly the greatest limitation to the operator's mechanical efficiency.

This chapter considers the structure and functions of the nerves and the sense organs. Chapter 3 deals with the ways in which the bones, joints and muscles are arranged and the limitations which they place on the body's movements.

SENSORY MECHANISMS

The basic unit which transmits all sensory information is the single nerve cell or neurone, and this comes in many shapes and sizes depending on its position in the body. It conducts the information in terms of very small potential differences (in the region of 70 mV), from one part of the body to another, through a system commonly known as the neural net.

Each neurone in the body essentially consists of three parts. First the cell body which contains the nucleus; second, a mass of hair-like protrusions extending from the cell body, known as dendrites; and third, a long, single, thin extension of the cell body, the axon. This may be from less than a millimetre up to more than a metre long, and ends as dendrites. In many neurones, the axon is covered by a fatty insulating sheath known as the myelin sheath.

The chain of command, therefore, is for the cell body dendrites to convey information to the cell body itself. This is transmitted along the axon as a burst of potential differences to other dendrites at the far end, which are closely entangled with the cell body dendrites of the next neurones. The information is transmitted across the dendrite gaps (synapses) and so on throughout the body.

The rate at which impulses travel along a nerve fibre depends on the thickness of the myelin sheath surrounding the axon and also, to some extent, on the diameter of the axon itself. When the sheath is thick, the rate of travel may be as high as 20 m/sec, while if the sheath is very thin or non-existent the rate of travel could be as low as 0.6 m/sec.

The transmission speed through the body also depends on the number of synaptic gaps between the neurones, since the synapses create a slight delay in the transmission process. Although the synaptic gap is only of the order of 100 ångströms (0.000 001 mm) the delay between the arrival of an impulse at the axon terminal and the initiation of an impulse the other side of the synapse is in the order of 0.5–1.0 msec. In that period, another impulse could be travelling a metre along the fibre.

THE SENSES

Various types of information are fed into the sensory system through receptors, which are classified into three groups. The *exteroceptors* receive information about the state of the world outside the body and so include the eyes, ears and touch receptors in the skin. Using the same terminology, the *interoceptors* inform the individual about the body's internal state, for example its state of hunger or fullness of the bladder. A specific subgroup of interoceptors which is of direct interest to ergonomists is the *proprioceptors* which are concerned with motor functions. These give information about the position of the body or parts of it in space and basically form two groups: kinaesthetic receptors in the muscles and tendons that supply information about the muscle and joint activity, and the vestibular system in the ears which inform the individual about the body's orientation in space.

Before describing the senses in more detail, it is useful to consider the difference between 'sensation' and 'perception'. Whichever sensory system is considered, sight, hearing, taste, touch or smell, the particular organ receives energy from the outside world, converts it into small potential differences and passes these along the system to the brain. This is the process of sensation (or *reception*). It is determined entirely by the stimulus quality and the particular organ and part of the nervous system, and it is an objective process. On entering the brain, however, the nerve impulses are interpreted to produce a recognizable pattern of sight, smell, sound, etc., and this process is influenced greatly by the individual's past experience, expectations, feelings, and wishes. This process of *perception* is entirely subjective in nature.

Thus the distinction between sensation and perception is very important: simply presenting stimuli in such a fashion that they will be *received* accurately does not mean that they will be *perceived* accurately. Furthermore, although two people may receive and sense the same object, they may not have identical perceptions. The implications of this for aspects of ergonomics such as designing appropriate displays should be clear. This distinction will be emphasized again in Chapter 4 when discussing in more detail the channels of communication which can be set up between two or more operators.

THE VISUAL SYSTEM

Of all the senses, vision has been the most thoroughly studied. It is also, perhaps, the system which is most overloaded at work. In essence the system consists of two eyes, each connected to the visual cortex of the brain by an optic nerve (see Figure 2.1). The two nerves meet at the optic chiasma at the base of the brain, where part of each nerve crosses over and terminates in the visual cortex on the opposite side of the brain to the eye from which it originated. In fact, fibres from the left-hand side of each eye terminate in the left visual cortex and those from the right-hand side of each eye terminate in the right visual cortex.

The effects of this crossing of fibres may prove to be important when information is presented in very short periods of time or when extremely fast responses are required. For example, it is now fairly well understood that the two halves of the brain do not 'perform' equally well for all types of material. For instance, speech appears to be analysed better in the left half (hemisphere) whereas the right hemisphere is dominant with respect to spatial ability. In terms of material normally presented to the visual system, the left hemisphere is better than the right at analysing words, whereas there is some evidence which suggests

18

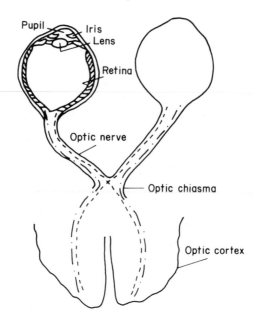

Figure 2.1 The eye and visual system, showing
the pathways of portions of the optic nerve

that numbers are recognized faster in the right hemisphere (Kimura and Durnford, 1974).

Depending on the nature of the visual material, therefore, it might be acted on more speedily or efficiently if presented to one-half of the visual field rather than the other. This right- or left-hand advantage, however, is likely to be noticed only when very fast responses are required. For example, Welford (1984) argues that a hemispheric advantage may be useful in situations such as the left/right placement of road traffic signs, when fast reactions could be required.

With regard to the eye itself, perhaps the easiest way to understand its structure is to compare it with a camera. A specific amount of light enters the eye through the pupil (aperture), the diameter of which is controlled by the coloured portion of the iris (stop). It is then bent and focused by the lens to fall on to the retina which acts as a photosensitive layer.

Although the analogy with the camera is suitable at a descriptive level, differences do exist between the structure of the eye and that of a camera which mean that the eye has more flexibility. First, the eye's lens is in a fixed position relative to that of the photosensitive area — it does not have to be moved to and fro to focus on objects at different distances as is the case with a camera. Focusing is accomplished by the muscles which surround the eye changing its curvature. Second, the photosensitive layer is curved which compensates for the curvature of the lens. Both of these differences allow quicker and more efficient focusing. Third, the pupil size is regulated by the iris. By influencing the amount of light able to enter the eye, along with the variable sensitivity of the retinal cells, this allows the eye to operate over a far greater range of illumination intensities than a camera which has to use a fixed type of film sensitivity at any one time. Fourth, the retina does not have the same level of sensitivity to light over its surface; it is highest at the centre and decreases quickly towards the periphery. A photographic film of this type would produce a picture with very good detail at the centre only, with reduced quality the farther away from the centre the image falls. To compensate for this, the eye constantly scans the visual field using a set of six muscles attached to each side, above and below the eyeball. In this way, different images can be pointed at the most sensitive part of the retina in rapid succession. Finally, by using both eyes together it is possible to obtain binocular vision. This helps us to perceive spatial relationships between objects and the environment, so that the eyes will record in three dimensions whereas the camera can only 'see' in two.

Perhaps the most important part of the eye itself is the retina. This is the layer at the back which acts in the fashion of a complex photodiode to convert luminous energy to electrical energy. It is made up of three layers of neurones, the most important being on the outside surface which contains two different neurones called the rods and cones (so called because of their shape). These appear to be the main receptor cells and, as shown in Table 2.1, they perform different functions.

Table 2.1 The different properties of rods and cones (*adapted from Morgan, 1965, and reproduced by permission of McGraw-Hill*)

Rods	Cones
Function at low levels of illumination (such as at night)	Function at higher illumination levels (such as during daylight)
Differentiate between shades of black and white	Differentiate between colours
Most sensitive in the greenish part of the spectrum	Most sensitive in the yellowish part of the spectrum
More numerous in the periphery of the eye	More numerous in the central part of the eye
Sensitive to very weak stimuli	Mainly involved in space perception and visual acuity

A number of important points emerge from Table 2.1. First because the rods, which function at low illumination levels, are primarily towards the periphery of the retina, we can see dim objects much more effectively if we look at them off-centre. This means staring a little to the right or left of the object to focus it towards the periphery of the retina where the rod density is high. Off-centre viewing is a trick used frequently by astronomers, those on night lookout duty and others who have to work in dimly lit environments. The corollary of this point, of course, relates to the distribution of cones in the retina. These are the cells used for 'normal' vision and are more numerous towards the central part of the retina (kown as the *fovea*). Since cones are the main receptors for differentiating between colours and are used in normal vision, for maximum perception it is important that visual information is presented centrally to the eye rather than to the periphery. Of course, the eyes can move around in their sockets to focus on an object but, before they can do so, the object has first to be seen. Images falling towards the periphery of the retina are less likely to be seen.

A second implication of Table 2.1 suggests that our sensitivity to light changes with variations in the ambient illumination level. At some point, for example at dusk, responsibility for the conversion of light energy to electrical impulses switches from the cones to the rods. Third, the rods and cones are sensitive to different wavelengths of light. These two latter points are important when considering the way in which we adapt to light and dark.

Light and Dark Adaptation

Because of the two types of receptors in the retina (the rods and the cones), the human eye is able to function efficiently over an extremely wide range of illumination levels. Cone vision provides acute vision at daytime (photopic) levels of illumination, whereas rod vision allows for the high degree of sensitivity essential for seeing when light levels are low (scotopic). With increasing or decreasing luminance levels, however, there will always be a point at which one set of photoreceptors ceases to operate as the other begins to take over. If the illumination change is relatively slow this adaptation to dark or light conditions is fairly smooth, but with fast changes in illumination the well-known experience of temporary blindness results. For example, moving from pitch darkness to bright sunlight sharply increases the illumination level falling on the retina so that the previously functioning rods are unable to cope and the cones have not had a chance to operate fully. In this case the eyes normally have to be closed, or dark glasses worn, to allow them gradually to become adapted to the change in the light level, after which time the eyes can again function efficiently within a new dynamic range of intensities.

Because the cones are relatively fast-reacting, their light adaptation is often complete within a minute or two. Rods, however, are much slower, and dark adaptation may take half an hour or even longer, depending on the previous illumination levels. For this reason, dark or coloured goggles are often worn by people having to work in dark environments (for example, radar operators or maintenance people) for some time before entering the dark room. Red is the colour normally used because it is one which does not greatly affect the visual pigment in the rods. Thus the cones may operate fairly normally during daylight while the rods are able to become adapted for the dark (see, for example, Cushman, 1980).

Visual Movement Perception

There are many situations in which a human operator might wish to perceive motion accurately. For example, a pointer moving across a dial, a vehicle along a track, or a falling object.

In general, movement can be perceived in two ways. In the first an object is kept in view by moving the eye, so the observer receives information about the object's speed and direction using information fed back from proprioceptive receptors in the muscles which surround and position the eye (this type of sensory information will be discussed in more detail later). The second case occurs when the eye is stationary and the object's image moves across the retina; the moving object is then perceived from the stimulation of different retinal cells. Under these circumstances the minimum velocity which can normally be detected is about 1–2 minutes of arc/sec. Faster movement than this will cause the normal reaction of the eye to track the object as it moves across the visual field, and so movement information is obtained from the eye muscles.

The *lowest* level of movement that can be detected (the movement threshold) will be reduced considerably (by an order of approximately 10) if another (stationary) figure is also present in the visual field. This provides a reference point against which the moving image can be compared and it is likely that other visual processes are also involved, perhaps concerning the ways in which we perceive spatial relationships.

Visual Spatial Perception

Perceiving the spatial relationships between a series of objects in the visual field is also normally accomplished by one or both of two processes: using visual cues provided by different objects in the visual field, and using proprioceptive feedback from accommodation and convergence of the eyes.

Two types of visual cues are normaly used, binocular and monocular. In the former the images received by the two eyes are compared by the brain and the disparity between them is used to indicate the relative positions of objects in space. For example, if a near and far object are both straight in front of the observer and the near object is fixated, on closing the right eye the left eye sees the far object as having moved to the left. Similarly, looking through the right eye only, the far object is observed to the right. Interpretation of these two different images by the two visual cortexes informs the observer something about the relative positions of the two objects.

The observer also uses a number of monocular cues to perceive spatial relationships, and each is related to past visual experiences. These cues include the relative sizes of objects (if two objects are the same size, the object further away appears to be smaller); covering and shadow (if one object is in front of another it may partially obscure it, or the degree of shadow may provide information relating to the distance between the two objects); and texture. Gibson (1950), for example, has argued that if there is any regular marking or visible texture in the object, for example on a floor, this texture undergoes a transformation in perspective so that in the retinal image there is a gradient of texture density. This gradient, then, suggests space.

In addition to binocular and monocular cues obtained from the images of different objects in the visual field, the fact that the eyes had to converge to fixate on the various objects also tells the observer about their relative position in space. Fixating on a far object, for example, causes double images of the near object and this disparity can be reduced by converging the eyes. This convergence may be used as a cue, implying that the second (nearer) object is nearer than the initial fixation point. Furthermore, the lens shapes are altered to accommodate the two, slightly different, images. The degree to which these two processes take place provides valuable information about the relative positions of objects in the visual field, and this information is obtained from the position (proprioceptive) receptors in the eye and lens muscle.

Visual Acuity

Having considered some of the principles underlying our ability to register spatial aspects of the visual scene, it is appropriate to turn to the topic of visual acuity. This is the process by which we are able to see fine details. Again many aspects of work require this ability — to register the fact that a very slowly moving pointer has moved; to detect differences in the position of two controls; to recognize the presence of an object in the visual field; to localize and to distinguish between two close objects in space, etc. The three types of acuity most commonly recognized are line acuity (the ability to see very fine lines of known thickness), space acuity (the ability to see two spots or lines as being separate, in other words to see a space between the lines) and vernier acuity (the ability to detect discontinuity in a line when one part of the line is slightly displaced) (Murrell, 1971).

In essence three factors are important in determining the degree of acuity under any given condition. First is the size of the pupil — acuity is fairly linearly related to pupillary diameter down to a value of about 1 mm. (High ambient illumination levels and some drugs, such as alcohol, for example, may cause the pupil to be constricted and this could be an important factor for the safe and efficient operation of machines which require high levels of acuity.) A second factor is the light intensity reflected from the object (its luminance). An object which is, perhaps, too fine to be seen at all in low illumination may become clearly visible when illumination is increased. (As was mentioned above, however, too high a level of illumination is likely to cause the pupil to become narrowed so reducing acuity. Indeed, in many respects it is the contrast between the object and its background that is important — as will be discussed in Chapter 11.) Over the range of illuminations normally found, acuity varies linearly with a logarithmic increase in illumination between a visual angle (that is, the angle subtended by the object at the eye) of about 0.2–1.5 minutes of arc. Finally, and within limits, acuity is related to the time allowed to view the object so that a reduced exposure time reduces acuity. The exposure times experienced in normal work, however, are usually above those needed for this to be a problem (above 200 msec at normal daylight levels of illumination).

Age and Visual Performance

The question of acuity becomes particularly important when considering how our visual senses fare as we become older. Unfortunately, from a fairly young age (some writers, such as Cakir, Hart and Stewart (1980), suggest from about age 10) all visual functions are subject to deterioration. We are normally able to compensate for such losses, however, since increasing experience and familiarity with a given object means that we require less information for the purposes of recognition. Nevertheless, as was explained in Chapter 1, such compensation might well bring with it further costs to overall efficiency.

A number of experimenters have investigated the course of visual depreciation with age (for example, Fortuin, 1963; Blackwell and Blackwell, 1971) and have shown that some of this reduction can be offset by increased luminance of the object. As Weale (1963) demonstrated, this is because of factors such as a yellowing of the lens which means that the amount of light reaching the retina of a 60-year-old person is about one-third that reaching the retina of a 20-year-old person. Thus Bodmann (1962), for example, found that 50–60-year-old subjects needed illumination in the range 100–400 lux to perform as well as younger (20–30-year-old) subjects working in 2–5 lux illumination.

Data such as these, therefore, imply that careful attention must be paid to the design of visual tasks in order to take account of the variations in visual abilities among different age groups. In many visual tasks involving reading printed text, it might be possible to raise the general level of illumination of the material to be read (although even this practice could have some difficulties since sensitivity to glare also increases with age due to changes that take place in the eye which results in more light being scattered in the optic media (Hopkinson and Collins, 1970)).

A further problem of decreased visual function with age relates to our ability to focus on objects at different distances — accommodation. This is normally performed by the ciliary muscles in the eye contracting and changing the lens shape. With age the functioning of these muscles may deteriorate, with the result that the nearest point to which the eye can be sharply focused (the 'near point') moves further from the eye (that is, we become longsighted). In addition, the speed of accommodation decreases with age, a problem that is particularly important when, for example, typing text at a computer keyboard. Thus, the eyes often have to move between the material on the manuscript to the VDU screen and, if these are at different distances from the eye, the eyes need to accommodate rapidly if blurred images are not to result. These problems are not entirely insoluble, however, since the ageing effects can be ameliorated using appropriate spectacles.

Visual Flicker

In many cases the human operator may be called on to respond not to a visual stimulus with a relatively steady illumination level, but to one which flickers. Flashing warning or indicator lights are, perhaps, the most obvious examples of such displays. Flicker can also be a negative feature of some environments; as will be discussed in Chapter 11, excessive flicker from structures such as fluorescent lights can be detrimental both to health and to working conditions.

Flicker is a temporal phenomenon; its perception depends heavily on the ability of the visual system to react to the fast changes in light intensity. In many cases, therefore, it may be considered as a type of acuity task, since the observer needs to 'perceive' the period of darkness between two flashes.

This task can be carried out fairly well for light flashes occurring relatively infrequently, when a flickering sensation will be created with separate flashes being perceived. As the flash frequency is increased, however, the flashes appear to merge to produce light which is indistinguishable from a steady state illumination. The frequency at which this merging occurs is normally called the critical fusion frequency (c.f.f.) and depends on a number of factors. It is often used as a measure of visual performance. C.f.f. has been shown to range from about two to three flashes per second at very low illumination levels (that is, scotopic vision using the rods) to around 60 flashes per second with extremely high levels (that is, at photopic vision). At the change-over point between scotopic and photopic vision, at illumination levels normally experienced at dusk, c.f.f. is around 15 flashes per second.

A great deal of experimental literature has been built up regarding the parameters of c.f.f. (see, for example, Hopkinson and Collins, 1970; Riggs, 1972). The main results can be summarized as follows:

(1) C.f.f. increases linearly with the logarithm of illumination intensity over a wide range of light intensities (this is the so-called Ferry–Porter Law, see Kelly, 1961).
(2) When the brightness of the stimulus and the surrounding area are the same, c.f.f. is at its highest. It reduces as they separate in intensity.
(3) At very small visual angles, the c.f.f. increases linearly with the logarithm of the stimulus area.
(4) C.f.f. is relatively independent of wavelength.
(5) C.f.f. decreases during dark adaptation.
(6) There is wide individual variability in c.f.f., but individuals are fairly consistent within themselves.
(7) C.f.f. is relatively independent of practice.

Colour Vision

A quick glance around a modern workplace will illustrate immediately the importance of colour. It is used to help the operator distinguish between different parts of the working area, controls, displays and parts of a display, files, action requirements, etc. It can create mood (it is generally accepted that the reds and yellows are 'warm' colours whereas blues are 'cool') and, using contrasts, colour can help to improve visibility.

Different colours are perceived as a result of the eyes receiving different wavelengths of light, either reflected from a coloured surface or emanating from a coloured light source. The normal eye is able to sense light in the visible spectrum with a range of wavelengths between about 440 and 700 nanometres (1 nm = 10^{-9}m). To these different wavelengths we attach various colour names, with the shorter wavelengths (around 450 nm) being described as 'blue' and the longer wavelengths (around 650 nm) as 'red'. The physical attribute of what is normally called colour is the *hue*.

The important dimensions of colour, however, do not end simply with hue. The *saturation* and *luminance* of the wavelengths contained in the light also have important implications for the quality of the colour experienced. The dimension of luminance is possibly easiest to understand and refers to the amount of light reflected into the eye. At one extreme the stimulus will be barely visible, at the other end it will appear almost painfully bright. Saturation, however, is sometimes less easy to conceptualize. It refers, essentially, to the amount of white light (that is light containing all of the visible wavelengths) contained in the light perceived. It is an index, therefore, of the hue's 'purity'.

These three attributes are often considered in terms of a cone-shaped arrangement on which different colours and shades can be defined, and is the basis of the Munsell Colour System (1929) (see Oborne, 1985).

Although the impression has so far been given that colour sensation depends on purely physical parameters, this is not strictly correct. Firstly, the retina is not equally sensitive to different hues. This means that different colours of the same intensity will appear to be either brighter or less bright according to their wavelength. When the eye is light adapted, the brightest spectral colour is at about 550 nm which gives an impression of yellowish-green and the brightness progressively diminishes as the wavelength approaches either the 400 nm (violet) or the 700 nm (red) ends of the spectrum.

Secondly, our cones in the retina and our interpretive mechanisms in the brain sometimes cause colour sensations to appear other than they actually are. Two phenomena are particularly important here: colour adaptation and colour constancy.

Colour adaptation refers to the process by which some colour sensations are altered by continuous exposure to others. For example, looking at a bright red stimulus for a few minutes and then at a yellow stimulus will cause the yellow to appear green. Gradually the eye will recover from the adaptive effects of the red field; the yellow content of the test field will gradually increase relative to the green and, after a few minutes, the field will again appear as normal. Similar effects occur through continuous exposure to green stimuli: a yellow field appears red. Along with this adaptation there will also be a reduction in brightness and changes in saturation. In both cases, then, it appears that the cones responsible for either red or green perception have been adapted out so that the other becomes prominent. (Most theories of colour vision suggest that there are specific types of cones in the retina that are sensitive to specific wavelengths, see Oborne, 1985.) Such effects, of course, have important implications for an operator who may have to spend many hours looking at a coloured display such as a computer screen.

Colour constancy is the name given to the psychological mechanism which makes us see colour as we think it ought to be rather than as it actually is. For example, near a sunlit window a white ceiling of a room with a blue carpet will actually reflect quite a lot of blue light from the carpet. However, it will look the same white colour all over because of the colour constancy effect.

The process by which all the colours and hues normally experienced are decoded are too complex to be explained here and indeed large gaps exist in our knowledge of this area. Of more interest to the practising ergonomist, however, is the proportion of the population who are deficient in their colour discrimination. These people, who represent about 6 per cent of the male and 0.5 per cent of the female populations (Morgan, 1965) may experience difficulty in work, particularly when colour is used to code various aspects of their machines.

Colour deficient people (note that the term 'colour blindness' is a misnomer — very few people are actually totally blind to colour) may be classified in a number of ways. The most common is on the basis of an ability to discriminate between the colours red, green and blue. Normal people are able to discriminate all three colours, hence they are called *trichromats*. The most common type of colour blind individual is the *dichromat* — this person might confuse red with green, or yellow with blue (red–green 'blind' individuals are considerably more common than yellow–blue individuals). The relatively rare person who is totally 'colour-blind' (0.003 per cent) sees only white, black and shades of grey. Such a person is described as a *monochromat*.

The presence of 'colour-blindness' may be fairly simply determined — perhaps the easiest being to use cards which make up the Ishihara colour test. Each card, which needs to be presented under standardized conditions, contains a number of different coloured dots, some of which form a pattern — either a number or a wavy line. Because of an inability to discriminate particular colours the 'colour blind' individual has difficulty in perceiving these patterns and the deficiency can be discriminated by an inability either to name the number or (for illiterate subjects) to trace the wavy line. Although the test appears simple to administer, it must be emphasized that it produces valid and reliable results only in the hands of a skilled tester under controlled lighting conditions.

THE AUDITORY SYSTEM

If the eye can be likened to a camera, the ear can be thought to perform like a microphone. In this case the ear's main job is to convert the noises received in the form of sound pressure waves into electrical patterns, which are then recognized by some sort of decoding apparatus. However, unlike the eye which is functionally superior to the camera, in many respects the human ear can be considered as being inferior to the highly sophisticated modern microphones which are available today.

The ear itself is composed of three recognizable sections: the outer ear, the middle ear, and the inner ear, and these are illustrated in Figure 2.2. What most of us commonly call the ear is to the anatomist the pinna of the outer ear. Animals like dogs and cats can move this in different directions to help 'collect' sound waves. In human beings, however, the pinna is a less effective sound trapper. The outer ear also consists of a tube which runs inwards from the pinna and terminates at the eardrum (the tympanic membrane). It is through these parts of the external ear that sounds are conducted to the middle ear and then to the inner ear.

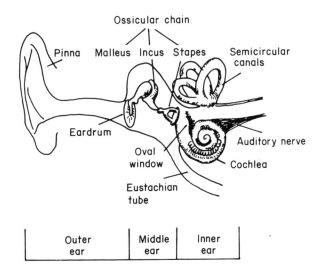

Figure 2.2 The structure of the ear

The middle ear performs two functions: to transmit sound waves and to protect the inner ear. Sound wave transmission is carried out by three small bones, the malleus, the incus and the stapes, which are collectively called the ossicular chain. They are so arranged that they span across the middle ear, and connect the eardrum to a thin 'oval window' on the other side. For this part of the ear to function properly, it is important that the air pressure remains the same as in the environment and this is achieved by a tube (the eustachian tube) which connects the inner ear to the back of the throat. However, sudden changes in the air pressure can close the eustachian tube thus creating pressure differences between the middle ear and the outside atmosphere. The effect of this may be to cause the excruciating pain sometimes experienced by air travellers, and may even lead to permanent hearing damage.

The outer and middle ear appear to have the function not only of transmitting sound to the inner ear, but also of protecting it from having to operate with sound pressure levels outside its capacity. Kryter (1970) points to three ways in which this can occur. First, the action of the eustachian tube may prevent pressure waves which have fast (less than 200 msec) rise times (the time taken for the sound pressure level to reach its maximum intensity) being transmitted to the inner ear. (Events such as explosions can easily produce sounds with extremely fast rise times.) Second, if high intensity pressure waves are experienced, small muscles in the middle ear can contract to stiffen the ossicular chain and attenuate the sound. Third, the mass and stiffness of the ossicular chain are such as to prevent the transmission of pressure waves with exceptionally fast rise times (of less than 50 msec).

The inner ear performs two separate functions: firstly hearing and secondly maintaining posture (this is discussed in the next section). The primary receptor organ for hearing is the cochlea, which derives its name from its coiled stucture that is similar in shape to a snail shell. It tapers slightly along its length, with the broader end incorporating the 'oval window' of the inner ear, and is filled with fluid. Running the length of the cochlea is a membrane (the basilar membrane) which acts in a similar way to the ribbon in an old carbon ribbon microphone.

Opinions differ as to the precise mechanism of hearing. However, a simple model would suggest that the sound pressure waves are transmited as vibrations across the inner ear from the eardrum to the oval window via the ossicular chain. These in turn set up hydrostatic travelling waves along the cochlea and basilar membrane, which cause the membrane to vibrate and its covering of hairs to be compressed. The sensation of pitch is produced because different parts of the membrane are sensitive to different frequencies: high-frequency sounds are perceived at the base of the basilar membrane whereas the apex is sensitive to low-frequency sounds. Loudness is discriminated by the extent to which the hairs are compressed.

Sound Localization

Although the action of the ear may be considered to be purely mechanical, our interpretation of what we hear is certainly not. For example, just as our two eyes enable us to perceive depth so having an ear on each side of the head enables us to tell from which direction a sound is coming. This information can be extremely beneficial. For example, in a dangerous situation being able to locate a warning sound, as well as registering its presence, could provide the 'split second' needed to take appropriate avoiding action.

As with visual depth perception, we use cues to localize sound sources. Instead of being related to the size of the object, however, these cues are in terms of the time differences taken by the sound to reach each ear.

It is possible to understand how sound localization occurs by imagining a sound source positioned to the right of a fixed head. Because the distance is slightly further to the left ear than to the right, it will take correspondingly longer for the sound pressure waves from the sound source to reach the left ear. As the sound moves to the centre of the head, the time difference is reduced. These time differences are long enough to provide cues about the left–right location of the sound source. Furthermore, in addition to the time cues there is likely to be an intensity difference at the two ears because of the shadowing effect caused by the head. Again, this provides cues about the position of the source relative to the two ears. Combinations of time and intensity cues, therefore, give us the ability to localize sounds accurately.

Accurate localization, however, only occurs when the second source is situated to the right or left of the listener. If the head is fixed, then front–back and up–down discrimination is poor. For this reason it is very important that the head is free to move to allow us to place the sound source along a left–right line relative to the ears. With head movement, of course, we also begin to integrate information derived from the neck and shoulder muscles (proprioceptive information) with that obtained from the time and intensity cues to localize the source more efficiently.

Tone and Loudness Discrimination

Frequency and intensity (and their corresponding subjective attributes, tone and loudness) are the two defining characteristics of any auditory stimulus. However, our ability to discriminate between (and thus act upon) different sounds is limited.

In this respect McCormick (1976) differentiates between two types of discrimination process. First, relative judgement in which there is an opportunity to compare two or more stimuli, for example comparing two sounds in terms of their loudness or two colours in terms of their hue. In the second, absolute judgement, there is no obvious opportunity to compare the stimuli. In this case the task becomes more one of identification or labelling. As might be expected, people are able to make more accurate discriminations on a relative judgement basis.

In most work settings, discrimination is likely to be based primarily on absolute judgements. An operator may have to decide to press the red button, to react to the 'soft' noise, or turn the 'small' control. Little opportunity for immediate comparison between stimuli exists in each situation. Unfortunately, however, the ability of people to make absolute discriminations between individual stimuli of most types is not very large. In this connection Miller (1956) refers to the 'magical number seven plus or minus two', implying that the range of such discriminations is somewhere around 7±2 (or 5 to 9). Thus we are able to discriminate four to five sounds of different loudnesses and about the same number of different tones.

If different dimensions are combined, however, the number of absolute judgements which can be made is increased. For example, Pollack and Ficks (1954) asked subjects to discriminate between over 15000 tones, each having different frequencies, intensities, durations, rates of interruption, on-time fractions, and locations in space. Under these conditions their listeners were able to discriminate about 150 separate tones without error, although their accuracy diminished as more tones were added. Miller (1956) sums up these and similar results by pointing out that 'as we add more variables (dimensions) ... we increase the total capacity but we decrease the accuracy for any particular variable. In other words we can make relatively crude judgements of several things simultaneously'.

In terms of auditory discrimination, therefore, the message is clear: our ability to discriminate between tones increases as we increase the number of dimensions carried in the meaningful sound.

THE PROPRIOCEPTIVE SENSES

The proprioceptive senses are those concerned with perceiving the body's own movement and with informing the individual of his or her position, and the position of the limbs, in space. In essence this sensory system is composed of two separate systems: the vestibular system in the ear which is mainly concerned with maintaining the body's posture and equilibrium, and the kinaesthetic (literally, 'feeling of motion') system which consists of sensors in the muscles, tendons and joints that indicate the relative positions and movements of the limbs and of different parts of the body.

The proprioceptive system is frequently overlooked when considering an operator's behaviour in a working environment. This is possibly because no one visible organ is responsible as, for example, the eye is the organ for vision or the ear for hearing. In many respects the system provides 'unconscious' information. A lack of consciousness, however, does not imply a lack of importance, for the proprioceptive system is absolutely necessary for notifying the operator about what the body is doing without each and every part of it having to be monitored. For example, we can walk and climb stairs efficiently because of the kinaesthetic feedback that arises from the muscles, tendons and joints used during locomotion; we do not have to look at our feet to know where to put them. Similarly, information from the kinaesthetic receptors in the hand, arm, and shoulder muscles allows an operator to use a hand control efficiently above the head or out of sight.

The Vestibular System

Situated within the inner ear and just above the oval window of the cochlea are sense organs which are collectively known as the vestibular apparatus. When describing this system it is usual to distinguish between two types of vestibular organs: the semicircular canals, and the vestibular sacs which contain the utricles. Each has a different structure and, to some extent, function. However, they do have a common feature in that they do not provide direct sensation in the same way that the eyes, ears, tongue, etc. do. As any 'poor' sailor will know, for example, the sensations of dizziness and nausea which can arise when the vestibular apparatus is violently stimulated by vigorous rotation is not centred in the inner ear!

The semicircular canals in each ear comprise three, almost circular, tube-like structures which are attached to one another in the vertical and two horizontal planes. Each canal is filled with a fluid which, by virtue of its inertia, flows through the canal whenever the head moves in the plane of that canal. This provides information about the direction and rotational velocity of head movements, and the signals produced by the fluid movements also generate reflex eye movements, termed nystagmus, which help to keep the visual world stable. Syringing the external ear with water, for example, causes the eyes to sweep slowly in one direction and then quickly back. (Interestingly, the water temperature determines the eye movement direction: hot water produces nystagmus with the quick phase to the side of the head being stimulated; cold water does the reverse.) Since each canal is part of a three-part system, then, when the sensations from all canals are integrated they will inform the person about the direction the head is moving as well as its speed. They can be conceived, therefore, of acting as both 'spirit levels' and angular speedometers which are capable of discriminating rotational movement in any direction as the head is moved (Reason and Brand, 1975).

The second organ, the utricle, is found in the utricular sac at the point where the three canals meet. The importance of the utricle is clear: it contains nerve endings necessary to preserve normal posture. As with the semicircular canals the utricle is filled with a fluid, but it also contains a flattish blob of jelly called the otolith which is covered with dense crystals. When the otolith moves in the fluid it probably stimulates hair cells around the cavity and this gives information about the head's orientation with respect to gravity. Thus the utricles inform the individual both about the tilt of the head and its linear displacement.

The vestibular receptors, therefore, enable man to maintain an upright posture and to control the body's position in space. The utricle informs the body about the static position of the head — whether the individual is upright, upside down or leaning over. The semicircular canals provide similar information about the head's rotation, its speed and direction and thus its equilibrium.

The Kinaesthetic System

Because people at work often need to know what different parts of their bodies are doing during any operation, the kinaesthetic senses form an extremely important system. This system comprises receptors situated in the muscles and tendons which convey information to the brain both about the extent to which these structures are being stretched and the rate of stretching.

Three types of kinaesthetic receptors are present in the body tissues. The first, which are spindle-shaped, are located in the muscles and provide information about the extent to which a muscle is being stretched and the rate of stretching.

The second type of receptor is located at different positions in the tendons. These provide information about the extent to which a joint is moved so that, again, movement speed and direction will be indicated. The third type of kinaesthetic receptor (the Pacinian corpuscle) is located in the deeper tissues. These furnish information regarding deep pressure and are sensitive to any deformation in the tissue in which they are embedded. In addition they can frequently be stimulated by a squeezing action whenever the body or the limb changes position, and they are thought also to be stimulated by vibration.

Each of these receptors will give the operator some idea of where the body or limbs are positioned in space, without the operator having to see them. For example, by integrating information from the biceps and triceps in the arm one can tell by how much the arm is extended. Further information from the biceps' and triceps' tendons and from the shoulder muscles, will provide sensations that imply by how much the arm is having to be supported — in other words its position with respect to the horizontal.

The kinaesthetic system is also critically important in training and performing skilled motor behaviours. For example, Fleishman (1966) has listed eleven important ability traits, found by himself and his co-workers, which underlie a large range of physical skills. The names provided are arbitrary but, as Dickinson (1974) points out, many of the abilities either include kinaesthesis to a greater or lesser extent or are totally measures of different kinds of kinaesthetic sensitivity. The eleven factors are:

(1) *Control Precision*: this factor is common to tasks which require fine, highly controlled muscular adjustments, primarily where larger muscle groups are involved.

(2) *Multilimb coordination*: this is the ability to coordinate the movements of a number of limbs simultaneously.

(3) *Response orientation*: this ability has generally been found in tasks which involve rapidly discriminating direction and orientating movement.

(4) *Reaction time*: this represents the speed with which the individual is able to respond to a stimulus when it appears.

(5) *Speed of arm movement*: this is similar to reaction time but represents the speed with which an individual can make gross, discrete arm movements where accuracy is not required.

(6) *Rate control*: this ability involves making continuous anticipatory motor adjustments relative to changes in the speed and direction of a continuously moving target or object.

(7) *Manual dexterity*: this ability involves skilful, well-directed arm–hand movements and is involved in manipulating fairly large objects under speed conditions.

(8) *Finger dexterity*: this is the ability to make skill-controlled manipulations of tiny objects using the fingers.

(9) *Arm–hand steadiness*: This is the ability to make precise arm–hand positioning movements; the critical feature, as the name implies, is the steadiness with which such movements can be made.

(10) *Wrist and finger speed*: this ability could be called 'tapping' and relates to the ability to move the wrist and finger quickly in time with some external stimulus.

(11) *Aiming*: speed and accuracy of placement are critical features of this ability.

From this list, it can be seen that the kinaesthetic system plays a major role in training all forms of skilled motor behaviour, since much of the development of complex motor skills depends on providing efficient feedback mechanisms. For example, in a skill such as typing the feedback obtained from the kinaesthetic receptors in the fingers, arms, shoulder muscles and joints allows the operator to be able to sense where the fingers ought to be placed without any conscious placement needed. In addition, efficient use of the kinaesthetic system (in other words when the skill has been learned fully) enables the operator to be able to sense when a limb is in an incorrect position and rapidly move to the correct position. Car drivers, for example, have learned that the right foot controls the accelerator and brake and the left foot the clutch. It takes a conscious decision to operate the brake with the left foot and, when this is done, the driver often feels 'uncomfortable' in the lower leg and ankle.

As Dickinson's list suggests, the kinaesthetic system is also used in skilled behaviour because of the information which it provides with respect to the timing of motor responses. In a large proportion of physical skills it is not enough merely to be able to predict appropriate responses; the timing with which a response is initiated is also important for smooth performance. For instance, when hitting a moving ball the subject needs to anticipate the arrival of the ball and to time a response so that the ball is struck at a specific position. In addition to providing information about where the hand and arm is placed so that correct placement can be made, therefore, the kinaesthetic receptors inform the skilled ball-player about the speed and direction of the arm movement so that the correct place can be reached at the correct time.

At this point it must be emphasized that kinaesthesis alone is not enough to allow fully skilled behaviour to occur. Vision is also important — possibly because the visual system helps originally to calibrate the kinaesthetic system. A number of authors, for example Gibbs (1970) and Norman and Fisher (1982) have argued that as the skill is learned vision gradually gives way to kinaesthesis as the important system for monitoring limb movements. As will be seen later, this is an argument advanced for the lack of significant performance differences using the QWERTY style of typewriter keyboard compared with other arrangements. Furthermore, recent evidence suggests that although kinaesthesis *has* a role in response timing it is not a sufficient system alone. Vision is also crucially important for accurate motor timing (Smith and Marriott, 1982).

Finally, it should be emphasized that muscles operate many parts of the body in addition to the skeletal system, and the role of kinaesthesis in these muscles should not be overlooked. For example, the eyes' positions are maintained by muscles which attach the eye to the socket, and the kinaesthetic receptors in these muscles provide information about the degree and direction of the eye's movement. Furthermore, if the eye is fixated at a particular point, kinaesthetic feedback from these muscles and those of the neck inform an individual of the body's orientation around the eye, and thus the orientation of the head. The role of the muscles' kinaesthetic system, therefore, should never be overlooked.

SUMMARY

This chapter has considered the roles of various aspects of the sensory nervous system in providing the channel for information to flow from the outside world to the human operator. Since they represent the first link in the man–machine system, the importance and modes of function of the visual, auditory and proprioceptive systems need to be understood before the efficiency of these channels can be increased. The next chapter will perform the same service for the body's motor processes — the communication channel in the other direction.

CHAPTER 3

THE STRUCTURE OF THE BODY

II Body Size and Movement

The sensory physiology and psychology discussed in the previous chapter essentially describe ways in which the operator receives and decodes information from the environment. Limitations of the operator's sensory and decision making apparatus are, perhaps, the first restrictions to the efficient working of the closed loop, man–machine, system.

Ensuring that the information is received and interpreted accurately, however, is only part of the problem; a man–machine loop is normally completed when the information has been responded to in some way. This means that appropriate actions have to be taken to transmit information *back* to the machine and these usually contain some motion component — pressing a button, throwing a switch, moving a lever, or even kicking the box! In terms of body structure, therefore, the second possible set of limitations for the closed loop system lies in the operator's ability to use the bones, joints and muscles that allow the body, or parts of it, to move in the desired way.

One of the more obvious restrictions of movement which the operator could experience is likely to be in terms of his or her own physical size. A tall person in a small room, a large hand operating a small control, a small pair of legs trying to cover a large distance each illustrates how the body dimensions themselves can restrict movement. The study of the operator's relevant body dimensions, often referred to as anthropometry, represents an essential aspect of any ergonomic study of a system.

Whereas the sizes of the bones and tissue may restrict movement in the initial stages, complete mobility can be brought about only by using the system of joints and muscles which connect the limbs. When considering such aspects as, for example, the role of the back muscles and joints during lifting or sitting, or the range of arm movements during reaching and of leg movements during walking, ergonomists enter the territory of the physicist and applied mathematician. Because the actions of the bones and joints are analysed and interpreted in terms of a complex system of levers and motions, this aspect of body mobility is known as biomechanics.

The purpose of this chapter will be to consider the ways in which people carry out and control motor behaviour and the factors which limit motor performance.

35

BODY MOVEMENT: Bones, joints and muscles

The 206 bones which make up the human skeleton perform one or both of two functions. A few, such as those which comprise the skull or the breastbone, protect the vital body organs from mechanical damage. The majority of bones, however, do not fulfil a protectionist role but give the body rigidity and enable it to perform its tasks — for example, the long bones of the arm and legs and the small long bones in the toes and fingers. A third group of bones can be added to these two groups of which the ribs are an example. These perform both a protectionist (of the lungs) and a working (aid to breathing) function.

In essence the body's bony skeleton consists of two lever systems, the arms and the legs, joined together by an articulated column, the spine. Since most bones in the body are designed to aid movement of the body parts they are connected to each other at joints and are held together by ligaments and muscles. The main rôle of the ligaments, therefore, is to hold the joints tightly together and to resist any sideways movement which may damage them. By doing so, however, they also tend to limit movement when a muscle is fully stretched.

In addition to being affected by the ways in which the muscles are distributed around the joints, the direction and degree of movement of body parts also depends on the shapes of the joint surfaces. At one end of the continuum are joints such as those in the fingers, elbows and knees which have simple hinge actions and allow movement in one plane only. Movement in joints such as those in the wrist and ankle, however, can occur in two planes because their surfaces are less flat. At the other end of the scale are the hip and shoulder joints which are shaped as a ball and socket and permit a wide range of movement. The fact that the ball of the hip joint is almost completely enclosed in a deep socket provides great mechanical strength but also limits the range of movement. In the shoulder, however, where a much wider range of movement is needed, the socket is more shallow — but a dislocated shoulder is fairly common as a result.

The joints in the spinal column are of a special type. Instead of the two smoothed surfaces of the joint moving against each other, they have between them a fibro-cartilage disc whose function is to act as a shock absorber and allow flexion and thus a wide range of body movements. The individual vertebrae in the spine are joined to each other by a series of elastic ligaments which help to maintain the normal curvature of the spine. As Murrell (1971) points out, they are probably the only ligaments which maintain a steady strain. The effect of the whole of this assembly (vertebrae, discs, ligaments) is that the body can bend forwards readily by about 180°, but not very far backwards.

In addition to bending, the spine also allows the body to rotate — the degree of movement varying between 90° in the neck vertebrae to about 30° in the lumbar region. Murrell (1971) emphasizes the importance of such rotational movements in being able to scan the area surrounding the body. Thus, the combined movement of the neck, lumbar region and the eyes enable the full horizon of 360° to be scanned with the pelvis remaining in the same sitting position.

The importance of the spine in maintaining posture will be considered later but it is useful to note here than an aching back may occur if undue strain is put on the mechanism. As will be seen later, more severe strain can cause damage to the muscles, to the elastic ligaments and, if the strain is sudden and prolonged, to the intervertebral discs. The result of this may be to cause part of the disc to be squeezed into the spinal canal producing the extremely painful back condition known as a 'slipped disc'.

Despite the perfect mechanical engineering of the body's bones and joints, no work could ever be done if the muscular system did not function adequately. Three types of muscles are present in the human body. The first controls the action of the main working bones and is known as striated (or skeletal) muscle. They are composed of long, thin, cylindrical fibres which are connected in bundles and are attached to the bones via tendons. These may be so short as to be invisible or quite long, such as the tendons which operate the fingers. Approximately 40 per cent of muscles in the body are striated and, except in some clinical conditions, their operation is under the operator's control. For this reason it is the striated muscle and its functioning that holds most interest to ergonomists. The second type of muscle, whose action is not under voluntary control, has a smooth appearance and maintains the functioning of vital body organs such as the stomach and intestines. Finally the heart is made from a muscle system unique to itself, cardiac muscle, which is similar to a mixture of both striated (for work) and smooth (involuntary) fibres.

Muscles are able to contract only in one direction, and when they do they become about one-half of their original length. This limits the amount of limb movement to a function of the length of its individual muscle fibres. On the other hand, the force which can be exerted by a muscle is not related to its length but to the number of fibres which it contains. Because of the way in which nerve impulses act, individual muscle fibres are only able to be in a state of contraction or non-contraction (a so-called 'all-or-none' functioning). Controlled, gradual movement, therefore, is brought about by additional fibres successively being brought into operation so that the greater the force required, the greater the number of fibres needed to be contracted. As was discussed in Chapter 2, such actions are monitored by kinaesthetic receptors in the muscles, and this provides the feedback loop needed to give the operator relevant information about the speed, direction and force of contraction.

Muscle Strength, Endurance and Fatigue

The amount of work that a human operator is called on to perform must clearly be within physical as well as cognitive capabilities. This is the reason for discussing such aspects as anthropometry and biomechanics in this chapter. However, it is often forgotten that the muscles themselves are constrained in their ability to carry out work. In the first place this is because of limits on their strength, secondly on their ability to maintain that strength (i.e. their endurance and their resistance to fatigue).

When discussing any of these factors a clear distinction must be made between the *types* of work which the muscle may have to do, i.e. between *static* and *dynamic* work. This distinction is normally made in terms of whether or not motion accompanies the muscular tension. The work is said to be static if no motion occurs, for example when holding a weight in the palm of the hand with the arm outstretched but not moving. If the arm moves up and down, however, then the upper arm and shoulder muscles are said to be doing dynamic work. The importance of this distinction will become clear when discussing some of the antecedents of muscular fatigue.

Muscular strength

Strictly defined, strength implies a situation in which static forces only are applied. For example, Kroemer (1970) has defined it as 'the maximal force muscles can exert isometrically in a single, voluntary effort'. Such a definition, therefore, would appear to remove from consideration most forms of work normally carried out within a dynamic environment. Restricting the definition to static situations, however, does ensure that the mechanics involved are easier to compute since, without movement, more complex considerations such as speed and velocity do not need to be considered. Furthermore, without movement the muscles do not change their shape (the movement is called isometric because the length of the muscle remains unchanged). Again, such a situation is more easily controlled and the effects more easily computed within a laboratory environment.

Information about isometric muscular strength, however, is often needed to suggest appropriate control and movement systems; to determine maximum and optimum control resistances; to define the forces required in various manual tasks and to ensure adequate arrangements for safe, efficient lifting or carrying. Levels of human strength are also relevant for the design of equipment which might have to be used under abnormal or special conditions such as space-travel: because of restrictions on features such as area and weight, conventional sources of power may be logistically impractical or expensive. Finally it is important to remember that most muscular actions which interest ergonomists commonly require the integrated exertion of many muscle groups. For example, pushing on a pedal requires turning the ankle, extending the knee and the hip and stabilizing the pelvis and trunk on the seat. In these cases the maximum force which can be exerted in a complex action will be determined by the weakest link in the muscular chain.

Many factors are related to (and perhaps influence) muscular strength, perhaps the most obvious being age: tasks requiring strength which are easily exerted by young workers may exceed the capacity of other, older groups. Damon, Stoudt and McFarland (1966) suggest that strength increases rapidly in the teens, reaches a maximum in the mid to late twenties and remains at this level for five to ten years.

Sex is another factor that is related to strength. Although skeletal muscle can produce the same force per unit area of muscle cross-section regardless of sex (O'Brien, 1985), since women generally have less developed musculature their overall strength tends to be lower than males. Indeed some authors, for example, Hettinger (1961) and Lauback (1976) have estimated that the general strength of women is about two-thirds that of males (although they accept that such a figure depends on the muscle groups under consideration). Such an assertion, however, represents a very broad generalization. It implies both that the differences in muscle strength between the sexes are the same for all muscle groups *and* that men and women use their limbs in the same way. Recently, a number of authors have argued that no evidence exists to support such a suggestion (for example, Redgrove, 1979; Pheasant, 1983; O'Brien, 1985). Pheasant (1983), for example, has demonstrated wide strength variability within a population of women, with one of the most important variables being the way in which strength was measured. Sex differences were also affected by the type of task used — for example, using a handle gripping and turning task the sex differences in strength increased as the size of the handle was increased. With knowledge of the sex differences that exist in hand sizes (Garrett, 1971, see p. 49) such results imply the need to consider the nature of the task as well as the strength required. A further example of this need is supplied by Corlett and Bishop (1975). In a pedal pushing task, they demonstrated that the optimum height of the pedal for both sexes was 25 cm below the chair seat. Although even at this height there was a male superiority of 9 per cent for exerting a force, this superiority increased by as much as 50 per cent at different pedal heights below the seat level. Ward (1984) urges that results such as these imply that greater care needs to be given to placing controls for women if equality of effort is to be achieved.

Behavioural differences between the sexes might also account for strength variations. In children, for example, trunk and upper limb muscles are stronger in boys and this might reflect the fact that boys tend to participate more in throwing sports than do girls. Furthermore, adult strength sex differences tend to decrease in the lower part of the body. O'Brien (1985) argues that this, again, may reflect usage — both sexes use their legs in habitual activities but in normal daily tasks men tend to use the upper body more than women. It may be, therefore, that some of the reported differences between the sexes in terms of their muscular strength reflects simply differences in patterns of activity, i.e. in the use and training of the muscles (Wilmore, 1975, for example, has shown that trained female athletes are stronger than untrained males).

Other factors that can account for strength differences, listed by Damon, Stoudt and McFarland (1966), include body position, fatigue, exercise, health, diet (hunger or inadequate diets decrease body strength), drugs, diurnal variation, environmental factors, motivation and occupation (although this may be related to the different amounts of exercise taken by people in various occupations). Additional factors include weight (Rasch and Pierson (1963) have demonstrated that body weight is an important determinant of arm strength)

40

and height (Caldwell (1963) obtained a correlation of 0.76 between pulling strength and height).

Muscular endurance

Endurance is the ability to continue to work or, in the static case, to continue to exert force even if fatigue has occurred. All of the data obtained in this area lead to the same conclusion: that the length of time for which a force can be maintained depends on the proportion of the available strength being exerted. Thus, the smaller the force required, the longer it can be exerted. This relationship between required strength and endurance has been shown to be non-linear (for example, Caldwell, 1963, 1964; Carlson, 1969; Monod, 1985) and this may be seen in Figure 3.1 (from Kroemer, 1970). This figure implies that while total strength may be maintained for only a few minutes (that is how strength is defined), if the contraction is to be maintained for long only about 15–20 per cent efficiency will be possible.

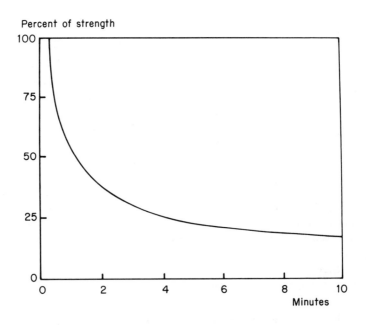

Figure 3.1 The relationship between strength and endurance limits. (*From Kroemer, 1970. Reproduced by permission of the Human Factors Society*, Inc)

At this point a distinction needs to be made between individual and group strength. Although the function shown in Figure 3.1 indicates the relationship between endurance and the percentage of each person's individual strength, the curve was obtained by averaging across many different strengths. Carlson (1969) and others, however, have demonstrated that whereas the relationship between strength and endurance shown in Figure 3.1 remains the same over different groups, weaker people are able to maintain proportionately greater endurances than stronger people. In other words, the curve is shifted slightly up or down according to the individual's maximum strength. Carlson suggests that this paradox is due to the fact that the stronger people, by definition of the term 'proportion of maximum strength', have to exert higher forces. This means that the muscles are working harder and require more oxygen carrying blood. However, because the muscles are more contracted they tend to occlude the blood vessels which limits the length of time that contractions can take place. (The importance of oxygen in reducing muscular fatigue is discussed below.) As evidence for this assertion, Monod (1985) has demonstrated that ability to maintain isometric contractions deteriorates rapidly when the blood supply to the upper arm is occluded using an arterial cuff. Whereas the normal 20–25 per cent strength shown in Figure 3.1 was able to be maintained after ten minutes and longer with no occlusion, with the cuff inflated strength dropped rapidly to zero after only six minutes.

Muscular fatigue

Fatigue is an important aspect of any situation in which work (both dynamic and static) is done. Depending on the degree of fatigue experienced it may cause discomfort, distraction, and possibly reduced satisfaction and performance. In many cases such factors rapidly lead to accidents. Muscular fatigue can often be avoided, however, if the manner in which it arises is understood, so that the task is designed to avoid factors which induce it.

For a muscle to contract (i.e. to do work) an extremely complicated chemical reaction is set up in the muscle itself. Described in its simplest form, the energy for the contraction is supplied by the breakdown of a chemical in the muscles called Adenosine Triphosphate (ATP) to Adenosine Diphosphate (ADP). However, the ADP must be regenerated to ATP before further contraction can take place, and the energy for this reversing action is provided by the breakdown of glycogen.

Unfortunately a by-product of the glycogen breakdown is an unpleasant substance with 'sharp' crystals called lactic acid, and this quickly accumulates in the muscles causing the muscular pain so well associated with fatigue. This is removed by a reaction with oxygen and converted into carbon dioxide and water. The function of oxygen, therefore, is to convert the by-products of the energy-producing reaction and this may continue for some time after muscular activity has taken place. The role of the blood is to transport oxygen to the muscles and to remove the carbon dioxide and water. The simplified reaction is shown in Figure 3.2.

It is interesting to note that the energy for muscular activity comes from a reaction which does not depend primarily on the presence of oxygen. Work can be done even if the immediate supply of oxygen is insufficient, and this allows

Figure 3.2 A simplified diagram of the process by which energy is obtained for muscle contraction

the body to make a sudden, extreme effort which would be quite impossible if the energy had to be obtained from the oxidation of some substance in the muscle fibre. So the importance of understanding the mechanisms that cause fatigue lies in realizing that the oxygen supplied by the blood, and the vascular system itself, are the sole agents for either reducing the level of fatigue or for increasing the length of time before this occurs. Conditions need to be designed, therefore, in which an efficient flow of blood to the muscles is maintained and even increased.

Blood flow is increased during dynamic work simply as a result of the action set up by the muscles doing the work. Blood is pumped through the blood vessels which supply the muscles, so helping to break down lactic acid and to remove the carbon dioxide and water. As long as the supplies of blood and oxygen can be maintained in sufficient quantities, therefore, and they are not exceeded by the production of lactic acid, muscular fatigue is likely to be kept at bay.

Under conditions of static load, however, no such pumping action occurs and the muscles soon become starved of the oxygen which they require. In addition, the contracted muscles also help to occlude capillaries and thus starve the blood supply. When this occurs muscles are said to be in 'oxygen debt'. (Oxygen debt can also occur in dynamic work if the supply of blood and oxygen is not sufficient.) This effect can be demonstrated well if the arms are stretched even for a short period above the head. With the shoulder and arm muscles under static load, the effect of gravity and the lack of muscle contraction serve to restrict blood flow to the muscles so causing an oxygen debt.

As Murrell (1971) has pointed out, the moral of the tale is that work should be designed to avoid forces having to be applied over long periods. As far as possible all muscular activity should be intermittent so as to allow blood to flow through the muscle and reduce the possibility of any oxygen debt building up, or to facilitate paying back a debt which has been incurred.

When discussing fatigue, it is not commonly realized that the main group of muscles which do static work continuously are those in the back and shoulders, since they are involved in maintaining posture. Although they have more red muscle fibres than muscles which do dynamic work, they often run into an oxygen debt if a rigid posture is maintained for too long. This is particularly important to the seated operator. For example, a typist may develop back and shoulder pain unless adequate opportunity is given to relax and contract the muscles, perhaps by walking about or by doing other work.

In this respect changes in working practice caused by new technology can create problems. Word processors, for example, enable typing to be done more quickly and efficiently than manual or even electric typewriters. However, because the new task no longer includes the natural breaks and movements required by the older technology, for example, changing paper, listening for auditory stimuli such as bells, etc., muscular fatigue often occurs more quickly and in different muscle groups. In addition, the design of the seat itself can help to reduce the degree of static load on the postural muscles, and this will be considered in Chapter 8.

As well as the oxygen that it transports, the other rôle of the blood supply should not be forgotten — that of removing waste-products from the lactic acid breakdown. Thus, the same sensations of pain and fatigue may, in some cases, occur after long periods of continuous work even if an oxygen debt has not occurred. This is caused by the fluid produced after the breakdown building up between the muscle bundles and being unable to be carried away by the blood. This causes the muscles to swell, which may then press on the intramuscular blood vessels so further reducing the flow of blood to the muscles. In most cases this fluid will eventually be dissipated by rest after the activity has ended but, if insufficient rest is allowed, then any more activity is likely to cause further increases in fluid level. Over time a muscle which is continuously used may become distended by intramuscular fluid and fibrous material can build up. This could ultimately interfere with the normal muscular contraction and may even cause permanent damage.

Heavy or repeated muscular exertion may have other consequences. For example, it is fairly common for frequently used muscles to become hypersensitive: they become more liable to contract than muscles which have not been exercised. Localized contractions or muscular spasm may result from such hypersensitivity, and perhaps a build-up of intramuscular fluid could cause local tender areas. In addition, whole groups of muscles may contract spontaneously to give what is commonly called 'cramp'. This can occur when some muscles are used continuously to exert a static force or on repeated movements of a comparatively short range. 'Writer's cramp', for example, is a common affliction among most authors!

Training the muscles

Being able to train the muscles is an important facility for anyone who depends on the work done by muscular activity. This is particularly so in sport but is also important in the case of heavy industries which include a great deal of lifting, pulling or pushing.

The two main aspects of muscular work in this context are strength and endurance. With regard to muscle strength, Hettinger (1961) produced the greatest improvements in the strength of different muscle groups by single, maximum, isometric muscular contractions for 1–2 seconds per day. No further increase in strength was obtained with more than a single maximum contraction per day, which implies that long, continuous periods of exercise are unnecessary for training. With one maximum muscle contraction every other day, the increase in strength fell to 80 per cent of that obtainable with daily sessions; with two sessions per week the comparable figure was 60 per cent; and with a single session weekly only 40 per cent.

Müller (1965), too, has demonstrated that standard isometric training over eight weeks increased the average static muscular strength by about 30 per cent, but it did not have similar consequences for dynamic strength or endurance. Dynamic training, however, did increase dynamic endurance, particularly at higher levels of work output. However, it still did not affect dynamic strength.

Müller explains these results by pointing to the fact that endurance depends on how much oxygen the cardiovascular system is able to pump to the working muscles in a given time. Since muscular training also helps to train the cardiovascular supply by making it have to deliver more oxygen carrying blood to the periphery, this helps to lower the load on the heart and produce a higher output per heart beat.

By relating the success of training methods to the amount of blood flow in the periphery. Müller suggests three further techniques to increase endurance. First massage during rest pauses. He obtained quicker recovery from work fatigue by manually supplying the contractions needed to pump the blood through the muscles without the muscles having to work (and thus produce lactic acid). The work which was possible in eight hours could be concentrated in two or three hours using massage. Massage has its limitations, however, since exhaustion was far greater after two or three hours work with massage than after the eight hours without massage. For this reason Müller suggests that massage has a potential for sports, but not for industrial work.

A second technique which he suggests is to restrict temporarily the blood supply to the appropriate muscles prior to work. He illustrates his argument by the observation that if one presses the skin with a finger hard enough to stop the blood supply, the pressed spot will become red (i.e. gorged with blood) when the finger is removed. Using a cuff placed around the thigh for up to ten minutes, Müller was able to demonstrate a 600 per cent increase in endurance on a pedalling task. Again, however, the cost of such increases in endurance is likely to be in terms of more long-lasting fatigue. In addition prolonged occlusion of the blood flow can be dangerous and should not be attempted by untrained personnel.

The final technique proposed by Müller does not increase fatigue. This involves cooling parts of the skin, so increasing the flow of blood to the periphery. He demonstrated that repeated five-minute periods of heavy pedalling work, interspersed with ten-minute rest pauses, could be continued for longer if the legs were immersed in water at 15°C during the pauses.

In summary, therefore, understanding the physiological and biochemical mechanisms of human movement is useful for two reasons. First, appropriate work and equipment design may be developed to reduce the number of situations in which restricted blood flow (and thus fatigue) can occur. Secondly the physiological principles may be used to increase human physical work capacity through training and other techniques.

BODY SIZE: Anthropometry

For many hundreds of years man has realized the importance of knowing something about his own body sizes. Indeed, measuring units of the 'foot' and the 'hand' are still used today, having been derived from the dimensions of standard body parts. The idea that the physical size of the person is somehow related to the ability to function in the world is so old that it is surprising how often the concept is neglected in everyday thought and design.

The term anthropometry is derived from two Greek words: *anthropo(s)* — human, and *metricos* — of, or pertaining to, measurement. Thus the sub-discipline is concerned with

The application of scientific physical methods to human subjects for the development of design standards and specific requirements and for the evaluation of engineering drawings, mock-ups, and manufactured products for the purpose of assuring the suitability of these products for the intended user population (Roebuck *et al.*, 1975).

The ergonomist, therefore, will use anthropometric data to ensure, quite literally, that the machine or the environment fits the person. Whenever the human operator has to interact with the environment it is important to have details of the dimensions of the appropriate body part. So, overall stature is an important determinant of, for example, room size, door height, or cockpit dimensions; the dimensions of the pelvis and buttocks limit the size of hatch openings or seats; the size of the hand determines the dimensions of controls and supportive stanchions; while it is necessary to have details of arm reach to be able to position control consoles at appropriate distances. The list of possible examples is almost endless.

Until recent years the main source of anthropometric data has been obtained primarily from military settings. This is possibly due to two reasons. First, large numbers of subjects need to be measured so that representative dimensions of a population can be obtained. The military scientists have at their disposal many thousands of available men and women, and this is particularly so during wartime. Secondly with the development of faster fighting machines (including tanks, boats, aircraft and space vehicles) space has been put increasingly at a premium. The need, therefore, effectively to build a machine around a single operator, but at the same time to build for a number of different operators, has meant that appropriate anthropometric data have been required. In addition anthropometric data are needed to design efficient clothing for use in a number of different theatres of war.

Unfortunately, however, data obtained from military personnel tend to be slightly misleading if civilian applications are envisaged. For example, conscripts measured during or just after a war may not have had a full diet or may have been working in difficult surroundings. Over time, factors such as these may affect the development of some body dimensions. In addition, as will be discussed later, the problem is further increased since anthropometric data obtained from members of one country, for example the United States of America, may not apply to those of another country, for example Great Britain.

The type of anthropometric data which mainly interests ergonomists can be divided into two categories: First structural anthropometry (often called static anthropometry) which deals with simple dimensions of the stationary human

Table 3.1 Details of some anthropometric surveys of civilian populations

Reference	Date	Sample size	Sex	Age
Kemsley	1950	27515	Male	14–75
		33562	Female	
Roberts	1960	78	Female	Average 71.65
Damon and Stoudt	1963	133	Male	Average 81.62
Ward and Fleming	1964	70	Male	?
Ward and Kirk	1967	100	Female	? (elderly)
Lewin	1969	87	Male	25–49
			Female	
Garrett (hand)	1971	26	Male	? (students)
		23	Female	
Andrew and Manoy	1972	323	Male	24–65
McClelland and Ward	1976	140	Male and female	18–30; 60+
Haslegrave	1979	1584	Male	17–64
		416	Female	
Guillien and Rebiffé	1980	8005	Male	20–60
Diebschlag and Müller-Limroth	1980	50	Male	?
Davies et al. (hand)	1980	92	Female	?
Office of Population	1981	7385	Male	
Censuses and Surveys		2889	Female	
Courtney (hand)	1984	100	Female	15–33

being. For example, weight, stature, and the lengths, breadths, depths and circumferences of particular body structures. The second category is called functional anthropometry (or dynamic anthropometry) which deals with compound measurements of the moving human being. For example, reach and the angular ranges of various joints.

For both types of anthropometric measurements, comparative data are slowly becoming available on selected civilian populations. Some of the more easily obtainable reports are listed in Table 3.1. In addition, Barkala (1961) provides details of some earlier surveys undertaken to estimate body measurements in relation to seat design; and the results of the majority of studies until 1971 have been collated and tabulated by Damon, Stoudt and McFarland (1971). However, these last two references deal mainly with data from military populations. A collection of papers edited by Easterby, Kroemer and Chaffin (1982) also provides useful civilian data.

Regarding functional anthropometry, the simplest forms of such data are tables which indicate the ranges of motion of individual body articulations. In this respect the definitive study of joint ranges remains that of Dempster (1955).

Variability in Body Shapes and Sizes

Even to the least observant, one thing must soon appear abundantly clear when considering body dimensions — there is wide variation between members of a population. Simply stand on any street corner and observe the differences in height, weight, shapes, etc., of people that pass by. With such variability it should be readily apparent that anthropometric data need to be used very carefully if they are to be of value. Unfortunately, it is not possible easily to present such a wide variety of data in a simplified fashion — even the simplest compound graphs, tables or slide-rules may serve only to mislead. Nevertheless Pheasant (1982a, b) does provide very useful information about ways in which anthropometric data can be estimated from available information concerning the heights of members of different populations.

Because the population does exhibit such variability in body dimensions, it is the normal custom when reporting anthropometric data to indicate both some average figure *and* the extent of the variability within the population studied. It has become common practice, therefore, to specify anthropometric data in terms of statistical numbers called percentiles, which simply indicate the percentage of the population who have body dimensions up to a certain size (i.e. that size or smaller). For example, a 95th percentile stature value will indicate the height of 95 per cent of the population. Using statistics of this type, the 'average' is taken as the 50th percentile (i.e. a value attained by 50 per cent of the population.)

Before discussing why anthropometric data are so variable, it is important to consider the meaning of this variability and of the statistics that are employed. In particular, it is necessary to question the concept of an 'average'. Often an 'average' dimension is of little use when used alone — take, for example, the design of a desk. If the height was arranged so that a person having an 'average' lower leg length would fit into it then, by definition, only half of the population (those with legs of average length or shorter) would fit. A feature such as desk height, then, needs to be designed to be *larger* than the average appropriate dimension. On the other hand, when dealing with a dimension such as reach, the distance employed needs to be *smaller* than the average reach of a population. If it was larger than average then, again by definition, the smaller 50 per cent of the population would be unable to reach.

Just how much larger or smaller than average a particular dimension needs to be depends on the importance and function of the feature being designed. For example, a joystick is useless if it is placed outside of the user's reach and so the reach dimension in this case would need to be related to the reach of the *smallest* member of a particular user population. At the other extreme, and taking a military example, an escape hatch in a submarine would need to be large enough to allow all (100 per cent) of the users through (with their clothes) in an emergency. Other dimensions, however, may not be so critical. For example, as long as adjustable chairs are available, a desk height does not need to be large enough to accommodate all users' heights and so could possibly be designed to accommodate, say, 90 or 95 per cent. For these reasons it is important also to have details of the variability of the various body structures in addition to the 'average'. For most purposes, a range of dimensions from the 5th to the 95th percentile (that is, from a dimension representing the smaller 5 per cent to one which represents 95 per cent of the population) is generally acceptable.

A further problem with the overuse of simple averages as statistical indicators should be pointed out. This is the fallacy of the 'average person'. Because the dimensions of various body parts are not related in a constant ratio, it is not possible to describe accurately the dimensions of one part by reference to another. Thus, it is not possible to say, for example, that because a person has an average height he or she will also have an average arm length. Robinette and McConville (1981) have demonstrated this fact both statistically and by practical example and, as long ago as 1952, Daniels demonstrated the fallacy of this 'average man' concept. He considered the dimensions of 1055 subjects who had an average stature and found that only 302 (29 per cent) also had an average chest girth, 143 (14 per cent) had average chest girth *and* sleeve length, etc. Indeed, when only six body dimensions were added to the equation he found only six of the original sample were 'average' in all six dimensions. (It should be noted that Daniels, conservatively, defined 'average' as falling in the central 25 per cent of the dimension distribution. Had he taken a true average of mean ±0 s.d., the proportion that are average in all dimensions would have been very much smaller.)

Sources of anthropometric variability

The wide distribution of body dimensions and shapes which may be encountered in any one population can often be due to slight genetic differences. However other, more readily observable, variables can also affect body dimensions and their variability, and these include age, sex, culture, occupation and even historical trends.

Age

The change in body dimensions from birth to maturity is well known and, indeed, the increases occur consistently although sometimes irregularly. For height, as for most other body lengths, full growth is attained for all practical purposes by the age of 20 in males and 17 in females (Damon, Stoudt and McFarland, 1971). Some 'shrinkage' of older people has also been noted (Stoudt *et al.*, 1965) and this is due mainly to biological changes that take place as a part of the normal ageing process — flattening of the discs between the vertebrae, general thinning of the weight-bearing cartilages, etc. It can also be related to some of the secular trends discussed below although, using a variety of statistical techniques, Trotter and Gleser (1951) were able to show a statistically significant decline of stature with age that was separate from any of the secular effects. Stoudt (1981) provides data showing the decrease in a number of body dimensions between the ages of 18 and 74 years.

Sex

With the increasing observance of sexual equality in the workplace, designing for differences in body dimensions between the sexes will become an important aspect of the ergonomist's task. In this respect males are generally larger than females for most body dimensions, and the extent of the difference varies from one dimension to another. Examples of this may be seen in the various hand dimensions provided by Garrett (1971). In each of the 34 different dimensions (hand length, thickness, and depth; hand, fist and wrist circumference; digit length and thickness, etc.), male sizes were larger than female sizes with the greatest differences occurring in the thickness dimensions (males' dimensions being approximately 20 per cent larger than those of the females). For the length dimensions (hand, finger) males were approximately 10 per cent larger than females.

Women, however, are consistently larger than men in the four dimensions of chest depth, hip breadth, hip circumference and thigh circumference. Pregnancy markedly affects certain female dimensions, mainly in the abdomen and pelvic regions but also the breasts. Such changes begin to reach anthropometric significance about the fourth month of pregnancy (Damon, Stoudt and McFarland, 1971), and Diffrient *et al.* (1974) suggest that the average female abdominal depth increases from 6.5 to 11.7 inches throughout pregnancy.

O'Brien (1985) details a number of specific anthropometric areas in which males and females differ.

Culture

The importance of national and cultural differences in anthropometry has been realized for some time but until recently there has been little concerted effort to implement the relevant data in the production of new plant and machinery. As Chapanis (1974) suggests, up to the present time ergonomics has been largely an American and Western European discipline. With more efficient communication and travel facilities, however, and with the emergence of newly industrialized countries, the need to design different environments to fit all populations is becoming felt. He further points out:

> Today Americans buy automobiles, typewriters, taperecorders and calculating machines made in France, Germany, Britain and Japan. We in turn sell our computers, aircraft and farm machinery to Europe, Africa, South America, Western Europe and perhaps soon to the People's Republic of China. Similarly the European Common Market has resulted in a free interchange not only of products, but of workers among the several countries belonging to that confederation. These are only a few of the internationalizations of business and commerce that have become an important fact of modern life.
> (*Reprinted from* Ergonomics *by permission of the publisher.*)

The implication of this statement should be clear: in addition to leading to poor worker performance, inappropriate anthropometric design may result in the loss of orders and exports to overseas countries.

The variability in anthropometric dimensions due to national and cultural differences may not all be as dramatic as the difference between the Central African Pygmy tribes (average male height, 144 cm) and the Northern Nitoles of Southern Sudan (average male height, 183 cm) (Roberts, 1975). However, for design purposes the differences are important. Kennedy (1975) illustrates this point with data relating to the range of heights of seven military populations: United States, France, Germany, Italy, Japan, Thailand and Vietnam. Relating these statures to cockpit design, he points out that it is customary in the US Air Force to design for the central 90 per cent of the population (i.e. from the 5th to the 95th percentile). Whereas this range would accommodate essentially the same percentage of Germans, as far as height is concerned it would fit only the upper 80 per cent of the French, 69 per cent of Italians, 43 per cent of Japanese, 24 per cent of Thai and 14 per cent of Vietnamese users.

Variations also appear to exist between people in different areas within the same country. For example, Guillien and Rebiffé (1980) analysed the statures of a large number of bus drivers from East and West France. Their data, shown in Figure 3.3, illustrates a large difference between the statures of sub-samples, although the decrease in stature with age is fairly similar.

For reference purposes White (1975) has collated anthropometric data for the weights, heights, sitting heights and chest circumferences of male, military samples from 19 countries.

Occupation

Differences in body size and proportions among occupational groups are common and are fairly well known. For example, many body dimensions of a manual labourer are on average larger than than those of an academic.

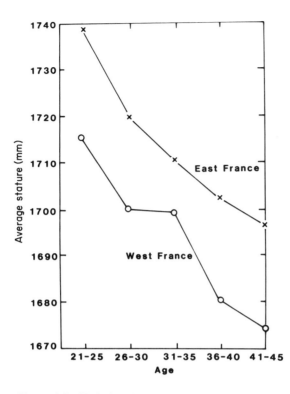

Figure 3.3 Variation in stature with age in people from two different areas of France. (Reproduced with permission from Guillien and Rebiffé, 1980, 'Anthropometric models of a population of bus drivers'. *In D.J. Oborne and J. Levis (eds)*, Human Factors in Transport Research, Vol I, *copyright by Academic Press* Inc. *(London) Ltd.)*

However, such differences may also be related to age, diet, exercise or many other factors, in addition to some degree of self-selection. For example, only males taller than 172 cm or females taller than 162 cm are accepted for recruitment for the British police force. Whatever the reasons for the differences, however, anthropometric variability in different occupations must be realized (a) for designing environments for the particular occupation, and (b) before using anthropometric data obtained from members of one occupation to design the environments of another.

Secular (historical) trends

Many people have observed that the equipment used in earlier years would be too small for efficient use today. Suits of armour, the heights of doors and the lengths of graves suggest the stature of people in former times, and each measurement is smaller than its modern counterpart. This has led to a suggestion that the average size of the population increases over time, perhaps because of better diet and living conditions. If true, such a suggestion would have important implications for the design of an environment that is to survive for some time — if we are getting taller, for example, then a design might need to take account of the statures of future generations as well as present-day users.

Some evidence exists to suggest that our body dimensions are increasing over shorter time periods than hundreds of years. For example comparing the statures, weights, sitting heights and chest circumferences of demobilized US soldiers from the First and Second World Wars, it appears that Second World War soldiers were, on average, 3 cm taller, 6.4 kg heavier, sat 0.9 cm higher with a chest circumference of 3.9 cm greater than their First World War counterparts. (Data drawn from White, 1975.) Unfortunately, however, such data are contaminated by the observation that the population's hygiene and diet have improved between the wars which could have provided more potential for growth. Thus, as Kroemer (1983) points out, body heights of families that have been well-off for generations no longer increase, while those of families still improving their socio-economic status show gains in stature. With favourable living conditions for most people, the increase might then diminish and body height, for example, will possibly level out (Stoudt, 1978). That this might have happened is implied by comparing the reports of two surveys of schoolchildren produced by Tanner (1962, 1978). In 1962 Tanner felt that the evidence pointed to an increasing secular trend and that puberty was occurring earlier. By 1978, however, he had pointed out that in some places, notably Oslo and London (for which data were available), the trend had appeared to have slowed down or stopped.

If the secular growth has not completely stopped, the significance of any secular changes that might occur over a decade or so (the usual life expectancy of modern machinery) also has to be considered. This problem has been well illustrated in a study by Guillien and Rebiffé (1980). They were concerned with producing adequately sized cabs for bus drivers, particularly since the vehicles are designed to be in service for two or three decades. From an anthropometric survey of over 8000 male bus drivers they were able to predict that the height of their drivers would increase by about 3 cm in ten years although, with the reduction of height with age, this figure would reduce to an increase in height of 2.3 cm over 15 years. Whether such small changes in stature will make much difference to the design of most technical equipment that is to be used over such relatively small time scales is a moot point.

BODY MOVEMENT: Biomechanics

The human body has been built to move by the action of its bones, joints and muscles, and the movement may take many varied and complicated forms. Because of this a separate sub-discipline, biomechanics, has been developed to consider the mechanics and range of human movement. Roebuck *et al.* (1975) define biomechanics as the

> Interdisciplinary science (comprising mainly anthropometry, mechanics, physiology and engineering) of the mechanical structure and behaviour of biological materials. It concerns primarily the dimensions, composition and mass properties of body segments, the joints linking the body segments together, the mobility in the joints, the mechanical relations of the body to force fields, vibrations and impacts, the voluntary actions of the body in bringing about controlled movements in applying forces, torques, energy and power to external objects like controls, tools and other equipment.

It is beyond the capacity of this section to consider the total range of interest of biomechanics, but the important actions of the person at work, namely those of walking and lifting will be discussed. The types of movements of the body segments and their respective angular limits may be obtained from reference texts (for example, Damon, Stoudt and MacFarland, 1971). However, it should be remembered when reading such figures that the ranges of joint motions vary from person to person due to anatomical differences, and also as a result of other factors such as age, sex, race, body build, exercise, occupation, fatigue, disease, body position and the presence or absence of clothing.

Locomotion

From an ergonomics standpoint, the mechanics of locomotion are important for a number of reasons. First, locomotion can lead to fatigue; secondly, understanding the way in which people walk may help in the design of suitable footware; thirdly, many accidents are caused by slipping (i.e. inadequate locomotion); and finally understanding how the normal legs work may help in the design of suitable prosthetic devices for the handicapped.

Walking from one place to another on two legs may seem to be a simple act. Actually it is the product of many complex interactions between the forces generated within the body and several external forces acting on it. These are co-ordinated in such a way as to produce not any 'step' but rather a particular pattern of movement known as 'normal step'. This is accomplished by means of a control system which automatically integrates changing conditions in the force–motion–position picture at a number of joints within the body and the changing pattern of external gravitational forces. As discussed in the last chapter, the vestibular apparatus in the ear plays a major part in this control system, which also corrects for changes in temperature, pressure, friction, loads being carried, obstacles, height, weight, and orientation in space.

In considering the way in which we walk, it is possible to make two separate levels of observations. The first is to observe the normal gait or movement of the legs and leg segments, and the second is to consider the more objective, but less easily observed, forces acting at the major joints.

To describe the biomechanics of gait, Peizer and Wright (1974) divide the cycle into two phases: stance and swing (see Figure 3.4). The stance phase begins

54

when the heel of one leg strikes the ground and ends when the toe of the same leg lifts off. The swing phase represents the period between toe off on one foot and heel contact on the same foot. As we alternate from swing to stance on each leg, there is a period when both feet are in contact with the ground simultaneously. This is called the period of 'double support' and occurs between push off and toe off on one foot and heel strike and 'foot flat' on the other (the absence of double support indicates that a person is running rather than walking).

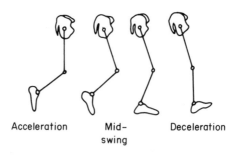

Figure 3.4 Diagrammatic representation of the stance and swing phases of human gait. (*After Peizer and Wright, 1974, and reprinted by permission of the Council of the Institution of Mechanical Engineers from* Human Locomotion Engineering).

At ordinary speeds, a single leg is in its stance phase for approximately 65 per cent of the cycle and in swing for approximately 35 per cent. The period of double support occupies between 25 and 30 per cent of the gait cycle time.

The forces which cause locomotion result from those created by the muscles and from external forces, principally the influence of gravity on the body.

When standing erect, the body's centre of gravity is in front of the hip, knee and ankle joints. This force tends to bend (flex) the hip, straighten (extend) the knee and bend (dorsiflex) the ankle. To begin walking we normally relax the muscles in one leg, allowing the body to fall forward to that side, and swing the leg forward at the hip.

Slipping and Tripping

The importance of analysing the normal gait and the motions which produce it may be seen in Figure 3.4. The section of gait producing the most instability is at the push off of one leg; at this point minimum contact is made with the ground. What contact there is occurs only through the toes of one foot. In addition, the pelvis is well forward of the contact point and stability is further reduced by the other leg being swung forward. It is at this point that most slips occur.

Slips can take place on turning, and sideways slips of the forefoot can also occur. The likelihood of such turning slips can increase if the person is carrying a load. In the unladen state arm swing is used to offset some of the rhythmical acceleration and deceleration of the trunk caused by the leg movements, and also to damp out the rotational forces on the trunk from the same causes. When holding objects these effects are not available, and increased rotational torques are needed at the foot–ground contact (Davis, 1983a).

Slipping is one of the most common causes of accidents on the job, and Davis (1983b) estimates that injuries resulting from slipping, tripping and falling can account for up to 40 per cent of lost-time accidents. Manning (1983) provides further analyses of such accident data, although he points out that whereas data are readily available that describe the antecedents and results of falls, equivalent slipping data are elusive.

Carlsoo (1972) suggests that there are two particularly critical phases of the normal gait at which slipping is likely to occur. The first is at heel strike at the beginning of the stance phase. The weight of the body is then lying behind the contact point of the heel and the ground, while the movement of the body's centre of gravity has just started the swing phase. The second critical instant is at the actual push-off when the body's centre of gravity lies in front of the pushing foot. Such assertions have been confirmed by Strandberg (1983) who filmed over 100 laboratory 'skids'. It could well be said that the first of these two instances presents the greatest danger since a person who slips when the centre of gravity is behind the foot is liable to fall backwards with little chance of using the hands to stop the fall. At least if the slip is during the second instant the body is bent forwards and is, therefore, likely to fall forwards.

The extent to which slipping occurs depends largely on the static friction which exists between the foot and floor prior to the slip. Carlson also suggests that slipping is highly likely to occur if the coefficient of friction between the foot is less than that required for normal walking (about 0.4).

Finally, it should be remembered that under relatively normal circumstances we are often able to walk on what would otherwise be slippery surfaces (for example, ice). This is because we adopt different postures and behaviours as a result of the environmental conditions. Thus, the coefficient of friction depends on two forces which act normally and tangentially on the foot. For any given combination of floor surface and footware the resultant coefficient of friction can be increased by using the ankle, leg and hip muscles to alter the forces which act on the foot — generally by shortening the stride. (Figure 3.5 illustrates the relationship between stride and the coefficient of friction necessary for stability.) If the muscles are used too frequently to overcome the tendency to slip, however, they will soon become fatigued. Once again, therefore, it is clear that the environment should be adapted to suit the operator, otherwise its poor design will soon become apparent.

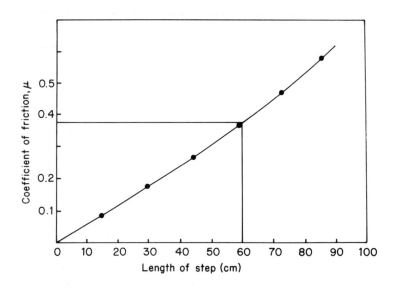

Figure 3.5 The calculated relationship between step length and coefficient of friction necessary for stability (after James, 1983)

Lifting

Lifting is an action which is frequently required in work. However, it is one which, if carried out incorrectly, may result at the very least in back pain and discomfort or at the worst in permanent disability. Benn and Wood (1975), for example, have estimated that over 13 million days a year are lost in industry due to painful back conditions. As they point out, this constitutes a greater loss of time than even strikes (between 6.8 and 11 million days in 1969 and 1970 respectively).

Although it is clear that back complaints are a significant cause of time lost at work, as with slipping accidents it is difficult to gather industrial data about the precise relationship between materials handling and back injuries. David (1985a), for example, points to very general category descriptions being used in accident reports which vary between different industrial sectors and even within the same sector from year to year. Fully meaningful interpretations of such data, therefore, are very difficult to make.

Despite such pessimistic comments it is possible to draw some conclusions from accident statistics and these imply a very strong relationship between inappropriate materials handling and the incidence of spinal injuries. For example, although Nicholson (1983) echoes David's comments regarding the quality of official accident reports, he used a confidential questionnaire which was administered to victims of accidents detailed in the official reports. Over a range of occupations his data suggest a very good relationship between the numbers of back injuries reported and those attributed by the victims to handling incidents. While a strong relationship does not imply a direct causal relationship, the data clearly demonstrates some link between handling and back injuries. They also show that approximately 25 per cent of all accidents gave rise to some form of back injury in the industries that he studied (telecommunications, electrical and construction workers).

Although such data should alert the ergonomist to considering the rôle of materials handling in accident causation, other features of the job should not be forgotten when considering the full relationship between lifting and back injuries. For example, Magora (1972) conducted a survey of over 3000 workers in Israel to determine the incidence of low back pain, and considered their occupational requirements in terms of sitting, standing and lifting. The results he obtained, shown in Table 3.2, are extremely interesting from a number of points of view. First, more workers experienced pain symptoms who rarely or never sat, stood or lifted in their jobs than those who did so often. Secondly, the distributions of back pain for weight-lifting jobs were not significantly different from the sitters or standers. Thirdly, they would suggest that the way to reduce the possibility of back pain is to introduce variability in the work.

Table 3.2 Proportions of workers complaining of lower back pain (LBP) having different occupational requirements for sitting, standing and lifting (from Magora, 1972)

Sitting	Proportion complaining of LBP (%)
Often	12.6
Sometimes	1.5
Rarely	25.9
Standing	
More than four hours per day	13.8
Variable	2.5
Less than four hours per day	24.9
Lifting	
Often	13.9
Variable	2.5
Rarely	28.1

Variables affecting the prevalence of back injury due to lifting

As with many other factors at work, attempting to detail the precise effects of any particular factor is extremely difficult because no one variable acts alone and no one variable is a single factor. The effects of specific features are often confounded with behaviour. Take age, for example. Although this is simple to measure it is related to other factors: there is degeneration of the body, the rate of which is different for different people (Brinkmann, 1985), as well as a reduction in strength of the trunk muscles that resist internal pressures when lifting (Stubbs, 1985). Also, with age there is often an increase in skill — more skilled individuals might handle the material in a more appropriate manner. Sex is another variable often considered in relation to lifting but any sex differences in lifting capacity can be attributed as much to experience as they can to structural differences of men and women's bodies. Occupational differences may be confounded as much by the fact that people often choose different occupations because of their abilities as to the possibility that different tasks may contribute more or less to back injury, etc. The effects of task-related variables, of course, for example the size, weight and carrying ability of the object, can greatly confound the effects of these individual (subject) variables.

Individual variables

With regard to age and occupation, in his questionnaire survey of workers in three types of industry Nicholson (1983) demonstrated the highest risk group to be aged somewhere in the thirties, although this was highly related to the type of work done. Thus, in the construction industry the highest accident frequency occurred in the younger age groups (16–30) whereas in the telecommunications industry the problem was faced more by older workers (31–45 years).

A confounding factor that affects the extent to which age and occupation can be seen as important variables is training: different industries provide different degrees and qualities of training for their younger workers. For example, Nicholson (1983) points out that apprentices in the construction industry rarely receive any instruction in the prevention of back injury accidents; younger workers tend to take pride in physical strength rather than manual skill. Apprentices in the telecommunications and electrical industries, however, undergo an extensive four-year training period during which time they are instructed and supervised, and attention is paid to the skill aspect of their jobs. It could be argued, therefore, that the age distribution of injuries noted above for these two industries reflects both the training given to younger workers and the behaviours adopted.

Of course, when discussing the effects of individual variables such as age on the prevalence of back injury, the attitudes and practices of organizations need to be taken into consideration. For example, occupations in which heavy materials have to be lifted generally expect the younger workers to perform that task. In addition some occupations do not allow workers to perform heavy work who have either had an injury previously or who have a history of back disorders. The variable of age, therefore, is confounded by experience and occupation.

With regard to occupation *per se*, it is clear that different types of workers have different degrees of risk — even within the same profession. Again, this might relate to training and to learned behaviours. The nursing profession, for example, presents a particularly high-risk group, with 67 per cent of the back pain being attributed to patient handling. Stubbs *et al.* (1983) report identifying significant differences in the occurrence of back pain between nurses of different status, showing that auxiliary and student nurses were most at risk of back pain from patient handling. Subsequent analysis, however, demonstrated the multifactorial nature of this problem, in so far as sex, full- and part-time nursing, status and ward speciality were also shown to have some effect.

With regard to sex as an individual variable, mention has already been made of its potential within the nursing profession. David (1985b) measured intra-truncal pressures in women and demonstrated lower optimal levels than in men. On average, the female limits were between 45 and 60 per cent those of men.

Task related variables

In addition to the operator's ability actually to lift the material, of course, the ways in which the material presents itself is likely to have implications for the lifting quality and efficiency. In this respect, the object's size, weight (and weight distribution), as well as its position in relation to the lifter, are important features to consider — as, too, is the frequency with which the object is to be lifted.

Size was shown by Cirello and Snook (1983) to have important effects on the maximum acceptable lifting load, although they point out that the important size parameter is the object's width. It is this which determines the angles at which the lifter can grasp the object when the usual side-wise grasp is made. These conclusions are confirmed by Garg *et al.* (1983), the maximum acceptable load decreases in a fairly linear fashion as the object width increases (they used widths between 30 and 65 cm).

Clearly, then, the extent to which an object can be lifted will depend on how well it can be grasped and thus the arm and hand postures that can be adopted. Grips and handles on the object can, therefore, influence the object's lifting abilities. In this respect, a survey by Drury *et al.*, (1982) demonstrated that very few boxes had handles and, even when handles were provided, frequently they were not used. Often the lifter's behaviour was to grasp the boxes at the corners. This begs the question, then, of whether the principles of Procrustes are being applied to handles: they may be provided but of such a shape, position, design, etc. that means they are difficult to use or cause more strain that if they were not used at all. Regarding handle design, Drury and Pitzella (1983) describe a number of variables, including shape, size and texture that should be taken into account.

Handle position is a variable that is more difficult to define since it will be determined by the task to be performed. In this respect, and following from the results of the 1982 survey and subsequent studies, Drury (1985) argues that for most movements of box-like objects an asymmetrical, diagonal handle position is best with the left hand being higher than the right (presumably for right-handed lifters). Of course, the position of the handle on the box will also affect the angle that the wrist makes to the lifting plane. In this respect Drury *et al.* (1985) have demonstrated significant effects of wrist angle on the maximum amount able to be lifted, with some changes in wrist angle producing an equivalent load to a 16 per cent variation in object weight.

In respect to handle position, a further consideration is the extent to which the grasp points are placed so that the object's centre of gravity is also well positioned. For example, Mital and Manivasagan (1983) demonstrated that the maximum acceptable weight lift is significantly reduced when the load's centre of gravity is offset towards either of the two hands, although less so if the offset is towards the preferred hand. Offsetting the centre of gravity in the other plane — that is, away from the body — means that the load distance from the body is increased, again causing reduced lifting capacity.

Finally, it should not be forgotten that sometimes lifting does not occur simply in a free environment. Often, environmental constraints are present with which the lifter has to contend: other machines, walls, even ceilings. Each can impose spatial restrictions that can interfere with lifting efficiency. For example, Ridd (1985) demonstrated performance reductions as soon as available headroom decreased below about 90 per cent of the lifter's stature. Barriers at both the front and side of the lifter also decreased lifting ability, although Ridd noted one beneficial effect of such barriers. When more than one barrier was present they sometimes combined to *reduce* the stress experienced — subjects often used them to provide extra support during the lifting task. Although the experimental design did not include barriers at the back, rear barriers may be particularly beneficial in providing this supporting function for the lumbar region.

Lifting methods

The evidence presented so far suggests that a number of variables, to do with both the lifter and what is being lifted, can interact to affect the extent to which lifting can take place with comparative safety. The final consideration must be the posture adopted by the lifter before and during the lift. Since the posture adopted can influence both the back stresses experienced and factors such as the object's centre of gravity and thus weight distribution, the lifting method employed can be crucially important.

There are essentially two ways in which objects are lifted. The first, commonly known as the derrick action, derives its name from its general similarity to the action of a derrick crane. Throughout the lifting operation the knees are kept fully extended and the back and arms flexed forwards to grasp the object. Lifting is done by extending, or attempting to extend, the lumbar region of the spine and hip joint. For this reason this type of posture is also called the back lift.

In the second method, known as the squat or leg lift, the grasp is made by folding the legs as in squatting. In this technique the trunk is maintained quite erect and the lifting action occurs primarily as a result of extending the knee joint which, in turn, extends the hip joint. There are two variations to this technique: in the first, the heel is lifted from the ground so that the load is borne by the muscles in the upper leg. In the second, the heel of at least one foot remains in contact with the ground giving more stability and allowing some of the forces to pass through more of the feet (Bendix and Eid, 1983) (see Figure 3.6).

Leg-lifting   Back-lifting

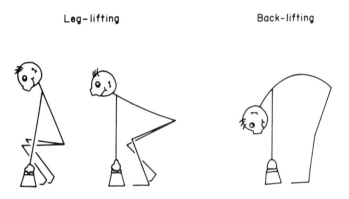

Figure 3.6   Three lifting techniques

Many workers, for example Davis and Troup (1964), have shown that manual activity is regularly accompanied by considerable increases in intra-abdominal pressure. This is due to the action which all of the muscles around the abdomen (the diaphragm, pelvic floor and anterior abdominal wall) have on the fluid contents of the abdomen. These pressure increases are related to the force acting on the lower spine, and Davis and Stubbs (1977a) have demonstrated that occupations in which peak intra-truncal pressures of 100 mm Hg or more are induced, have an increased liability to report back injuries. (This was particularly so for the mining and construction industries.) Such pressures can be monitored by swallowing a small pressure sensitive radio pill and, using a device of this nature, Davis and Stubbs (1977a,b; 1978) have produced a series of levels of the single loads or forces which can be lifted safely by fit young males, standing, sitting, kneeling and squatting with the back erect. Their data, however, were obtained from a military population and care must be taken if they are to be used for civilian applications. However, Davis et al. (1980) have reported that a male industrial population produced very similar data up to the age of about 40 years, but the maximum loads which they could lift safely decreased to about 75 per cent of the military data after about age 50.

Because the stresses resulting from different lifting postures will be borne by different parts of the anatomy, and because the postures will result in different positions of the body's centre of gravity (Bendix and Eid, 1983), it is clear that the lifting posture adopted is likely to have significant effects on the intra-truncal pressures and the amount of muscular loads experienced. This has been found to be so by a number of authors, with the combined wisdom suggesting that the back lift method is hazardous to the lower back. Thus Eckholm et al. (1982) measured the forces acting on the lumbar vertebrae during different types of lifting. They demonstrated significantly lower compressive forces during the leg lift rather than the back lift. These conclusions were confirmed by Leskinen et al. (1983). They also demonstrated that, during leg lift, significantly more of the force was conducted through the feet than in the back lift; during back lift the spinal discs (measured between the last lumbar and first sacral vertebrae — see Chapter 9) received significantly higher compressive forces.

With regard to the two forms of leg lifting technique (heel flat and heel off) Bendix and Eid (1983) have demonstrated that the heel off position allows the object to be lifted much closer to the body — so reducing the load placed on the lumbar vertebrae. Nevertheless, such a posture is possible only if the object can be lifted between the outstretched knees — for larger objects the arms will need to be extended and thus the knees kept together. In such a situation, it may be that the object passes the knees at a greater distance from the body with leg lifting than with back lifting. Again, then, the complex interactions of variables contributing to safe lifting is apparent.

Finally, it should be remembered that such conclusions are based solely on forces exerted using the different techniques and takes little account of features of the body during lifting. For example, Davies (1972) emphasizes that bending and twisting during a lift causes spinal injury and this is more likely to occur during a back lift. Furthermore, in addition to causing potential damage to the spine, the increased pressures in the truncal region predisposes the operator to a hernia.

A pamphlet Lifting in Industry (Anon., 1966) has been prepared to advance the correct lifting technique. In essence it describes the knee action in terms of (1) the feet should be far enough apart for balanced distribution of the weight; (2) the knees and hips should be bent and the back kept as straight as possible with the chin tucked in; (3) the arms should be held as near to the body as possible; (4) wherever possible, the whole of the hand should be used to grasp; and (5) lifts should be made smoothly without jerks or snatches.

The following formulae (from Poulsen and Jorgensen, 1971) may be used to predict the maximum lifting load using this type of action:

males: maximum load = 1.1 × isometric back muscle strength
females: maximum load = 0.95 × isometric back muscle strength – 8 kg

These figures, however, refer to a single lift. Jorgensen and Poulsen (1974) have demonstrated that lifting ability falls dramatically when repeated lifts need to be made. The relationship follows closely the one seen between strength and endurance. Thus the authors suggest that only between two or three lifts per minute should take place if the load to be lifted is 75 per cent of the maximum load possible. For a load of only 10 per cent of maximum, six to nine lifts per minute can be tolerated. Ronnholm (1962), however, has demonstrated that if such lifts are able to be interspersed rhythmically with short rest periods, efficiency and output may be increased and the work-load may be reduced. The sex, age, height and body weight of the lifter, however, may affect these conclusions, as was shown above.

Before concluding the discussion of lifting, it should be noted that Procrustes is starting to rear his head. One might well question whether, by instructing industrial man to adopt the knee action, one is attempting once again to fit man to the environment rather than make the environment fit the person. If the derrick action is the natural lifting posture, then the mere fact that heavier loads might be able to be lifted more safely by some other action should simply mean that reductions should be made in the maximum loads able to be lifted — not that man should be trained to adopt an unnatural posture. As was illustrated in Chapter 1, training may become ineffective under conditions of stress.

SUMMARY

This chapter has considered some of the structures in the final link in the man-machine–man system — the bones, joints and muscles. No matter how efficiently a mechanical system has been designed — how fast it works, how reliable it is, how aesthetically pleasing it appears — if the operators cannot fit into it or around it, if they cannot pull the levers or push the buttons with sufficient force for a sufficient length of time, or if they cannot reach the controls in the first place, then the mechanical system is at the least effectively useless and at worst potentially dangerous.

CHAPTER 4

MAN–MAN COMMUNICATION: WORDS AND SYMBOLS

Chapters 2 and 3 discussed in detail the physiological aspects of people that have implications for their efficient interaction with their environment. It is now time to turn towards their psychological functioning and features of their behaviour that can influence the efficiency of a man–machine system. Underlying this interaction is the information that is passed between actors within the system — people and machines.

In many respects information is the cornerstone of our civilization. Without it governments could not govern, generals would be unable to win battles, and industrial organizations would not be able to function properly. However much we might complain about the bad news we hear and see each day, as individuals we would find it difficult to function adequately without constant, accurate, updated information about the state of our world and our interactions with it. The transmission of information between individuals, therefore, plays an extremely important, indeed a fundamental, role in everyday living and working.

As was outlined in Chapter 1, in some respects ergonomics itself can be viewed as the science of ensuring efficient information communication between important parts of the man–machine system. Of course, this information does not appear simply as the written or spoken word — information implies an increase in knowledge and so can take any form. Thus you, the reader, are presently gathering information (hopefully) from this book, but at the same time you are also gaining knowledge about your body state (from, for example, proprioceptive receptors in your muscles), about the environment (from your ears, temperature receptors, etc.) and about people around you (from your ears, nose, etc.). Similarly, a person at work collects information from a variety of sources. For example, an operator is likely to need information about how a machine works, how to operate it safely, what to do when it breaks down, and so on. Much of this will obviously be obtained from colleagues, a supervisor or a manual, but information is also transmitted from the machine via its displays informing the operator, for example, about its heat, speed, or activity.

The operator also communicates with the machine — via controls — 'telling' it what needs to be done: to go up, to go down, to turn right, or to increase speed.

Information, then, is important in the working environment but so, too, is the way in which the information is transmitted. In many respects it is as crucial as the message being conveyed.

Put in its simplest terms, any communication system comprises only two components: a transmitter who (or which) communicates information through some medium to a receiver. Only if the receiver interprets the information in the way intended by the transmitter can proper communication be said to have occurred. The point may perhaps be illustrated by an example in which two people who speak different languages are trying to converse. Any difficulties experienced arise largely from the receiver being unable to translate correctly the ideas conveyed by the transmitter. In such cases 'sign language' possibly helps the communication process by placing the message in a different medium — but one which can be understood by both. The communication problem, however, might be increased if one of the two can speak a smattering of the other's language but interprets the message incorrectly. In this case the communication system is likely to break down because of misunderstandings.

Because effective communication is so important for efficient working, and because inefficient communication can cause the man–machine system to break down, one of the ergonomist's primary functions is to design systems which will enhance the chances of the message being received and understood correctly. For this reason the present, and following two, chapters will consider different aspects of this communication process.

Since either a person or a machine can act as the transmitter or the receiver, four possible combinations of transmitter and receiver can be envisaged: a person communicating with another person; a machine communicating with a person; a person communicating with a machine; and a machine communicating with another machine. Since the first three of these options involve human behaviour in that the operator interacts with the environment, they are within the realms of ergonomics and will be discussed in this and in the next two chapters. The fourth option (machine–machine communication) lies more in the domain of the cyberneticist or the engineer and will not be discussed in this book.

The present chapter will consider the problems presented by 'man' to 'man' communication — primarily those involved in the written communication of information and instructions. Detailed considerations of purely verbal interactions lie well outside the boundaries of this book, although indications of the importance of understanding verbal behaviour and some the the variables that influence efficient behaviour will appear in this chapter. Chapter 5 will continue the communication links by considering the question of communication between the machine and the operator, while the channels for reply (from the operator to the machine) will be discussed in Chapter 6.

MEANING, COMMUNICATION AND THE MESSAGE

The process underlying communication can perhaps best be understood when one realizes that the linguistic origin of the word is the Latin *communis*, meaning 'common'. One clear characteristic of meaning in human communication, therefore, is its 'commonness' — an essential prerequisite being a common understanding by those involved in the communication process. However, this quality of commonness does not necessarily mean that all participants in the communicative process have to have *identical* understandings of the symbols or thoughts transmitted, so long as some understanding is common to them all (Fisher, 1978). Communication can take place, therefore, even if the transmitter and receiver do not 'speak the same language' — as long as the basic ideas being transmitted in the message are received accurately.

The role of ergonomics, then, is to arrange a situation which enhances the chances of the transmitter and the receiver having a maximum common understanding. However, before looking at the ways in which this state of affairs may come about it is interesting to consider briefly some of the reasons why the two may not display this commonness — why meanings and messages might be misinterpreted.

First personalities might be involved. A receiver who dislikes or mistrusts the transmitter could be unreceptive to what is being said. Indeed, the receiver's understanding of the message could well be distorted by negative opinions of the transmitter or by imputed motives. Secondly even if the receiver is receptive to the message it may become distorted by personal preconceptions (or 'set'). As Bartlett (1950) has argued, one of the chief functions of the active mind is to 'fill up gaps', that is constantly to try to link new material with older material to make it more meaningful. So a message might be distorted by the receiver placing it in a context in which it is not meant to be placed, simply because of a 'set' to the message.

Thirdly, there is the problem of interest and attention. If the receiver is not attending to the message, perhaps because of boredom, part of it may easily be missed or misinterpreted. Finally messages can become distorted because of our limited capacity to process the transmitted information. This concept has already been discussed briefly when dealing with our ability to store different stimuli but it also applies to the storage of complex, meaningful material such as ideas and concepts. If the message is too detailed or too long it may overload our memory system and become distorted, lost or simply unable to be retrieved. In summary, therefore, the common channel for communication may be distorted by social influences, by personal attitudes and expectations, by boredom and a lack of interest, or by information overload.

Messages which have to be transmitted between people take many forms, and Miller (1972) divides them into three groups according to the physical appearance of the stimulus. These he terms verbal (including written words and signs), vocal (including spoken words and voice variations) and physical (including gestures and movements) stimuli. The remainder of this chapter will consider, primarily, the influence which ergonomics can play in facilitating the transmission of 'verbal' stimuli (including written communication). As the reader will become aware, many of the principles involved with verbal stimuli may also be applied to vocal stimuli but, because other aspects of the environment may possibly be important (for example environmental noise, or social and organizational factors), the specific problems of speech communication will be dealt with in Chapers 5 and 10. The role of non-verbal stimuli in the communication process (body signs, gestures, etc.) is one which is too wide for the scope of this book. However, texts such as those by Argyle and Cook (1976) or Morris (1977) may prove interesting. Christie (1981) illustrates the extent to which such non-verbal cues can influence the efficiency of electronic communication between people.

PERCEPTUAL PROCESSES IN WRITTEN COMMUNICATION

Before considering how written communication (text, pictures, graphs, etc.) may be designed to enhance the communication process, it is appropriate to discuss aspects of the receiver's perceptual behaviour that might affect how the message could be perceived and recognized. Two features are important in this respect: first, the ways in which the eyes are made to move over the presented information and thus begin the process of *reception*. Second, how the observer integrates and organizes the information. This is the process of *perception*.

Eye Movements

Whereas it is possible to hear speech and sounds quite passively, reading words and pictures is a very active process. Because the most acute part of the retina is towards the centre, near the fovea, the eyes constantly have to be moved to bring appropriate parts of the displayed material into view. Since a stable image is only formed when both the eyes and the object are stationary, however, visual scanning during reading is characterized by a succession of fast movements and stationary periods. The fast jerks are called *saccades* and the stationary points are termed *fixations*. (Even during these fixation periods the eye makes relatively small tremors.)

The existence of saccadic eye movements during reading has been known since the turn of the century and so there is a fair amount of experimental literature available which deals with the subject (see Matin, 1974, for an historic review). It is only in more recent times, however, with the development of sophisticated equipment, that the investigation of these movements and their implications for understanding the cognitive processes involved in reading and comprehension has been able to be performed with any accuracy (see Young and Sheena, 1975, for a survey of the techniques).

The two important parameters of saccadic movements that relate to reading efficiency are the duration of each fixation and the number of fixations required.

In this respect, the average length of a saccade appears to be about two degrees of visual angle (which is about six ten-pitch or eight twelve-pitch character spaces) and, for skilled readers, the average fixation durations lie between 200 and 250 ms (Rayner, 1977). However, there is a great deal of individual variability in this matter. For example, Rayner (1978) reports that even for a single person reading a particular passage, saccade lengths often range from 2 to 18 character positions or more, and fixation durations range from 100 to over 500 ms. This variability in reading skill can be related to an individual's reading efficiency.

A simple exercise in introspection, of course, would indicate that saccadic eye movements do not take the form simply of continuous movement from, for European texts, left to right over the page. The eye's movements also include a third characteristic of saccadic movements — *regressions*. A regression is a movement in the opposite direction to the normal saccadic scan (that is, for English, in the right-left direction) and occurs approximately 10–20 per cent of the time in skilled readers (Rayner, 1978). They are assumed to occur when the reader has difficulty understanding the text, misinterprets it and/or when the reader overshoots the next fixation target. They also occur, of course, when the reader reaches the end of one line and needs to start processing the text on the next (although Rayner, 1978, argues that these movements should be distinguished from a regression, both because they are necessary to continue the reading proces and because there is some suggestion that they involve different cognitive control processes).

Discussing the relationship of line saccades to the reading process, Bouma (1980) points to the importance of typographical design:

> The horizontal extent of line saccades is controlled by visual information in the left visual field, concerning the far left-hand margin, which should therefore be in a straight vertical line ... with a sufficiently wide margin. ... The vertical extent of line saccades is controlled by perceived inter-line distance. If this vertical component is inaccurate, the eye may mistakenly jump over two or perhaps even three lines.

Thus use of such information to the appropriate design and layout of text will be considered later.

PERCEPTUAL ORGANIZATION AND VISUAL SEARCHING

The ways in which the eyes move over the printed material, then, influence the extent to which the material will be at least received efficiently. However it has been argued, for example Rayner (1977), that eye movements are controlled by the observer's cognitive processes occuring at the time. This *process monitoring hypothesis*, then, suggests some form of complex interplay between our perception and understanding of what is being read and eye movement control during reading. Following this line of argument, to ensure appropriate layout for ease and speed of perception it is as important to understand how we organize our perception as it is to understand how we control our scanning process when reading.

Perceptual organization

A number of models exist to explain how we organize our perceptual world (see, for example, Vickers, 1979) but one of the most enduring theories to have emerged over the years arose in the 1920s from the German *Gestalt* school of psychology. The Gestaltist's predictions regarding perceptual organization provide some very simple suggestions as to how textual (and other) information should be arranged for easy perception.

The essential feature of the school of thought is that individual stimuli are grouped together during perception into wholes or *Gestalts*. These Gestalts posses features of their own that are not obvious from an examination of their individual parts. Take, for example, the object that you are now observing: what you see is **a book**. This book is an entity in itself; it has meaning to you as a book. Although the book is composed of separate pages, each page containing printed words, each word being composed of individual letters, each letter having different features, you do not see the object in this way. You see it as a 'whole'; the words, paragraphs or pages themselves do not imply the book — it is the whole book that implies the book. One of the principal aims of the Gestalt psychologists has been to specify the principles by which individual items are combined into larger, organized wholes. They also seek to find the principles by

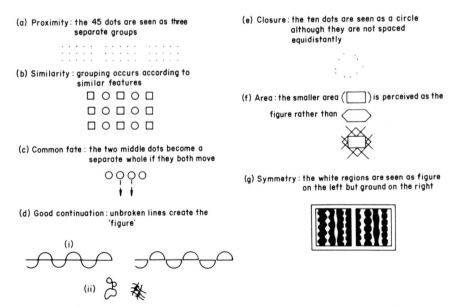

Figure 4.1 Examples of Gestalt principles for perceptual organization

which these wholes are perceptually segregated and separated from other wholes. In other words, how the figure stands out from its background. Many of these principles are described by Wertheimer (1958) and are based on subjects' reactions to simple patterns of dots and line drawings. Examples of these principles are shown in Figure 4.1.

Perhaps one of the most important of the principles is *proximity* which states that organization of individual elements into groups occurs on the basis of distance: the smaller the distance between elements the more likely they will be perceived as a whole — as a figure that stands out from the ground. As an example, simply flick through the pages in this book: small sections of text, with headings, stand out as being separate from the remainder of the text because of their distance from the last line of the previous section.

Along with proximity is the principle of *similarity*. Similar features are likely to be grouped together so that, for example, the pictures in this book are seen to be different from the text — as in Figure 4.1 which is composed of small figures. Figure 4.1 is perceptually organized as *a figure* because the similar smaller figures are grouped together and are different from the surrounding text. Using special highlighting features such as colour or underlining can help to create an appearance of similarity. If a particular pattern conforms both to the principles of proximity and similarity, Hochberg and Silverstein (1956) demonstrated that the principle of similarity is stronger than that of proximity.

Two elements will also be organized together if they share the same *common fate*. Thus, if two portions of the text on a computer screen are flashing, or two areas or graphic symbols move in the same way, they will be treated as a whole — possibly as endpoints of an imaginary moving line.

This suggestion of an imagined continuation line between two common features is extended in the fourth Gestalt principle, that of *good continuation*. This states that the elements that are organized into wholes are those that produce few interruptions or changes in continuous lines. Of course, where interruptions do occur, the principle of closure (described below) might be invoked to produce a set of smaller, individual 'wholes' (see Figure 4.1d(i)). This principle also explains why it is sometimes difficult to perceive a particular shape embedded in another. For example, the continuation lines on the number 5 in Figure 4.1d(ii) make the whole shape into the 'figure' and the white paper surrounding it into the 'ground', rather than the '5' standing out as the figure and the remainder of the image as the ground.

Related to the principle of good continuation is the principle of *closure*. This states that we tend to organize elements so that they form simple, closed figures that are independent of other continuation, similarity or proximity properties. Such closed figures are often referred to as 'good figures'.

One major principle for determining whether a complete figure will be perceived as figure or ground is that of *area*: the smaller of two overlapping figures will be perceived as the figure and the other the ground. For example, in Figure 4.1f, the smaller square is seen as the figure against a grid background, rather than the hexagonal shape. A second principle of segregation, *symmetry*, states that the more symmetrical a figure is the more likely it is to be seen to be being a closed figure, and this isolates it from the ground.

Finally is the principle of *simplicity* which, as Hochberg and McAlister (1953) argue, probably underlies many of the other principles. They suggest that our perceptual processing system organizes input into the simplest interpretation possible. Gestalt principles such as closure, good figure, etc., then, are simply statements about which elements of a stimulus are the simplest to group.

In summary, the importance of these Gestalt principles should be quite evident. Since we perceive stimuli in terms solely of the ways that we arrange our perceptual world and since, as has already been discussed, our understanding of the information presented is guided largely by such perceptual organization, employing many of the principles suggested by the Gestalt school should make it possible to ensure that the operator perceives the material presented in the ways intended. This will be discussed in the next section but, before doing so, it is important to consider one further aspect of the ways that we extract detail from the information presented — that is how we organize our perceptual searching facilities. After all, when information is presented the operator generally has to perform some type of search task to perceive the fact: the eyes need to be directed towards the relevant part of the material before the information can be processed.

Visual scanning and search

The available data relating to the visual search process can be divided, essentially, into studies which have considered the effects of different display arrangements on the task and those dealing with the subjects themselves.

Display features

Perhaps one of the first important aspects to be considered when discussing display characteristics and scanning and search behaviour is the position of the information in the material-to-be-searched. Clearly, this can determine the part of the retina on which the stimuli fall and, because the retina is differentially sensitive, is likely to affect search performance.

A number of experimenters have shown this prediction to be true, both in terms of the probability of correctly identifying characters (for example, Bouma, 1973; Wolford and Hollingsworth, 1974a) and the time taken to identify characters (for example, Schiepers, 1980). In all cases, the evidence suggests that the further a character is displaced from the gaze fixation position, the less likely will it be identified correctly and the longer will it take to be identified. Of course, it should be remembered that the 'central point' in these studies implies the point at which the eye is fixated initially — not necessarily the centre of the material. The eyes can be drawn to highlighed parts of the material, for example, so that these areas become the fixation point. This might then mean that information at the central part of the material falls on the periphery of the retina.

Regarding the serial position of characters in a display, some evidence exists to suggest that identification is enhanced when gaps appear in the character string. Both Estes and Wolford (1971) and Wolford and Hollingsworth (1974b) have shown that a gap improves reporting accuracy for the letters that appear on either side of it. For example, take the following two arrangements of a character string:

A   V   F   T   Y   U   I   O   P   L   E

A   V   F   I   O   P   L   E

Accuracy for reporting the 'F' and the 'I' would be about 20 per cent better in the second than in the first string. This is possibly because, as the Gestalt school would argue, the gap enhances the principle of proximity. This creates the appearance of two substrings and allows attention to be directed to the letters on either side of it. As Gould (1976) suggests, 'people fixate on contours much more frequently than they fixate on homogeneous areas'. Furthermore, the evidence suggests that the letter preceding the gap (F) benefits more from the gap than that following it (I). Adequate spacing of displayed material, therefore, is likely to lead to increased detectability of individual items.

Detection efficiency is also related to the material that is displayed — particularly in terms of the display complexity and the distinguishability of the display items.

In terms of material complexity, Teichener and Krebs (1974) have reviewed a number of laboratory studies and have shown that the detection time for stimuli presented as arrays (like, for example, a complex table) increases dramatically with array densities above about 200 stimuli.

Another feature of display complexity concerns the number of different *types* of elements that make up the displays. For example, letters, numbers, pictures, and highlighted material. In this case, the evidence suggests that if too much information of this type is presented, the reader's cognitive capacities are likely to be overloaded and thus search performance reduced. For example, although using colour can considerably reduce search time (Christ, 1975), Green and Anderson (1956) concluded that search time was slightly longer for multi-coloured than for single-coloured displays.

The distinguishability of the displayed items is clearly likely to be an important factor in determining the efficiency of any search activity. In their literature survey, for example, Teichener and Krebs demonstrated that search efficiency was related to the extent to which the target stimulus stood out from the surrounding material. For example, when asked to detect squares in circles, subjects' performance deteriorated when only about ten stimuli at a time were presented. The deterioration point for black triangles among black circles, however, was not until about 200 stimuli were presented. With even greater distinguishability between the array elements, for example in detecting a large black circle among small black circles, very little deterioration occurred even with about 2000 display elements.

Subject features

Possibly the most important individual variable affecting processing performance concerns the information that the person wishes to extract from the display. This is related, of course, to the reasons for looking. For example, Buswell (1935) demonstrated that faces and hands are the most fixated areas of pictures containing people among other things. (Kolers, (1976), describes in detail some of Buswell's findings regarding perceptual span in reading and looking at pictures.) Mackworth and Morandi (1967) showed that the parts of pictures rated as being most informative by one group of subjects were fixated most by another group of subjects.

Related to display meaning in terms of importance is the individual's motivation for viewing the display — thus, people often search displays for meaning rather than to perceive specific targets. That observers are able to vary their search or scan patterns with their intentions was demonstrated well by Yarbus (1967). He showed subjects pictures of different scenes, such as a group of individuals in a room, and asked them to infer different things from the picture. For example, when asked to estimate the ages of the individuals, most eye fixations occurred around the facial regions; when asked to consider their social standing, most fixations related to the clothes and furniture, etc. Clearly, then, the observer's search and fixation pattern was related to the search intent.

TYPOGRAPHICAL FEATURES OF WRITTEN COMMUNICATION

The points made above concerning the ways in which the eyes scan over the text and how we search for material within the text have clear implications for presenting material. For written information to be communicated efficiently, the message needs not only to be read (and interpreted) correctly but it should be assimilated in the shortest time possible. Fast reading is important because of economy of time and, perhaps more importantly, it ensures that our long-term storage memory capacities are not overloaded. For example, the longer a reader needs to decipher a word or a symbol on a page (perhaps because of bad handwriting or because the fifth carbon copy or a faint photocopy is being used), the slower will be the comprehension rate. Furthermore, it seems likely that such factors play quite a large part in determining whether the material will be read at all (McLaughlin, 1966). It is only comparatively recently, however, that those involved in presenting written information have considered, in any systematic way, the question of typographical factors such as the type and quality of the print and the page layout, despite the fact that it is these aspects which convey the message.

Print Features

Type size

Type size is conventionally specified in terms of the height of a line of print, the unit being the 'point' which is 0.0138 in (about 1/3 mm) high.

Using two measures of readability, the amount read and the degree of comprehension, Burt (1959) compared the readability of passages composed of different sizes of Times Roman print (designed in 1932) ranging from 8 to 14 pt. Unfortunately, he did not provide any data to support his claim, but was able to state that the 10 pt prose was the most legible. Most students found the 9 pt print equally as legible as the 10 pt, while older people often did best with 11 pt or even 12 pt. These results were replicated by Poulton (1969a) when he asked housewives to search for particular words in lists of ingredients printed in 10, 7.5, 6 and 4 pt lower-case type.

Tinker (1965a) investigated the ways in which type size affected eye movements during reading. His results are very much in line with Burt's and Poulton's in so far as the 10 and 11 pt type was read most quickly with fewer fixations and longer saccades. Smaller and larger type sizes were read more slowly — mainly because fixations were more frequent. Smaller type sizes meant that the characters were harder to discriminate; larger sizes meant that the average saccade traversed fewer characters resulting in more fixations.

These conclusions, of course, are related to the number of characters on a line — as will be discussed below.

Upper and lower case

Irrespective of its size, alphabetic information can be presented in capitals, lower-case letters or a combination of both. The different modes, of course, affect both the character outline and distinctiveness, and the amount of space available between the lines. Lower-case ascenders and descenders (for example, the top parts of 'b', 'd' or the bottom parts of 'g', 'y') means that the space available between lines of text varies. For Example, more interline space is available when the letter a is above c than when it is above b because of the ascender on 'b'. In the same way, just a glance at the characters on this page will show minimum space between, say, a p and a b. For these reasons it is important to consider the question of character case for ease and speed of reading.

Most of the work in this area has been carried out using printed material — usually for the newspaper industry. For example, in 1946 Paterson and Tinker investigated the relative value of upper and lower-case letters in newspaper headlines. At normal reading distances, their results indicated that on average more words were read when using lower-case letters than when using headlines printed in upper case in the same type face and point size (in this case 24-pt Cheltenham Extra Condensed). These results were replicated by Poulton (1967) who showed a 9 per cent advantage in reading ability of lower-case over upper-case headlines. A similar advantage was obtained by mixing upper and lower-case letters, although they were not read any more reliably than headlines printed entirely in lower case. Poulton and Brown (1968) and Poulton (1969a) have also demonstrated a lower-case advantage, as did Fox (1963) who compared reading speeds and comprehension using 'gothic elite' (capitals) and 'standard elite' (lower case) typefaces. Interestingly, however, this advantage occurred only when the standard elite text was read before the gothic elite text. When the results from the other group of subjects (those who read the gothic text before the standard) were added to the data, no case advantage was observed.

Paterson and Tinker (1946) and Poulton (1969b) have suggested that the reason for any superiority of mixed over upper-case letter probably lies in the shape of the envelope surrounding the whole word (rather than the individual letters). Words presented in capitals do not have any distinctive shape since all the letters are the same height. Word shapes using various lower-case letters, however, are more likely to be different because of the ascenders and descenders on different letters. For example, the shape of the envelope surrounding the word *dog* is different from that around *cat* due to the extensions of the *d* and *g* in *dog* and the *t* in *cat*. The envelopes around *DOG* and *CAT*, however, are not greatly different, and this lack of distinctive shapes means that the reader has to examine some of the intermediate letters to identify the words, so increasing reading time.

A distinctive envelopes explanation for the lower-case advantage has been challenged by Phillips (1979) — at least when a search task is employed. He compared subjects' abilities in searching for place names on a map when the names were typed all in lower case, in lower case but with the initial letter a capital, all in upper case, and in smaller sized upper case with the initial letter larger. His results demonstrated that names set entirely in lower case took significantly longer to find than names in the other conditions; the shortest time was taken for names in capitals with the larger initial letter. On the basis of his results, Phillips suggests that, for search tasks at least, the important aspect of the word is not the overall shape but the initial letter and, by making this distinctive, the word should be found more quickly.

Finally, another exception to the lower case advantage findings should be mentioned. Foster and Bruce (1982) asked subjects to read aloud text composed of 'nonsense' phrases written either in lower case with the first letter of the sentence in upper case, or all in upper case. Their data showed no significant advantage of lower over upper-case letters, although there was a slight trend towards faster mixed case reading. It is likely, however, that their task — reading aloud — may have reduced any advantage of using the lower case arrangement. Thus the experiments described so far have asked subjects either to read to themselves or to read for comprehension. Silent reading can be performed more quickly than reading aloud since the processes involved in translating the the cognitive stimuli into vocal responses are not required. Thus, although perhaps lower-case letters and words may be perceived and 'registered' quicker, it is possible that the speed advantage is reduced if a vocal response is required.

In summary, therefore, it would appear that for general comprehension and reading, text composed in both upper and lower case letters (as in this book) is superior both for reading speed and accuracy. The advantage is reduced, however, when the task includes components of search and reading aloud.

Punctuation marks

Unfortunately relatively little work has been done on the legibility of punctuation marks. Prince (1967) has reported on the difficulties of poor vision readers in distinguishing between the comma and the full stop. He suggests that the comma should be 55 per cent and the full stop 30 per cent of the height of the lower-case letters used in the text. Reynolds (1983) argues that similar difficulties are often encountered with carbon copies of text, where commas, semi-colons and full stops may be virtually indistinguishable.

Layout Features

Sectioning prose

Dividing the text into meaningful sections has three advantages for the reader. First it provides structure to the prose, informing the reader where one set of ideas ends and a new set begins. Secondly, through the Gestalt features discussed earlier, it allows the material's structure to be organized perceptually. Thirdly, it provides a chance for the reader to collect some thoughts and to prepare for the next section. Regarding the design aspects, Hartley and Burnhill (1976) have suggested that leaving an empty line between paragraphs is a more effective cue for the reader than simply indenting the first line of a new paragraph. Spacing between paragraphs, then, helps the reader to group and separate those parts of the text which have similar content. In Gestalt terms, the paragraph is seen as a 'whole'.

A further possibility for sectioning prose, suggested by Wright (1977a), is to colour either the print or the background. Problems with the use of colour in the text, from the point of view of presenting too much information to the reader, have already been introduced but Wright's suggestions could be used to reduce the reader's burden. She argues, then, that a coloured background can provide supplementary indexing information, for example, as with a book appendix. It enables the reader to turn quickly from the text to the beginning of the appendix without having to look for page numbers.

Headings

A common way of sectioning prose is to use appropriate headings, and these serve a number of different purposes. Most obviously they assist readers who are searching through a display or printed material for particular sections. Perhaps less obviously they are also extremely valuable to those who have to read the entire material since they provide a structure which enables the information to be integrated as it is being read. Each of these may help to increase the reader's comprehension and memory of what is read, as Dooling and Lachman (1971) have demonstrated. Unfortunately, as Wright (1978) has pointed out, no specific research evidence is available to suggest either the type of text that would benefit most from headings or the form that headings should take.

One aspect of headings that has received consideration concerns ways of numbering them. Numbering can serve two purposes: it may help to make clear to the reader the way in which the sections are nested together (thus replacing, perhaps, the need for subheadings) and it enables the reader to refer to specific sections that are smaller than a page.

Perry (1952) has suggested that Arabic numbers are preferable to Roman numbers, although this is possibly so only for the smaller values — compare, for example, the ease of interpreting the sets of symobls iv and 4, and xxviii and 28. In addition, Wright (1977a) suggests that numbers are probably better for indexing than letters of the alphabet, and the larger the sequence the greater is the advantage for numbers. For example, people are more certain that 8 precedes 10 than H precedes J.

The size of display area and line spacing

Whereas dividing text into distinct areas facilitates the reader's scanning and search behaviour, the question of the size of the text area relates more to the normal reading and comprehension processes. These involve saccadic eye movements and the division of words, phrases and sentences so that they are not frequently split in places that make comprehension difficult.

With regard to saccadic eye movements, it will be remembered that each saccade encompasses about 6–8 character spaces. It will also be remembered that the available evidence suggests that we do not sweep our eyes over the text in a rigid left–right direction, but often make recursive movements, perhaps to correct mistakes or to aid comprehension. Thus, although unfortunately no evidence is available to help decide on the optimum width of the text area, it should be clear that it should be neither too small nor too large. If the width is too small, only a few saccades may be possible on any one line, thus necessitating recursions to previous lines with the attendant problems of directing the eyes to the beginning of another line. If it is too large, too many saccades may be needed to scan the line. More importantly perhaps, it is necessary to ensure that when the eye is at the extreme right-hand end of one line it does not have too far to travel back to begin the next line (again, the occular control mechanism can lead the eye to the beginning of the wrong line). In this context, Bouma (1980) relates the length of a line of text (i.e. the distance between the left and right-hand margins) to the angle over which the eye travels to reach the next line. This, he suggests, should be approximately 2 degrees. Within reason, therefore, for long lines of text the interline spacing should be reduced.

The number of characters in a line needs to be related to the distance of the observer from the text. This determines the visual angle that each character presents to the eye.

Columns

Subsumed under the topic of display width lies the question of whether text is better presented as a single block or in a column format as appears, for example, in newspapers and magazines. Again, this concerns eye movement control between lines. With very long text lines (as would occur in a newspaper that did not use a column format) the interline spacing would have to be extremely small to retain the optimal 2 degree recursive movement to the beginning of the next line. Columns, then, help to keep the line length short.

The experimental evidence that has been produced to support such a contention suggests that column formats are advantageous, but only under certain circumstances. Thus, Tinker (1965b) demonstrated that both speed and comprehension are superior when text is arranged in a two-column layout compared with an arrangement in which it is spread across the page. However, Kak and Knight (1980) report that this column format was beneficial only for normal reading speeds. Subjects who had been taught to 'speed-read' showed no advantage when using such a format, and even some disadvantage. It may be, of course, that the training that these subjects underwent during the speed reading course (for example, to control recursive eye movements, to scan efficiently) may have directly interfered with the eye movement patterns needed for column formats.

Text justification

Whenever characters at the left or right-hand margin are vertically aligned with one another (as, for example, in this book) the respective margins are said to be justified. Whereas left justification clearly has advantages for the control of line recursive eye movements — the line always starts the same distance from the page edge — the advantages of right justified text are less tangible. Unless words are to be broken at sometimes inappropriate places (thus causing difficulties for word recognition), a constant line length can only be maintained if the amount of spacing between the words is varied. In lines which contain a fair number of words, of course, this will not be too noticeable but for shorter lines the unpredictable interword spacing may cause problems for the reader. For this reason Burt (1959) recommended the use of the unjustified style in books for small children.

Gregory and Poulton (1970) performed a number of experiments designed to investigate this question, using both good and poorer readers. As stimuli they used three justification formats: right justified, not right justified and not right justified but with words broken by hyphens in appropriate places. Their comprehension results demonstrated that the better readers neither benefited from nor were disadvantaged by the different format styles. However, the poorer readers obtained lower comprehension scores for the justified than for the two non-justified formats. A second experiment, using the poorer readers, demonstrated that the non-justified format advantage no longer held when the line length was increased from about seven to twelve words. In this case, then, the disadvantage caused by the variable interword spacing was reduced.

Coding and cueing

One clear result that emerged from the discussion of visual search processes was that the more conspicuous is the target area, the better is the search performance. Clearly, then, highlighting important areas of the display, by increased display luminance, by typographical techniques such as underlining, italicizing, bolding, capitals, etc. or by colouring different sections can help the reader pick out salient parts of the display. With regard to written text, for example, Fowler and Barker (1974) found that library textbook readers had inserted some form of cueing such as underlining or asterisks in over 90 per cent of the books.

As well as helping the observer in his or her search task, of course, many of these typographic techniques can also be used to code certain display areas or types of information. Colour coding, for example, is a well known technique in many areas: a flashing red display is often used to indicate 'danger'; green usually signifies safety, etc.

The available research regarding the effectiveness of different typographical cueing techniques is inconclusive — primarily because of scarcity. For example, the little evidence available suggests that the occasional use of italics for emphasizing significant points may be no better than plain text for comprehension, and a complex cueing system may actually impair study.

The research on underlining as a means of cueing is similarly inconclusive. For example, Cashen and Leicht (1970) showed that students who had received offprints with relevant passages underlined in red were better at answering questions both on the underlined statements and also (possibly because the underlining helped comprehension) on the adjacent, uncued passages. It would appear, however, that this advantage is only apparent if the reader is not under some time stress to complete the passage. For example, in a study in which all subjects were allowed the same time to read a passage, Crouse and Idstein (1972) found that cueing led to higher scores when the readers were given some time to study a 6000-word text, but not when they were given a shorter time. Furthermore, it may well be that underlining may actually make the text harder to read because it reduces the blank space between lines.

Foster and Coles (1977) considered the relative merits of using capital letters and bold type as cues. Their results indicated that the bold type was a better all-round cueing technique. Although the capital letters led to higher scores on the cued material, when the subjects were tested on the uncued material they performed worse than those who had not had cueing. The authors suggest that when readers used the capital letter cueing technique it hindered their reading performance, perhaps by affecting their reading behaviour so that they had less time available for perceiving the uncued portions of the text.

Finally, the use of colour needs to be considered. Certainly for coding visual information, colour appears to be the most useful technique. For example, Hitt (1961) compared five types of code: numbers, shapes, letters, stimulus position and colour and demonstrated that numerical and colour coding were equally the most efficient. Similar results were obtained by Smith and Thomas (1964) who demonstrated that a colour code consisting of five different colours was more effective than any geometric shape code that they used. In addition, Christ (1975) has reviewed a number of similar experiments and has shown that colour is superior to size, brightness and shape coding for identification tasks. However, in some instances the use of letters and digits were shown to be more efficient, but this is not altogether surprising since the tasks used were essentially to identify objects. When tasks which involved searching displays were reviewed, colour was superior in all cases. As far as coding is concerned, therefore, colour would appear to be the most useful 'all-round' method. However, it should be remembered that it does have its own limitations — particularly in environments containing coloured ambient illumination, and if the observers are 'colour blind'.

Regarding the effect of colour as a highlighting cue for text comprehension, Fowler and Barker (1974) found that subjects who were questioned a week after having read material were more likely to answer correctly questions concerning the highlighted parts of the text than the non-highlighted material.

In summary, although the evidence suggests that highlighting may have beneficial effects on reading performance and comprehension, caution should be taken about the over-use of such techniques. Thus, it has previously been pointed out that visual search times can be increased if the operator is presented with too much information (or, more specifically, too much uncertainty). Within the present discussion too much information implies, perhaps, too many cueing categories. Whereas using one or two colours may increase searching performance, using too many may actually degrade it. (Jones (1962), suggests that the normal observer can identify about nine or ten surface colours, primarily varying in hue.)

The second caution relates to the possible distracting influence of the cueing techniques and their deleterious effects on perceptual organization. For example, Engel (1980) argues that, although colour can be a powerful means of improving the legibility of text displays, over-use (or non-optimal applications) can break up the display's Gestalt. Perhaps more insidiously, colour can create artificial groupings of material. This can happen particularly in displays which consist of non-prose information such as tables or menus. As a check to ensure that this does not happen, Engel suggests converting the alphanumeric charac-ters in the display into rectangles of the same size and colour. In this way the influence of the colours on the layout will become apparent.

ALTERNATIVE WAYS OF PRESENTING INFORMATION
AND INSTRUCTION

The large number of books, journals, magazines, manuals and newspapers available to us every day would seem to point to the fact that we crave for the printed word. Whenever a new product is marketed it needs to be advertised, and words and phrases are used to present it in the best light. It also normally often carries an instruction manual to tell the operator how it works and how to work it, and a maintenance manual giving details of what to do if it breaks down. In addition, the machine itself is likely to carry small pieces of symbolic information to help the operator — for example, small information labels that might say 'danger', 'on/off' or 'position control'. Each of these communication media attempt to reach a different audience and will provide different levels and types of information. Each, therefore, has its own problems of information presentation, but some general points do apply and these will be discussed below. However, as with most design recommendations, it should be remembered that the most appropriate means of communication for one situation may not be so for another.

The first question to be answered is how should the information be presented? As Wright (1977a) points out, for example, people who keep information and refer to it when necessary (for example when using reference manuals) may have different requirements from those who, having studied the information, will be retrieving it from memory. Similarly those who read a report from beginning to end will use the material in a very different way to readers who wish only to understand specific information or answer particular queries and do not intend to read the entire document. Even among those who read all the information, there may be some who read it in order to take a decision but, once the decision is made, they no longer have any interest in the technical details.

Studies of alternative ways of presenting complex material have shown that some non-prose formats can increase the reader's ability to use the information. As an example, Dwyer (1967) provided subjects with information on the structure of the heart either orally or using simple line drawings. He showed that the line drawing was more effective when the subjects were subsequently tested on their memory of the heart's structure. However, for tests which examined the subjects' understanding of the heart's function the oral presentation was most effective. Dwyer's results appear to suggest, therefore, that simple information is better presented visually, but when any action is to be taken, perhaps to integrate the information, it may be better to present it orally, with all of the different emphases that the voice can attain.

When deciding on the appropriate communication mode, as well as the use to which it is to be put, it is also important to consider the type of information to be communicated. Booher (1975), for example, showed that if the information is 'static', that is merely informing the operator about, say, the location of controls on a machine, then it is better to present it as a series of pictures. 'Dynamic' information, on the other hand, for example informing the operator how to switch the machine on, is better presented as pictures and words.

The problem facing the ergonomist (or indeed the designer of any technical information), therefore, is to decide on the most appropriate way of presenting the information (or instructions) to the predicted audience. In doing so the first decision is to choose through which of the two senses, visual or auditory, to present the information. Even this choice can be limited, for example by environmental constraints. Thus spoken instructions may be more costly to produce and are certainly less effective in a noisy environment. Since more will be said in the next chapter about presenting auditory information, the remainder of this chapter will deal with the visual presentation of information and instructions. In this case the designer is likely to have to choose between prose or some pictorial presentation such as graphs, bar charts, pictures, flowcharts and tables for the information channel.

Graphs and Bar Charts

Graphs are used in a number of situations to present numerical information. They have the distinct advantage that they give the reader both the numerical data itself and illustrate any apparent trends. This is particularly so if two or more functions are plotted on the same graph — variations in their relative trends can be seen easily.

Some data are available to help the designer draw graphs to their best advantage. For example, Milroy and Poulton (1978) have shown that if more

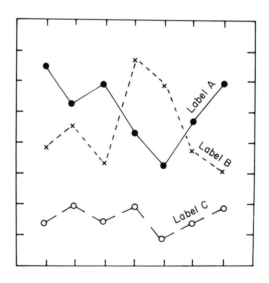

Figure 4.2 An hypothetical graph illustrating the principles of direct labelling and extending the axes

than one curve is drawn on the same graph, and each needs to be labelled, then labelling each curve directly (rather than putting labels elsewhere on the graph or even under the legend) is likely to result in the quickest readings without any loss of accuracy. This is probably because direct labelling requires the reader to make fewer visual scans of the graph and so puts less strain on short-term memory.

The number of curves that can be included on the same graph without any loss of intelligibility will clearly depend on the degree to which the curves overlap each other. If there is a fair amount of overlap, Wright (1977a) suggests a simple rule-of-thumb: three curves may well be the maximum for clarity. Indeed it may also be advantageous to break graphs down into smaller units rather than have too much information presented on a single graph.

Finally, Wright reports other work which has indicated that presenting the axes of a graph as a square (i.e. extending the 'x' and 'y' axes on the top and right-hand side respectively) increases the ease with which the values of extreme points on the graph may be read. This is possibly because, following Gestalt principles, the squared axes help to produce the perspective of a 'whole' figure. Some of these suggestions are illustrated in Figure 4.2.

Despite the fact that they are used extensively, particularly in the advertising industry, little comparable work has been carried out regarding bar charts. Wright (1977a), however, has summarized their advantages and disadvantages in the following way:

> One of the a priori advantages of bar charts would seem to be the ease to which they can be used to present many differently related variables. Some alternative ways of doing this are shown in Figure 4.3. Experimental comparisons among these different formats are hard to find but some of the formats will be more suitable for a specific purpose than others. For example, Figure 4.3a conveys the most information in the least space and very clearly shows the growth in total expenditure over time; but comparisons may be error prone either between items in the same year (e.g. in 1951 more was spent on defence than on education, but this is not obvious in Figure 4.3a) or between different years for the same item (e.g. defence in 1968 and 1973). Indeed there may be two different ways of displaying the information to facilitate these two different comparisons. For example Figure 4.3c enables a comparison of items within the same year but comparisons between years are still very difficult; on the other hand, Figure 4.3b facilitates comparisons between the years but the distance between different items of expenditure may cause errors for these comparisons (e.g. education versus housing plus roads in 1968). Figure 4.3b makes it easier to compare the change in expenditure on particular items over time, whereas the lack of alignment between the different items makes this difficult in Figure 4.3a.

Flowcharts

The flowchart (sometimes called an 'algorithm' or 'logical tree') presents information to the reader as a set of choices and pathways and looks very similar to the computer programmer's flowcharts so much in evidence these days. On the surface at least, they appear to provide the reader with easily 'digestible' information, since the more complex textual structure is illustrated by the ways in which the pathways join the flowchart boxes. These routes, then, give an

Figure 4.3 Alternative ways of displaying information using bar charts. (*From Wright (1977a), reproduced with permission from* Instructional Science.)

overview of the various relationships between different aspects in the information.

Although a case has been made to consider flowcharts as means of presenting information, there is evidence to suggest that they may not be beneficial in all circumstances. If relatively simple information is transmitted, under some circumstances flowcharts may actually create problems. For example, although Wright and Reid (1973) have demonstrated that presenting difficult information as flowcharts produced fewer subsequent errors when compared with prose, short sentences or tables, flowchart presentation of easy problems produced no advantage. Furthermore, if the material had to be remembered, the performance of subjects who had been presented with flowcharts deteriorated faster. It would appear, therefore, that flowcharts are more efficient if complicated information needs to be acted on immediately, but have little value (and may even be detrimental) if the information is otherwise easy to understand or needs to be retained.

A few research findings are available to help to design an efficient flowchart. Kamman (1975) compared the efficiency of two types of flowcharts for finding information in part of a telephone directory. The first design used essentially a vertical structure although horizontal pathways were included. A series of question boxes led, via arrows, to further question boxes or to 'action' boxes. The second consisted of a streamlined flow of short captions arranged horizontally only. Other layout changes included the pathways being made thicker and standing out against a grey background, each decision point could branch into three or even four pathways although more appropriate decision points were provided, and the number of words in the chart was reduced. Comparing these two forms Kamman showed that the second (streamlined) chart produced significantly fewer errors than the first. Both designs, however, produced more efficient performance (fewer errors, faster comprehension) than the standard telephone directory format.

The value of horizontally streaming the choice points has been emphasized subsequently by Krohn (1983) who compared horizontal (right–left and left–right) streaming with top–down. Whereas for simple problems there was little to choose between the three formats, streaming from right to left (i.e. against the normally accepted reading direction) produced significantly more errors and increased reading time when subjects were asked to use the flowchart to solve complex problems.

Although Kamman's study demonstrated the value of reducing the number of choice points within a flowchart, in some cases it may be neither practical nor desirable to do so. In such cases Gane *et al.* (1966) have suggested producing small subcharts, each of which deal with separate sequences in the operation. A more radical solution has been advanced by Jones (1968) who suggests that the material can be rewritten in a 'branching list' structure so that the information is listed vertically and the reader has to jump to other questions. For example, the question might read 'Is the motor turning? If YES continue with question 2. If NO go to question 15'. Wright (1977b) argues that such a format may be useful in providing specific answers to specific questions, but it loses some of the other advantages of flowcharts — particularly the visual appearance of the decision-making structure emphasized earlier.

As well as reducing the number of choice points and words, Wright suggests other ways of increasing flowchart efficiency. First, it is often the case that the various outcomes are not equally likely to occur. The designer may, therefore, decide to produce a flowchart in which the most frequently used decision path is the shortest possible — rather than reducing the average path length. Secondly, there may be occasions when it makes better sense to emphasize particular aspects of the choice. For example, the fact that some of the outcomes may be more important than others might be an argument for putting the important decisions at the top of the tree; or different choices may have different levels of uncertainty attached to them, so making it reasonable for the decisions to be made in order from the most to the least certainty.

Pictures

Illustrations are widely used in modern communication systems, for example with technical terms, and pictorial information is increasingly being employed to communicate instructions for using equipment. This is particularly so when the equipment is to be used by people of different nationalities and literacy levels. Other advantages of pictures are that in some circumstances they produce better responses where viewing conditions are degraded (Ellis and Dewar, 1979) or viewing times are short (King, 1971). They can also be used during problem-solving to answer specific questions which arise and they can even influence the type of problem-solving strategy adopted. This, in turn, will determine the type of information sought (Szlichcinski, 1979a).

It must be emphasized, however, that pictures do have their limitations. For example, Vernon (1953) reviewed the results of wartime research on the visual presentation of statistics and concluded that people needed special training to understand diagrams and make proper use of them. She also argued that diagrams and pictorial charts are less likely to be effective than prose if the concepts being presented are too complex for the readers to understand. This was demonstrated well by Szlichcinski (1979b) who found that his subjects had great difficulty in carrying out a fairly complex task when given only pictorial instructions.

Despite these negative points it is likely to be the case that pictures will be used increasingly more frequently to present both static and dynamic information. At the very least, the constant need to sell goods to people of different nationalities should ensure this. Furthermore, the observations that pictures may produce poorer performance under some circumstances must be tempered by the argument that such results will depend on the quality of the material used in the experiments. Poor pictures, for example, are likely to produce poor results. Indeed, Szlichcinski (1977) showed that simply using three-dimensional pictures, rather than two-dimensional representations, tended to improve performance. It may be the case, therefore, that the pictures need to be designed well to produce better performance, and so it is up to ergonomists to produce guidelines for their efficient production.

In essence two types of pictures may be used: discrete symbols or more complex compilations of illustrations.

Discrete pictographic symbols are already in widespread use on equipment, for example vehicle controls, and for public information and warning, for example road traffic signs. Unfortunately, despite their extensive use, it is only relatively recently that some research has been carried out to consider their appropriate design (Zwaga and Easterby (1983), for example, describe a series of evaluation procedures suggested by the International Standards Organization).

Two features need to be considered when designing a pictographic symbol to give a single piece of information: the content of the symbol and the extent to which it is perceptible.

Features that affect the picture's perceptibility can be gleaned from the discussion earlier relating to the principles expounded by the Gestalt school. Thus Easterby (1970) has suggested a number of factors, the more important of which are:

(1) A solid boundary to the figure provides good contrast between the figure and its background (see Figure 4.4a).

(2) Simplicity: a simple shape is perceived more readily than one which contains too much detail (see Figure 4.4b).

(3) Closure of the figure helps to provide the 'whole' (it may be remembered that Wright advocated this principle for the production of graphs, suggesting that the axes should form a square) (see Figure 4.4c).

(4) Stability: because our perceptual system attempts to impose form on the incoming sensory information, some types of figures are inherently 'unstable'. For example, most people will know of the picture showing two faces in silhouette (Rubin's vase-profiles pattern). Depending on the observer's 'set' either two faces looking at each other or a Grecian vase against a dark background will be seen. Once both possibilities are seen the

Figure 4.4 Some of the principles important in symbol design. (*Reproduced from Easterby (1970)*, Ergonomics, **13**, *149–58*, by permission of Taylor & *Francis Ltd.*)

perception tends to keep changing from one to the other. The same effect can be seen in Figure 4.4d in which the arrow appears to be indicating, alternately, clockwise and anticlockwise movement. Because of this instability the picture becomes ambiguous, but removing part of the arrow reduces this ambiguity.

(5) Symmetry: to make recognition easier, the various elements in the picture should be as symmetrical as possible — as long as the production of a symmetrical figure does not mislead the observer. Szlichcinski (1979a) however, argues that there are some circumstances in which an asymmetrical figure may provide more information than one which is symmetrical — for example, his study mentioned earlier in which three-dimensional pictures (asymmetrical) produced better performance than the symmetrically drawn two-dimensional pictures.

Before concluding the discussion of pictogram appearance, the point made in Chapter 2, about increasing the dimensions (cues) present in information, should not be forgotten. The number of different dimensions able to be incorporated within simple pictograms is limited but can include shape, size and colour. Welford (1984), for example, points to the design of international road traffic signs which use the shape dimension as an initial identifier: circular signs are mandatory, triangular signs are advisory. In Great Britain colour is also used: green signs are used on major roads, blue signs are used on motorways. Giving such initial coding systems helps the observer put the sign into 'perspective', i.e. it provides the 'set' from which the (hopefully correct) identification can be made.

What pictures should actually go into the pictogram is the other important question. Welford (1983) argues strongly that designs need *not* be pictorially accurate, often more abstract symbols can do the job just as well. An arrow, for example, universally implies motion; a diagonal bar across a figure implies negation ('do not ride', 'do not cross'). However, Barnard and Marcel (1983) caution that the understanding of such abstract symbols is often culturally determined and ought to be used with caution.

Cultural influences also appear when considering the actual picture to be used. Easterby and Hakiel (1981), for example, have demonstrated that the recognizability of a symbol is possibly the most important criterion for its comprehension: prior experience of the sign was found to increase comprehension rate by 150 to 200 per cent. But prior experience does not mean simply having used the sign before — it means also having had 'experience' of the picture. For example, Barnard and Marcel (1983) point to the use of a penguin to imply frozen goods. This involves an inferential relationship between the picture (penguin) and what it is intended to signify (frozen goods). As long as the inference is made, then the connection should also be made. However, people who have never seen a penguin or know where it comes from may not understand the picture's meaning.

Although discrete symbols can be used to represent a great deal of information, their usefulness is mainly restricted to informing about specific features of the environment. When more complex information, such as instructions, needs to be conveyed then individual pictures may have to be combined in some way to form a sequential message. It is at this point that problems can emerge since the sets of pictures have to fulfill many of the functions of natural language without having the benefit of some of the features that accompany language: voice intonation and stress, gestures, repetition, etc. The ways in which the pictures are arranged, then, and the shapes from which they are formed need to convey both their meaning and the message structure and logic in a similar fashion to the ways in which words and grammatical structure determine the meaning of simple sentences.

Barnard and Marcel (1977) carried out a fairly comprehensive study to determine how pictures should be designed and arranged to convey information. In essence they investigated:

(1) Part versus whole representation of equipment: whether each picture in the sequence should display only the important part to be considered (for example, a dial or a switch), or whether it should represent the whole apparatus with the important part accentuated.

(2) The order of representing the status and actions: whether or not individual pictures should be linked — the first showing the action to be taken (for example throwing a switch) and the second the consequences of the action (for example, a light illuminated).

(3) The use of insets to illustrate aspects of the actions.

Using subjects' reports of what they thought different sets of pictures were instructing them to do, Barnard and Marcel demonstrated the need to include details of the relevant parts of the machine in each picture (in other words the 'whole' representation). Surprisingly, however, the use of insets resulted in poorer understanding than did comparable instructions without insets. Overall, the action-state representation yielded the best results.

Tables

Tables are probably the most frequently used ways of presenting discrete pieces of information. However, perhaps because they are in such common use, little thought is generally given to their design.

A table is little more than a systematic arrangement of different items of information which can be numerical, as in timetables, or non-numerical such as the table of chapters in the front of this book. A variety of ways is available to arrange the information. For example the items could be listed alphabetically or in numerical order, or they could be grouped with reference to a common feature. Furthermore, as Wright and Fox (1970) point out, it is always possible to provide aids such as spatial cues by aligning items vertically or in rows, or typographical features such as variations in the size, style or colour of the print.

The many forms of tables which can be seen in present day usage differ, primarily, in the amount and kind of work which they require the user to perform. In this respect Wright and Fox (1972) refer to explicit and implicit tables. Explicit tables are those which give the reader all the information which may be needed, for example a bus timetable which lists each time the bus will arrive. An implicit table, on the other hand, gives some information only and leaves the reader to infer any additional information that is required. The bus timetable which tells the reader that the bus will arrive 'every 20 minutes after 11.00 a.m.' is an example of such a table.

For the designer, the main advantage of the implicit over the explicit table lies in the space which is saved. However, they are disadvantageous as far as the reader is concerned since further calculations are needed, to which the wrong answer might be obtained.

With regard to the explicit types of table, Wright and Fox (1970) suggest that there are two main variants: linear and two (or more) dimensional (the latter are sometimes called matrices). In the linear version the authors argue that the reader searches through what is effectively one long list to find the information required — as in, for example, a tax code or a telephone directory. With the matrix version on the other hand, the reader has to make two or more searches for different parts of the information required, and then has to co-ordinate the results of this search in a particular way. For example when reading a train timetable to determine the arrival time at a particular station, a passenger will first scan the rows to find the train, then scan the column to find the station. The arrival time is given at the intersection of the row and column.

In many respects, of course, the linear type of explicit table may be viewed simply as an implicit version of a matrix table. Take the telephone directory as an example. To use it as a linear table to find the telephone number of a Mr H. K. Williams one could start at the beginning of the directory and work through until the required name is read. This is clearly not the way in which a directory is used — in fact a number of dimensions are (implicitly) imposed. Thus one first looks for the initial of the surname (dimension 1). The second dimension would be the second letter (or even the second couple of letters), etc. In this way the search time is reduced considerably.

From the available research it is difficult to draw general guidelines as to which type of table should be chosen, since users and the type of information to be conveyed differ markedly from situation to situation. However, from their studies Wright and Fox (1970) suggest that some people were completely unable to use matrices, and their difficulty persisted even when the experimenter worked through examples with them. In addition conversions were made slightly more rapidly, but much more accurately, with the explicit than with the implicit table. Thus they argue that linear, explicit tables are generally better than either matrix or implicit tables, particularly if they are to be used by the general public.

Nevertheless many situations exist when a multidimensional table is more desirable, perhaps because of space limitations or because the user population is known to be more capable. In such cases guidelines regarding their design may be able to be gleaned from understanding the ways in which people use tables. In this respect Wright (1980) points to three features of a table that require consideration: the table's logic, layout and function. Translated into the reader's behaviour, these relate to comprehension, searching for information and decision making on the basis of the interpreted information.

As far as the table's logic is concerned, Wright argues that one of the reader's first tasks is to understand the underlying principles on which the table was structured. The concept of compatibility has already been discussed (and will be discussed further in Chapter 7) and it should be apparent that it relates as much to written communication as it does to communication via other channels. Thus, we expect tables to be arranged in certain ways — particularly two-dimensional ones. For example, the two main variables on the left and top sides with the 'answer' in the main body of the table. Arrangements which do not conform to these expectations are likely to lead to confusion and/or increased reading time.

The table's logic may also be emphasized by improved layouts, for example by reducing the number of dimensions in the table. In this respect Wright (1977a) has shown that subjects made fewer errors and performed quicker when only two dimensions were given than when the table required four decisions. Thus, arrangement 4.5(a) was preferred to 4.5(b). This is probably because whereas the reader merely has to scan in one direction for each dimension in table (a) two directions need to be scanned for table (b). To find alternative F2 in table 4.5(b), for example, the reader first needs a horizontal scan to 2, then a vertical scan to F, so potentially increasing the time taken and the errors made.

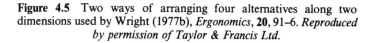

Figure 4.5 Two ways of arranging four alternatives along two dimensions used by Wright (1977b), *Ergonomics,* **20,** 91–6. *Reproduced by permission of Taylor & Francis Ltd.*

Layout may also be improved by grouping group items together rather than having them equally spaced. Tinker (1960), for example, has shown that grouping items into blocks of five was more helpful to the reader than grouping by tens, but grouping by tens was better than no grouping at all.

Spaces between items will also help to structure the table and provide a Gestalt, although thick ruled lines appear to be as effective as spaces for marking distinctions between rows and/or columns (Sprent *et al.*, 1983). Wright and Fox (1970) make the following comment regarding the size of the gap between the grouped items:

> Although there seems to be no direct experimental evidence on the point, it is a common observation that when there is a large gap between the item that is looked up in the table, and the information which is as a consequence read off from the table, it is easy for the eye to misalign the two columns and so err by reading off information either directly below or above that required. Indeed, it was to the lessening of such difficulties that Tinker attributed the beneficial effect of grouping items within columns. Therefore it would seem advantageous to have the space between corresponding items within a table as small as possible ... even if lots of space within a table makes it easier on the eye, too much space in some places may make it harder on the user.
> (*This material appeared in Vol. 1, pp. 234–242 of* Applied Ergonomics, *published by IPC Science and Technology Press Ltd, Guildford, Surrey, UK.*)

With regard to arranging the table so that relevant items can be searched for quickly, again this returns to a question of layout — making the relevant information 'stand out'. Typographic cues such as bold type and colour can be valuable in this respect.

As far as the column and row headings are concerned, it would appear that it is not too critical where a heading is placed with respect to its column. Thus Hartley *et al.*, (1975) have shown that column headings are as effective if they are aligned with the left-hand edge of the column as they are when centred. Column headings written horizontally, however, are easier to read than when written vertically. Tilting the headings by 45 degrees to the horizontal makes them easier to read than if they were vertical, but increases the risk that they will be thought to relate to an adjacent column.

Finally, Wright (1980) argues that the table's designer needs to know and to understand the use to which the tabular information is to be put. Often, for example, users may wish only to have approximate information rather than precise figures. It may be better, for example, to present train arrival times rounded to the nearest minute (or five minutes!) rather than to the second. This is because our use of time is often not more precise than this. Another use of tabulated information is often to compare information within parts of the same table or with information from another table. For example, a passenger may read a train timetable not only to find out the arrival time but also to see whether another train or a different route might be quicker. In these circumstances, the table's layout and typography may serve to help or to hinder. Of course, if considerable comparisons need to be made — particularly in the form of trends — then graphs and bar charts may present the information more efficiently.

Forms

That form design is important from the viewpoints both of economics and efficiency can readily be seen by the number and range of forms that are in use today. Miller (1983), for example, points out that the United States government alone issues nearly 10000 different kinds of forms and receives over 500 million responses per year. Furthermore, Wright and Barnard (1978) have reported that in at least one London borough several local authority staff are employed full-time to assist people in completing their forms for benefits. As they point out, if to such staff costs are added the administration time and the postage that normally accompanies returning incompleted or wrongly completed forms, some idea can be obtained of the total cost and wasted time which can accompany poor design.

From the previous discussion it is clear that layout and typography are important when designing tables — structures that provide information for the reader but which the reader has to 'use' before the information becomes apparent. In this respect forms are very similar to tables: again, they interact with the user; often they look like tables. However, they differ from tables in one very important respect: the reader provides the information and the form determines the way in which the information is provided. As with tables, however, some ways of asking the questions and laying out the form have been shown to be more efficient in obtaining the required information than others. Many of these features have been discussed already — structuring the form; using aspects such as colour and lines; providing the reader with a logical flow and helping the respondent to move from one relevant question to the next; using typographical features such as cueing, letter size and shape to ensure adequate perceptibility of the questions, etc. Other aspects will be discussed in the next section when dealing with the prose that constitutes the instructions. This section will consider some of the problems specific to form design — that is, questions that relate both to the user's responses and to the administrator's interpretation of the responses.

Barnard and Wright (1976) investigated the effects of character spacers in the response boxes. These vertical lines that separate the respondent's characters are frequently seen these days, particularly on forms that are used in conjunction with computers. They help to ensure that the maximum number of characters allowed by the computer program is not exceeded. However, Barnard and Wright have demonstrated that the spacers break up the familiar shape of a word, impairing both writing and reading. Wing (1979), however, has demonstrated that the illegibility is not so great when the spacers occur as small marks at the top of the line, rather than at the bottom or as complete separators. This is probably because respondents will write smaller and so form their letters below the marks. Wright (1983) also points out that using character spacers can make typing the responses, and reading typewritten responses, particularly difficult since the character spaces on the finished forms do not always match the usual ten- or twelve-pitch typewriter character spacings.

Prose

The use of prose for instruction and information has purposefully been left until last to give the reader a chance to consider the value of alternatives such as tables or flowcharts. However, it is the case that most information transmitted between people is carried out by combining words (either verbal or visual) into (sometimes) meaningful sentences. Before considering appropriate ways of presenting information as prose, it is useful to discuss briefly some of the processes by which we *comprehend* text.

Anderson (1980) argues that comprehension can be analysed into three stages. The first comprises the *perceptual process* by which the message is originally encoded. Secondly is the *parsing* stage in which the words in the message are transformed into a mental representation of the word's combined meaning. Finally is the *utilization* stage, in which the reader actually uses the mental representation of the sentence's meaning to answer a question, to store information, to obey an instruction, etc. As Anderson points out, these three stages can occur sequentially or they can overlap. For example, while reading part of a sentence readers might make inferences about the meaning and implications of what has already been read.

Parsing

The ways in which we break up sentences, known as *parsing* can significantly affect both our reading efficiency and our understanding of the message being transmitted. This can be seen in a small illustration designed by Graf and Torrey (1966) (and described by Anderson, 1980). They argued that a sentence would be more easily understood as its constituent structure becomes more identifiable. Thus, they presented subjects with two forms of a sentence that had been split over a number of separate lines. In the first the break at the end of each line corresponded with a major constituent boundary; in the second it did not. For example:

Form A (Split according to constituent boundaries)
During World War II,
even fantastic schemes
received consideration
if they gave promise
of shortening the conflict.

Form B (Split haphazardly)
During World War
II, even fantastic
schemes received
consideration if they gave
promise of shortening the
conflict.

As they expected, their subjects showed better comprehension in Form A than in B. Such conclusions are also substantiated by Anglin and Miller (1968) who found that recall was higher when phrases in a prose passage were intact than if the phrases were broken, and Cromer (1960) who reported similar findings for comprehension.

A number of other factors can influence this parsing procedure, and each is related to the way in which the text is constructed. These factors include the presence of ambiguity, the imagery contained in the sentence, the sentence length, the degree of activity or passivity implied by the sentence, whether or not it is couched positively or as a negative and, for instructions, the order of words used.

Ambiguity

Parsing so far has been discussed as a syntactic (rules based) process. However, it must be remembered that the words themselves convey meaning and that parsing syntactically may not produce the understandings of a message that was intended by its transmitter. This can apply particularly when the sentence is ambiguous, that is when the semantic patterns do not necessarily relate to the syntactic patterns. Because different interpretations are able to be placed on the same piece of text, ambiguity can cause major problems for the reader's comprehension and subsequent behaviour.

In essence, linguists distinguish between two main forms of ambiguity: structural and lexical ambiguity. *Structural* ambiguity arises when an entire phrase or sentence can have two or more meanings; *lexical* ambiguity, on the other hand, arises when only a word in the sentence can have two or more meanings — for example 'light ("set fire to" or "illuminate") the paper'. In addition it is useful to distinguish between *permanent* and *transient* ambiguity. Thus, the ambiguity in a sentence which is permanently ambiguous remains even after the sentence has been completed. During transient ambiguity, however, the ambiguity is resolved by the words contained in the remainder of the sentence — before the sentence is completed; for example, 'the briefs were read by the lawyer'. Clearly, permanent ambiguity can lead to misunderstanding whilst transient ambiguity, depending on the extent of the ambiguity, can lead to increased comprehension time. Such results were obtained by Bever, *et al.*, (1973) who asked subjects to complete partial sentences having differing degrees of ambiguity. Interestingly, however, they also showed that once a reader has resolved the ambiguity of a constituent in a sentence, and has settled on a particular interpretation, the ambiguity has no further effect on processing the remainder of the sentence or text — providing that no further change in interpretation is made.

Both forms of ambiguity can arise in a number of ways. For example, if apparently redundant words are removed from the text, meaning can be affected due to the various possibilities that result from alternative parsing.

Ambiguity arises not only because apparently redundant words are removed, but also when prose written in one language is translated into another. Slight changes in the arrangement of translated words can radically alter the meaning or the comprehensibility of the message, as can subtle differences in the meaning of words in different cultures. For example, to an English car mechanic 'gas' implies the exhaust whereas an American counterpart would think of petrol; 'boot' in the United Kingdom is the same as 'trunk' in the United States, and so on.

As an example of this problem Sinaiko and Brislin (1973) asked Vietnamese airforce mechanics to perform various maintenance tasks using manuals which were written in either English (American); or in high quality, lesser quality or poor quality translations of the original. Although their Vietnamese subjects made many errors when using the American material (61 per cent), their error rate increased to 89 per cent when they were provided with the poor Vietnamese translations.

Finally, ambiguity can also arise if the information presented to the operator is incomplete, misleading or if it is too verbose. Chapanis (1965b) presents a number of examples to illustrate these points, in each of which the ambiguity results from the receiver having to restructure the information (often erroneously) into a message that can be understood.

Imagery

The effect of imagery on a number of cognitive processes has been studied extensively for many years. For example, high imagery words are recalled faster than those which do not easily conjure up an image (Paivio, 1971; Postman, 1975). Similar results have been obtained concerning the memorability of high-imagery sentences (Marschark and Paivio, 1977). Furthermore, Ernest (1979) has shown that subjects with high imagery ability are able to recognize unfamiliar pictures more quickly and at lower threshold levels than subjects with low image ability.

If imagery is so important in these cognitive processes, it is not unreasonable to suggest that it also mediates sentence comprehension. Indeed, this was shown to be the case in a study by Eddy and Glass (1981), and Holmes and Langford (1976) have also related comprehension to the concreteness or abstractness of sentences. As an explanation of these types of results, Begg and Paivio (1969) have suggested that we code abstract and concrete sentences differently in memory. Thus they proposed a dual coding hypothesis which suggested that concrete sentences can be coded in the form of non-verbal spatial imagery as well as in a verbal association form. Abstract sentences, however, can be coded imaginally only with difficulty.

The implications of such results, that picturable material is easier to understand than non-picturable material, are summarized thus by Paivio and Begg (1981):

The thoughtful student can readily see some of the implications of this for such matters as the appreciation of literature. One reason why Shakespeare is so appealing, for example, may be the fact that his plays are unusually high in literary imagery.

As an aid to choosing the most image provoking words, Paivio *et al.*, (1968) produce data relating to the 'concreteness', 'imagery' and 'meaningfulness' of nearly 1000 nouns.

Sentence length

The end of a sentence allows the reader to take a short pause before taking in further information. Since we have a limited capacity to process information, if the sentence is unduly long the reader will either begin to forget some of the earlier information in the sentence or will impose an individual structure. In this case readers will break up the long sentence themselves, perhaps in the wrong places, and obtain a slightly different meaning to the one intended.

The problem appears to be particularly prevalent in government, legal and even military circles as the following example given by Chapanis (1965b) illustrates:

This radio uses a long life pilot lamp that may stay on for a short time if radio is turned off before radio warms up and starts to play.

As Chapanis suggests, this 29-word statement could have been more explicitly put as 'the pilot lamp stays on for a while after you turn the radio off' (16 words).

Wright and Barnard (1978) suggest that to be readily understood each sentence should contain only one clause. To implement this they suggest that writers should scrutinize sentences with more than one verb, looking for alternative ways of expressing the information.

Sentence activity

It is often possible to convey the same message in different forms, one distinction being along an activity dimension. Thus, a sentence can often take the form simply of a passive statement or can be made in an active or an imperative fashion. For example, a passive instruction could be 'The button is pressed', whilst its active counterpart would take the form: 'Press the button'.

The available evidence suggests that comprehension time is reduced for the active form of the text. For example, Gough (1965) demonstrated that active sentences are verified as being 'true' quicker than are passive sentences. Similar results were obtained by Greene (1970). Olsen and Filby (1972), however, demonstrated that the relationship is a strong function of the *focus* of the sentence. Thus, the active sentence advantage is maintained only when the receiver of the sentences can identify with the active part of the sentence. When the event described by the sentence was coded in terms of the receiver of the action, passive sentences were more easily verified. The same results were found for answering (rather than simply identifying) active and passive sentences.

Finally, there is also evidence to suggest that the active advantage holds only for text in which a sensible active-passive transformation can be made. For example, Slobin (1966) measured the verification time for reversible sentences such as *The boy is being hit by the girl* (in which the subject and object can be interchanged to the active form 'The girl hits the boy'), and non-reversible ones such as *The boy is raking the leaves*. He found that active reversible sentences were verified more quickly than passives, but that the verification time did not differ for active and passive non-reversible sentences. Paivio and Begg (1981) suggest that such results arise because in non-reversible sentences it is easy to determine which noun is the logical subject so that passives do not cause any problem. With reversible sentences, however, it is more difficult to determine the subject, so that passives are more difficult.

Positives and negatives

Just as a sentence can be couched in terms of different degrees of activity so, too, can it be arranged along a dimension of positive to negative. For example, the positive instruction 'Press button A' could also be put into its negative form 'Do not press button B'. Words such as *not, except, unless* each have negative elements as, in some circumstances, do words such as *reduce* (Wright and Barnard, 1978).

Again, the evidence appears to suggest an advantage of one form over the other — in this case the positive form of a sentence is generally comprehended faster than its negative counterpart (for example, Gough, 1965; Greene, 1970).

Despite this general conclusion, however, it would appear that contextual aspects can, again, affect the positive form's advantage. Thus Wason (1965) has argued that if the negative form carries with it more information than its positive counterpart — if it is both plausible and performs its natural function of contrasting and distinguishing the exception from the norm — then the positive form is no more easy to comprehend. This he calls the *plausible denial* hypothesis. For example, since most people go to work in the morning saying 'I went to work yesterday' carries very little information. The statement 'I didn't go to work yesterday', however, tells us something new. In such cases Wason found that the reaction time to plausible negatives were significantly shorter than to both positive and negative implausible forms of the sentence. Nevertheless, it was still the case the plausible, positive sentences were reacted to fastest. These results have been confirmed by Arroyo (1982).

Temporal order of the words used

If a series of actions is either to be described or performed, it is better if they are written or spoken in the order in which they are to be carried out. Broadbent (1977) illustrates this point with the following example: if an action involved pushing in the carburettor control and then starting the engine, it is better to write the instruction 'depress the carburettor plunger before starting the engine' than 'before starting the engine depress the carburettor plunger'. In the first case the words are matched to the actions, in much the same way as, in ergonomics philosophy, the environment is matched to the person.

READABILITY

Having finally decided on the appropriate wording of instructions and information, a designer may wish to check that the prose produced is the most readable that is able to be devised. In many respects, readability is largely subjective with individual styles of writing being able to be discerned in different pieces of work. As Klare (1963) points out, however, although there are rules for efficient writing, careful adherence to them does not guarantee good writing. Writing is an art not a science. However, he points to three general principles of which the writer must bear in mind. First to know something of the type of reader — educational level, motivation and experience. Second the writer's own purpose for writing should be considered — what is intended; perhaps to help the reader read more efficiently; to judge whether the material is acceptable; to read for comprehension, learning and retention; to understand orally presented material; or to accomplish some combination of these and other purposes. Third as emphasized above words should be selected carefully. It is the words used and their construction into sentences which make the prose readable.

To produce some standard in the readability of material, various readability formulae have been proposed which operate by analysing the words used in selected passages in the prose. Klare (1963) describes many such formulae, but perhaps the most popular was produced by Flesch in 1948.

To compute Flesch's 'Reading Ease' score, a 100 word sample passage of the prose to be analysed is first chosen. Then the number of syllables (w1) in those 100 words are counted in the way in which they are read aloud. For example 1980 will have four syllables (*nine-teen-eigh-ty*). Secondly the formula requires the average number of words per sentence (s1) to be computed. With this data reading ease can be calculated as:

$$206.835 - 0.846w1 - 1.015s1$$

This score puts the piece of writing on a scale between 0 (practically unreadable) and 100 (easy for any literate person). As a more detailed guideline,

Table 4.1 The range of Flesch 'reading ease' scores (from Flesch, 1948)

Score	Description of style	Typical magazine	Syllables per 100 words	Average sentence length in words
0 to 30	Very difficult	Scientific	192 or more	29 or more
30 to 50	Difficult	Academic	167	25
50 to 60	Fairly difficult	Quality	155	21
60 to 70	Standard	Digests	147	17
70 to 80	Fairly easy	Slick-fiction	139	14
80 to 90	Easy	Pulp-fiction	131	11
90 to 100	Very easy	Comics	123 or less	8 or less

however, Flesch produces a table of typical scores for different types of prose as shown in Table 4.1.

SUMMARY

This chapter has considered communication in its most basic sense — the transmission of information and meaning from one person to another. After considering the meaning of meaning, and the ways in which the communication system may be corrupted, the remainder of the chapter discussed the various processes involved in transmitting information using the printed page: typographical aspects and the use of various communication media such as tables, graphs and pictures. Finally, some of the problems involved in the efficient communication of prose were considered.

CHAPTER 5

MACHINE-MAN COMMUNICATION: DISPLAYS

Chapter 4 demonstrated our need for information and the various ways in which it can be presented. Thus, the man–machine system thrives on information; without it the whole working system will soon degrade and, even if information is given, if it is given badly poor performance is still likely to occur. Communicating information and instructions from one person to another, therefore, can be viewed as being the first link in the working chain. Once initial instructions have been given, however, much of the information which the operator subsequently receives will come not from another human being, who can perhaps be questioned further in the case of misunderstandings, nor from written instructions which can be read a few times to ensure that they are understood, but from single or composite instruments which display information about the state of the system. Since an appropriate response can only be made on the basis of the operator's interpretation of the information provided by the display, it is clear that this aspect of the system needs to receive careful consideration.

In practice the 'best' display is normally chosen by trading off the criteria of speed, accuracy and sensitivity in communicating the important information. Since the communication act requires the receiver to interpret correctly the transmitter's message, however, these criteria refer just as much to the operator's performance as they do to that of the machine. It is for this reason that the needs of the task and the operator have to be made explicit. In some cases it may be that the speed of assimilating the information is more important than other criteria, for example when a pilot reads the rapidly changing height information from the altimeter on take-off or landing. In other cases accuracy may be as important — avoiding errors or ambiguity. It is of little value, for example, for the pilot to be able to read the altimeter quickly if either it is inaccurate or is read inaccurately. In other situations the display may need to be very sensitive (i.e. able to detect the slightest change in the variable being measured). For example, a heart-rate monitor in an intensive care unit should respond immediately to any change that occurs in the patient's condition. It would be a useless machine if the nurse was able to read (quickly) the fact that the patient's heart had stopped beating (accurate) three minutes ago (insensitive).

101

This last point, then, emphasizes that although speed, accuracy and sensitivity are the primary criteria on which a display's value is judged, they are not independent criteria. A display which is able to be read quickly is valueless if its readings (either the readings which it gives or the interpretation of the readings) are inaccurate; a display which communicates slight changes in machine state is worthless if it takes a long time to read; etc. For this reason it must again be emphasized that both the operator's and the system's requirements need to be considered before the appropriate display is chosen.

Displays, therefore, represent the sole means by which a machine is able to communicate information about its internal state to the operator. As Rolfe and Allnutt (1967) put it, 'The display translates what is at first imperceptible to us into perceptible terms'. As such it can only function in one of the operator's five sensory modes: vision, hearing, touch, taste or smell. Under normal circumstances only the first two (or sometimes three) of these senses are used. To understand fully the ways in which the display's requirements can be matched to the operator's capabilities, therefore, much of the information regarding the human sensory system which was discussed in Chapter 2 needs to be remembered.

Before discussing visual and auditory displays in more detail, it is useful to compare the two types and to consider briefly situations in which they are more usefully employed.

In general, *visual displays* are more appropriate when:

(1) The information is presented in a noisy environment. Under such conditions auditory displays may not be perceived.

(2) The message is long and complex. Compare, for example, a written sentence on a computer screen (visual) and the same information presented from a tape-recorder (auditory). Because the eyes are able to scan the visual material more than once, short-term memory capacities are less likely to be overloaded. Unless the (auditory) taped message is translated into written material, the decoded words somehow have to be stored in memory while other words in the message are being decoded.

(3) The message needs to be referred to later. Visual information can produce a permanent record; unless auditory recording equipment is used, acoustic information is stored only in memory.

(4) The auditory system is overburdened — perhaps because of too many auditory displays or (as in (1) above) in a noisy environment.

(5) The message does not require an immediate response.

Visual displays are more appropriate, therefore, for providing continuous information to the operator. On the other hand, *auditory displays* are more useful when:

(1) The message requires an immediate response — they are more attention getting. It is for this reason that warning messages are normally presented using a klaxon or a bell.

(2)   The visual system is overburdened — perhaps because of too many visual displays or in glaring conditions.

(3)   The information needs to be presented irrespective of where the operator is facing. The drawback of visual displays lies in the fact that the operator needs to be looking at them before they are able to communicate the information. Auditory displays do not have such restrictions. This is another reason why they make such acceptable warning indicators.

(4)   When vision is limited — for example in darkness, at night, or when it is likely that the operator will not have had time to adapt to the light or dark conditions.

VISUAL DISPLAYS

Types of Display: Digital and Analogue

Visual displays are possibly the most commonly used instruments for communicating information from the machine to the operator. They are also, however, frequently badly designed — with sometimes disastrous results. For example, Fitts and Jones (1947a) analysed 270 errors made by pilots in reading and interpreting their instruments, each of which could have led to an accident. Their results suggested that there were a number of different ways in which visual displays could be misread. These include 'simple' misinterpretations of the instruments (for example, misreading the altimeter by 1000 feet); reversal errors (for example, interpreting the bank indicator as showing a left bank when, in fact, the aeroplane was banking to the right); misinterpreting visual warning signals; substitution errors (confusing one instrument with another) and illusory errors (for example misreading the altimeter because of an illusory conflict between body sensations and the instrument indication). Clearly, a display which can be misinterpreted is effectively worse than useless (particularly if the misinterpreted information leads to a totally inappropriate control action).

Visual displays generally take one of two forms: digital and analogue. The digital display, which has become more apparent in recent years with such consumer-oriented products as pocket calculators and digital watches, presents the information directly as numbers. With the analogue display, on the other hand, the operator has to interpret the information from a pointer's position on a scale, from the shape, position or inclination of a picture on the screen, or from some other indicator which is analogous to the real state of the machine. For example, a conventional clock face is an analogue display since if the minute hand points at '9' it has travelled $\frac{3}{4}$ of the way around the face and indicates a position which is analogous to $\frac{3}{4}$ of the way through the hour. The pilot's pictorial artificial horizon display (which indicates the attitude of the aircraft relative to the horizon) is also an analogue display since the positions of the 'aircraft' and 'horizon' indicators in the display are analogous to the respective positions of the aircraft and ground in the real world. Finally, a warning light is an analogue display since the state of the light (on or off) is analogous to the state of the machine (danger/safe) in the real world.

Using visual displays

In many respects the ways in which a display is to be used determines the type chosen although, of course, exceptions to this rule exist as will be discussed later. Displays may be used:

(1) To make quantitative readings — to read the state of the machine in numerical terms: the temperature in degrees centigrade, the height in feet, the speed in m.p.h., etc.

(2) To make qualitative readings — to infer the 'quality' of the machine state. For example, whether it is 'cold', 'warm' or 'hot', rather than its precise temperature; whether the aircraft is banking 'shallowly' or 'steeply' to the right or to the left, rather than its precise angle, etc. Also subsumed under this heading is the use of displays to make check readings — i.e. to compare the state indicated by one display with that shown by another.

(3) In combination with controls to set the machine, or to track (maintain) a steady machine state.

(4) To warn the operator of danger, or that a specified machine state has been reached.

When deciding on the type of display to be used and its characteristics, Murrell (1971) points out that it is important to consider what information the operator needs so that the job can be done effectively, and then to question how this can be presented quickly and unambiguously. Sometimes the same type of display might be used in different ways. Take, for example, a voltmeter: sometimes this might be used to indicate whether the machine is on or off; at other times a direct numerical (voltage) reading may be required; while in other cases the operator may wish simply to compare the information with that obtained from other displays. It is only possible to decide on the appropriate type of display when it is known what proportion of time the display is used in each case, and this information is 'weighted' in terms of the importance of each operation in the particular situation.

Quantitative Readings

Both digital and analogue displays may be used for making quantitative readings, although it is only with increased electronic sophistication that digital displays have become a viable alternative to analogue displays. A mechanical type of digital display which is operated by a system of reels (as may be seen, for example, in the **milometers** of most types of car) has two major drawbacks: first a number may not always be fully visible as it moves around a continuously revolving wheel; instances can occur when only the bottom half of one number and the top half of the next is visible. Clearly this can lead to either misreadings or to increased reading times. Second, because the number is actually moving the image will not be in the same place on the retina and may even cause blurring. As will be seen later, this is not the case with electronic displays in which the character is varied by illuminating different segments or dots.

Given that appropriate digital displays are now available, the important question is under what circumstances the analogue or digital display should be used? In this respect, much of the work carried out has concerned the design of suitable aircraft displays (usually the altimeter) but the principles which have evolved may be extrapolated to any situation in which people need to interact with machines.

The results of early experiments to resolve the question tended to suggest that digital displays produce fewer reading errors and faster reading times than do analogue displays. For example, Murrell and Kingston (1966) describe results from an experiment with skilled journeymen using graduated and digital micrometers. Whereas about 3 per cent of the readings were in error using the graduated micrometer, the same men made only 0.05 per cent errors when they used a digital micrometer. Similarly, Zeff (1965) compared conventional and digital clockfaces for reading speed and errors. He showed the digital clockface to be read faster than the conventional clock, with only 10 per cent of the errors.

One of the earliest investigators to compare the effectiveness of dials and counters was Grether (1949) who recorded the reading time and errors made by

Figure 5.1   Speed and accuracy in reading altitude from different types of instruments (from Grether, 1949)

trained pilots and college students. He presented photographs of altimeters bound into booklets, each photograph showing a different height on one of eight analogue arrangements or a counter (see Figure 5.1). His results indicated that the standard three-pointer altimeter used extensively in aircraft (one pointer indicates ten thousands of feet, another thousands of feet, and the third hundreds of feet) caused the highest error rate and longest reading times. The digital display was associated with the lowest error rate and fastest reading times.

It is, perhaps, useful at this point to realize the implications of making reading errors in these types of circumstances. For example, the skilled journeymen in Murrell and Kingston's experiment misread their graduated micrometers by up to one hundred thousandths of an inch, a not insignificant amount in precision engineering terms. Perhaps a more sobering example is provided by Rolfe (1969a) who quotes the reports of investigations into two airline crashes, of which the following is an example:

> On the evening of 28th April 1958, a BEA Viscount airliner fitted with modified three-point altimeters was making a final approach to land at Prestwick Airport at the end of a flight from London. The captain reported to the ground that he was 14,500 feet and descending. As he descended he reported he had passed through 12,500 feet. Soon after the last report the aircraft struck the ground. The subsequent investigation ... showed that the captain had misread his altitude by 10,000 feet and had perpetuated his misreading error until the aircraft struck the ground and crashed.
> (*This material appeared in Vol. 1, pp. 16–24 of* Applied Ergonomics, *published by IPC Science and Technology Press Ltd, Guildford, Surrey, UK.*)

This report has more than simply historical interest. It illustrates a further aspect when making quantitative readings — a misreading error from a badly designed display may not necessarily be a 'one-off' event. Often a 'set' is introduced that causes the error to be perpetuated on subsequent readings. Thus, not only did the captain misread his altimeter once, he continued to misread it by the same amount until he hit the ground.

The impression may have been gained, so far, that numerical information should always be presented digitally. Indeed, some authors tend to argue strongly for this. Digital displays, however, do have their drawbacks, particularly in dynamic situations when the rate of change of information is particularly fast, when the display is used as a predictor as well as providing numerical information or, as discussed earlier, when mechanical digital displays are used. In addition, as will be discussed later, tasks in which displays are used to compare values (check reading) are often best served using analogue rather than digital presentations.

Fast-changing information and blurring

Many of the earlier experiments that compared the efficiency of digital and analogue scales for quantitative readings presented the stimuli as static pieces of information: each stimulus was either shown to subjects for a specific short period or the subject was timed reading the display. Under these circumstances the results demonstrate quite conclusively that digital displays produce fewer reading errors and faster reading times than do analogue displays.

In the dynamic (real-life) situation, however, values indicated by the display will often be constantly changing, sometimes very quickly. Under such circumstances the image may become blurred, and this can have serious consequences if the numbers have to be read with some precision. As anyone who has tried to read the fast-changing times provided by a digital clock at a sports meeting will know, the blurred image makes reading the information practically impossible.

Fast-changing information does not appear to affect the efficiency of analogue displays to such a large extent, however. This is because the pointer that is lacking in digital displays, itself provides some additional cues for the operator. Thus spatial (the direction in which the pointer is moving) and rate-of-change (how fast it is moving) information gives the reader further information and helps interpret the reading.

Using spatial cues for prediction

It is very rare that an operator will simply read the values indicated on a display. In the majority of cases, although possibly not immediately obvious, operators use the information received to make predictions — perhaps about the state of the machine or about the machine's future behaviour.

This unconscious prediction can be illustrated by the following example: an operator knows that the machine is likely to explode when the display indicates 10 'units'; although the display indicates only 9½ units, the pointer is moving upwards. At this point the understandable reactions (possibly of panic) will be due to predictions of the machine's future state!

A second example concerns the conventional (analogue) watch face: the large (minute) hand may point at 7 and the small (hour) hand somewhere between 11 and 12, indicating that the time is 11.35. Within the same glance, however, the position of the minute hand also provides spatial cues to enable the reader to predict, quickly, that 25 minutes are left of the hour. Digital displays do not give this information so readily — the operator needs to carry out fast numerical computations (with all of their attendant problems) to achieve the same result.

The efficiency of analogue displays in providing such spatial cues has been demonstrated by Simon and Roscoe (1956). They presented subjects with display information intended to represent an aircraft's present altitude, the predicted altitude after one minute, and the final altitude to be reached. One of four types of display were presented: (a) a vertical (strip) display incorporating three pointers; (b) a circular (dial) display with three pointers (similar to the three-point altimeter); (c) three separate five-digit counters; and (d) three separate circular, single pointer displays.

From this information subjects had to decide:

(1) Whether they were diving, climbing or flying level,
(2) In order to reach and/or maintain their final altitude, whether they should climb, dive or continue flying level,
(3) If they should climb or dive, whether they should increase, decrease or maintain their present rate,
(4) Whether they should eject!

In terms of the time taken to complete the task, the results showed the vertical displays produced the lowest average time in a series of ten problems (56.3s). The combined circular display came second (64.2s), the digital displays third (74.6s) and the separated circular displays fourth (79.7s). In terms of errors, however, the digital displays had the highest (approximately 7 per cent) and the vertical strip displays the lowest proportion (approximately 3 per cent).

Discussing their results Simon and Roscoe argue that the digital display's poor showing, both for speed and accuracy, was related to its failure to provide any direct spatial cues.

In summary, therefore, it would appear that for recording quantitative information, digital displays make the task easier for the operator (faster reading time and less errors) than do analogue displays. The superiority of digital displays is reduced, however, in situations where the values change quickly, where the operator might need to predict the future 'conditions' of the machine, and, as will be discussed below, where some sort of check reading is required.

Qualitative Readings

In some situations an operator may use the display not to record precise readings but to register the machine's qualitative state. For example, rather than needing to know the temperature in degrees centigrade, it may simply be necessary to know whether it is 'hot', 'neutral' or 'cold', or whether it is 'safe', 'dangerous' or 'critical'. In these circumstances numerical values are not recorded and so the digital display's advantage may be reduced. Indeed, analogue displays may be more effective than digital displays.

Visual coding

As McCormick (1976) points out, the ideal display designs for qualitative readings depend on what needs to be read. If the whole range of machine states can be divided into a limited number of 'levels' then the best way of representing these levels is to code different areas separately on the dial face. A number of visual coding methods are available that enable different features of a display to be distinguished, and some of the coding methods which Morgan et al. (1963) list include colours, shapes (both numbers, letters and geometric shapes), and brightnesses.

The efficiency of various coding techniques was discussed previously in Chapter 4 (p. 79). At this point, however, it is pertinent to emphasize the cautions expressed regarding the over-use of colour as a coding system for qualitative displays — particularly if coloured ambient illumination is used or if there is a chance of normal light being reflected from a coloured surface. Since colour is perceived as a result of a particular wavelength of light being reflected from a surface, it is clear that if a coloured light is used to illuminate a coloured patch, the resultant colour perceived will not be what would be expected under daylight illumination. (This problem may occur even when fluorescent illumination is used — fluorescent lights are not normally white; they contain high proportions of light in the yellow part of the spectrum.) These effects may cause the colour coding system either to be lost entirely or to be altered.

A further limitation of colour coding systems is if 'colour-blind' operators are likely to be employed. As was discussed in Chapter 2, approximately 6 per cent of healthy adult males have marked reduced sensitivity to colours, most having difficulty in distinguishing between red, green or blue colours.

Pictorial displays

Pictorial displays are a particular type of qualitative display which, as the name suggests, present the operator with a pictorial representation of the machine state. Examples of this type of display may be found in many large process industries when they provide information about such aspects as which stage of the process has been reached. Large panels, then, give the operator a 'picture' (usually a representational picture in terms of interconnecting lines) of the system and its operation: parts of the display may be colour coded and/or illuminated to indicate special features. In some respects, then, these may be considered to be large types of flowchart.

Another example of a pictorial display is the artificial horizon seen on most pilots' control panels, which indicates the airplane's position with respect to the horizon. The relationship between the airplane and the horizon is generally shown by the relative positions of a horizontal bar and an outline symbol of an airplane.

The overriding principle in pictorial display design is to ensure that the picture which they give is as realistic to the true life situation as is possible. For example, if a section of railway track is represented pictorially by a series of interconnecting lines on a signalman's panel, the length of the lines should, as near as possible, be in proportion to the relative lengths of the track sections, the points should be in their relative correct positions, and the speed of the 'train' (perhaps indicated by a moving light) should be proportional to the real train speed. If principles such as these are adhered to, a pictorial display will provide the operator with both useful and readily available information.

In some cases, however, it may be difficult to decide what is a 'real-life' representation. For example, with the artificial horizon in the pilot's cockpit the question has arisen whether it is more true-to-life for the airplane symbol to move and the horizon bar to remain static, or vice versa. From the point of view of a person standing on the ground watching an airplane bank, there is no doubt that the plane moves with respect to the horizon. From the pilot's position looking out of the aircraft, however, the horizon appears to move while the world (the aeroplane) remains 'stationary'. The question, then, concerns whether a pilot's interpretation of such a display relates to perceptions of the vehicle when on the ground or when in the air.

The many studies which have been carried out to investigate this specific type of pictorial display have concluded that the moving airplane type of pictorial display is interpreted quicker and with less errors than the moving horizon display (Johnson and Roscoe, 1972). The reason for this may be explained when one considers that the pictorial display represents a figure–ground configuration, with the figure being whatever is the moving part of the display and the ground the stationary part. When a pilot is looking out of the cockpit window the horizon, normally being accepted as a stable frame of reference, is the ground against which the moving aircraft is a figure. However, when the pilot's eyes move to accommodate on the panel containing the artificial horizon display, the panel itself becomes the ground with the moving horizon bar becoming the figure. In this way it is quite possible to misinterpret the display elements and make a control movement that aggravates the condition. As with the symbols discussed in the last chapter, therefore, it is important to determine the figure–ground relationships of the various elements before an adequate pictorial display is designed.

Check Reading

This will be discussed in more detail in Chapter 7 when ways of grouping displays are considered. In the meantime it is useful to remember that displays are often used not just to obtain precise, quantitative information. They are also used to compare readings or to check that a certain value is or is not being indicated. For example, Murrell (1971) discusses data from a survey of HM ships in 1952 which indicated that, on electrical and steam equipment, only 18 per cent of the dials were used for quantitative readings whereas over 75 per cent were used for some form of checking. Similar conclusions were reached by White, *et al.*, (1953) who report that pilots flying on instruments fixate on their instruments on average for only 0.5s, suggesting that aircraft instruments are typically used in a check reading manner.

For check reading, the available evidence suggests strongly that some form of analogue display produces more efficient performance. This is probably because of additional spatial cues that the pointer provides (for example, the angle between the pointer and 'north', or the angular difference between two pointers). Digital displays lack this information and so the operator has to compare numbers before any check reading can be made. For this type of task, then, digital displays may increase both the time needed to read the instruments and the number of errors made. For example, Connell (1948) mounted four displays side-by-side on a panel. She found that the average time taken to determine whether or not the same reading appeared on each of four digital displays was half a second longer than when the subjects were presented with four, circular, scale and pointer instruments. The number of errors also increased.

Setting and Tracking

Little work has been carried out to find the optimum type of display for use when settings have to be made.

Comparing the merits of analogue and digital displays for this type of task, it would appear that analogue displays are easier to use. For example, Benson, et al., (1965) asked subjects to maintain a constantly changing display reading at a steady position (i.e. to carry out a tracking task). At the same time they were required to react to a light which was illuminated at irregular intervals. (This use of a secondary task ensured that the subject's total attention is employed.) Two types of display were used: a combined analogue and digital display, or a single digital display. Whereas the subjects' performance on the two displays was not significantly different, their performance on the secondary task was worse when the digital display alone was presented than when they were presented with the combined analogue and digital display. This, coupled with the fact that the subjects' heart rate, sweat rate, muscle activity and respiration rate all increased when the digital display alone was used, suggests that the digitial display made the subjects work harder to maintain their performance.

The possibility that analogue and digital displays may differentially affect the quality (rather than accuracy) of an operator's performance on a setting task was also considered by Rolfe (1969b). His subjects were asked to alter their 'altitude' using either a digital or a combined analogue/digital (counter/pointer) display. Again, no significant differences in either speed or accuracy were reported between the two types of display when the experiment was carried out in the presence of a secondary task. Differences in the *type* of error were apparent, however. Using the combined display, 62 per cent of the 21 errors made were caused by the operator 'levelling out' too early (for example, levelling at 25 000 ft when being asked to ascend to 26 000 ft). Using the numerical display, however, the majority of the 26 errors (69 per cent) were caused by the subject 'overshooting' the required setting (i.e. exceeding it by more than 150 ft and then returning to the correct setting).

Again, therefore, it would appear that adding the analogue component to the display alters the operator's behaviour, to create a more 'conservative' and, perhaps, cautious setting.

Table 5.1 summarizes the relative advantages and disadvantages of analogue and digital displays as discussed above.

Table 5.1 The respective merits of analogue and digital displays

Function	Analogue display	Digital display
Quantitative readings	Best if a precise reading is not required, or if the task contains predictive or checking components	Best for accurate reading of slow changing values; poor if the task includes any predictive or checking component
Qualitative readings	Best for warnings, checking and prediction; useful to have visually coded areas	Poor
Setting and tracking	Best	Poor

VISUAL DISPLAY DESIGN

From the foregoing discussion it is clear that it is extremely important to choose the correct type of display if the system's efficiency is to be maximized. To do this one needs a full analysis of the task that the operator has to undertake, and this can then be matched against the display's abilities to carry out these requirements.

Unfortunately, knowing which type of display is useful in which circumstance is only half of a solution to the problem. Just as the previous chapter illustrated how communication between people can go hopelessly wrong if, for example, the words are not put together in a suitable fashion, so too can the right type of display give a wrong (or misleading) communication if it is poorly designed.

The purpose of this section will be to consider the second half of the problem — visual display design. Naturally very few people will be in a situation to design suitable displays, but many are in a position to purchase them. This section, therefore, should provide some guidelines for making a realistic choice.

Display Design for Quantitative Readings

Analogue displays (dials)

The design aspects of a dial simply to take readings of the machine state have been investigated from most possible aspects. These studies were carried out in the early years of ergonomics, with some of the recommendations being embodied in British Standards (for example, BS 3693 Parts 1 and 2 (1964, 1969)). They have been discussed at length by Murrell (1971).

Possibly the two most important criteria to consider when choosing a dial are the ease and the accuracy of making a reading. Translated into design features this implies simple, uncluttered, bold design (McCormick, 1976).

The first requirement is that the dial should be large enough to be read comfortably by an observer positioned some distance (the reading distance) away. This distance, of course, may change with the dial's position on the console. For example a dial placed above the operator (not a reccommended position, as will be discussed in Chapter 7) will probably be further from the eyes than one directly in front. In addition, since most of the information needed will be obtained from the scale itself, the size and length of the scale plays a large part in determining the dial size. For all practical purposes, the British Standards Institute (1964, Parts I and II) has suggested that the length of the scale (L) is related to the reading distance (D) by the formula $D = 14.4L$. So, for example, if the dial is placed one metre from the operator the scale base length (the distance around the scale between 'minimum' and 'maximum') should be at least 7 cm long.

Having chosen an appropriately sized dial, the second question which a potential purchaser should ask concerns the scale divisions and markers: their number and size.

The distance between the scale markers represents possibly one of the most fundamental factors which determines the readability of the scale. For any particular scale base this will be a function of the number of markers used. Thus, as the space between two successive markers is reduced while the distance between the dial and observer is maintained, the visual angle which the space subtends at the eye will also decrease proportionately. If this visual angle falls below a critical value then the observer will begin to make reading errors, and the frequency of such errors increases linearly with the logarithm of the decreasing visual angle. Murrell (1958) has demonstrated that, for most reading applications, a visual angle of 2 minutes of arc is the critical point. This would imply, therefore, that for a reading distance of D units a gap of approximately $0.0006D$ units between the markers is required — i.e. a minimum scale gap of just less than 1 mm for a reading distance of 1 metre. It must be remembered, however, that Murrell's studies were carried out under ideal viewing conditions. Under poor illumination, for example, the critical visual angle would be increased and so require a larger scale gap. Practice and poor vision also play an important role in acuity tasks of this nature. For these and other reasons, McCormick (1976) recommends minimum scale gaps of between 1.25 and 1.75 mm.

The desirable length and thickness of scale markers have also been the subject of a number of investigations. These have generally indicated that within limits some variations can be accepted without influencing reading ability to any great extent. However, it is obvious that the major scale markers (i.e. those associated with particular values) should be emphasized, and the British Standards Institute (1964) suggests that each major marker should be twice the length of the minor markers. Regarding the thickness of the markers, Morgan et al. (1963) suggest that the major markers should be between 0.125 and 0.875 mm for good to poor illumination conditions, and McCormick (1976) appears to agree with these dimensions.

Regarding the arrangement of scale markers, the body of opinion which has evolved appears to suggest that a system which progresses in 1s or 10s (1 ... 2 ... 3 ..., or 10 ... 20 ... 30, etc.) is the easiest to use. A system increasing in 2s would appear to be slightly less effective, whereas progressions of 4s, 8s, 25s or decimals is not recommended. (It may be postulated, of course, that these results simply reflect our practice of counting in tens rather than in fours.) The minor markers should help the observer's accuracy in interpolating between major markers and so, for this reason, the divisions need to be sensible. Since people can be fairly accurate in interpolating into fifths or even tenths of a scale division (Cohen and Follert, 1970), however, the number of minor markers may not be too critical.

No readings would be able to be made without some sort of pointer, and details are available concerning appropriate pointer design (Spencer, 1963). In summary the pointer should be pointed rather than blunt and the tip should meet, but not overlap, the base of the scale markers.

If the pointer is placed away from the dial surface, parallax problems may occur. These can perhaps be demonstrated by envisaging reading a dial first from the left, then in front and then to the right. In each case a slightly different reading will be made because of different sight lines between the dial number, the pointer and the eye. To minimize the chance of parallax errors some dials have a small, thin mirror positioned behind the pointer. Only when the pointer obscures its reflection in the mirror will the observer be positioned in front of the dial and a true reading made.

Finally, of course, there is the question of the design of the numbers presented on the dial face. In this case the two important features are the character shape and size.

Regarding the shape, two criteria apply — confusibility and readability. Unfortunately, as was demonstrated by Smith (1978), these two requirements are sometimes in conflict; shapes designed to reduce confusibility may also lead to reduced readability.

Confusibility is often a function of the extent to which characters are composed of the same basic shapes. For example, the numbers 0, 3, 6, 8 and 9 are sometimes confused since they usually have curved or rounded outlines. This dilemma can be increased when letters are introduced, for example B, 8 and 3 are commonly confused.

The effect of different number shapes on readability does not appear to be too great. Most conventional alphanumeric fonts can be read with reasonable accuracy under normal conditions where size, contrast, illumination and time permit. For this reason the only recommendation which Buckler (1977) makes is that font styles are kept clear and simple.

Although the character's shape may not be too important to legibility, its size certainly does matter: characters that are too small may be difficult to read; too large and they waste space. This depends on such factors as the reading distance, contrast, illumination and time allowed for viewing. After reviewing the relevant literature and performing an experiment of his own, Smith (1979) demonstrated the range of readability to lie between a visual angle of 7 and 24 min of arc. This means that a dial placed 1 metre from the observer needs character heights of at least $2\frac{1}{2}$ mm for readability (7 min). Using Smith's data, 90 per cent readability will be obtained with characters $3\frac{1}{2}$ mm high (10.5 min), and 100 per cent with 7 mm high characters (24.5 min).

In summary, therefore, a potential purchaser should pose the following questions:

(1) Is the scale base length large enough to be read at a 'normal' reading distance?
(2) Is the gap between scale markers at least a millimetre?
(3) Are the major markers able to be differentiated easily from the minor markers?
(4) Is the numbering system in 1s or 10s?
(5) Is the pointer designed adequately?
(6) Do the characters subtend a visual angle of at least 10 mins of arc?
(7) Are the characters legible and non-confusible?
(8) Does the dial, as a whole, look uncluttered and easy to use?

Digital Displays (counters)

Digital displays may appear as any of three forms: mechanical, electronic and computer generated using a cathode-ray tube (CRT). In the mechanical type of display, the numbers are printed on either a revolving drum or on pieces of metal which 'flip' over. However, with the discovery of crystals and diodes which become illuminated when a current is passed through them, mass-produced and very cheap electronic digital displays have become available. Computer generated displays are, of course, also a form of electronic displays but their advantage lies in the easy generation of letters as well as numbers. Ergonomists, therefore, must also consider the production of alphanumeric displays.

Mechanical counters

Two aspects of the counter are important: First the way in which the numbers change over. Second, the design of the numbers themselves was discussed above.

If the numbers do not change in a 'snap' action, but revolve around a drum, an undesirable situation will sometimes arise in which only parts of the number are shown in the display window, for example the bottom half of the number 8 and the top half of 9. Naturally this will increase the time needed to read the number and may possibly lead to errors.

Electronic displays

Electronic displays now play an important part in the working environment. They range from computer linked visual display units (VDUs) to the small crystals which can be seen in digital watches and calculators and which become apparent when a current is passed through them. Because VDUs have some ergonomic problems associated with them which are additional to the problems associated with the crystal displays, they will be discussed later in this chapter.

The advantages of electronic displays are threefold: First, because a particular number is produced by different display 'segments' being illuminated, the character is always in the same part of the observer's retinal field. There are no problems with numbers 'flicking' or rolling over. Second, the LED display generates its own illumination, enabling it to be read in the dark without additional light sources. This is not the case with LCD displays: since the segments appear black, background illumination is needed for adequate contrast. Third, both LED and LCD displays can be computer driven and this provides greater flexibility in terms of both the design and the content of the displayed information. Finally, multicolour LCDs will allow products to be colour-coded if necessary (for example, the numbers may change from green to red if the machine state changes from 'safe' to 'danger').

Many of the design considerations discussed earlier apply also to electronic displays. However, the segmented characters produced by LEDs or LCDs do have further problems: because it is composed of segments (usually 7) the character's appearance differs from that of a drawn number. This means that the normal curves are lost. A secondary problem, shown in Figure 5.2, concerns the spacing between different numbers: because the character is formed by illuminating different segments the spacing between numbers varies, depending on the number to be read. For these reasons, Plath (1970) has cautioned against the over-use of segmented numbers.

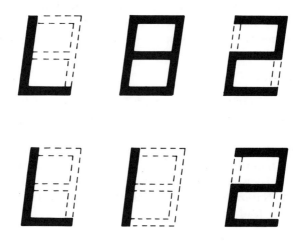

Figure 5.2   The different spaces produced by different combinations of electronic, seven- segment numbers

Plath's caution is also reflected in the efficiency of seven-segment characters. The available evidence suggests that seven segment displays using either LCDs or LEDs produce worse performance (more errors — usually errors of confusion

— and slower reading) than both conventional (printed) characters (Plath, 1970) and dot matrix produced characters (Orth, Weckerle and Wendt, 1976). Ellis and Hill (1978), however, have demonstrated that such conclusions apply only when the reader is placed under time stress. Where time is not critical, reading segmented numbers is as efficient as reading conventional ones. Furthermore, even with time stressed reading, appropriate training was able to overcome difficulties in reading segmented numbers. Unfortunately, without the opportunity for continued practice the skills acquired decreased significantly within a month.

Van Nes and Bouma (1979, 1980) have suggested that the inferiority of seven segment characters is likely to be caused by the design of the segments themselves. On the basis of their own experiments they suggest that:

(1)   The smaller the number of segments from which a digit is built up, the better it will be recognized. For example, the number 1 (which is composed of two segments) is recognized more quickly than 9 (which is composed of 6 segments).

(2)   The probability of confusing two different numbers decreases as the difference between the number of segments making up the two numbers is increased.

(3)   Not all segments appear to be equally important for perception.

Using these suggestions, and data from their own experiments, they have produced a new set of segmented numbers which have variable segment thickness. As can be seen in Figure 5.3, the top and right-hand segments of a seven-segment number are about two-thirds the thickness of the other four segments. The authors do emphasize, however, that these new designs are still at the experimental stage.

Figure 5.3   Proposed designs of seven-segment numbers based on analyses of confusion errors (Van Nes and Bouma, 1980). *Reproduced by permission of the Human Factors Society*

The design of alphanumeric characters will be discussed further later when considering visual display design.

A combined analogue and digital display

When discussing earlier the relative merits of analogue and digital displays for making quantitative readings, it was shown that each have their advantages and their disadvantages in different situations. For example, analogue displays were shown to be more valuable for recording fast changes whereas digital displays were more appropriate for making static readings; digital displays, on the other hand, were more useful when having to read precise values, etc. A sensible compromise, therefore, would seem to be to produce a display which has both analogue and digital components.

Only one detailed study reported in the literature has considered this compromise. After producing such a display Rolfe (1969a) carried out both a pilot opinion survey and a laboratory experiment to investigate whether the digital display should be separate from (that is, above) or an integral part of (that is, inside) an analogue altimeter display. Using static trials (subjects were presented with photographs of each altimeter showing different readings), no difference was obtained between either of these two combined forms, although a significant difference was obtained between these two displays and an analogue-only display: the average reading time for both counter-pointer displays was consistently about 30 per cent faster than for the analogue display. No errors were made on either of the counter-pointer displays, while 20 per cent of the readings made on the analogue display were in error by 100 'feet' or more.

Dynamic trials, however, pointed to the 'counter-inside' display being more valuable than the 'counter-outside' display. This was also reflected in the pilots' opinion survey which suggested that the counter-outside display tended to appear as two independent displays demanding an alternation of attention. Remembering the Gestalt principle of closure — that a solid boundary leads to more efficient perception because it gives the appearance of a 'whole' — it is not surprising that the counter-inside display was read more efficiently.

Display Design for Qualitative Readings

The available evidence discussed earlier indicates that an analogue (dial) display represents the most efficient means of presenting qualitative information to the operator. The pointer position, and its movement speed and direction, provide the operator with relatively low-level information of the machine state which, coupled with coded areas on the dial, enable fast qualitative judgements to be made.

Colour coding

When discussing the various types of coding available to the designer (p. 108) it was apparent that colour provides the most efficient coding system. This is possibly reflected in the fact that most indicators used for qualitative readings include colour coding. However, two important questions need to be answered before an appropriately colour-coded display can be produced. These are: what colours should represent which type of machine state, and how many colours should be used overall? The maximum number of colours which ought to be used in the coding system would appear to be around ten. For example, Jones (1962) suggests that normal observers can identify about nine or ten surface colours, primarily varying in hue. On the other hand, Morgan *et al.* (1963) suggest a maximum of 11 different colours. It is possible to increase the optimum number quite significantly if stimuli vary along a number of different dimensions, for example size, luminance levels, hue and colour purity (Jones, 1962).

Having decided on the number of colours the next question relates to *which* colours should be used. In this respect it was pointed out earlier that many colours are already associated with different moods or conditions, so it is important that the colours chosen should be compatible with the operator's stereotypic ideas of what they represent. Unfortunately, little research has been carried out to answer this problem so most of the colours used in modern displays are chosen on the basis of 'common sense'. In this respect Morgan *et al.* (1963) have suggested the meanings and uses of a number of different colours (Table 5.2).

Table 5.2 The suggested meanings of different colours (*adapted from Morgan* et al., *1963, and reproduced by permission of McGraw-Hill*)

Colour	Meaning	Use
Red	Hazard	Fire: Alarms, extinguishers, hose Danger: Symbols Stop: Signs on machinery, road signs Emergency
	Hot	
Orange	Possible danger (but not immediate hazard)	Dangerous parts of machines and guards
Yellow	Caution	
Green	Safety	First-aid equipment
Blue	Caution	
	Cold	
Purple	Radiation hazards	

Finally, Poulton (1975) has pointed out that colour coding can often be used to indicate sizes, for example some stores code cloth sizes according to colour; and electrical resistor values have been colour coded for some years (black = 0 ... white = 9). On the basis of a small survey in which he asked people to say what colour they thought represented the largest size, etc., Poulton was able to recommend an 'ergonomic colour code' for sizes in which red represents the largest size and white the smallest. Intermediate sizes should be represented by colours arranged in rainbow order.

120

Pictorial qualitative displays

Pictorial displays which illustrate the state of the machine were discussed above (p. 109). In this respect it was shown that the overriding design principle is that the display should be as 'true to life' as possible.

Display Design for Check Reading

Although comparing two readings (comparison) or ensuring that a value has or has not been reached (checking) are frequent tasks, very little research appears to have been conducted to help design appropriate check reading displays. This is possibly because colour coding is generally used to differentiate the important areas of the dial for check reading, although this may not be the most useful way of helping the operator. For making comparison readings, for example, the most useful technique is to arrange the displays in a particular way, and this will be discussed in detail in Chapter 7.

An interesting design for a check reading dial face has been proposed by Kurke (1956) who suggested a face which was so arranged that when the pointer is indicating, say, a 'danger' reading a high-contrast wedge-shaped 'flag' appears

Figure 5.4 The value of a warning flag appearing on a display to indicate 'danger' (*From Kurke, 1956. Copyright © 1956 by the American Psychological Association. Reprinted with permission.*)

on the dial face. This is not present when the machine is operating in 'safe and 'normal' conditions. Kurke demonstrated significantly reduced errors and operation times when using this type of dial compared with one which had a colour-coded (red) area permanently on the dial face and with one which had no obvious aids (Figure 5.4). With this display, therefore, the operator has only to perceive the presence or absence of the flag. A display with colour-coded portions requires the operator first to find the pointer and then decide whether or not it is in the red area; a display without aids requires the additional load of having to decide on the meaning of the reading. Clearly, having only to decide whether a flag is present or not is likely to be a considerably easier task.

Cathode-ray Tube and Visual Display Units

The cathode-ray tube (CRT) and its more computer-jargonized relative, the visual display unit (VDU), offers the designer a more flexible man–machine communication system than either analogue or digital displays alone. Being computer linked, in many respects it represents an amalgam of all types of display, allowing alphabetic characters, numbers and even diagrams to be displayed. Indeed, Chorley (1973) suggests four main advantages of these displays: first, they are sometimes the only suitable means of presenting certain types of information (for example, radar or television). Second, with limited panel spaces and with increased amounts of information to be shown, some type of time-sharing display becomes possible. Third, using appropriate software the electronic display's versatility allows flexibility of formats — for example, the order in which information is presented (for example, emergency signals can be programmed to override normal communications) and the way in which different information is emphasized. Fourth, VDUs generate their own illumination and can therefore be used in the dark.

The operating principles of VDUs have not changed significantly since the times of early television sets. Indeed, both have as their basic mechanism the cathode-ray tube. This is essentially an evacuated glass tube with a 'gun' at one end and a phosphor-coated 'screen' at the other. The gun fires a stream of electrons at the phosphorized screen which interact with the phosphor material and cause it to glow at each point of impact. An observer viewing the face of the screen will perceive, at each point of impact, a bright spot of light which dims as soon as the beam has moved. Indeed, since the glow decays rapidly as soon as the beam has passed, the screen needs continually to be refreshed to present a stable, flicker free image. The speed with which this happens is called the 'refresh' or 'regeneration' rate and this is also determined by the way in which the beam of electrons is moved over the screen.

When the scanning control circuitry sweeps the electron beam across the surface of the CRT screen, the character images are 'written' on the screen by switching the beam 'on' and 'off' as it travels through its scanning pattern. These scanning lines are generally made horizontally, as on a television, and it is the density of these lines which determines the display's resolution and thus the character size and clarity. Jones (1976) and Cakir, Hart and Stewart (1980) describes the various ways in which scan lines are produced on the screen and the ways by which distortion due to the screen curvature is eliminated.

The most common procedure for producing text on VDUs is the dot matrix method in which each character is composed of a series of bright dots (sometimes called 'pixels'). The required dot positions for each character are stored in a dot matrix memory in the computer. The matrix resolution is defined by the number of horizontal and vertical dots — usually 5×7 or 7×9 — and the character is written to the screen in a 'sliced' form. Thus the tops of all characters in the line are written first, followed by successive horizontal slices until the bottoms are reached some seven or so lines later.

Radiation

Before discussing the design of VDUs and their displays in more detail, it is appropriate to consider, briefly, the question of the radiation which they emit. For a VDU to operate it must produce a considerable amount of radiated energy — otherwise the characters would be invisible. This type of radiation, however (electromagnetic radiation in the visible spectrum), is quite safe; what many operators fear is the possibility of other radiation wavelengths being produced by the cathode-ray tube — radiation that cannot be perceived through our normal, biological sensors. Luckily, however, all of the available evidence strongly suggests that both ionizing and non-ionizing radiation levels produced by commercial cathode-ray tubes fall far short of any levels set for occupational exposure to such radiation. Indeed, in measurements of ionizing radiation from a number of terminals, Terrana, Merluzzi and Giudici (1980) have demonstrated that the levels produced are often no higher than the normal background radiation to which we are constantly exposed. (See also, Grandjean, 1980a; Cakir, Hart and Stewart, 1980.)

VDU DESIGN AND USE

Two aspects will be considered: firstly the user's needs with respect to physical characteristics of the display — its brightness, colour, etc. Secondly the needs from the point of view of the information displayed — in a sense the 'software' aspects.

Physical Aspects of the Display

Illumination and luminance

From the earlier discussion of the way that the eye operates, and from experience, it is obvious that we can only see objects when light enters the eye, either directly from the object or reflected from it. The light which falls on an object is termed the illumination, while that which enters the eye from an object is known as the luminance. (Brightness is the term used to define the subjective experience of luminance.) These terms will be discussed more fully in Chapter 11.

Regarding the luminance of visual display units, Gould (1968) points out that the amount of light reflected from the usual paper pages which people read these days under ambient house and office illumination is around 160 cd m^{-2}. He, therefore, suggests that this level may be used to estimate the recommended luminance for symbols on VDUs. Comparing different VDUs of the time, Gould considered that most fell within this loose specification. More recently Läubli, Hünting and Grandjean (1981) measured the luminances arising from terminals in more modern offices and recorded average (median) luminance of 163 cd m^{-2} on terminals used for data-entry, and 108 cd m^{-2} on 'conversational' terminals. (The main difference between the two types of terminals was in the task performed: with data entry terminals the operator had to keep moving the eyes from the terminal to the source document on which the data were recorded, and back again. Conversational terminal use, however, was typified by the operator interacting only with the screen.)

Schmidtke (1980) points out that the range of display luminance is a function also of the overall illumination levels in which the screen is to be used. Thus in normal office environments having illumination levels between 100 and 1000 lux, a range of symbol luminances between 10 and 150 cd m^{-2} would be required. In much darker environments, for example in military operations control rooms, however, the range must be able to be extended downwards or else the symbols will appear too bright. On the basis of his own experiments he suggests a range

Figure 5.5 Suggested ranges of display luminances in different environments (Schmidtke, 1980). Reproduced by permission of Taylor & Francis Ltd.

of 0.2 to 200 cd m^{-2}. The data from which these suggestions were made are shown in Figure 5.5.

Finally, as Schmidtke points out, the symbol luminance is controlled by a potentiometer. If its control resistance characteristics are linear, a small deflection of the potentiometer will brighten the screen to such an extent that the operator's adaptation level may be disturbed if the display is used under dark conditions. He suggests, therefore, that a non-linear control resistance is used as the dimmer. The same control deflection will then lead to a small increase of symbol luminance under dark conditions, with larger increases under daylight conditions.

Contrast

Coupled with overall luminance is the factor of luminance contrast between the characters and the background. Too low a contrast level will prevent the characters from being readily and accurately identified; too high a contrast, however, can cause glare problems.

The contrast problem is further exacerbated when a dot matrix type of character generation is used since the luminance levels of the dots that make up the character are not uniform. Whereas, for example, the luminance from any one of the characters on this page is constant, a symbol (or light spot) produced on a VDU is composed of a spread of illumination levels with the brightest part in the centre where the electron beam strikes and gradually becoming dimmer towards the edges. This means, of course, that the contrast between the edge of the symbol and its background is not as high as between its centre and the background, resulting in a slightly 'hazy' symbol. Fellman et al. (1982) have demonstrated wide variations in character sharpness between different makes of VDUs. To overcome the slight burring effect from dot matrix displays Gould (1968) suggests both reducing the level of ambient illumination (and thus the amount of illumination reflected from the background) and adding a darkened filter to the screen.

The question whether light symbols should be viewed against a dark background (positive contrast), or vice versa (negative contrast), has been posed recently by a number of investigators. The evidence which has emerged appears to demonstrate, fairly conclusively, that performance is increased using the *negative* contrast (dark symbols against a light background) technique. For example, Bauer and Cavonius (1980) found that changing the contrast from the normal positive contrast to negative (by setting the letters to be as dark as possible and increasing the background illumination), the success rate for recognizing nonsense words increased by 23 per cent and the speed of recognition increased by 8 per cent. Radl (1980) suggests that the reason for the negative contrast advantage lies in the type of task which a VDU operator has to perform: to move the eyes from the VDU to a printed sheet which, itself, is negatively contrasted (i.e. black letters on white paper); the screen and data sheet, therefore, appear the same. Furthermore, having a light background reduces the possibility of glaring reflections on the screen which might mask the displayed symbols (see Chapter 11).

Resolution

As was discussed earlier, the usual way of producing characters on the VDU screen is to build them up as a sequence of bright dots. Each character, then, is composed of a number of scan lines and the size and definition of the character (the resolution) will be related to the number of scan lines used. In this respect, an important parameter involved in perceiving an object correctly is its size or, more accurately, the size of its image on the retina. For this reason the minimum acceptable character size for VDUs has been determined by some experimenters in terms of both the number of raster lines and the visual angle (i.e. the angle subtended at the eye by the object). Essentially, the research has indicated that about ten raster lines per character height are needed for accurate detection of individual characters, and somewhat fewer are needed to detect words.

Elias, Snadowski and Rizy (1965) reported fairly good performance with alphanumeric symbols composed of as few as 5 lines per character, although reading speed increased progressively from 5 to 11 lines. These figures, however, are averaged over all alphanumeric characters — the authors also found quite high variability in performance with different characters. For example, when using 4 scan lines approximately 90 per cent of the subjects recognized the letter 'L' correctly whereas only about 30 per cent recognized the number '8'.

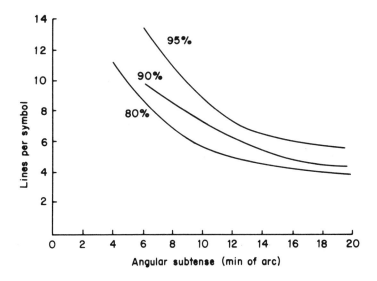

Figure 5.6 The relationship between the number of VDU raster lines and the angle between the lines subtended at the eye for 80, 90 and 95 per cent correct detection. (*From Hemingway and Erickson, 1969, and reproduced by permission of the Human Factors Society.*)

Hemingway and Erickson (1969) discuss a number of studies which have investigated the effects of resolution on recognizing geometric symbols. From such data, they conclude that about ten lines per symbol are required for good (80 per cent) identification with about twelve lines being required for 90 per cent identification, although the results of their own study showed that at least eight raster lines and a visual angle of at least 10 minutes of arc are required per geometric symbol. With an average viewing distance of 66 cm (Grandjean *et al.*, 1982) this would imply a minimum character height of about 2 mm. This is slightly smaller than one suggested by Giddings (1972) of approximately 4 mm for words and 4.6 mm for digits. Hemingway and Erickson have produced a family of curves relating lines per symbol and the angle needed to be subtended at the eye for 80, 90 and 95 per cent correct detection (see Figure 5.6).

Flicker and regeneration

As was discussed previously, when the electron beam has passed a particular spot on the screen the phosphor glow declines and, unless it is regenerated on the next scan, it will disappear. If the regeneration rate is too slow, therefore, characters will appear to flicker and this could lead to the eye muscles having to work more to keep the image in focus, causing operator fatigue. As will be discussed later, excessive flicker can cause other physiological reactions such as epilepsy. In a survey of VDU users Stammerjohn, Smith and Cohen (1981) found that 68 per cent of the operators complained of flicker from the screens. To ensure that this does not happen, relevant data regarding an observer's ability to perceive flicker is important.

If a light is repeatedly turned on and off at a fairly slow rate, then it appears to flicker. As the frequency of reversals is increased, however, there comes a point at which the flickering appears to stop and the light appears to fuse. To ensure that the characters do not appear to flicker, therefore, it is important that the screen regeneration rate is faster than this critical fusion frequency (c.f.f).

As discussed in Chapter 2, because flicker depends on so many variables it is not possible to state precise regeneration rates to ensure that flicker is overcome. However, Gould (1968) suggests that the normal electric mains regeneration rates that are used (50 Hz in the UK. and 60 Hz in the USA) are probably sufficient to prevent the perception of disturbing flicker. Furthermore, the regeneration rate can be reduced if screen phosphors having longer persistence are used.

Flicker and photosensitive epilepsy

One consequence of flicker that should be considered is its potential for inducing minor epileptic seizures. A small proportion of the population (estimated to be about 1 in 10 000 — Jeavons and Harding, 1975) suffer recurrent convulsions in the presence of flickering light stimuli. Of course, the most common 'natural' cause of such stimuli at work is likely to be the VDU. The probability of an adult VDU operator reacting to the screen in this way, however, is likely to be much less than the 1 in 10000 since the age distribution of patients who complain of these seizures is markedly skewed towards the age of puberty (Harding, 1979). Using complex striped patterns to affect the brain's responses (measured by electroencephalography — EEG) Wilkins (1978) was able to determine aspects of the display which were likely to trigger an epileptic onset, without actually inducing seizures in his patients. His results suggest that the primary correlate of such seizures is the number and intensity of retinal cells stimulated. In particular his data suggest that the epileptogenic attributes of VDU screens can be reduced firstly by reducing the area of the retina stimulated. This can be achieved by using a small screen, by displaying light characters on a dark background, by limiting the amount of text on the screen, and by seating the operator further from the screen.

Secondly the tendency can be reduced by reducing the overall luminance of the display, perhaps by the observer wearing dark glasses (Wilkins notes that this is quite common among TV studio managers who have to watch TV displays for long periods). However, the glasses would have to have a transmission rate of only 10 per cent or so to be effective.

Finally, work by Wilkins, Darby and Binnie (1979) suggests that reducing the screen-surround contrast will also reduce the potential for seizures. Thus, with a contrast ratio of 0.2 the probability of seizures was about 25 per cent of that when the ratio was 0.3.

Colour

For some years technological advances have allowed coloured symbols to be used on VDU screens. This section will discuss only the use of colour for character presentation and the screen background. The use of colour for highlighting, coding or making specific parts of the displayed information more interesting was discussed earlier in Chapter 4.

Possibly because the use of colour in VDU displays is quite a recent advance, little published work is presently available to suggest which colours should be used. Radl (1980) investigated operator performance and preference for different coloured phosphors and filters (white (monochrome), green, two types of orange and three types of yellows). His results indicate that both performance (a letter transcribing task) and preference were maximum for the yellow phosphors. Of the yellows, the true yellow phosphor produced maximum performance and preference, although a monochrome screen with a yellow filter was nearly as 'good'. The reason for this discrepancy is probably related to the luminances of the screen: whereas the yellow phosphor transformed the full energy of the electron beam into the yellow colour, the yellow filter is likely to have removed some of the luminous energy.

Radl also considered the combined effects of different coloured characters and backgrounds. Using five character colours (red, blue, green, yellow and violet) and seven background 'colours' (red, blue, green, yellow, violet, grey, and grey with 'noise'), he showed that the different colour combinations produced combined error rates (wrongly named colour and character not detected) which varied between 4 and 95 per cent. As is shown in Figure 5.7, not unreasonably the maximum error rates occurred when the character and background colours had wavelengths close to each other (for example, violet on blue, yellow on green). This is in line with the results of experimenters, such as McLean (1965) and Ohlsson, Nilsson and Rönnberg (1981) for example, who have shown that legibility and text scanning speed increase with increased colour contrast. However, Radl's results also showed that *minimum* overall error was obtained when coloured characters were presented on a *grey* background.

Figure 5.7 Error rate for the different VDU symbol/background colour combinations (Radl, 1980). *Reproduced by permission of Taylor & Francis Ltd.*

Aspects of the Software

As well as the hardware aspects of visual display design, it is also important to consider the actual characters which are displayed and the ways in which they are produced. For example, whether or not characters should be presented in lower case and whether lower-case characters should be produced with their descenders. The relative value of mixed case over simply upper-case characters was discussed in Chapter 4.

Character shape and design

Vartabedian (1971) reported a study in which he compared recognition speed and the numbers of errors made for different CRT displays. In essence, two forms of displays were used — four types of dot matrix and two types stroke display (in which the electron beam traces the character shape on the screen). The dot matrix display was either a 5 × 7 matrix, using circular or elongated 'dots', or a 7×9 matrix, using circular or slanting 'dots'. The stroke displays were either upright or slanted.

The results indicated, fairly conclusively, that the 7×9 circular dots produced fewer errors and faster reaction times than did the other forms. Whereas the 5×9 circular dots produced roughly similar numbers of errors to the 7×9 matrix, the characters took rather longer to recognize. The two slanted displays (7×9 elongated and stroke) produced a higher proportion of errors and slower reaction time than their upright counterparts. Finally, Vartabedian also demonstrated that elongating the 'dot' also affected legibility.

On the basis of this work Vartabedian (1973) produced a set of alphanumeric characters for a 7×9 dot display. A similar matrix was used by Huddleston (1974), although his display was composed of square rather than circular dots. In addition Maddox, Burnette and Gutman (1977) have produced recommendations for a 5×7 dot matrix display.

Pastoor, Schwarz and Beldie (1983) considered the efficiency of larger dot matrices, including 9×11 and 11×15. Their results demonstrated greater efficiency with both the 9×11 and the 11×15 matrices, although the difference in both performance and suitability ratings between the two were not significant. On the basis of these data, since the 9×11 matrix requires less room than one which is 11×15, the authors suggest that a 9×11 matrix should be used.

Another dimension of character shape relates to the character's height : width ratio. In this respect, Beldie, Pastoor and Schwarz (1983) demonstrated that character sets which are composed of variable width characters — as in proportional spacing, for example — produced faster reading times and fewer errors than fixed-width character sets.

The cursor

The cursor is a very important aspect of a visual display since it performs two major functions: first, it acts in the same manner as the carriage position on a conventional typewriter and indicates where the next character is to be placed. Second, it directs the operator's attention to specific parts or features of the display. Its twin roles, therefore, are first an information presenter and second an attention seeker.

Cakir, Hart and Stewart (1980) suggest that cursor types can be divided into three categories, defined by their effect on the character they are meant to be indicating. They describe these categories as 'superimposing', 'replacing' and 'enhancing'. *Superimposing* cursors do not affect the character at all; the cursor, for example a box, simply adds to the character. A *replacing* cursor is one that actually replaces the character, although it perhaps alternates with the character. Finally, an *enhancing* cursor highlights the character in some way, perhaps by intensifying the character or by colouring it.

Unfortunately, there is very little published work regarding cursor design — either to choose between the types outlined above or to determine their parameters (size, speed of flashing, brightness, shape, etc.). However, it is well known that we orientate our eyes towards a novel stimulus and so a flashing cursor is likely to prove most effective for the attention-seeking aspects of its task. With regard to the frequency of flashing, Cakir, Hart and Stewart suggest that a blink rate between 3 and 5 Hz minimizes both search and tracking times. Although it may be effective as an attention seeker, however, a flashing cursor can be distracting to the operator when, say, simply typing data from the keyboard (particularly if the operator has to think while doing so — for example, when composing text). For this reason they suggest that facilities should be provided for turning off the blinking cursor to provide a steady symbol.

AUDITORY DISPLAYS

Although the visual modality is the most extensively used medium for presenting information to the operator, auditory displays do have their value — particularly if the visual system is already overloaded or if the operator needs to have the information irrespective of the head's position at the time. In addition, as Colquhoun (1975a) has pointed out, combined auditory and visual displays can often make monitoring performance superior to using visual displays alone. Auditory displays, therefore, are suitable primarily for presenting qualitative information — as warning devices — although they are used in some circumstances to display information about the machine state. These aspects will be discussed below, but it should also be remembered that in some cases quantitative information can be displayed in the auditory mode. The hourly chimes of a clock or morse code dots and dashes are examples of such uses.

Warning Displays

A warning sound is probably the simplest type of auditory display since it conveys information of an 'on–off' nature. Either the system is 'safe' or 'unsafe' and its state is indicated by the absence or presence of the sound. To be effective, therefore, a warning sound should be both perceptible and attention getting.

Unfortunately, little scientific data exists to guide the designer in chosing suitable warning displays. Murrell (1971), for example, suggests that to be effective the sound intensity should be at least 10 dB higher than the background noise, although he offers no supporting evidence for this assertion. As will become clearer in Chapter 10, because of masking effects the warning sound should be louder than the background noise, but by how much is not clear since masking levels depend on such factors as the signal's frequency and duration. Unfortunately, no authors other than Murrell suggest a minimum level.

As long as it can be heard, possibly a more important criterion is the need for the warning display to be attention getting. Again, few design data are available although it would appear sensible to use sound to which the ear is maximally senstive — i.e. in the range 500 to 3000 Hz. McCormick (1976) has drawn

Table 5.3 Types of auditory alarm — their characteristics and special features *(from Morgan et al., 1963, and reproduced by permission of McGraw-Hill)*

Alarm	Intensity	Frequency	Attention-getting ability	Noise-penetration ability	Special features
Diaphone	Very high	Very low	Good	Poor in low-frequency noise Good in high-frequency noise	
Horn	High	Low to high	Good	Good	Can be designed to beam sound directionally Can be rotated to get wide coverage
Whistle	High	Low to high	Good if intermittent	Good if frequency is properly chosen	Can be made directional by reflectors
Siren	High	Low to high	Very good if pitch rises and falls	Very good with rising and falling frequency	Can be coupled to horn to directional transmission
Bell	Medium	Medium to high	Good	Good in low-frequency noise	Can be provided with manual shutoff to ensure alarm until action is taken
Buzzer	Low to medium	Low to medium	Good	Fair if spectrum is suited to background noise	Can be provided with manual shutoff to ensure alarm until action is taken
Chimes and gong	Low to medium	Low to medium	Fair	Fair if spectrum is suited to background noise	
Oscillator	Low to high	Medium to high	Good if intermittent	Good if frequency is properly chosen	Can be presented over intercom system

together most of the available evidence regarding the qualities of the sounds which are suitable for auditory warning signals. In addition to using signals in the 500 to 3000 Hz range, he suggests that if the sound has to travel far then frequencies below 1000 Hz should be used. If they have to 'bend' around major obstacles or pass through partitions, then the frequency should be reduced to below 500 Hz. He also suggests that a modulated signal (1-8 beats per second or warbling sounds varying from 1-3 times per second) are different enough from normal sounds to demand attention. Finally, McCormick argues that 'high intensity' sudden onset signals are often desirable for alerting an operator, and these could be presented dichotically (alternating the signal from one ear to the other) if earphones are used. Overriding all these considerations, however, is the requirement that the quality of the warning sounds different from any other sound which the operator is likely to experience in his workplace. Fidell (1978), for example, demonstrated that signals that were equally detectable were equally efficient in producing an effective response to an emergency.

Table 5.3 describes the relative advantages and disadvantages of different types of auditory warning displays.

Other Qualitative Auditory Displays

Just as a visual display can present the observer with relatively low-level qualitative information — for example whether the machine is 'hot', 'cool' or 'cold' — so too can auditory displays. In this case the coding is usually made in terms either of the tonal pitch or some other quality.

The present day telephone provides an ideal example of this use. As soon as the receiver is raised a tone is heard which indicates that the system is working and is ready to be used. On dialling or keying a number a different tone is presented depending on the new state of the system: number ringing, engaged or unobtainable. Other examples of the use of auditory information in this way can be conceived but, in all cases, it is essential that the tones indicating the different machine states are easily distinguishable.

Tracking Displays

Auditory tracking aids have been used for sometime to help pilots maintain a steady course, perhaps the simplest of which was the A/N signal system. This consisted of a continuous 1020 Hz tone being heard when the pilot was flying on course. Deviations to the left, caused the the tone to become more of a morse 'A' (dot-dash) signal, whereas an 'N' (dash-dot) signal (which interleaves with the 'A' signal to form the continuous 'on course' tone) would become apparent with deviations to the right. Although some success was claimed with this system it does depend, again, on the distinguishability of the two (A and N) codes. As McCormick (1976) points out, however, under adverse noise conditions the difference between the two signals may not be properly identified.

Hoffman and Heimstra (1972) report an auditory tracking system which proved to be superior to a visual display. In this case the subject was required to maintain a particular random course using a hand-wheel, in which no noise was heard if the pointer remained on target. Deviations by more then 5 per cent, however, caused a noise signal to be heard in either the right or left ear, depending on from which side of the track the deviations occurred. Using this system, more time was spent on target using the auditory than the visual display.

From these two examples, therefore, it is clear that acoustic displays can be used to provide simple, one-dimensional tracking information, although great care needs to be taken to ensure that the various displayed states are easily distinguished.

SUMMARY

This chapter discussed various ways by which the machine can present information presented to the operator — through its displays. Although many types of displays are available, it soon became apparent that the most appropriate display depends to a considerable extent on the nature of the task for which the information is to be used. In the visual modality the choice is essentially between an analogue and a digital display, although a number of different ways of presenting these two basic types were discussed. In the auditory modality, the designer's choice is more restricted.

The following chapter will consider the third main sensory system which is used at work — the sense of touch. Although the main theme of the chapter will be to discuss ways of enhancing the information flow in the other direction — from the operator to the machine via controls — it should not be forgotten that each time the operator operates a control, for example using a push-button, the control shape, dimensions and movement, etc. are also passing information from the machine to the operator.

CHAPTER 6

MAN-MACHINE COMMUNICATION: CONTROLS

By allowing the operator to return information to the environment, controls represent the alternative link in the man–machine closed loop system and are very much the complement of displays. Indeed, the value of a well designed display (reduced reading errors; faster reading time) could be seriously affected if the many features important in operating its associated control are not considered. Display design was discussed in Chapter 5, and so the present chapter will consider factors which are important from the viewpoint simply of designing the operator's controls and tools.

That poorly designed controls alone may lead to inefficiency and breakdown in the man–machine system is well illustrated in a survey carried out by Fitts and Jones (1947b). In a complementary study to their investigation of aircraft display reading errors, they analysed 460 'pilot error' experiences in operating aircraft controls. Sixty-eight per cent of the errors were related to poor control design. The remainder were due either to mistakes occurring because of a lack of compatibility between the display and the control (6 per cent) or to poor control placement on the cockpit panel (26 per cent). (Chapter 7 will discuss these points.)

Controls, therefore, are important components in the system. However, a number of factors need to be considered before an effective control system can be designed that will match the operator's expectations, abilities and behaviour. The operator's task needs to be analysed to determine the degree of accuracy, force, precision and manipulation, etc. required, and these features have to be compared with the operator's abilities to carry out such tasks. If abilities do not match requirements, then changes in the mechanical part of the system have to be considered — perhaps involving different types or designs of controls and control systems.

This chapter, therefore, will first consider the types of controls available for different types of operations. Secondly some of the factors important in control design and aspects of the system which could affect control effectiveness will be examined. Finally, the discussion will consider the extent to which such factors have been incorporated in producing specific types of control.

TYPES OF CONTROL

Controls are commonly classified into two groups according to their function. The first includes those used to make discrete alterations in the machine state, for example switching it 'on' or 'off', or switching to different levels of machine activity. Secondly are controls which are used for making continuous settings. For example, a radio volume control allows the user to increase the volume gradually, and to stop at any of an infinite number of intensities within its operating range. McCormick (1976) further subdivides these two functions into:

Discrete
- Activation — for example, turning a machine on or off.
- Data entry — as on a keyboard to enter either a letter or a number.
- Setting — switching to a specific machine state.

Continuous
- Quantitative setting — setting the machine to a particular value along a continuum, for example turning a radio-frequency control to receive a specific radio station.
- Continuous control — continuously altering the machine state, usually to maintain a particular level of activity (commonly known as tracking). For example, steering a vehicle using the steering wheel.

Different controls will be more appropriate for some of these activities than for others. The respective advantages of controls for different activities are shown in Table 6.1.

It is unlikely that any single control would be appropriate in all circumstances. Take the case of the ubiquitous push-button, for example. After reviewing the literature concerning various types of single-switches, Chambers and Stockbridge (1970) showed that in terms of operating speeds the most efficient activation control was the push-button followed by the rocker switch, the slide switch and the toggle switch. The order for accuracy was reverse that of speed, however, because the push-button is usually associated with a 'ballistic-like movement which resulted in increased speed but reduced accuracy'.

Finally, as McCormick cautions, the usefulness of any control can be limited by such features (if relevant) as the ease to which it can be identified, its location and size, its relationship to the appropriate display, and the type of feedback which it gives to the operator. The next section will consider some of these factors.

FACTORS IMPORTANT IN CONTROL DESIGN

Feedback

Feedback has been discussed already in previous chapters. It refers to the information received, both from outside and from inside the body, which helps

Table 6.1   Types of controls and their functions

Control type	Activation	Discrete Setting	Data entry	Quantitative setting	Continuous control
		Discrete		Continuous	
Hand push-button	Excellent	Can be used, will need as many buttons as settings—not recommended	Good	Not applicable	Not applicable
Foot push-button	Good	Not recommended	N/A	N/A	N/A
Toggle switch	Good—but prone to accidental activation	Fair—but poor if more than three possible settings to be made	N/A	N/A	N/A
Rotary selector switch	Can be used, but on/off position may be confused with other positions	Excellent—provided settings are well marked	N/A		N/A
Knob	N/A	Poor	N/A	Good	Fair
Crank	Only applicable if large forces are needed to activate—e.g. open/close hatch	N/A	N/A	fair	Good
Handwheel	N/A	N/A	N/A	Good	Excellent
Lever	Good	Good—providing there are not too many settings	N/A	Good	Good
Pedal	Fair	N/A	N/A	Good	Fair

the operator to assess his or her performance, body position, etc. In relation to hand controls, for example, feed back obtained from the eyes, shoulders, arms, wrists and fingers informs the operator by how much a control has been moved and its final position. In addition, feedback from the more sensitive pressure receptors in the skin provides information about the nature of the control being operated: its size, texture and any tactile coding characteristics. In many respects, therefore, feedback can be considered to relate to the control's 'feel'.

Burrows (1965) points out that control 'feel' arises from two separate sources. Firstly, as just discussed, it occurs as kinaesthetic feedback from the muscles, for

Table 6.2 The characteristics of static and coulomb, elastic, viscous and inertial control resistances

Type of resistance	Example of incidence	Characteristics	Advantages	Disadvantages
Static and coulomb	1. On/off switch 2. A 'stuck' control	The resistance is maximal at the start of the movement, but falls considerably with further force, i.e. the control slips	Reduced chance of accidental activation	Little precision control once the control has begun to move
Elastic	Spring-loaded control	Resistance is proportional to control displacement	1. Kinaesthetic cues may be maximally effective 2. Control returns to null position	Because control returns to neutral, operator's limb needs to be constantly active
Viscous	Plunger	Resistance is proportional to the velocity of the control movement	1. Good control precision—particularly rate of movement 2. Reduced chance of accidental operation 3. Operator can remove limb and control remains in position	
Inertia	Large crank	Resistance is caused by the mass of the control	1. Allows smooth movement 2. Reduced chance of accidental operation due to high force required	1. May cause operator fatigue 2. Does not allow precise movement because of danger of overshooting

example telling the operator where the arm is at the time and the speed with which it is moving through space. As was discussed in Chapter 2, this is a very efficient form of feedback, particularly for learning different skills. Secondly, 'feel' is determined by the control itself in terms of the amount of resistance to movement which is built into it, its looseness, etc. Of course, to these sources should be added any tactile, visual or auditory feedback loops which may help the operator (for example 'clicks' or marks on the control surface).

Resistance

The control's resistance to movement is possibly the most used feedback cue. In the majority of cases, particularly when continuous settings are to be made, some inbuilt resistance is desirable since it allows the operator to make settings with some degree of precision. Resistance also often helps to guard against accidentally activating the control. However, if too much resistance is incorporated, or the wrong type of resistance is used, the operator could experience fatigue and performance may be reduced. Understanding the nature of different types of resistance, therefore, should make it possible to choose controls which have characteristics that will minimize any possible negative effects while, at the same time, maximizing performance.

Control resistance takes four main forms, and their advantages and disadvantages are shown in Table 6.2. From this table, it would appear that static friction is most appropriate for discrete setting controls since it reduces the possibility of accidental operation. For continuous setting controls, however, elastic or viscous resistance will allow greater precision due to the nature of the kinaesthetic feedback which it provides.

Regarding the level of resistance to be introduced, it is difficult to suggest any particular figure since it will be related to the type of operator, control location, and the frequency, duration, direction and amount of control movement required. Clearly, however, the maximum level set should lie within the range of abilities of the operating population, for which texts such as those of Damon *et al.*

Table 6.3 Minimum resistances required for different controls (*adapted from Morgan* et al., *1963, and reproduced by permission of McGraw-Hill*)

Control	Minimum resistance
Hand push-button	10oz. (2.8 N)
Foot push-button	4lb (17.8 N) if foot does not rest on control; 1.25lb (5.6 N) if foot rests on control
Toggle switch	10oz. (2.8 N)
Rotary selector switch	12oz. (3.3 N)
Knob	0–6oz. (0–1.7 N) depending on function
Crank	2–5lb (9–22 N) depending on size
Handwheel	5lb (22 N)
Lever	2lb (9 N)
Pedal	4lb (17.8 N) if foot does not rest on control; 10lb (44.5 N) if foot rests on control

(1971) and Roebuck *et al.* (1975) should be consulted. For minimum levels Morgan *et al.* (1963) suggest that, for all hand controls except push buttons, resistance should not be less than 2–5 lb, since below this level the hand's pressure sensitivity is very poor. If the full weight of the arm and hand rest on the control the minimum resistance should be 10–12 lb. Table 6.3 summarizes some of the data available for maximum resistances for different types of control.

Size

Control sizes and dimensions clearly need to be related to the anthropometric dimensions of the limbs used. Thus the diameter of a push-button should be at least that of the fingertip (approximately 16 mm); the size of a knob on a lever equal to the breadth of grip (49 mm); etc. Garrett (1971) provides a set of these various dimensions for the human hand but it should be remembered that these dimensions will be altered, sometimes considerably, if the operator is wearing gloves.

Not only is it important to relate the size of the control to the dimensions of the limb which operates it, it is also important to consider the action required. All controls require some degree of manipulation. For hand controls, therefore,

Figure 6.1 A classification of hand control functions. (*Adapted from Grieve and Pheasant, 1981, reproduced by permission of Cambridge University Press.*)

different types of manipulative tasks will require different control dimensions, depending on the part of the hand used to operate the control.

Most manipulative tasks can be placed along a continuum of 'gripping' to 'non-gripping' activities. In gripping activities the fingers and parts of the palm form a closed chain and act in opposition to each other to exert compressive forces on the object to be gripped. In non-gripping actions the forces are exerted either through all of the hand or through the fingertips in an open chain. As well as the amount to which the fingers are closed, a second manipulative dimension concerns the degree of hand/object contact. From such a two-dimensional classification it is possible to determine the anthropometric dimensions required for any particular task, and also the forces and torques needed. Some of these dimensions, with examples, are illustrated in Figure 6.1.

Weight

The weight of many controls becomes important only when the inertia is enough to cause undue resistance (for example as with a crank handle), otherwise the weight will be supported by the machine itself. However, some controls are used away from a machine (particularly as hand-tools) and in these cases the tool's weight may obviously play an important part in its effectiveness.

In addition to the overall tool weight, its weight distribution is an important feature. For example, a rod held in the hand which is in a relaxed, neutral position makes an obtuse angle of approximately 102° to the forearm (Tichauer, 1978). Major deviations from this will cause the wrist muscles to be under static load. If most of the weight is distributed towards the front or the back of the tool, therefore, so that the wrist needs to work to maintain its natural posture, the static load will soon cause fatigue. The ideal weight distribution, then, will be one which places the maximum weight over the place where the tool is held and maintains the 102° angle.

Texture

Since the control acts as the interface of information flowing between the operator and the machine, it might be thought to be an obvious point that the quality of the control action will depend largely on the extent to which the operator's limb is able to remain in contact with it. As with many aspects of the working situation, however, ensuring that this occurs is not so simple. For example, it is obvious that the surface of hand-held controls should not be so smooth as to make a firm grip difficult to accomplish. This is particularly important if the hands are likely to be moist from sweat. In addition, a highly polished surface may cause glare, perhaps adversely affecting the operator's performance on a visual task. On the other hand, surfaces which are to be grasped or which are likely to be rubbed against should be free of any abrasive properties (rough surfaces are often contaminated with sand or dirt, etc., and so it is likely that an abraded wound would eventually become infected). A balance must be struck, therefore, between the two extremes and so the question becomes to what extent the control should be textured. Many of these problems are solved by using a non-reflective, rippled coating, but the ripples should not be raised so much that they cause painful pressure spots.

When the operator applies a force to a hand control, the direction of the force may act either transversely across the palm as in the case of a steering wheel, or longitudinally as with a lever. (Feet also exert longitudinal forces along a pedal.) In both cases the rippled texture described above may help the designer to minimize the possibility of the hand slipping. However, the two types of force suggest that the directions of the ripples need to be considered in so far as they should be at right angles to the likely direction of force.

Coding

The value of highlighting different aspects or areas of the machines to ease identification was discussed in the last chapter. For qualitative displays colour coding different areas was shown to increase performance and reduce errors.

It is, of course, possible also to colour code controls. However, because they are usually operated by a limb it is probably more appropriate to code them along some tactile dimension. This allows the eyes to be released to accept other, visual, information. Unfortunately, however, touch is a less accurate sensory mode for perceiving differences than is vision, and this may lead to uncertainties in the operator's actions and probably slows down discrimination time. For this reason Moore (1976) recommends that tactile identification of controls should only be used as a final check on the control's identity, rather than as the primary coding method. Adequate labelling, he suggests, is probably as efficient. Like colour coding, however, labelling also needs to be seen to be effective and, as was discussed in Chapter 4, requires careful design.

In many cases controls may have to be put in places where labels or colours are not easily seen and in such cases shape, texture, size and location coding, or any combination of these, may be used. With each of these techniques, the aim is to produce groups of controls such that the controls within each group are rarely confused with each other.

Coding by shape

An operator is able to distinguish different shapes mainly by pressure differences over the hand tissue caused by various protrusions in the shape. For this reason shape coding is normally useful only to ungloved operators.

A number of sets of unconfusable shapes have been produced by different investigators over the years (e.g. Hunt, 1953; Jenkins, 1947; Moore, 1974). In general the work has demonstrated that simple forms are easier to discriminate than are more complicated ones. Furthermore, learning their use can be simplified and made more efficient if the controls also have shapes which, either by design or by convention, look similar to the part of the machine which they operate.

Coding by texture

As well as its shape the control's texture may also be coded, for example the edge may be differentially rippled or knurled. As Bradley (1967) demonstrated, as long as the textures are distinct enough confusions will not occur. He produced smooth, fluted and knurled textured control-wheel edges which would not be confused. Furthermore, appropriate training and practice may significantly improve an operator's ability to distinguish between textures (Eckstrand and Morgan, 1956) — although the cautions expressed in Chapter 1 concerning the value of training alone should be remembered.

Like shape coding, but perhaps to a lesser extent, the stimulus perceived from using textured controls is related to different patterns of fingertip deformation. This is what the operator learns to recognize and any impediment to the perfect transmission of this information from the control to the operator could result in errors being made. Gloves provide a good example of this problem. Even if the gloves are thin enough to allow the operator to manipulate controls under normal circumstances, they may impair (or perhaps more importantly distort) perception of the surface texture. Dirt and grime collecting in the textured surface may cause similar problems.

Since the important stimulus is the amount and the pattern of skin and tissue deformation, texture coding does not need to be confined solely to 'smoothness', 'rippledness', or 'knurledness'. Moore (1974), for example, describes an experiment designed to investigate discriminability between different raised surface shapes on push-buttons. By asking subjects to feel (blindly) the surface of different push-buttons and to compare them with pictures, he was able to produce a set of six discriminable surface textures.

As far as tactile shape coding is concerned, Moore recommends the following five principles:

(1)   Shapes to be distinguished by touch should have as gross a shape as possible, covering an area which can be touched by one finger.
(2)   Geometric shapes, numbers or letters should be formed from outlines rather than from solids.
(3)   Shapes should be made to vary along as many tactile dimensions as possible.
(4)   If at all possible, the buttons should be designed or chosen to ensure that the shapes remain in the same orientation at all times and do not revolve.
(5)   The shapes should not be uncomfortable or difficult to use.

Coding by size

The size of the control itself may provide useful visual or tactile cues, but size alone generally is not as useful for coding as is shape or texture. Again the different sizes used should be such that they are discriminable from one another. In this respect, Moore (1976) suggests that the sizes used should follow a logarithmic progression with at least a 20 per cent difference between each.

Coding by colour

Colour coding has previously been discussed in relation to visual displays, and similar principles exist for coding controls. Unlike visual displays, however, the prime function of controls is not to present visual information and so they may not be in a position which can easily be seen by the operator. Indeed, they are often put in places which enable them to be operated while the operator is looking elsewhere, perhaps at the display. In these circumstances colour coding — which is essentially a visual aid — is often of little value for controls which have mainly manual and tactile features.

FACTORS THAT AFFECT CONTROL EFFECTIVENESS

In many respects the majority of topics discussed in this book will affect control effectiveness: the quality of the information reaching the operator; the operator's position with respect to the control; environmental factors (both social and physical); fatigue; stress, etc. However, this section will consider aspects of the interaction which are not discussed elsewhere and which are specific to control design — namely, operator handedness, the wearing of clothing (in particular gloves and shoes), the control shape, and the way in which the control is used.

Handedness

For everyday use, an individual's handedness (or, more accurately, hand preference) may be classified as being 'left' or 'right' simply on the basis of the writing hand. For complex tasks, however, this simple dichotomy clearly becomes insufficient; an individual may have different hand preferences for various actions and this could cause problems from the viewpoint of determining which hand should operate which control. Taking the action of tightening a screw as a very simple example; a right-handed person would need to rotate the wrist with a movement of the palm upwards, i.e. twisting the wrist away from the body (supination). The operator with a left-hand preference will need to protinate the wrist (palm moved downwards, wrist twisted towards the body). Unfortunately for the left-handed person, however, supination allows a greater torque and range of movement than does protination (Damon, Stoudt and MacFarland, 1971).

The problem of left-handed operators, however, does not simply rest with considering the strengths and types of left- and right-hand movement. Controls, particularly tool handles, are often designed for use by right-handed operators. Left-handed operators frequently find them difficult or uncomfortable to use and this may lead to fatigue and possibly accidents.

A solution to the problem caused by hand preference, however, is not simple. A number of estimates of the incidence of left-handedness have been made and vary from 2 per cent to 29 per cent (Hardyck and Petrinovich, 1977), although generally less than 10 per cent of any large national population is left-handed (or at least has a left-hand preference for most activities) (Kimura and Vanderwolf, 1970). Since ambidexterity, in the sense of equal preference, is extremely rare the question must be posed whether it is possible to accommodate fully the requirements of the left-handed operator. Naturally, sometimes right and left-handed tools may be available, when the different handle shapes and directions of movement will need to be considered. In other cases, however (for example, the question of control placement with respect to the operator's own position), it may not be possible (or economical) to produce both right and left-handed versions. In such cases it is even more crucial to assess the requirements of the job and to match them to the operator's capabilities.

Clothing and Protective Clothing

The type of clothing most likely to interfere with efficient control action are gloves covering the hands and shoes on the feet. Both may affect relevant control dimensions and both are likely to alter the operator's ability to use the control adequately.

Although gloves are designed to protect the operator's hands they may have a number of undesirable consequences, particularly in relation to manipulating the control and obtaining feedback from it. As an example, the normal sensation of 'grip' probably results from the pressure perceived when the flexed fingers around the gripped object press against each other. A working glove which is too thick in these regions can cause high pressures to be generated between the fingers before the hand is firmly closed around the tool handle or equipment control, and this may result in an insecure grasp. A thick glove can also interfere with the fingers and stop them from wrapping around the handle sufficiently for a firm grip. On the other hand, of course, an operator who is aware of these problems may grip the control unnecessarily tightly so increasing fatigue in the finger and other muscles.

After carrying out a series of experiments to determine the degree to which gloves interfere with control manipulation and operation speeds, Bradley (1969a) concluded that the efficiency with which instrument controls may be operated by a gloved hand depends on the glove characteristics, the physical characteristics of the control, and the type of control operation. Specifically, snugness of fit and resistance to slipping were shown to be the two most important glove parameters, and under some circumstances a snug glove which did not slip over the controls actually improved performance. In many cases, however, gloves are worn for protection against injury, and snugness and even resistance to slipping may be absent. In such cases the control sizes need to be increased to allow adequate manipulation and, as discussed earlier, the control ought to be textured to reduce slipping.

In addition to interfering with grip, gloves can often impede the perception of any coded texture differences on various controls. As was discussed earlier, such texture differences cause different pressure patterns on the observer's skin and these could be occluded by the gloves.

In a similar fashion to gloves interfering with the operation of hand-held controls, shoes sometimes affect the efficiency of foot-pedal operation. Heavy, protective footwear, for example, may not allow the feet to be moved with the required precision since the necessary feedback may be either missing or of poor quality.

A second interfering feature of shoes which is often forgotten is the height of the heels. As will be discussed later, most foot pedals are designed for the forces and angles produced by a foot having 'average' dimensions and the presence of high heels can alter these parameters. For example, Warner and Mace (1974) demonstrated that the average brake response time of female drivers was increased by 0.1s when wearing platform (having a heel higher than 2in and a sole $\frac{1}{2}$in thick) as opposed to 'normal' shoes — despite that fact that the subjects were used to wearing platform shoes. (This is simply a further example of training being unable to overcome the effects of poor equipment design.) Translated into vehicle stopping distances, this represents an increase of 1.42ft for each 10m.p.h. speed increase, which could mean the difference between safe and unsafe stopping.

Control Shapes

Control shapes can have an important influence on the way in which an operator uses the control. This may, in turn, affect the posture. Awkward postures can put undue stress on the musculoskeletal system causing fatigue over long periods. This applies particularly to the use of hand controls.

Many tools are used which, under normal operational conditions, require the wrist to be bent either downwards or upwards. This causes the tendons connecting the finger muscles to the forearm bones in the elbow region to bend and to become subject to mechanical stress. Whereas infrequent use of such a tool and posture is unlikely to lead to any ill effects, under continuous operation the effect will be to cause muscular fatigue and thus loss of efficiency. As Tichauer (1978) points out, it is much safer to bend the tool than to bend the wrist.

Shape is also important when considering the cross-sectional configuration of a hand tool. If high grip forces are required, the handle should distribute the forces to as large a pressure-bearing area on the fingers and palm as possible, while still being small enough to allow the fingers to wrap round the handle. To this end, Pheasant and O'Neill (1975) have demonstrated that muscular strength is maximal when using handles around 5cm diameter. Below 3–4cm and above 5–6cm both the amount of hand contact with the handle and the amount of torque able to be exerted, fell dramatically.

Movements Required for Different Controls

Different types of controls require different types of operation and this can significantly affect the effectiveness with which the control is operated.

As an example, consider the types of control operation described earlier in terms of open and closed chain operation. The movement required to operate a keyboard is characterized by an 'open chain' approach, with the hand having little contact with the control. Thus, the operation is performed using more of a 'pointing' movement which has a ballistic nature (Chambers and Stockbridge, 1970). Essentially, therefore, the problems facing the operator are considerations of speed and accuracy: to place the fingers accurately over the appropriate keys, and to strike the keys as quickly as possible. The muscles involved include those in the shoulder, arm and wrist, in addition to the muscles needed to operate the appropriate fingers.

The operations required to use controls such as a pen, however, are different. These involve rather more hand–object contact, particularly because more than one finger has to hold and operate this type of control. Thus, more muscles are employed and, because of the nature of the controlling task, they are maintained under tension for longer. Inevitably this will lead to more static load and to a higher risk of muscle fatigue.

A further biomechanical problem associated with controls occurs when they have to be positioned or operated at some distance from the body. Since more stability occurs as the operation is carried out nearer to the body, it follows that operations such as touching a pen to a computer screen at arm's length, or turning a valve above the head may be less accurately performed than pressing a key on a keyboard near to the operator. The reason for this is twofold: First, as the arm is extended forces on the shoulder muscles are increased because the centre of gravity of the hand–arm complex moves away from the body. More work will be required from the muscles, therefore, to maintain a stable position — to counteract the force of gravity. Indeed, this was demonstrated well by Mead and Sampson (1972) who measured hand steadiness while subjects performed various types of movements. The amount of tremor was considerably reduced, and thus accuracy increased, when subjects made ballistic-like 'in–out' movements than when they were required to move a stylus 'up–down'. Secondly, as the arm is extended the wrist orientation has to change. This means that the degree of finger-control contact tends to be reduced — unless the operator takes specific steps to counteract this tendency. Doing so, of course, will increase the amount of static load on the finger muscles.

THE DESIGN OF SPECIFIC TOOLS AND CONTROLS

When discussing the development of modern ergonomics, many sceptics describe the era of the 1950s and early 1960s as being the period of 'knobs and dials' investigations. By this they imply that ergonomists were interested mainly in the design aspects of specific types of displays or controls — rather than considering how these pieces of equipment function as parts of the total work system. Although a cursory examination of the published literature of this period tends to support this observation, it could well be argued that basic research of this nature needed to be carried out before the advantages of different types of display or control in the system could be considered. Because it is important to be able to recognize good 'ergonomic' control designs, this section will provide a very basic description of the design recommendations for different types of control as elucidated by the research of the period. Chapter 7 will consider the use of such controls within the total system. When discussing these recommendations, however, it should be realized that some of the data are based on experiments using comparatively small numbers of subjects. Given the wide variability of performance abilities shown by individuals, therefore, it is not possible to provide figures for diameters, loads and so on with absolute certainty. Nevertheless, as Murrell (1971) points out

At the best (the figures) give a reasonable estimate of the design parameters concerned, at the worst they are better than guesswork on the part of the designer who, if he follows them, may rest assured that the equipment which he is producing is being designed in accordance with the best knowledge available at present.

Hand Controls

Naturally the basic considerations of all hand controls concern the anthropometric and biomechanical capabilities of the operator's fingers, hands and wrists.

Knobs

The knob is a cylindrical-shaped control which is operated by gripping the thumb and forefinger around its circumference and moving them in opposition. Knobs may be used for making fine, continuous adjustments or as rotary selector switches.

It is important that the diameter of this type of control is not too small to prevent it from being gripped and turned easily. On the other hand, panel space should not be wasted by using controls which are larger than those required for efficient operation. For this reason Bradley (1969b) asked 48 subjects to make various clockwise and anticlockwise 'standard' operations, using knobs with diameters ranging from 0.5 to 3.25 in (1.2 to 8 cm), in 0.25 in (0.6 cm) increments. Two levels of shaft friction (torque) were used: normal (77–85 inch grams; 0.5–0.6 Nm) and heavy (171–181 inch grams; 1.2–1.3 Nm). Using turning time as his main measure, Bradley demonstrated that a knob diameter of approximately 5 cm was optimum for both normal and heavy friction. As the shaft friction increased the turning time was magnified significantly as the knob diameter deviated from the optimum.

As control panels increase in complexity, more and more instruments may have to be crowded into a limited panel space. One possible means by which this might be accomplished is by grouping controls together. In the case of concentric controls, this would mean ganging several control knobs perpendicular to the panel by mounting them on concentric shafts. Unfortunately, however, ganging control knobs probably increases the chance of inadvertently operating adjacent knobs. While turning one of the knobs the operator's fingertips or knuckles might scrape against the face of the knob immediately behind it, or the fingers or palm may rub against one of the knobs in front of it, so altering the setting of the knob which was inadvertently operated.

Bradley (1969c) investigated the optimum dimensions for such controls. In a similar experiment to his determination of optimum knob diameters he demonstrated that, for three-ganged controls, if the diameter of the centre knob is 5 cm (optimum knob diameter) the diameter of the front knob should be less than 2½ cm and that of the rear knob about 8 cm. His results also indicated that the front and middle knobs should each be 8 cm thick, whereas the back knob could be as thin as 0.6 cm. Bradley further argues that concentrically ganged knobs should only be used if enough shaft friction is present to prevent accidental operation.

Push-buttons

Push-buttons are small, single action controls which operate in one direction only. They are usually activated by the fingers but sometimes by the foot. They range in size from comparatively large 'on' or 'off' buttons for heavy machine-tools to small, individual finger-controlled buttons of which modern electric typewriter keyboards are examples. Three types of push-button are commonly available: 'latching' (push-on, lock-on), 'momentary' (push-on, release-off) and 'alternate action' (push-on, push-off). All three modes are found in hand-operated buttons, but the latching mode is seldom found in foot-operated buttons.

The important physical parameters of push-buttons are their size, separation, shape, operating force, the provision of feedback, and the separation between the buttons. Of these factors the shape of the button has already been discussed and the separation between buttons will be discussed in the following chapter — particularly in terms of grouping buttons together to form a keyboard.

Regarding button size, the limiting factor must be the dimensions of the fingers which are to operate the controls. In this respect, a minimum diameter of 13 mm is often suggested for finger-operated controls and 19 mm for those operated by the base of the thumb (for example, an emergency stop button). Unfortunately few data are presently available to enable comparisons between these dimensions and the size of the average finger-tip.

As an indication of the importance of ensuring that the size of the keys is optimum, Deininger (1960) reports a study which investigated button size as a variable in different keyboard arrangements. By increasing the dimensions of a square button from 9.5 to 17.4 mm, he was able to show a reduction in keying times from 6.35 to 5.83 s, and reduced errors from 7.1 to 1.3 per cent.

For use when designing key sizes and spacings to fit the operator's hand, Garrett (1971) provides a number of anthropometric dimensions for different parts of the adult human hand. His data suggest that the top of the finger joints have an average breadth of approximately 1.7 cm for males and 1.5 cm for females. Ninety per cent of the male population falls into a range of from 1.6 to 1.9 cm, and of the female population 1.3 to 1.6 cm. Naturally, the width of this joint is not the same as that of the finger-tip, since fingers tend to taper, but data such as these are presently the nearest available.

As was discussed earlier, key resistance performs two functions: first, it provides the operator with kinaesthetic feedback relating to the extent to which a key has been pressed. Second, by requiring force to depress the key, resistance can prevent accidental operation. Because of its properties of acting against movement, however, resistance is likely to increase muscular fatigue and so needs to be set to a type and level that is optimum. Moore (1975) suggests a range of push-button resistances from 283 to 1133 g if one finger is used, 140–560 g if different fingers are used, and 283–2272 g for large, thumb-operated controls. Chambers and Stockbridge (1970) emphasize, however, that caution must be given against reducing the resistance by too much since it becomes easier to operate the button inadvertently. A hair-trigger on a gun, for example, requires a safety catch to prevent accidents.

With regard to the maximum force able to be exerted, Alden, Daniels and Kanarick (1972) report a study performed by Haaland, Wingert and Olsen (1963) in which the maximum pushing force for each finger of the adult male hand was measured. As can be seen from Table 6.4, quite wide variations occur over the five fingers and Haaland *et al.* attribute this to differences in the finger musculature. Furthermore, they observe that individuals whose fingers bend back when pushing perpendicularly could not apply as much pushing force as those whose fingers remain rigid.

Table 6.4 Maximum finger pushing force (g) (Haaland *et al.*, 1963)

	Finger				
	Thumb	Index	Middle	Ring	Little
Mean	1055	684	627	513	342
Range	855–1226	485–884	485–741	342–627	171–542

Of course, the maximum force able to be pushed will not necessarily be the ideal force required for a keyboard. It is, therefore, important to consider what is the *optimum* force for maximum speed and minimum fatigue. For example, Droege and Hill (1961) demonstrated that variations in key resistance can have important implications for performance.

In his experiment investigating different key arrangements, Deininger (1960) found that varying the key force from 3.5 to 14.1 oz (100 to 403 g) or varying the maximum displacement from 0.03 to 0.19 inches (0.08 to 0.48 cm) produced insignificant differences in his subjects' keying performances. However, later reports from the subjects indicated a general preference for the light touch keys and a definite dislike for the keys requiring greater displacement. Unfortunately as Alden, Daniels and Kanarick (1972) point out, many of Deininger's results are questionable given his lack of experimental controls. Nevertheless the subjective reports have some use and the results do relate favourably to other studies in the area.

For example, Bergenthal (1971) reports a study in which sixty subjects were required to push buttons having a range of forces from 3 to 48 oz (86–1371 g). His results demonstrate a strong preference for buttons having a resistance of approximately 10 oz (286 g). Preference fell significantly as resistances departed from this value. It should be pointed out, however, that Bergenthal's study was performed with subjects pressing the buttons sequentially with a 'stiff' finger and this may not be an appropriate type of action for all forms of push-button operations. Typing, for example, is performed using the fingers in a bent posture, the control being operated by the finger-pad rather than the finger-tip.

Finally, feedback: as has already been discussed, effective feedback is essential if the control is to be operated efficiently; the operator needs to know that the control has functioned correctly. Although this feedback may be visual, in the case of push-buttons it is most usefully given by feel or by an audible click. The eyes can then be released for other work. However, the resistance needed to produce such a click should not exceed the maximum resistance suggested above or fatigue may occur after continued use (users of some calculator keyboards will have experienced this fatigue). Finally, modern control panels often use indicator lights as feedback devices but, as Moore (1975) rightly points out, they are only useful if they can be seen by the operator. He also emphasizes that the value of indicator lights usually bears an inverse relationship to the number alight at any one time; the more alight the less that each new one will mean to the operator.

Switches

Switches have one of two shapes; either rotary selector switches, which look like knobs but which are used to make discrete settings, or a toggle type of switch which has the appearance of a miniature lever. These switches generally have two positions — 'on' or 'off'; speed and ease of operation may be sacrificed with additional settings.

Few data are available on which to base the design of toggle switches, although Morgan et al. (1963) suggest that the maximum length should be 2½ cm with a minimum of 3 mm. Murrell (1971), however, would allow toggles up to 5 cm long but agrees with the minimum dimensions. Both agree that the switch should 'snap' into position and should not allow the possibility of intermediate positions.

The advantage of a rotary selector switch lies in the increased number of positions which may be used (Chapanis, 1951, suggests between 3 and 24). Most of the dimensions discussed for rotary control knobs are relevant to selector switches, apart from the resistance. As with the toggle switch, the resistance should be applied to enable the switch to 'snap' into position — i.e. it should be reduced at each position.

Perhaps the most important design consideration for rotary selector switches is the way in which the settings are indicated. This is usually done by moulding either the whole switch or the top part of it into a pointed shape, or marking the switch surface. Whatever method is employed it is essential that no ambiguity can exist regarding the position selected (see Figure 6.2).

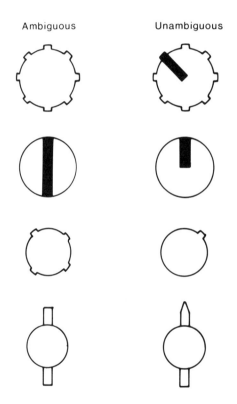

Ambiguous   Unambiguous

Figure 6.2 Some examples of ambiguous and unambiguous switch shapes and markings

Levers and joysticks

The difference between levers and joysticks is simply that joysticks operate in two dimensions whereas levers only operate in one. For this reason, joysticks are used more often for complex tracking or positioning tasks (for example, vehicle guidance) whereas levers are used in situations in which only one dimension is altered (for example, changing vehicle speed or direction).

Because joysticks are used when precision adjustments are made, it is desirable that only the hand and fingers are used since these muscles are more densely supplied with nerves than are, for example, those in the arm. For this reason, joysticks will generally be smaller than levers. To aid precision they should have resistance in all directions with, perhaps, a return to centre position if the hand is removed. Morgan *et al.* (1963) further suggest that the joystick should be designed to enable the operator to rest the wrist while making the movements, and that the pivot point should be positioned under the point at which the wrist is rested. As will be discussed in Chapter 10, however, the value of resting the wrist when making tracking movements may be reduced considerably if the joystick is to be used under vibrating conditions.

Few data are available for chosing the optimum length of either lever or joystick handles, perhaps because the important consideration relates more to the extent to which the display alters in relation to the control movement. This factor, the control–display ratio, will be discussed more fully in the next chapter.

Hand-operated computer input controls

With the advent of computers a number of new types of hand-operated controls have appeared which are used essentially to move a cursor about the screen. These are controls which operate as discrete entry controls or for continuous movement.

Touch displays

Touch displays allow the user to control the machine's operation simply by touching an appropriate part of the computer screen or some representation of the screen. In this way the computer screen becomes, essentially, a bi-directional instrument in that it both presents information to and receives information from the operator. With appropriate software, different parts of the screen can represent different responses as different displays are presented to the operator. For example, a screen may first present a list of actions available to the operator, who choses a particular action by touching — say the centre of the screen. The centre of the screen for the next display, however, may represent a totally different choice.

Both Hopkin (1971) and McEwing (1977) discuss the advantages of screen-based displays, which can be summarized thus:

(a) *They are easy to use.* Such displays present a direct, 1:1, relationship between the information presented to the operator and the response required. Indeed, the two are the same. Being easy to use, training time is reduced (Usher, 1982) so that the need for careful selection of operators is also reduced.

(b) *They are fast to use.* In a small pilot study, McEwing compared the speed of inputting information using typewriters and touch displays. Touch displays took about one-third of the time taken when using typewriters.

(c) *They minimize errors.* Because they limit the choices available to the operator and because of the close proximity of the responses to the choices, touch displays minimize the occurrence of keying errors (Hopkin, 1971).

(d) *They are flexible.* Because touch displays are under software control they are extremely flexible, both in the variety of ways in which sequences can be arranged and in the comparative ease with which modifications and additions to sequences can be made.

(e) *Operator reaction is generally favourable.* Usher (1982) for example, describes an experiment carried out to compare the efficiency of a touch-sensitive screen with a conventional keypad. Nearly five times as many subjects preferred the touch display to the keypad as vice versa and, for emergency operation, this ratio increased to ten times as many. Hopkins (1971) also reports that 'operators enjoyed using the touch display and immediately formed favourable attitudes towards it'.

Against these advantages, however, Pfauth and Priest (1981) suggest a number of disadvantages of touch displays. These include an initial high cost for the system, increased programmer time, reduced flexibility for some types of input, possible screen glare, physical fatigue from reaching to the screen, and the finger and hand blocking the operator's line of sight to important areas of the screen.

An alternative type of touch pad to the screen-based display is one which is (topographically) associated with, but not actually situated on, the screen. The advantages of this types of touch display is its increased mobility. Like a remote keyboard it can be moved around to suit the operator's posture. For example, as Bird (1977) and Pfauth and Priest (1981) emphasize, over time continuous pointing to a vertical, or near vertical, screen is likely to cause fatigue; the ideal angles of the surface for vision and for touching may not be the same. Also, in the act of touching the screen, the fingers or part of the hand may obscure the rest of the display. An 'off-display' touch panel mounted on a desk surface below the screen may reduce some of these potential problems. Unfortunately, although it may be biomechanically more convenient, such a display lacks the immediate visual feedback on finger position in relation to the displayed information. Operators, therefore, have to translate information presented from the screen in the vertical plane to responses made in the horizontal plane.

Nevertheless, the evidence appears to demonstrate that off-display types of touch pad do not carry any performance penalties. For example, Hopkin (1971) reports a study in which performance on a touch-wire display was compared with that on a 'remote labelled keyboard'. Using these two variations of the touch input concept, Hopkin reported no significant differences between the devices. Furthermore, when subjects trained on one type of device were asked to transfer to the other, complete transfer of training resulted; the subjects showed no marked preference for either device. Whitfield, Ball and Bird (1983) have also demonstrated no *significant* performance penalty using off-display touch pads for three types of task: menu selection, tabular display and target acquisition.

Light-pens

Like touch displays, light-pens are fully interactive control devices. They can be used effectively to position the cursor on the screen or to select responses from a 'menu' displayed to the operator. The user simply touches the appropriate part of the screen with the 'pen' and, through the photosensitive diode situated in the end, the computer is able to compute the pen's position on the screen. The operation of the pen, therefore, is very similar to that of the finger on a touch display. Indeed, Goodwin (1975) demonstrated that for selecting particular words or characters from a text display as, for example, in text editing, a light-pen appears to be much faster than using keyboard cursor controls.

Despite the positive features of light-pens, however, if the task requires the operator to mix modes of data entry (say to type using the keyboard but, on occasions, to use a light-pen to respond to questions) then using the light-pen can be quite detrimental (Earl and Goff, 1965). Thus the operator needs to stop using the keyboard, reorientate the hands (to pick up and to operate the light-pen), and then return to using the keyboard.

Although little information is available for designing the pen itself, it should be possible to predict some of the problems which constant light-pen users might face — in particular those to do with muscular fatigue in both the arm and the wrist. Thus, as argued earlier, as the arm is extended the hand's prehensile grip on the pen varies so that higher forces are required to maintain the pen support. Secondly, continuous working of the hand both away from the body and high up causes the upper arm and shoulder muscles to be under static muscular load. Thirdly, the pen's weight distribution is important to ensure that undue forces are not placed on the wrist. A relatively 'heavy' cable connecting the end of the pen to the computer, which is needed to transmit information from the pen to the computer, *could* detrimentally affect the weight distribution and thus increase static muscular load on the wrist. Finally, when operating any pen the forces acting on the pen itself are in an opposite direction to that in which the pen is pointing, i.e. from the screen towards the operator. This being so, to stop the fingers slipping down to the tip of the pen the operator has to grip hard with the fingers. Any design which will increase the finger/pen resistance, such as using a non-slippery surface or by putting grooves *around* the barrel (i.e. opposite to the direction of slipping) will help reduce the amount of grip required and thus the amount of static load.

Bar-code scanners

These are devices which both look and operate very much like light-pens. However, they are not used interactively with the computer screen, rather they are passed over alternate black and white bars, the composition of which contain the information to be input. In some installations, the pen remains stationary and the operator has to pass the code over it.

As with light-pens, little work has been published that considers the appropriate design and operating characteristics of a bar-code reading system.

However, the increased use of such devices in all aspects of work seem to attest to their perceived usefulness. Thus Gilchrest and Shenkin (1979) report that the obvious savings for one large US supermarket chain through using bar-code scanners arose in the following way: 37 per cent increased checker productivity; 21 per cent easier cash register checking and balancing; 21 per cent automatic produce weighing and pricing; and 14 per cent eliminating pricing, reading or keying errors. It is not certain, however, from their figures, whether the increased productivity arose from the reduced keying errors, etc., or whether it occurred because data entry using a scanner is faster.

Supermarket checkout customers ought also to see advantages using scanners. Wilson and Grey (1984), for example, argue that a faster through-flow of customers can be accomplished, with itemized till receipts and lower prices as a result of more efficient stock control. Another advantage emphasized by Hoffman and Cramer (1981) is that the system reduces the operators' cognitive and motor workload — although Wilson and Grey question whether further reducing the load of an otherwise boring job is really an advance.

As far as the operator's performance is concerned, bar scanners do have a major advantage over light-pens in that their operating postures are not constrained by the computer system itself. Thus, the arm and hand does not need to be maintained under static load to enable the pen to touch the screen. The code on the product can be read at any angle desired by the operator. However, Wilson and Grey (1984) point out that the fixed 'pen' system of scanners, in which the material to be read is passed over the scanner, can create postural difficulties for the operator. In their study of supermarket scanners, they demonstrated that the fixed nature of the device and the amount of reach required created problems for operators with smaller stature. However, these are problems associated with the workplace rather than with the device itself.

The roller ball and mouse

As the name suggests, 'roller balls' are spherically shaped objects which the operator can rotate in any direction. Their distinctive characteristic is that they rotate within a socket; thus they are fixed pieces of equipment. The 'mouse', on the other hand, operates in a similar fashion to the roller ball but it is not fixed; the operator is able to move it around, much like a pen is moved around paper to form characters. In most other aspects, however, the two devices are similar.

Card, English and Burr (1978) demonstrated the superiority of these input devices over the conventional keyboard when used to move a cursor around the screen. Despite their apparent superiority in this type of situation, however, little research appears to have carried out to determine their optimum parameters.

Roller balls can be manipulated in a number of ways. Thus, as Jackson (1982) illustrates, the fingers can be placed on the surface and moved, so drawing the ball surface along in continuous contact, or the ball can be flicked into ballistic motion by the fingers, with further flicks for additional motion. Friction pressure is then used to halt the ball abruptly. The palm of the hand can also be used in the same manner as the fingers.

From these descriptions, it would appear that an important parameter in the ball design is the amount of surface area exposed to the operator, since this determines the extent to which displacement can occur without relocating, for example, the fingers. The surface area, of course, is a function of the ball diameter. The size of the ball is also related to the friction and inertia that it presents to the operator; these will increase with ball dimensions. Unfortunately, information is not available on the sensitivity of operator performance to such variables as inertia and friction, although Bahrick (1957) has suggested that operators quickly learn the physical 'feel' of a control. They balance its friction and inertia against the amount that they want it to move, and gauge their manual input by this 'feeling'. The result is that each control movement takes roughly similar times to accomplish. In a study performed in 1963, Rogers used a $3\frac{1}{2}$-in ($8\frac{3}{4}$ cm) ball to determine the optimum velocity at which the ball could travel for correct placement of the cursor on the screen. From his results, he recommended a maximum surface velocity of 28in/s (0.71 m/s). When considering these recommendations it is important to remember that the velocities used by his subjects were related to the distance of the target from the cursor. Thus an inertial system which allowed this velocity would produce fastest and most accurate responses.

Foot Controls

Pedals

Pedals are frequently used when large forces need to be applied with relative speed, but they are rarely used for the primary control process — this is usually reserved for hand controls. Historically this has arisen because it has been felt that the feet are slower and have less precision than the hands. However, as Kroemer (1974) points out, such assertions are based upon very little data. Indeed, his own experiments suggest that an operator can be trained to use the feet with almost as much effectiveness as the hands (consider, for example, the precision with which an experienced motorist can control the speed of a car accelerator pedal). Since the hands always appear to be the overloaded control channel (like the visual system and displays), efficient use of the feet may reduce operator overload.

Apart from the pedal size, which is clearly related to the amount of space available, the important parameters of foot pedals are the position and angle of the fulcrum (if the pedal is hinged) and the maximum force required to operate the pedal. These factors are clearly interrelated as was demonstrated by Hertzberg and Burke (1971). They measured the force able to be exerted by 100 subjects using pedals set at different angles to the floor. As may be seen from Figure 6.3, an optimum angle of between 25 and 35 degrees produced the highest forces. This was verified by asking the subjects to rate their ankle comfort at each angle. Eighty per cent preferred angles between 25 and 35 degrees.

Figure 6.3 Maximum pedal forces able to be exerted in various leg and foot positions (*From Hertzberg and Burke, 1971, reproduced by permission of the Human Factors Society*, Inc)

The angles suggested by Hertzberg and Burke are the initial pedal/floor angles — not the operating angles of the pedal. This should be related to the possible range of movement at the ankle, otherwise fatigue is likely to occur very quickly. In this respect, Damon, Stoudt and MacFarland (1971) suggest that 95 per cent of the population can attain an ankle angle of 20 degrees, and so it would appear sensible not to exceed this angle by any large amount.

In their experiment Hertzberg and Burke used fit, male aircraft personnel as their subjects, who were asked to push their feet against the pedal as hard as possible. As can be seen from Figure 6.3, under these circumstances forces of approximately 140lb (623N) were obtained with a 'neutral' leg position. Mortimer (1974), however, has demonstrated that although 95 per cent of his male subjects were able to attain these forces, a similar proportion of his female subjects were able to press with a force of only 70 lbs (311N). Once again, therefore, this demonstrates the need for the design of the equipment to take account of the type of operator who is to use it.

SUMMARY

With the efficient transmission of information to the machine via controls, the communication link is completed. However, as this chapter has demonstrated, the choice and design of appropriate controls are not independent considerations, they are highly related to the type of task, operator and clothing. Only when all aspects of the system have been considered can the information be transmitted from the machine to the person and back again in an unimpeded fashion.

CHAPTER 7

WORKSPACE DESIGN

So far the discussion has centred around principles concerning the design of specific aspects of the operator's immediate work environment, particularly various machine components. So, an operator receives information (perhaps instruction) about the task or the machine from a colleague or a manual (Chapter 4) or from the machine itself (Chapter 5). Chapter 6 considered the ways in which the operator communicates with the machine via controls. Such features, however, although extremely important to enable information to be communicated efficiently to and from the operator, are unfortunately not the only aspects that need to be considered. Any advances gained from the ergonomic design of displays and controls, for example, may be negated entirely if these individual components are inappropriately arranged 'in front of' the operator. This immediate area is often called the *workspace* — a term which should not be confused with the 'workplace' which refers to the arrangement of different workspaces. This latter aspect will be discussed in the next chapter.

This chapter will consider principles that govern ways in which controls and displays ought to be arranged around the operator to guarantee their most efficient use, i.e.:

(a) The position of controls with respect to other controls;
(b) The position of displays with respect to other displays;
(c) The position of controls with respect to displays, and vice versa;
(d) The shape and dimensions of the operator's workspace.

Although much of the discussion will centre around the relatively concrete concepts of a 'panel' that contains displays and particular controls, the wider workspace concept should always be borne in mind. For example, included in a car driver's immediate workspace will be the dashboard (which includes both displays and controls), a steering wheel and foot pedals (controls). These are obvious. Taking the extended concept of a display as any feature that provides information, however, the car windscreen can also be considered to be part of the driver's display system. It displays a great deal of information regarding the machine's (the car's) operation *vis-à-vis* the road. Other displays are also present outside of the vehicle, for example signals, road signs and even other vehicles. In the future discussion, therefore, notions such as 'display', 'control' or 'panel' should be taken in their widest sense — primarily in terms of the direction in

159

which information is transmitted and arrangements used to aid this trans-mission.

Determining where controls and displays should be placed within the operator's workspace is not a simple problem to solve. Not only do aesthetics and styling need to be considered, but also such factors as the operator's comfort and safety, the closeness of controls for ease of use, the control separation for avoiding mistakes, the balance of work between limbs, avoiding operator overload, the need to satisfy a wide range of operator sizes, the layout of components to help operator understanding, and many other factors which are possibly not quantifiable. Because the problem is so complex, a few computer programs have been developed to help the designer arrive at a solution. Such computer-aided design packages allow the user to simulate practical situations on the computer screen and to test out various arrangements. Nevertheless, the final decisions still rest with the human designer and will have to be made in terms of practical criteria based on ergonomic principles.

GENERAL PRINCIPLES OF WORKSPACE DESIGN

When deciding how controls and displays should be arranged in front of the operator the overriding considerations are that they should be able to be used quickly, accurately and without fatigue. For this reason an attempt is normally made to ensure that complementary sets of components are arranged so that they suggest to the operator how they should be used. Groupings are made, then, in terms of the sequence in which they would normally be used, their frequency of use and their importance. However, superordinate to these considerations is the basic requirement that the components should be accessible to the operator when they are needed. Relevant data concerning anthropometry and the positions adopted by operators performing the task, then, are required. In addition, as discussed in previous chapters, any restrictions placed on the operator's movements, by clothing or by other equipment, will affect these considerations.

Sequence of Use Principle

Time sequence

This principle suggests that if controls or displays are normally operated in some sequence, for example switching on a lathe, increasing r.p.m., moving spindles together, etc., then they should be arranged in that sequence. All that the operator then needs to do is to follow the arrangement provided, rather than work in an apparently random fashion.

A slight variation to arranging components according to a temporal sequence was described by Shackel (1962) — in this case the temporal sequence related to reading the setting made by five rotary switches (note that this is an example of a component acting as both a control and a display; the switch is used as a control to make the setting and a display to read the setting). In an original prototype five switches arranged on a console in front of the operator were used to make a five digit setting (see Figure 7.1a). Unfortunately, however, the position of the switches did not suggest to the operator the order in which they should be used. The correct sequence was executed in the form of a capital letter W with the top left switch setting tens of thousands, the bottom left setting thousands, the top middle hundreds, etc. Since a 'natural' setting sequence would be to set the first three digits using the top trio of controls and the last two the bottom pair, errors were clearly likely to occur. For his redesigned console, illustrated in Figure 7.1b, Shackel simply rearranged the controls in a linear, sequential order.

(a) Original W pattern

(b) Redesigned sequential pattern

Figure 7.1 Rearranging five switches to be used in temporal sequence (both settings read 54345)

Functional sequence

Having arranged the panel components according to a temporal sequence, it is also possible to arrange them in terms of their function — either within the temporal sequence or in terms of a temporal sequence of different functions. For example, the workspace around a pilot may include components concerning the altitude, attitude, speed, radio contact, etc. It is common sense to suggest that all of the controls and displays which are related to any one of these functions should be grouped together. However, it may also be the case that the different *functions* are used in a temporal sequence — for example the radio, then the speed, then altitude, and then the attitude, etc. In such a case it is sensible not only to group the components according to their function (perhaps in terms of a sequence of usage order within each group), but to arrange the groups in the order in which they are to be used.

Frequency of Use Principle

As its name implies this principle suggests that controls and displays should be arranged in terms of how frequently they are used by the operator. Thus, the more frequently used components should be placed within easy sight and reach (usually directly in front) of the operator.

Importance

The frequency of use principle provides a useful guide to design but if it were taken to extremes situations might arise in which a rarely used, but nevertheless very important, component might be positioned well outside of the operator's effective area. Obvious examples include emergency controls. By their nature these are operated infrequently, but when they are used they need to be operated quickly and accurately. The frequency of usage principle, therefore, must be tempered by importance.

POSITIONING CONTROLS WITH RESPECT TO OTHER CONTROLS

Spacing

Having ensured that the controls have been placed in the optimum area in front of the operator (that is having regard to sequence and frequency of use, function and importance), the next question concerns the specific position of each control. In this respect the amount of space allowed between each control can be a very important consideration. Too much space is likely to make the operator move the limbs unnecessarily or, if a large number of controls are to be arranged, will result in a less than optimum spatial arrangement. Too little space, on the other hand, may cause the wrong control to be activated accidentally.

The minimum spacing required between each control is determined largely by the type of control to be operated (and thus the limb to be used), the way in which it is operated (sequentially, simultaneously or randomly), and the presence or absence of protective clothing.

The need to design controls that fit the limb or part of the limb that operates them should be clear. For example, controls such as push-buttons which are operated by the fingertips will require less intercontrol space than pedals operated by the feet. Similar 'common sense' can be applied to the manner by which the control is to be operated. Using levers as an example: if two levers have to be operated simultaneously the space between them will need to accommodate two hands (or at least the parts of two hands which overlap the lever handles). Sequential operation, however, is likely to be made using one hand only and this would require less intercontrol space. Again, if more than one lever is to be operated at once and by the same hand, the intercontrol spacing should be reduced sufficiently to allow the fingers to spread easily to each control.

Similar arguments may be advanced for other controls. For example, Bradley (1969d) measured the time taken to reach and to turn four concentric controls arranged about a central point. He varied the spacing between the knobs (0.5in to 1.75in (1–4cm)), the knob diameter (0.5in to 1.5in (1–3.5cm)) and the knob configuration, and recorded the number of inadvertent touchings of adjacent controls.

Bradley's results indicated that performance increased rapidly with distances between the knobs up to 1 in (2.5 cm), after which it continued to increase but as a much slower rate. Interestingly, too, his results indicated that 'inadvertent touchings' of knobs depended on their position. Figure 7.2 shows the frequency of touchings when one, two or four knobs were arranged around the knob to be operated. Whenever any knob was arranged horizontally to the one that had to be operated, the right-hand knob was always the one to be touched inadvertently. With a vertical arrangement, however, the lower knob was most vulnerable. These results, of course, might have been predicted since

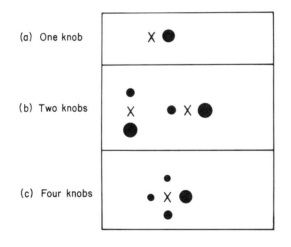

X Operated knob

● Crowding area – represents the frequency
with which the knob was touched

Figure 7.2 The effect of the number and orientation of adjacent knobs on the likelihood that they will be inadvertently touched. (*From Bradley, 1969d, and reproduced by permission of the Human Factors Society. Inc*)

Table 7.1 Desirable separations between different types of controls (in cm) (*adapted from Morgan et al., 1963, and reproduced by permission of McGraw-Hill*)

Type of operation		Finger		Hand			Foot	
		Push-button	Toggle switch	Lever	Crank	Knob	Foot pedal between pedals	between centres
Simultaneously		–	–	12.5	12.5	12.5	–	–
One finger/ hand/foot	Sequentially	2.5	2.5	–	–	–	10	20
	Randomly	5	5	10	10	5	15	25
Different fingers/ hands/ feet		1	1.5	–	–	–	–	–

right-handed subjects were used. Thus, when using the right-hand the right control knob would normally have to be passed over to operate the central knob. Similarly with a vertical orientation an upward movement of the hand is likely to be used. The results are interesting, however, in so far as they illustrate that the position and direction of movement of the operating limb needs to be considered as well as the position of controls on the panel. Table 7.1 indicates the desirable separation between different controls (from Morgan *et al.*, 1963).

Accidental Operation

This problem has already been introduced when discussing the spacing between controls. For example, the 'wrong' control may be activated if too little space is provided between adjacent controls or if the controls are arranged so that the operator's limb movements will be such that they pass over (with the danger of touching) another control.

Even if controls are in ideal positions, however, they can still sometimes still be activated accidentally. These mishaps need to be guarded against, and a number of techniques are available:

(1) Recessing the control;
(2) Orientating the control so that the normal direction from which any accidental activation may occur will not cause it to be operated. For example, if the operator needs to reach over a lever (so that the arms move in a vertical direction) orienting the lever to operate horizontally may reduce the possibility of an accident;
(3) Covering the control with a hinged cover;
(4) Locking the control;
(5) Operationally sequencing a set of controls. If controls need to be operated in sequence it is often possible to ensure that control 2 cannot be operated until control 1 has been activated;
(6) Increasing control resistance.

Control Position on the Console

Even if the controls have been arranged with an ideal spacing between them and all necessary guards against accidental operation are incorporated, one further consideration still remains — locating the controls on the console for optimum reach and performance.

Reach is clearly a problem which relates to the operator's anthropometric dimensions, and this will be discussed further in the next chapter. Overall 'performance', however, depends on a number of factors including speed and accuracy. One of these factors, speed, was investigated by Sharp and Hornseth (1965). They placed three types of control (knob, toggle switch and push-button) in different positions on a console situated about 30 in (76 cm) from the seated operator. Their results, shown in Figure 7.3, demonstrate different performance 'maps' for the three different types of control. Thus the knob, for example, is able to be placed in a much wider range of positions than the toggle switch before the same decrease in performance is observed, implying that locating the toggle switch is more critical than the knob. Other, similar, types of conclusions may also be drawn from Figure 7.3.

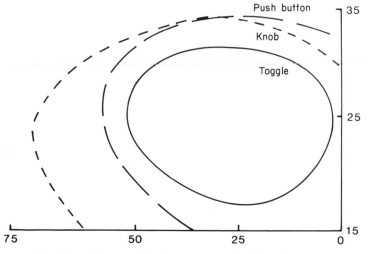

Position of control in degrees to the left of centre

Figure 7.3 Ten per cent reduced performance contours for the toggle, knob and push-button controls placed in front of and to the left of the operator (from Sharp and Hornseth, 1965)

SPECIALIZED GROUPS OF CONTROLS — THE KEYBOARD

Although controls are often thought as being single, or sometimes pairs, of units used by the operator to alter a machine state (for example, a switch to turn the machine on or off, or a knob to increase speed) these single units are sometimes used for extremely fast, sequential use, presenting information in bursts. The typewriter, data entry and digital telephone keyboards are instances in whch controls are used in this manner. Because the operator works with groups of either letters or digits, the key arrangement needs to take account not only of the control spacing but of an optimum control grouping. If the arrangement is not ideal, since a full-time typist may press up to 75 000 keys each day (Klemmer, 1971), fatigue may be induced in both the finger muscles and in the muscles maintaining posture in the back. (Ferguson and Duncan (1974), for example, have demonstrated that the finger loads using a standard keyboard layout are maldistributed, with the ring and little finger being overloaded relative to their strength — see Figure 7.4.)

167

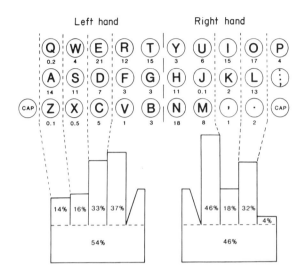

Figure 7.4 Distribution of finger strokes of each hand on individual keys using the QWERTY keyboard (Ferguson and Duncan, 1974). The figures below each key represent the percentage of times the key was pressed when the particular hand was used

In essence three types of board can be produced: first, *alphanumeric keyboards*, containing alphabetic, punctuation and numeric keys. These are used, primarily, for processing text. Secondly, *numeric keyboards* (sometimes called key-pads) which contain only the numeric keys with associated function keys (plus, minus, etc.) for keying in numeric data. Finally, are the *chord keyboards* which are used to input both alphabetic and numeric information. Their characteristic lies in the fact that each letter or number is 'composed' by pressing groups of keys — rather than separate keys as with the alphanumeric boards and key-pads.

Alphanumeric Keyboards

The normal typewriter keyboard (often called the QWERTY board because these letters occur at the beginning of the top line) has been in existence since before the beginning of this century. It was designed by C.L. Sholes and his colleagues in 1874 (patented in 1878) to conform to the mechanical constraints of contemporary typewriters. The problem was that typists were able to press keys at a faster rate than the machines, with their mechanical links and reliance on gravity to return the keyhead, were able to respond. The resulting key jamming was overcome by an apparent haphazard arrangement of the letters. The QWERTY board, therefore, was designed originally to *slow down* typists.

Various authors have suggested different reasons for the QWERTY arrangement. The first is a machine-based argument. For example, Norman and Fisher (1982) suggest that the arrangement is such that the keys are typed successively as far apart on the keyboard as possible, so that the type bars will approach each other at a relatively sharp angle with minimum chances of jamming. Hackmeister (1979) supports this argument but adds one further observation: the top row contains all of the letters in the word 'typewriter', and it was Sholes who designed the first 'Typewriting Machine'!

Secondly is an operator–performance argument. For example, Martin (1972) argues that the arrangement is such that the letter most likely to be typed next is obscured by the operator's hand. Biegel (1934) has suggested that the board produces less efficient performances because of anthropometric, biomechanical and perceptual factors. Thus:

(a) The ring (third) finger and little fingers have to be stretched when moving from the home keys to the third and fourth rows. This reduces the strength of the stroke and leads to the edge of the finger-tip rather than the centre being used to hit the keys.

(b) Dividing the keys into parallel but oblique vertical 'strips' for the different fingers means that the strips for the fingers of the right-hand present the same shape as those for the left. This is despite the fact that the hands are not congruent, but are inverse images of each other.

(c) Tracks from the home keys are difficult to follow so that often the wrong key is struck.

One positive feature of the QWERTY board suggested by a number of authors (for example, Kinkead, 1975; Cakir, Hart and Stewart, 1980; Noyes, 1983a) is the workload that it places on each hand — rather than on each finger. Thus, when typing English text almost all keystrokes alternate from one hand to the other. Noyes (1983a), for example, argues that common letter sequences typed on the QWERTY board involve either alternate hands being used, the whole hand being moved over the keyboard, or non-adjacent fingers being moved sequentially.

Despite this positive aspect of the QWERTY arrangement, and despite (or possibly because of) the fact that many millions of typewriters have been produced using the arrangement, a number of alternative keyboard arrangements have been proposed. All are based on the frequencies that letters and letter pairs occur in the English language. The two which have captured most experimental time are the Dvorak and the Alphabetic boards.

The Dvorak board (patented by A. Dvorak in 1932) was produced as a result of a decade of physiological and language research. The main principles behind the arrangement are as follows:

(a) Layout is arranged on the basis of the frequency of usage of letters and the frequency of letter patterns and sequences in the English language.

(b) All vowels and most used consonants are on the second (or 'home') row, so that something like 70 per cent of common words are typed on this row alone.

(c) Faster operation is possible by tapping with fingers on alternate hands (particularly the most used index fingers) than by repetitive tapping with one finger. Since the probability of vowels and consonants alternating is very high, all vowels are typed with the left-hand and frequent (home row) consonants with the right-hand.

(d) Finger travel and consequent fatigue are thus greatly reduced.

Using these principles, the arrangement shown in Figure 7.5 was produced which, Dvorak claims, provides a more even distribution of finger movements and a bias towards the right-hand. This is also shown in Figure 7.5 (compare these figures with the finger analyses for the QWERTY board shown in Figure 7.4). Dvorak also claimed that this arrangement reduces the between-rows movement by 90 per cent, and allows 35 per cent of all words normally used to be typed on the middle row.

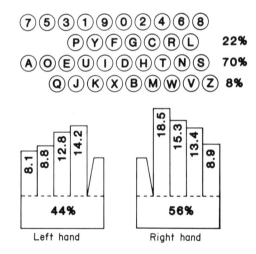

Figure 7.5 The Dvorak keyboard layout and workload distribution in typing English text. The row figures relate to the proportion of times the keys in each row are used

Controversy presently exists as to the relative merits of the QWERTY and the Dvorak boards. For example, a US government sponsored study in 1956 demonstrated little difference between the advantages of each arrangement (Alden, Daniels and Kanarick, 1976). Martin (1972), however, discusses (unreported) novice training experiments carried out in Great Britain which demonstrated a 10 per cent saving in training time using the Dvorak board.

Furthermore, Dunn (1971) argues that the Dvorak board is superior in terms of ease of learning, reduced likelihood of error and fatigue, and increased speed of data entry.

In the alphabetic board, keys are arranged as the name suggests: from A to Z. The argument behind the use of this arrangement is, quite simply, that an alphabetical ordering of the keys makes logical sense, particularly to inexperienced typists who presently need to spend considerable time learning the QWERTY arrangement.

Despite the apparent logic of using an alphabetically arranged board, Norman and Fisher (1982) point out that the available studies do not support the view that inexperienced typists find the alphabetic board easier to use. Indeed both Hirsch (1970) and Michaels (1971) have shown that for semi-skilled typists, keying rates and error correction are better using the QWERTY board, and the performance on the two boards is essentially the same for novices. Norman and Fisher have also shown that typing speed is faster with the QWERTY board.

Norman and Fisher suggest two reasons for these apparently paradoxical findings. Firstly, an experimental one in that it is difficult to find subjects who have not had some exposure to the QWERTY arrangement. Secondly, although logically superior the alphabetic keyboard still requires considerable visual search and mental processing (to remember, for example, that 'm' appears after 'k'). At the novice stage at least, therefore, all keyboard layouts are equivalent. Once the skill has been learned, visual feedback gives way to kinaesthetic feedback so that the different board arrangements are likely to be equally efficient.

In summary, it would appear that, from the point of view of key arrangement alone, it makes little difference which type of board is used. Since the high cost of converting machines and of retraining typists to use the alternative boards are likely to ensure the continuation of the QWERTY arrangement, more valuable time could possibly by spent in redesigning the physical arrangement of the board to make it fit more the anthropometric and biomechanical properties of the user.

Before concluding the discussion of alphabetic input, one final point should be emphasized. All of the discussion so far has centred around the arrangement for entering Roman characters into the computer (Cakir, Hart and Stewart (1980) describe some experimental boards for Spanish and German languages). However, as Chapanis (1974) points out, there are large numbers of different languages and forms of script, and the problems outlined above are increased markedly when languages which do not use the Roman alphabet are considered — Japanese, for example, uses between 2000 and 4000 characters. To this end Brown (1974) describes the development of a Japanese card punch machine which, as with the Dvorak concept, puts the most frequently used characters on a special high-usage region of the board. For example, about 70 per cent of ordinary Japanese can be written with 600 of the most frequently used characters. Grouping these characters decreased the search time and the average distance needed to be reached when keying in ordinary text. Using these principles Brown was able to show that skilled Japanese operators could key about the same average number of words per minute, and almost as accurately, as skilled American card-punch operators working in English.

Numeric Keyboards

Compared with those investigating alphanumeric arrangements, there have been fewer studies performed to determine the optimum arrangement of numeric keys (0–9). This is possibly because, with only ten keys, there are fewer sensible key arrangements.

A number of these arrangements were investigated by Deininger (1960) in a study of push-button telephone sets. Four designs, shown in Figure 7.6, were shown to be roughly equally acceptable on criteria such as keying time, errors and 'votes' for and against. For 'engineering' reasons, however, Deininger suggests either arrangement 1 or 2 is used for telephones. Indeed, the 'standard' telephone arrangement has now become that shown in arrangement 1; i.e. a 3+3+3+1 matrix starting with 1, 2, 3 on the top row and ending with 0 below the third row.

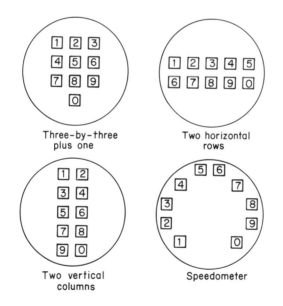

Figure 7.6 Four efficient numeric key arrangements found by Deininger (1960)

Although this arrangement has become standard for telephone key-pads, it is not that currently used for numerical input on keyboards such as calculators.

This is normally the reverse of the telephone arrangement, the keys on the 3+3+3+1 matrix having the order 7,8,9: 4,5,6: 1,2,3: and 0.

Conrad and Hull (1968) compared the keying efficiency of these two types of arrangement. No significant differences were obtained in terms of the speed of data entry, but they did obtain significantly fewer errors using the telephone keypad (1, 2, 3: 4, 5, 6: etc.) than with the calculator pad arrangement (7, 8, 9: 4, 5, 6: etc.) (6.4 per cent versus 8.2 per cent).

Chord Keyboards

In the search for improved ways of keying data, particularly alphabetic data, the possibility of reducing the number of keys by requiring the operator to press more than one key at a time has often been suggested. Such key arrangements are called *chord keyboards* and they appear in many different forms. Some are operated by one hand only (usually with five keys — one for each finger), while others are operated by both hands (with 10 keys). (Litterick (1981), describes some of these boards, and Noyes (1983b) describes the history and development of chord keying.) Some boards use groups of keys to form different letters whereas others, usually the larger boards, also enable words or parts of words to be formed. By pressing combinations of keys, then, a large number of characters can be formed, in fact with N keys 2_N-1 sensible combinations can be made (one combination — no keys pressed — is not sensible in this context).

The main impetus to reduce the number of keys arises, clearly, from a wish to reduce the amount of time that fingers travel over the keyboard and the possibility of errors being made. Thus, Fitts (1954) has shown that the difficulty of making small hand movements is determined largely by the extent to which the hand has to move and the size of the target. If the fingers are hovering over chord keys (as they appear to do during 'normal' typing), the argument goes, the time taken to form characters and the number of errors should both be reduced.

Unfortunately, the little evidence available does not support this argument fully. For example, both Ratz and Ritchie (1961) and Seibel (1962) required subjects to react quickly to combinations of lights by pressing corresponding keys under the fingers. Between the best and the worst of the 31 possible chord combinations, reaction time increases of about 70 ms were recorded while the error rate increased by about 400 per cent. Not surprisingly, the fastest time and the fewest errors were recorded when only one stimulus light needed to be reacted to — the analogous situation to typewriting.

Very few experiments have been performed to compare directly keying performance using a typewriter and a keyboard. As Conrad and Longman (1965) point out, this is probably because of difficulties in obtaining matched groups of subjects and being able to train them for very long periods using the same instructor.

Bowen and Guiness (1965) compared performance on a semi-automatic mail-sorting task using either a typewriter, a small (12 key) chord board, or a large (24 key) chord board. Both chord boards resulted in more items being sorted correctly per minute than the typewriter, with the small board proving superior. McCormick (1976) attributes this observation to the fact that the small keyboard did not require such difficult finger patterns as the large board.

The superiority of chord keyboards over typewriters has also been established by Conrad and Longman (1965) who, like Bowen and Guiness, used a letter-sorting task. However, they continued the experiment for nearly a month. Their subjects used either a two-handed, 10-key chord board (with some associated control keys) or a typewriter. Their results suggested that subjects trained on the chord board learned the key arrangement quicker than those on the typewriter (with an average of $12\frac{1}{2}$ days as opposed to $20\frac{1}{2}$ days) and, once learned, operated the machine faster. It should be pointed out, however, that most of the letter and number sequences used by Contrad and Longman were postcodes — apparently random pairs of letters and numbers. Whether or not the typewriter would maintain its inferiority with recognizable chunks of English is an unanswered question.

Finally, the impression should not be gained that chord keyboards will automatically be more efficient than standard keyboards. Thus, as McCormick has pointed out, much is likely to depend on the combinations of keys needed to be pressed to produce particular letters. In this respect Seibel's (1962) data are important in showing how different combinations of keys can lead to varying keying times and errors. Furthermore, the time required to learn particular key combinations is bound to be a strong function of the ease of remembering the logical arrangement of the keys to be used, and this is determined by the quality of the system used to code combinations of keystrokes (Seibel, 1964).

POSITIONING VISUAL DISPLAYS WITH RESPECT TO OTHER DISPLAYS

The main consideration when placing visual displays on the operator's console concerns the physical relationship between the display and its associated control(s). This will be discussed in more detail in the next section. However, two features peculiar to displays need to be considered. These are the display's visibility and the ways in which the pointers are aligned when groups of analogue displays are used for check reading purposes.

Visibility requirements

Since the value of a visual display depends entirely on the operator's ability to perceive it, making sure that displays are within the line of sight is an extremely important aspect of the panel design. However, it is an aspect which is sometimes overlooked, since the problem can take two forms.

First, visibility might be impaired because the display is obscured (either fully or partially) by another component on the console. This is not an unusual occurrence, particularly when controls and displays are placed close together.

174

For example, a display located towards the periphery of a console may be partially obscured by part of a nearby control, simply because of the operator's position with respect to the control and the display. This aspect will be considered in more detail in the next chapter. Less obvious, perhaps, is the case when reaching out to operate a control can easily cause a display to be obscured by the hand or arm.

The response to a display can also be impaired because, although the operator's visual field may be quite wide, response speed and accuracy depends largely on the stimulus position in the visual field. Within a narrow range of positions, for example, it was shown in Chapter 2 how foveal perception is both faster and more accurate than image perception towards the retinal periphery — towards the parafovea. Haines and Gilliland (1973) measured the response speed of seven subjects to separate lights placed in different areas of their visual field. Figure 7.7 illustrates their results and shows the various boundaries of equal reaction time over the visual field. The fastest response, therefore, was obtained within an area bounded by about 8 degrees above and below the central sight line, up to 40 degrees to the right, but only 10 degrees to the left of the mid-point. This general 'oval but skewed to the right' trend can be seen in the other equi-response time boundaries — although the right side superiority reduces towards the edge of the visual field.

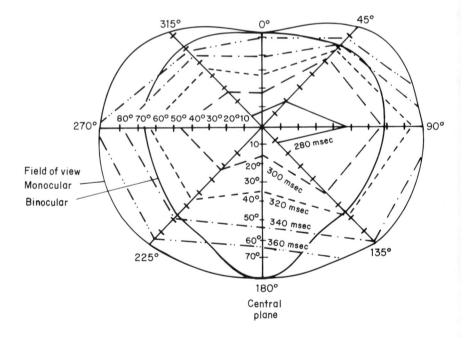

Figure 7.7 Equal response times for displays in the visual field. (*From Haines and Gilliland, 1973. Copyright © 1973 by the American Psychological Association. Reprinted with permission.*)

Haines and Gilliland suggest that Figure 7.7 can be used to aid the designer in placing important displays (particularly warning displays) in front of the operator. By superimposing the contours over a scaled-down model, the positions for the various displays may be pinpointed.

Grouping displays

For check reading

As was discussed in Chapter 5, displays are not only used for making quantitative readings but also for simply checking that the machine state is within certain (safe) boundaries. Since the operator makes readings largely in terms of the amount by which the pointer deviates from a particular position, rather than from the precise dial reading, the task would appear to contain a fairly large memory component. Using coloured 'danger' areas on the dial helps to reduce the operator's load, as does the arrangement of the dial so that when showing a normal state the pointer is orientated to, say, 9 o'clock (White, Warrick and Grether, 1953).

If a number of displays are used for check reading, however, they may be arranged so that each facilitates the reading of the other. Johnsgard (1953), for example, has demonstrated that pointer symmetry (i.e. arranging the pointers to form a pattern) is possibly better than a pointer alignment (arranging the pointers to point in one direction) for check reading. He compared four

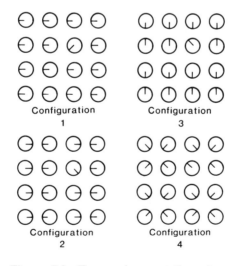

Figure 7.8 Four pointer configurations used by Johnsgard, 1953 (one pointer in each case is indicating 'non-normal'). (*Copyright © 1953 by the American Psychological Association. Reprinted with permission*)

arrangements of a bank of 16 dials for check reading accuracy. In the first arrangement the dials were each rotated so that, under 'normal' conditions, all pointers were aligned at the 9 o'clock position. For the other conditions the dials were rotated so that the pointers produced different patterns under 'normal' conditions (see Figure 7.8). Any deviation of any pointer would be highlighted by a break in the pattern.

Johnsgard's results clearly demonstrated that the configuration in which the pointers were arranged to point to the centres of groups of four dials (number 4) was less effective than any of the other three. However, arranging the dials so that the pointers were vertically symmetrical (configuration 3) produced significantly more correct responses than simply a horizontal alignment. Similar results were obtained by Ross, Katchmar and Bell (1955), although they were unable to support the contention that a symmetrical (patterned) alignment produces more correct responses than a simple, uniform alignment.

The use of patterns such as these was taken one step further by Dashevsky (1964) who extended the lines made by the pointers under 'normal' conditions on to the console (see Figure 7.9). Comparing these extension lines, with the open (no line) arrangement, he produced an 85 per cent reduction in error rate over a uniform alignment, and a 92 per cent error reduction when the dials were rotated as in Johnsgard's condition 4.

For flow diagrams

Different displays can often be grouped to provide the user with a 'working model', or flow diagram, of the process or machine, illustrating parts of the

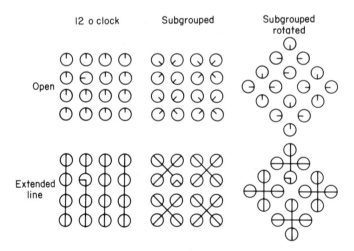

Figure 7.9 Groups of displays used by Dashevsky (1964) to investigate whether extensor lines between displays aid check reading. (*Copyright © 1964 by the American Psychological Association. Reprinted with permission*)

working system from which the information is arriving. For example, large panels are commonly found in modern railway signalboxes which graphically depict the rail sector under the signalman's control, the position of the points, and the movement of the train through the sector. Such displays help the operator to interrelate different aspects of the total system which are displayed, and allows speedy location of faults or delays. Although such composite displays are now more frequently used in large process industries, Morgan *et al.* (1963) caution that they are limited in terms of the additional space required for the connecting lines between displays. In addition much of the value of the display is lost if too much information is presented in too complex a form. Nevertheless, flow diagrams allow the operator to feel that he or she has some involvement with the system being controlled.

POSITIONING DISPLAYS AND CONTROLS

One theme which has been emphasized continuously throughout this book is that the information which flows from the machine to the operator and back can be seriously disrupted if any part of the chain is deficient (for example the display, the operator's processing capacities, or the control). However, even if each separate component is operated at its peak efficiency the process may still be interrupted if the information received from one component does not 'fit' the requirements of the next link in the chain. For example, information displayed too quickly may overload the operator's perceptual and decision-making capabilities; a control with an inappropriate type or amount of inbuilt resistance may be difficult to operate because the operator lacks enough arm strength, etc.

Taking this argument further it is apparent that, for information flowing in the display–operator–control direction, the operator's workload may be further reduced if a display is compatible with its associated control(s). Then, just as a well-considered display or control will help the operator because it 'fits' his or her capacities, components which are compatible with each other will require less work to complete the display–operator–control link. Of course, it is just as important to ensure that links in the opposite (control–display) direction are also compatible.

Before considering in detail the concept of display and control compatibility, as was discussed earlier it is important to remember that the term 'display' must be taken in its widest sense. Thus, any aspect of the operator's environment may display information about the machine and its state. The way that the machine itself behaves (for example, the speed at which a drill moves into a piece of wood or metal) is information displayed, as is its behaviour with respect to the rest of the environment: the way in which a car moves along a road is displayed to the driver through the windscreen. In this case, then, both the windscreen *and* the car's movements represent the display.

Control–display Compatibility

In effect, a display and a control may be said to be compatible if one suggests the way in which the other should be operated. Compatibility effects can possibly best be exemplified by a simple experiment carried out by Crossman (1956) (which is described by Welford, 1976). Crossman presented his subjects with up to eight stimulus lights, to any one of which they had to respond as quickly as possible by pressing the appropriate numbered key. Two conditions were presented. In the first condition (high compatibility) each button was located below its light. In the second (low compatible) condition the buttons were arranged randomly. Crossman's results demonstrated that faster response times were produced when the lights (displays) and keys (controls) were compatible than when they were incompatible. As Welford explains it:

> presumably in the first (condition), once the light was identified the key was also, whereas in the second arrangement the light had to be identified first and then its number used to locate the corresponding key. In other words, in the second condition the data had to be recoded from digital to spatial form before a response could be chosen, so that the translation mechanism had more 'work' to do than when each light was located above its corresponding key.

In the low compatible condition, in other words, the display did not 'suggest' the appropriate key response.

In addition to an increased response speed from using compatible displays and controls, Murrell (1971) suggests two further reasons why compatibility should be aimed for. First, learning time for operating equipment on which controls and displays are compatible will be much shorter than if they are incompatible. In Crossman's experiment, for example, the subjects had to learn the new (random) arrangement before they could respond quickly. Secondly, under stress an operator's performance on equipment with incompatible display/control relationships will deteriorate as he or she reverts to the expected relationship. The example has already been given of a press operated by a lever that needed to be lifted to make it fall. Whereas under 'normal' circumstances this incompatible operation was carried out efficiently, when a stressful occasion occurred and the operator needed to *raise* the press quickly the 'natural' reaction was to lift the lever — thus compounding the problem by making it fall.

Fitts and Seeger (1953) suggest that this occurs because a response which a person makes can be considered to be a function of two sets of probabilities:

(a) the probabilities (uncertainties) appropriate to the specific situation in which the operator works — training, instructions, past experience, successes, failures, etc.; and
(b) the more general and more stable experiences or habits based on the operator's experiences in many other situations.

They suggest that training will nearly always lead to changes in the former but will have relatively little effect on the latter. Loveless (1962) continues this argument a little further by suggesting that the new (trained) behaviours do not replace the old behaviours which were learned as a result of past experiences and expectations — they merely overlay them. Certain situations may arise in which the old behaviours may be stronger.

> During training the old response is weakened sufficiently to allow the new response to appear, and the latter is then strengthened by further practice; but the old habit has been suppressed rather than eliminated. The suppression is likely to be in part temporary, so the old response may reappear after a period away from the task.

He further suggests that 'it can also be predicted on theoretical grounds that habit regression will occur when the operator's motivation is decreased, when he is fatigued and when he is subjected to any novel change in the working situation'.

The suggestion is made, therefore, that compatibility arrangements are learned, that there are more examples of compatible relationships in everyday living than there are incompatible ones and that the more that one is exposed to these relationships the more likely will they be expected. This begs the question whether there are developmental trends in the learning and durability of compatible relationships, but unfortunately few data are available concerning this question.

In the mechanical environment two main ways of arranging compatibility between control and display exist. First, *spatial compatibility*, in which the two components are compatible if the position of one on the console suggests that of the other. Crossman's lights and buttons in the first condition had high spatial compatibility. Second, *movement compatibility*, in which the control's movement suggests the way in which its associated display is likely to move, and vice versa. For example, by turning a knob clockwise an operator would expect its associated display to indicate an increased reading. Such movement relationships which are expected by the majority of the population are described as population stereotypes. (Petropoulos and Brebner (1981) point out that the 'clockwise=increase' stereotype does not apply when the control releases material which is stored or contained under pressure of force — taps that control water or gas flow, for example, are turned anticlockwise to increase the flow.)

Although spatial and movement compatibility are applied to *physical* controls and displays, the advent of computers and other forms of information technology has helped to bring the question of compatibility between 'controls' and 'displays' back to a cognitive/information type form of concept. With computers, for example, a display may be considered to be as much a type of result (say storing data on disk) as a piece of hardware such as a screen. Similarly, a computer command such as 'PUT' may be considered to be as much a control as the keys on the QWERTY keyboard. In these cases, then, the third type of compatibility that needs to be considered between display and control represents more of *cognitive compatibility*.

180

Spatial compatibility

As evidence that the need for spatial compatibility exists on all types of equipment, Chapanis and Lindenbaum (1959) investigated different control/display positions using four-burner gas and electric cookers. In this case the burners represent the displays. Four arrangements were investigated and the results indicated fewer errors as the control's position matched more that of the displays' (see Figure 7.10). Thus, in arrangement I, when the burners were staggered to be in the same sequential order as the controls, no operating errors were detected. The same sequence of controls, but with non-staggered burners produced some errors, but far fewer than incompatible arrangements. Chapanis and Mankin (1967) followed this study with an investigation of ten control/display relationships. In this case, however, the controls were in the same plane as the burners (displays), an arrangement commonly used with 'split level' cookers.

Figure 7.10 Four control–display arrangements used by Chapanis and Lindenbaum (1959). *Reproduced by permission of the Human Factors Society.* Inc

Whereas population stereotypes exist for control/display movement relationships, as will be discussed later no such stereotypes seem to exist for spatial relationships. Thus Shinar and Acton (1978) asked over 200 subjects which sequence of controls they considered was most appropriate using the burner arrangement described by Chapanis and Lindenbaum. Of the four most obvious arrangements (ABCD, ABDC, BADC, BACD) the first three were suggested by very similar numbers of respondents.

This being the case, it would appear that some further aid to spatial compatibility is required. Two suggestions have been made. First to use linking 'sensor lines' between controls and displays (Chapanis and Lockhead, 1965) and second to colour code the display and its appropriate control (Pook, 1969). In both cases the experimental results were remarkably similar in so far as the aids produced no increase in performance when the display and control had maximum spatial compatibility. When they were arranged incompatibly, however, large improvements in accuracy and response time were obtained (up to 95 per cent reduction of errors on large panels using sensor lines, and approximately 40 per cent faster response using colour coding).

Although the discussion of spatial compatibility has so far centred around visual displays, displays that use other sensory modalities may also be arranged to be 'spatially' compatible. For example, Simon and Rudell (1967) demonstrated that information presented to the right ear was reacted to faster by the right-hand, whereas a left-hand advantage was obtained for information presented to the left ear. Since we have fairly accurate abilities to localize sounds, particularly at the lower frequencies used, for example, for warning klaxons, these data suggest that the emergency controls associated with such an auditory display should be located in the same direction as the display. Wickens, Vidulich and Sandry-Garza (1984) discuss the need for maintaining mode copatibility.

Movement compatibility

Controls and displays are composed of moving (or in the case of digital or auditory displays, apparently moving) parts. Since the two components are related both in the machine and in the operator's 'mind' it is important to ensure that the directions of their moving parts are compatible with each other and conform to the operator's movement expectations. Again it must be stressed that the display represents the means from which the operator receives information. A windscreen, for example, displays as much information as does a dial.

The commonly expected control–display relationships which might arise have been fairly extensively researched and documented and can be divided into two subsets.

The first group include relationships in which the control and display are in the same plane — perhaps on a console panel. In these cases the general movement rule, using either linear (for example, a lever) or rotary (for example, knob or switch) controls, is 'up or clockwise' for an increased or right moving reading, and 'anticlockwise or down' for a left or reduced reading. In addition, to make the operator's task easier it has often been suggested that the controls and their displays should have the same appearance — that strip displays are associated with linear controls and dial displays with rotary controls.

If the type of control and display are mixed, for example a rotary control and a strip display, curious effects which sometimes deviate from these generalizations may sometimes be noted. This was first documented by Warrick (1947) (and is discussed by Brebner and Sandow, 1976) who pointed out that the indicator is expected to move in the same direction as the point on the control closest to the display. Whereas the expected movements of vertical controls and displays may simply conform to Warrick's principle, if the display is vertical and the control rotary then Warrick's principle implies that the side of the display upon which the control is situated is important. Thus a clockwise movement on the left of the display would be expected to produce a reduced reading since the part of the control next to the display is moving downwards. The same control on the right, however, would need an anticlockwise movement to produce an expected fall in the reading (see Figure 7.11). Brebner and Sandow (1976) note that this effect is enhanced if the scale values are placed on the side of the vertical display which is opposite that of the control.

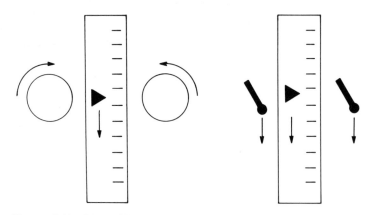

Figure 7.11 The different control actions required according to Warrick's principle, when the control is on the left and right sides of the display

The second control–display relationship occurs when the two components are situated in different planes, perhaps with the display positioned vertically with the control on a horizontal console. Using this type of arrangement the appropriate movement relationship is that which would occur if the two planes were imagined as being one simple plane. Warrick's principle may then be invoked (see Figure 7.12).

Control–display ratio

When discussing movement compatibility, it is also important to consider the amount by which the moving parts of the control and the display actually move. This has implications for the sensitivity with which the control is to be adjusted. A small control movement which is associated with a large display 'deflection' means that the operator has to deal with a highly sensitive system; as with a 'hair trigger' on a gun, a small movement produces a large response. At the other end

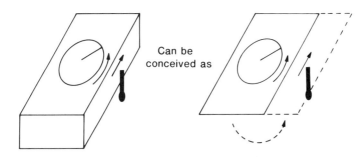

Figure 7.12 The application of Warrick's principle to cases in which the control and display are in different planes

of the continuum lies the low sensitive system in which a large control movement is required to produce a small movement on the corresponding display. (Like the terms 'control' and 'display', 'movement' must also be taken in its widest sense. This includes not only linear distances but, perhaps, degree of turn, number of revolutions, or even, as with the gun analogy earlier, the intensity of a reaction.) The ratio between the control and display movements is, naturally, known as the control–display ratio and is an index of the system sensitivity. Thus a low C/D ratio (small control:high display movement) indicates a highly sensitive system, whereas a high C/D ratio suggests the reverse.

The optimum ratio for a control–display system depends entirely on the system requirements and properties, and so on general formula exists to help decide on an appropriate ratio. However, the optimum ratio for a particular system can be determined experimentally, as was demonstrated by Jenkins and Connor (1949).

Whenever a continuous control is used, the operator effectively performs two types of movement. First is a relatively crude, gross motor movement to position the control in the vicinity of the final setting. Jenkins and Connor describe this as the travel phase. Second there appears a much finer movement, the 'adjustment' phase, in which the operator regulates his or her motor control to bring about the final control setting. The optimum control/display ratio, Jenkins and Connor argue, will be when both of these movements occur in the shortest time.

Figure 7.13 illustrates these relationships. Taking, for example, a system which has a low C/D ratio (small control : high display movement), the proportion of the control time used for adjustment will be higher than for travel. However, as the amount of control movement needed to produce a corresponding display movement increases (i.e. as the C/D ratio increases or the system sensitivity decreases), the time spent travelling will also increase. At some point the two times will intersect, and Jenkins and Connor argue that this will be at the optimum C/D ratio for that system.

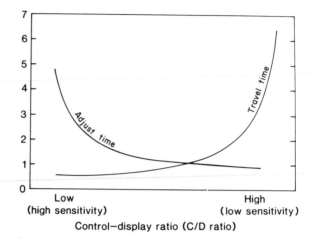

Figure 7.13 The relationship between adjustments and travel time for varying control–display ratios (from Jenkins and Connor, 1949)

Cognitive compatibility

Just as it is necessary to ensure physical compatibility between the user through controls and displays, so it is important that they are compatible at a cognitive level. This means that the machine's conception of what the user is able to do needs to be compatible with what the user actually can do and vice versa.

The importance of such cognitive compatibility generally appears when dealing with computer systems. This has been highlighted by workers at the Applied Psychology Unit in Cambridge (Morton *et al.*, 1979; Barnard *et al.*, 1981; Hammond *et al.*, 1981; Barnard *et al.*, 1982). Their concern was the concept of computer-centricity; that is, that computer programmers often work to a model in which the computer is at the centre of events. This might not be compatible with the user's expectations. In essence, they extract three forms of cognitive incompatibility which can occur: linguistic, memory and perceptual.

Linguistic incompatibility can occur at both a syntactic and at a semantic level. As an example of the syntactic level, consider interactive commands that are often used by computer systems such as DELETE (to delete an entry or a file), MOVE (usually to move one piece of file to another area), INSERT (to insert information into a file), etc. Accompanying each of these commands are usually two further pieces of information: the information to be deleted, moved or inserted and the file or memory area from which or to which the information is deleted, moved or inserted.

The incompatibility often arises because the information following the commands DELETE, MOVE, INSERT, etc., often have to be used in abbreviated forms, such as DELETE X, Y; MOVE X, Y; INSERT X, Y. In 'natural' language, the operator's own language, the above abbreviated commands might well be interpreted as DELETE (information X) from (file Y), or MOVE (information X) to (File Y), or INSERT (information X) into (Area Y). If this is how the computer programmer or system designer intended the actions to take place, then there is no syntactic incompatibility. Often, however, commands of the form such as DELETE X, Y imply the reverse of what is expected in natural language, that is DELETE Y from File X, with disastrous results!

Semantic linguistic incompatibility can occur in a similar way, that is the system designer's view of the user's behaviour is at variance with the user's expectations. In this case, however, the problem arises over command meanings — particularly when the commands are computer-centric. Carroll (1982) discusses some of these semantic incompatibility problems. Examples might include the terms PUT and GET or LOAD and DUMP. Both of these pairs of operators are often used to transfer information from the computer to some storage medium and vice versa. However, the *direction* of the transfer is only immediately obvious if the user has already accepted that the computer is at the centre of the operation. Then PUT, for example, implies putting information onto the storage medium and GET suggests retrieving it. However, if the operator shifts attention from the computer towards the storage medium itself, so that this is seen temporarily as the centre of the operations, then the actions of PUT and GET become cognitively incompatible. Similar problems also exist with the commands LOAD and DUMP. Although a computer-centric user would possibly understand that information is DUMPed to a file, the word LOAD does not immediately imply that the information is LOADed from the file to the computer.

The second form of cognitive incompatibility which has been suggested is a *memory* incompatibility. In this case, the machine's requirements of the user's memory capabilities can be incompatible with the user's actual abilities. Again, linguistically incompatible terms can increase the memory load required because they require the user to remember, for each command, the relationship between the variables X and Y.

Finally, there is proposed *perceptual* incompatibility. This relates primarily to the presentation of information as displayed on the computer screen and its relationship to the operations required of the user. As such this returns more to the spatial and movement compatibility concepts discussed earlier.

THE WORKSPACE SHAPE

By this point the reader should have a good idea of where individual components (principally its controls and displays) should be placed. The final consideration is how the machine, the panel, the console should be arranged around the operator.

Regarding the complete console, again few experimental data are available to guide the designer in a choice of shapes. This is probably because 'common sense' and 'aesthetic' principles (which are by no means complementary) have arisen over the years.

The 'common sense' approach to shaping the workspace argues that an appropriate shape is one which allows the operator to reach all of the controls easily and to see each of the displays. Thus full details are needed about the anthropometric dimensions of the user population: arm reach, hand sizes, sitting height, eye height, etc.

As Morgan *et al.* (1963) point out, the most appropriate shape to ensure that the operator can reach all controls easily is one with a continuously curved surface which effectively wraps around in front of the operator. However, this is often difficult to produce, particularly if large, flat displays need to be mounted on the console face. To overcome this problem, therefore, a sectioned console may offer the next best alternative, having angled side panels which can, again, be located around the operator. For this type of design, Siegel and Brown (1958) demonstrated that side panels at 50–55 degree angles produced the lowest number of operator body movements.

The problem is not so under researched, however, when smaller panels are considered — partiuclarly the size and shape of keyboards. This is understandable, of course, since the keyboard is one of the most prominent features of modern computer systems.

The physical dimensions of alphanumeric and numeric keyboards are clearly determined by the dimensions and arrangements of the keys which they contain. In this respect, the anthropometric dimensions of the fingers and hands discussed earlier are important. So, too, are the ways in which the keys need to be pressed — sequentially or in groups. This will determine the minimal interkey spacing.

With respect to keyboard angle, or tilt, both Alden, Daniels and Kanarick (1972) and Cooper (1976) point out that there is a relatively small literature on the question of typing performance as a function of the keyboard tilt. Furthermore, the few studies that are available suggest that, providing the board does not deviate too far from the optimum tilt, performance is not greatly disrupted. For example, Alden, Daniels and Kanarick report a study by Galitz (1965) who investigated the effect of a computer keyboard tilt on typing performance. He used slopes of 9, 21 and 33 degrees to the horizontal, and found no significant performance differences between them. However, his subjects did appear to prefer the 21 degree slope. This 'idealized' slope of about 20 degree is substantiated in a study by Scales and Chapanis (1965). They used keyboard slopes of between 0 and 40 degrees to the horizontal, and their subjects were asked to perform a task of keying ten-character alphanumeric characters. Although no significant differences were obtained in either typing speed or errors, the 'operator preference data' suggested that some slope was desirable. Half of the preferences occurred between 15 and 25 degrees.

Regarding numeric, as opposed to alphanumeric, keying Alden, Daniels and Kanarick point to studies by Creamer and Trumbo (1960). They used a keytapping task in which subjects were required to tap keys in a particular sequence, alternating fingers and hands. Five tilt angles were used (0, 22, 44, 66 and 88 degrees). Although the maximum number of errors were made at 0 degrees, the variation in errors after 22 degrees was only very slight. Using an actual number keying task (telephone numbers) Cooper (1976) again showed that the 'best' keypad angle appears to be around 25 degrees to the horizontal, since this produced least keying time and errors. However, he also points out that his data indicate that the effects of a deviation either way from this angle was quite small.

In summary, therefore, the optimum keyboard angle appears to lie between 20 and 30 degrees to the horizontal.

As an extension of the idea of tilting the keyboard, and taking account of biomechanical data regarding the ways in which the wrist and forearm have to be extended during typing, Kroemer (1972) describes a new type of alphanumeric keyboard (called the K-board) which is split at the centre and hinged backwards at angles of either 30 or 50 degrees — each half being operated by each hand. The main feature of the K-board is that the keys are arranged in straight columns (rather than offset as on a conventional board) and in curved rows. The space bars, one for each sectional keyboard, are bent from the inside of the keyboard to below the bottom row. Such an arrangement reduces the tendency to twisting the forearm into the body noted by Ferguson and Duncan (1974) and prevents operating the wrists in the 'abnormal' (protinating) posture. Kroemer (1965) reports that normal keyboard tilts of 15 degrees proved significantly slower and more fatiguing than the experimental K-board. With regard to the K-board itself, Kroemer (1972) reports an investigation in which four angular tilts (0, 30, 60 and 90 degrees) were used. Inclinations of 30 or 60 degrees produced significantly faster and less fatiguing stroking performance than either the 0 or 90 degree inclination. Nakaseko *et al.* (1985) describe an extension of this split board concept, with variations in both lateral and horizontal angles. Initial results from both biomechanical observations and subjects' reports indicate strong preferences towards this type of arrangement when compared with the normal, flat type of keyboard. Thus preferences tended towards a system of two half keyboards with an opening angle of 25 degrees and angled laterally (that is, lifted at the centre) by 10 degrees.

SUMMARY

Having decided on the appropriate controls and displays, this chapter considered how they should be arranged around the operator — within the workspace. The overriding principles to consider are to arrange the components in terms of their sequence and frequency of use, and their importance. Having estimated these parameters, however, careful consideration needs to be given to where displays should be placed with respect to other displays, controls with respect to other controls and, finally, displays with respect to controls (and vice versa). Only when these aspects have been assessed will the link between the operator and the machine be able to work to its best advantage.

CHAPTER 8

WORKPLACE DESIGN

Having designed the operator's immediate workspace — displays, controls and consoles — the final problem concerns ways in which the various components in the total working environment (an environment which comprises groups of both people and machines) should be arranged around the operator within the workplace. Just as the efficiency of a display or a control can be reduced by an inadequately designed console, so can the usefulness of different machines if they are poorly positioned. In this case, 'usefulness' probably reflects the ease of use rather than speed or accuracy. If speed is a factor, it is important more in terms of the operator's mobility around the environment, rather than the faster reaction times which have been considered so far.

When discussing placing people and machines in the workplace the social relationships of operators themselves also need to be examined, an aspect which so far has not been considered. As was discussed in Chapter 4, the types of communication links set up between individuals and between groups of individuals may facilitate or hinder activity. Existing social relationships can easily influence these communication links. Needs for privacy, peace and territory are various aspects of the social environment that will be discussed later in this chapter.

Perhaps the first decision that needs to be made when designing the workplace, however, is whether or not the operator is to be seated. Specific aspects of seating design will be discussed in the next chapter, but suffice it to say at this stage that although a seated operator will experience less fatigue, mobility is also likely to be reduced.

This chapter considers first the physical aspects of the environment important when considering where people and machines should be placed, and then discusses some of the social factors.

PHYSICAL REQUIREMENTS IN THE WORKPLACE

Anthropometric Considerations

The importance of designing the environment to fit the operator's anthropometric dimensions has been stressed throughout this book. They are, per-

188

haps literally, the most basic considerations for ensuring that a person is able to fit into the working situation.

Passageways

Anthropometric details are no less important when considering the ideal arrangement of machines in the system. For example, if people have to walk down passageways or between machines, the space available needs to be at least greater than the shoulder breadth so that both arms can be accommodated, as well as any clothing which the operator is likely to be wearing. For 99 per cent of the population, Damon, Stoudt and McFarland (1971) suggest the following minimum dimensions for various kinds of passageways (including corridors, aisles and tunnels:

Height: at least 195 cm or 160 cm if stooping is permitted (although this is undesirable).
Width: at least 63 cm.

If space is at a premium, the passageway can be trapezoidal in shape, 63 cm wide at shoulder level and 30 cm at the feet. For gangways in which two or more people may pass, Damon, Stoudt and McFarland suggest the same height but increasing the width by approximately 50 cm for each extra person likely to walk abreast.

Whereas these figures apply specifically to passageways which are bounded on each side by walls, it is likely that similar dimensions will also be required for gangways between machines. Indeed, a case might be made for increasing the width since, unlike walls, machines often have protruding controls which could possibly be knocked by a passing operator, resulting in injury or accidental activation of the machine.

Stairs and ramps

Anthropometric and biomechanical considerations are also important when the operator needs to move between different levels — using either stairs, ramps or ladders.

Corlett *et al.* (1972) compared the average energy required by eight male subjects to climb either stairs or ramps which had slopes ranging from 10 to 30 degrees. Using oxygen consumption, heart rate and maximum knee-joint angles as their comparison measures, the authors demonstrated that the physiological cost of stairs was always less than that of a ramp of equal slope. However, they also point out that stairs impose a particular gait on the user which causes increased knee-bending. For old or infirm people (and even those carrying loads which sometimes create an awkward gait) this makes ramps easier to use — regardless of the energy cost. In addition it should be remembered that ramps allow the operator to push or to pull large loads between levels (within the constraints discussed in Chapter 3). Stairs make this activity more difficult and, if the operator is carrying goods, ramps are likely to be safer than stairs.

Although for normal purposes stairs require less effort than ramps, they still need to be designed to fit the user. Four aspects of the stair geometry appear to be important in determining their ease and safety: first, the riser height (the vertical distances between one step and another); second, the tread depth (the distance between the front and the back of the step); third, the steepness (slope) of the stairs; and finally, the tread texture. The first three factors determine the amount of energy required, and the fourth affects the likelihood of slipping.

Regarding the riser height and the tread depth, many architectural codes of practice still embody an eighteenth-century formula derived in about 1792 by Francois Blondel, Director of the Royal Academy of Architecture in Paris. From personal observation he concluded that the normal pace in level walking (said to be about 60 cm or 24 in) must be decreased by a regular and fixed amount to allow the foot to be raised in climbing stairs. His formula stated that the pace should be decreased by 5 cm (2 in) for every inch of riser. In other words, the tread depth should be 60 cm (24 in) minus twice the height of the riser.

Fitch, Templer and Corcoran (1974) point out that this formula has been passed down almost unaltered through generations of architects. This is despite the fact that in stairways which span either larger or smaller gaps than usual the rule produces either extremely narrow or extremely wide treads, corresponding to the higher or smaller risers. In addition, as was discussed in Chapter 3, the average human body is bigger now than in the eighteenth century, and today's inch is shorter than that used by Blondel in his calculations.

As Corlett et al. (1972) and Fitch, Templer and Corcoran (1974) demonstrate, all stairs impose an individual gait on the user due to the knee and pelvic angles required. As a result of proprioceptive feedback this gait soon becomes learned as a person moves up or down the stairs, so that any irregularity in either riser height or tread depth might cause a misstep to occur. (This was well understood by castle builders in the Middle Ages who added an irregularly spaced 'trip step' near to the botton of the stairs to catch the unwary intruder.) In this respect a worn step caused by continued use may be enough to make the user stumble.

Although the gait adopted when climbing or descending stairs can provide useful feedback cues to the user, if it is irregular or accentuated it can also cause discomfort and increase the energy expenditure. Corlett et al. (1972) for example, demonstrated that subjects used less oxygen when climbing stairs with a 6 in (15 cm) riser than with a 4 in (10 cm) riser and, naturally climbed the stairs faster. A larger riser height was also suggested by Fitch, Templer and Corcoran (1974) whose data suggested that increasing the height from 6 to nearly 9 in (15 to 22 cm) reduced the number of missteps.

The ideal tread depth clearly ought to be related to the user's foot size since, as Ward and Beadling (1970) have noted, as the size of the tread decreases a point is reached where the shod foot can no longer fit on the step without being twisted sideways. This awkward movement induces a crab-like gait and a poorly balanced posture. If stairs are to be adequate for the largest people, therefore, Fitch, Templer and Corcoran (1974) suggest that the tread will need to be about

$11\frac{1}{2}$in (27 cm) deep. This allows a nominal $\frac{1}{4}$in ($\frac{1}{2}$cm) between the heel and the riser, and the toe of the shoe to overhang the step by 1.75in (1.5cm) (on decent). Finally, all authors appear to support the contention that the steeper stairs cause less energy to be expended. Corlett *et al.*'s results, for example, showed that almost twice as much oxygen was used on a 30-degree slope than on a 10-degree slope.

Although the dimensions of a stairway may be designed eventually to fit the user, accidents can still occur if the tread texture is too smooth. This was illustrated in Chapter 3 when discussing how reduced friction between the walker and the floor can result in slipping. Kroemer's (1974) data, for example, illustrates how different combinations of shoe and floor material can aid or hinder slipping.

Finally, accidents using stairs may be able to be reduced if the user is provided with handrails which enable a more stable movement to occur, as well as helping to provide extra movement forces. In this respect, two factors would seem to be important: handrail diameter and shape, and handrail height. The first will determine the amount of grip able to be exerted on the handrail; the second affects the forces able to be generated and thus the stability in moving up the stairs.

Maki, Bartlett and Fernie (1985) investigated the optimum height of handrails for generating stabilizing forces and moments when moving up and down stairs. Their results indicate a fairly linear relationship between forward and backward force generation and handrail height, although an optimum height of about 90 cm was demonstrated at both a biomechanical and a preference level. In a subsequent study the authors demonstrated that, within bounds, this optimum height was fairly independent of stair pitch.

Ladders

Apart from using lifts, which are space-consuming and extremely costly to install, the other practical means by which an operator can move from one floor to another is by ladders. These are particularly useful when slopes greater than the 20 to 30 degrees discussed above are employed.

Ladders, however, are more dangerous to use than stairs. Data are not available which compare the probability of accidents occurring using ladders rather than stairs, but the Royal Society for the Prevention of Accidents (1977) suggest that about 10 per cent of all falls from a height in industry involve ladders. Buck and Coleman (1985) report that 17 per cent of the nearly 46000 industrial accidents reported in 1982 that resulted in a fracture were classed as 'falls from a height'. Clearly such a category includes sites other than ladders, but the figures do support the contention that falling represents a significant feature of the accident data.

Dewar (1977) describes an analysis of one set of 248 ladder accident reports. Sixty-six per cent of accidents occurred when the ladder slipped, either during climbing or when working on the ladder. Of the remaining 34 per cent a large proportion was attributed to misplacing the feet or otherwise stumbling when climbing. It would appear, therefore, that two aspects of the interaction between the user and the ladder are important: first, the forces which restrain the ladder on the lower level, and second, a person's climbing action. For this second factor Dewar suggests two further influencers: the ladder angle, which affects the awkwardness of the climbing action and the climber's stature, which alters the knee and pelvic angles required to move up the ladder.

Regarding the climber's behaviour, simple observation would suggest that all of the limbs are involved. Ladder climbing is characterized by both the hands and the feet being used; the hands helping both to propel and to stabilize. Using films of climbers ascending ladders with different inclinations, McIntyre and Bates (1982) demonstrated four distinct climbing patterns: In the *lateral gait*, the arm that is on the same side as the moving foot is used both for propulsion and stability and is moved at the same time as the foot. The *four-beat lateral gait* is similar except that the hand moves slightly later than the foot. Less frequently used were the two *diagonal* gait patterns which operated in a similar way to the lateral gaits but the arm opposite to the moving foot was used.

Clearly, therefore, since the hands are used to such a great extent in all types of ladder ascent, sufficient detail needs to be given to the design of the part of the ladder that the hands use — either the rungs or the ladder side. Unfortunately no data are available to make recommendations in this respect.

For an environment with fixed machinery it is likely that the ends of the ladder will also be fixed, thus ruling out any ladder slippage. For situations without fixed or secured ladders, however, Hepburn (1958) suggests that the 'quarter length' rule should be used: that is, the horizontal distance from the foot of the ladder to a point vertically below its top should be one-quarter of the ladder length. This represents a gradient of 4 in 1 or approximately 75 degrees.

This suggestion has been challenged by Dewar (1977). After recording the hip and knee-joint angles of both tall (average height 181 cm) and short (average height, 167 cm) men climbing ladders set at 70.4 and 75.2 degrees (representing gradients of 3:1 and 4:1 respectively), he demonstrated that the steeper (75 degree) ladder caused the body's centre of gravity to be further back from the ladder than was the case for the 70-degree ladder. This means that more reliance has to be placed on the hands for support. Under such circumstances, therefore, he argues that if the hands slip there is less chance that the person would be able to regain his or her balance.

With regard to stature, Dewar's data indicated a slight, although non-significant, increase in the amount of leg movement associated with the shorter subjects. In other words, taller subjects ascended the ladder with a less 'natural', 'stiffer-legged' posture. This difference increased with the steeper ladder. Since a forced and unnatural posture may result in increased errors, Dewar's data suggest that taller people are more at risk as the angle of a ladder becomes steeper. Hepburn's suggestion of adopting the quarter length rule, therefore, might need slight revision.

Communication Considerations

As had been stressed constantly, the operator's communication requirements consist of links in all directions with the machine and with other operators. These may occur via any of the operator's sensory systems, although the visual (for example, displays), auditory (for example, speech) and tactile (for example, controls) systems will most often be used. This means that the operator must be able to see the machines, move around and quickly operate them, and be in a position to hear and communicate with other operators and machines. The anthropometric and biomechanical requirements for moving around machines have already been discussed, so this section will consider the operator's visibility and auditory requirements, and the necessity to arrange machines so that movement from one to another is reduced.

Movement considerations

To reduce movement time between components, the principles governing the arrangement of people and machines in the workplace are similar to those suggested for arranging controls and displays in the operator's immediate working area. These are that the most important machines are placed within easy access of the operator, as are those which are used most frequently. Machines or workplace areas should be grouped according to function and, whenever possible, operator movement from machine to machine should follow some sequence of use.

Unfortunately, few data exist with which one is able to evaluate these guidelines. However, an experiment carried out by Fowler *et al.* (1968) (discussed in McCormick, 1976) indicates that when controls and displays are arranged on the operator's console according to one of these principles, the average time to carry out a task was lowest for the sequentially arranged components. The 'functional', 'importance' and, finally, the 'frequency' arrangements respectively took progressively longer. Translating these results to the gross body movement time of an operator moving between machines, however, is difficult and no comparative data exist. Nevertheless, without any evidence to suggest the contrary, it would appear sensible to arrange machines as far as possible according to these principles.

Visual considerations

Having ensured that the operator is able to move safely and quickly between machines, a further consideration is to ensure that visibility is not impaired — both of machines for which the operator is responsible and other operators who may need to be consulted. Such visibility requirements could be hindered in two ways: first, if the illumination level is too low to be able to see accurately (this is discussed in more detail in Chapter 11). Second, if lines of sight are obstructed by other equipment or by other operators. This is a problem which concerns placement of both machines and operators.

The problem may be overcome during the design process by very simple procedures which involve mapping the operator's sight lines. Usually this takes the form of running pieces of cotton or string from where the operator's eyes would normally be to the machines (and to the important parts of the machines) which should be under his or her control. (Scaled models are often used for this purpose.) As long as the cotton is able to run in a straight line, the operator's visibility requirements will be unimpaired. Bends in the cotton indicate features of the workplace which will be in the way.

Sell (1977) used a very similar procedure to design the structure of a moving crane cab used to transport steel in a mill. The shadow thrown by a small illuminated light bulb, placed at the position of the operator's eye in a scaled down model of the cab, provided a preliminary idea of the directions in which obstructions to vision (caused by, for example, girders) would occur. He was then able to obtain more detailed information by running a thread from the place where the operator's head would be to the various points that have to be viewed. Using these threads, it was easy to measure the sight line angles and thus to design the cab structure on this basis.

Finally, rather than providing for maximum visibility to as many parts of the operator's environment as is feasible, in some cases (or in some sight directions) it may be more sensible to ensure that visibility is obscured — perhaps by erecting screens. This is particularly so in two cases: first, when requirements for privacy override communication needs (this is discussed in more detail below when landscaped offices are considered). In the second case, machines might be sited to shield the operator from too high a glare source, for example, from a furnace.

Visual strain and fatigue from close work

A feature of the visual workplace that has received some considerable attention in recent years, particularly with the advent of computer work-stations, is the relationship of the workplace to the visual load placed on the operator. In some respects, of course, this relates as much to the workspace as to the workplace, but it is considered here because the problem does involve as much the arrangement of workspaces as the workspaces themselves.

Dainoff (1982) presents a comprehensive and recent view of studies investigating the effects of both short and prolonged use of VDUs on visual fatigue. As Table 8.1 shows, all studies report significant fatiguing effects, although it should be pointed out that many of the earlier studies lacked good control groups against which the results could be compared (groups of equivalent workers who did *not* use VDUs), and some of the more recent studies simply asked operators what effects they *felt* VDUs had (this is not the same as asking what effects they actually had).

With regards the nature of the complaint Läubli, Hünting and Grandjean (1981) asked a number of VDU operators to provide details of the visual impairments that they felt were caused by VDU operation. From the responses

Table 8.1 Summary of studies showing visual problems of workers who use VDUs (adapted from Dainoff, 1982). *Reproduced by permission of Taylor & Francis Ltd*

Name	Proportion complaining (%)	Types of workers and comments
Hultgren and Knave (1973)	47	VDT operators No control group
Gunnarsson and Osterberg (1977)	46	VDT operators No control group
Gunnarsson and Soderberg (1979)	62	Newspaper compositors
	83	VDU users in office
Technical University Berlin (in Cakir et al., 1980)	85	Workers on incentive schedules
	68	Workers not on incentive schedules
Rey and Meyer (1980)	75	VDT operators (50% in control group)
Shipley et al., (1980)	61	Newspaper workers
Ghiringhelli (1980)	50	VDT operators
Coe et al. (1980)	51	VDT operators —analysis made in terms of type of *task*
Läubli et al. (1981)	50–70	VDT operators—analysis made in terms of type of *complaint*
Dainoff et al., (1981)	45	Clerical workers with varying VDT experience
Smith et al. (1981)	–	Investigated effects of VDUs on mood as well as eye strain
Mourant et al. (1981)	–	Compared fatigue from VDU use with fatigue from using normal writing

they were able to extract two eye impairment factors as shown in Table 8.2. Thus the major group is composed of a 'discomfort' dimension, whereas the minor group of factors comprises, essentially, a visual impairment dimension.

As far as the effects of the task are concerned, Dainoff (1982) provides an excellent description of some of the work in this area. In particular he describes an extensive series of studies carried out in New Zealand by Coe *et al.* (1980) who sampled nearly 400 employees from 19 different firms.

The data from these studies were analysed according to the type of symptom, and a significant difference was obtained between the VDU users and the controls (50 versus 33 per cent) but only for the *fatigue-like* symptoms. Creative workers (for example, programmers group) reported fewer symptoms than any other type of task. Furthermore, full-time operators were significantly more likely to report asthenopic complaints (both fatigue and irritation) than were part-time operators.

Table 8.2 Factor analysis of eye impairments of VDU users (Läubli, Hünting and Grandjean, 1981). *Reproduced by permission of Taylor & Francis Ltd*

Factor	Proportion of variance	Name	Symptoms
1	81	Visual discomfort	Pains Burning Fatigue Shooting pain Headaches
2	19	Visual impairment	Blurring of near sight Flicker vision Blurring of far sight Double images

This task duration effect has also been reported by other investigators. For example, Rey and Meyer (1980), in their study of VDU users in a Swiss watchmaking factory, found that VDU operators who worked 6–9 hours per day at their terminals were significantly more likely to have visual complaints (73 per cent) than those who used their terminals for less than 4 hours per day. These patterns of complaints appeared to be the same for both young and old operators. Ghiringhelli (1980) also found that complaints of eye irritations increased for workers who used terminals for more than 3 hours per day, and they were significantly greater than for control (clerical) workers.

One reason for the relationship between eye strain complaints and the type of task probably lies with the amount of work which the eye muscles are called on to do — particularly the ciliary muscles which control the lens shape. To perceive near and far objects, the lens shape constantly has to be altered to focus the image on the retina — a process known as accommodation. For practical purposes all objects further than 6m from the normal eye are sharply in focus and the nearer the object is to the eye the greater is the amount of muscular effort required to maintain the correct lens curvature. With 'normal' visual work, then, the ciliary muscles are continually varying in the level of contraction and, because they are performing dynamic work, are able to pump blood to maintain their oxygen supply, etc. For the type of work normally done at a computer terminal, however, this does not necessarily happen. The copy and the screen are generally placed close to each other and the operator's eyes rarely have a chance to vary the accommodation level from one which requires the ciliary muscles to be under constant static load. This argument is supported by findings of Starr, Thompson and Shute (1982) who showed that if operators wear correctly prescribed glasses, the incidence of complaints from VDU users is no greater than that from other workers.

Finally, Läubli, Hünting and Grandjean (1981) investigated how different aspects of the display affected these complaints. In particular, they considered the effects of luminance contrasts between the screen and the surround (arising from, say, windows and reflections off the copy) and the quality of the displayed characters.

With regard to contrast, their data suggest that it is the high contrast displays which cause more eye complaints. Indeed, significantly more members of the high contrast group reported that the complaints continued after work and even until the next morning. In addition, the extent of reflections off the screen correlated well with operator annoyance, although there was no relationship between measured reflection luminance and actual eye complaints.

Regarding the characters themselves, the authors measured the extent to which the character luminances oscillated in brightness. Complaints of eye irritations and red eyes were more frequent from operators who had used displays with strongly oscillating luminances. Character luminance oscillation was also related to performance — with high oscillation leading to reduced visual acuity.

Auditory considerations

Whereas the operator's communication channels from machines will be mainly in the visual mode, apart from non-verbal information, communication with other operators usually occurs in the auditory mode. For this reason, assessing the levels of environmental noise and attempting to reduce the noise levels is important, as will be discussed in Chaper 10.

Noise is usually reduced at source by some methods of noise absorption, for example, by placing padding around the noisy machinery or by using sound absorbing wall and floor materials. However, it is also possible to reduce noise levels by a few decibels simply by an appropriate arrangement of the equipment. For example, Corlett, Morcombe and Chanda (1970) suggest that altering the positions of movable pieces of equipment produces both screening and reduces levels of reflected sound. They demonstrated a drop in sound level of 5 to 10 dB by judiciously arranging storage of work-in-progress material. Although this appears to be a small amount when compared with much larger reductions from sound-deadening materials, they suggest that small reductions can be beneficial by permitting considerable increases in tolerance and speech communication. However, they concede that the siting of such storage areas (or, in the context of the present discussion, other machines) should not override the other considerations discussed elsewhere in this chapter.

SOCIAL REQUIREMENTS IN THE WORKPLACE

So far, the discussion has centred around the concept of physical aspects of the working environment which may interfere directly with the operator's ability to carry out the task. However, it is important to remember that the environment also contains other operators who are likely to interact with one another, and these interactions can also affect performance. The physical arrangement of both men and machines, therefore, may inhibit or facilitate these more social interactions and can have important implications. Unfortunately, despite the fact that the operator's environment includes other men and women, little attention has been given to the influence of social environmental parameters on performance, safety or comfort. Two important aspects of the social space requirements are personal space and territoriality and these are discussed below.

Personal Space

Personal space has been defined as an area with invisible boundaries surrounding a person's body into which intruders may not enter (Sommer, 1969). It may be considered as a series of concentric globes of space, each defining a region in which certain types of interaction may occur. The regions, however, are not necessarily spherical, sometimes they extend unequally in different directions. Savinar (1975), for example, has shown that people have space requirements in both vertical and lateral directions. If the available space is limited in one dimension (for example, by reducing the ceiling height), then a person's spatial needs will increase in the other directions.

A. Intimate distance
B. Personal distance

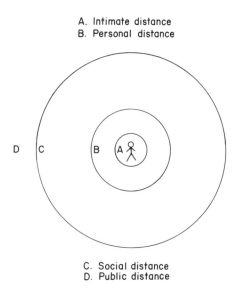

C. Social distance
D. Public distance

Figure 8.1 Personal space zones (to scale)

Hall (1976) broadly divides the social space areas surrounding a person into four distance zones from the centre: intimate, personal, social, and public distance (Figure 8.1), each zone having both a close and a far phase. However, as discussed below, the boundaries of each zone are not necessarily constant — they sometimes fluctuate under different conditions. The importance of these distances to the present discussion lies in the observation that only certain classes of people are allowed to enter each space area. The behaviour of a person whose space is violated may change considerably if the 'wrong' person infringes the 'wrong' zone.

At intimate distance (close phase 0–15 cm; far phase 15–45 cm) the presence of the other person is unmistakable and may sometimes be overwhelming because of increased sensory stimulation. The close phase is typified by actual physical contact which, in many cultures, is considered taboo between strangers. Within the far phase the degree of physical contact is slightly reduced but increased visual awareness of the other person is maintained. As Hall describes it: 'The head is seen as enlarged in size, and its features are distorted ... The iris of the other person's eye seen at only 6–9 in is enlarged to more than life size. Small blood vessels in the sclera are clearly perceived, pores are enlarged.'

Although, as its name suggests, personal distance is concerned with friendly contact, fairly large differences may exist between behaviours associated with the close and far phases (45 to 76 cm and 76 to 120 cm, respectively). The close phase is reserved for 'well-known' friends since a stranger moving into this distance may imply a threatening situation. The far phase begins at about arm's length and is the area in which normal social contact is made. The personal distance, therefore, may be conceived as a buffer zone between an area reserved for intimate acquaintances and one in which less personal contact takes place. Perhaps because physical violence may be perpetrated, only well-known friends are allowed to enter.

Less personal business is normally conducted within social distance (close phase 1–2 m; far phase 2–3.5 m). People who work together tend to use close social distance. It is also a common business distance for people who are attending a casual social gathering. If business is conducted at the far phase it has a more formal nature. Hall suggests that a feature of the far phase of social distance is that it may be used to insulate or screen people from each other: 'The distance makes it possible for them to continue to work in the presence of another person without appearing to be rude'. Public distance (close phase 3.5 to 7.5 m; far phase 7.5+ m) is well outside the circle of social involvement and, at this distance, other communication problems may occur similar to those discussed in Chapter 4.

A stranger who violates a person's space (that is, enters a particular zone that is not reserved for the invader) may cause tension, discomfort and flight. For example, Sommer (1969) intruded mental patients' space by sitting to close to them on benches. The patients' typical reaction was to face away, become rigid, and pull in their shoulders. Within 2 minutes, 33 per cent of the victims departed while none of the control patients whose space had not been violated did so. Within nine minutes, 50 per cent of the experimental subjects and only 8 per cent of the control subjects had departed. In another study reported by Sommer (1969) female students working alone at a table in a library departed much faster than control subjects when another female subject occupied the adjacent chair and moved it closer to the subject. Interestingly, the 'defence behaviour' is typified by a lack of verbal responses to the invasion. Only two of the 69 mental patients and only one of the 80 students asked the invader to move over. As Sommer suggests, this provides support for Hall's (1959) contention that 'we treat space somewhat as we treat sex. It is there but we don't talk about it'.

Flight is an extreme reaction to personal space invasion. McBride, King and James (1965), however, showed that subjects' arousal (measured by skin resistance, GSR) rose more sharply when they were approached from the front compared with a lateral approach. Both of these directions produced greater GSR changes than invasion from behind. Other less extreme reactions were recorded by Patterson, Mullans and Romano (1971) who describe both 'leaning away' and 'blocking out' responses, both of which were designed to 'exclude' the intruder. These responses increased in frequency as the intruder seated himself closer to his victim. Mahoney (1974), however, was unable to replicate the increased 'leaning' and 'blocking' responses when using control subjects whose space was not violated. This was primarily due to their subjects 'tensing up' and 'freezing' rather than actively moving to block out the violator. Consistent with this interpretation are the findings of Mehrabian and Diamond (1971) who showed that relaxation decreased as chairs were located so as to increase immediacy.

Another study which demonstrated the arousal that can result from personal space invasion was reported by Lundberg (1976). He measured the level of catecholamine (a pharmacological stress indicator) in the urine of selected passengers both before and after crowded or empty train journeys. Significant increases were obtained under crowded conditions and his findings were supported by subjective responses of increased feelings of discomfort as the number of passengers increased.

As an example of how the discomfort and stress that might result from personal space invasion could affect performance, Middlemist, Knowles and Matter (1976) recorded performance in a mens' lavatory. In a three-urinal lavatory a confederate stood either immediately adjacent to a subject, one urinal removed, or was absent. They showed that both the onset and persistence of micturition was delayed significantly in the adjacent condition compared with the other conditions. Leaving aside the ethical questions of privacy which such a study raises, the results do indicate that personal space invasion may cause reduced performance, probably because the person's arousal is increased to a greater level than optimum. As was discussed in Chapter 1, for example, over-arousal is likely to lead to reduced performance.

It is clear, therefore, that the invasion of a personal space zone by someone who should not normally enter causes a complex series of behavioural responses. The purpose of these responses would appear to be to 'distance' the intruder by the victim leaning away, turning, or more simply, 'withdrawing' from the situation. In this way, an individual may temporarily shrink his or her personal space zone so that invasion is not perceived. For example, Sommer (1969) observed that people in a very crowded situation (for example, a crowded train) seemed to control their potential discomfort from the overcrowding by behaviours such as staring at the floor or into space, thus relating to those close by as if they were 'non-persons'. The importance of such invasion, therefore, lies in increased feelings of unease, discomfort and stress with a possible loss of performance.

Many variables affect the distance of these different space zones and include personality, sex, age, culture and the status of the individuals involved.

Personality

Many studies suggest that subjects with personality abnormalities need more personal space, although findings are not totally conclusive (Evans and Howard, 1973). Several studies have also been carried out to examine the relationship between personal space and personality types. Patterson and Sechrest (1970), for example, found that extraverts have smaller personal space zones than introverts, but Meisels and Canter (1970) found no such relationship.

Sex

An examination of sex differences in the way we use space indicates that females have smaller personal space zones, and hence can tolerate closer interpersonal contacts, than males (Liebman, 1970). When opposite sex pairs are mutually attracted it is not surprising to find that the magnitude of such buffer zones decreases considerably (Allgeier and Byrne, 1973). One striking difference between the sexes is in the positions which each adopts: research on attraction indicates that males prefer to position themsevles *across from* liked others while females prefer to position themselves *adjacent to* liked others (Byrne, Baskett and Hodges, 1971).

Age

Very little research has been reported which explores the developmental aspects of personal space. Willis (1966) studied three age groups: older, younger and peer (within 10 years) and found that peers approached one another more closely than they approached those who were older. Age differences, however, are often confounded with status differences and the effects of these are discussed below.

Culture

Clear differences appear to exist in the spatial behaviours of members of different cultures. For example, Hall (1976) observed that Germans have larger personal space areas and are less flexible in their spatial behaviour than are Americans. Latin Americans, French and, particularly, Arabs, on the other hand, were found to have smaller personal space zones than Americans. Sommer (1968) found no significant differences in personal space between English, Americans and Swedes, but showed that Dutch have slightly larger, and Pakistanis slightly smaller, personal space areas. Sommer does suggest, however, that such studies are difficult to interpret fully because of language barriers which sometimes make it difficult for subjects to understand the purpose of the experiment.

Status and familiarity

In general, studies support the contention that external sources of threat (by meeting a higher status individual or one who is not known) lead to increased personal distance. Correspondingly, those who wish to convey a friendly impression or a positive attitude choose smaller interpersonal distances than neutral or unfriendly communicators (Patterson and Sechrest, 1970).

Territoriality

Like personal space, territoriality is a concept which invokes social, unwritten rules of behaviour, with infringement causing discomfort and/or other behavioural reactions. It is a concept which is widely understood in the animal world but has only been considered comparatively recently in relation to humans. Territoriality differs from personal space, however, in that territories have fixed locations and do not move around with the person. Furthermore, the boundaries are often quite visible, being marked by recognized stimuli which may either be personal (like a coat) or impersonal (like a fence).

Although different societies and political systems have different rules governing territoriality, there appears to exist a commonly shared distinction between territory (or property) which is private and territory which is public. A private territory (for example, a house) may be occupied or owned *in absentia* by a single person who has the authority to decide who may or may not physically enter it. Public territory (for example, stairs, streets, workplaces, etc.) is accessible to many diverse people and cannot be owned by a single person other than on a temporary basis.

Of interest to designers are the cases when a semi-private territory is set up in what is otherwise public territory. For example, reserving seats in a canteen, marking seat boundaries in transport, or the 'ownership' of machines and office areas.

Fried and DeFazio (1974) observed the territorial behaviour of travellers in a New York City underground train. The seating accommodation in each car consisted of four long benches (two on each side of the car), each of which seated up to eight passengers, and two, 2-passenger, seats. No armrests or other means of delineating territory were present. The authors' interest centred on the use of the two-passenger seats. Under low-density conditions (up to 15 passengers) it was observed that only one passenger ever sat on a two-passenger seat, and the other seats were used in such a way as to provide a large degree of separation between passengers. Clearly, therefore, the two-passenger seat was regarded as 'territory' which remained sacrosanct even under medium-density conditions (16–40 passengers). Indeed, many passengers were observed to prefer to stand rather than to sit in the 'free' space on the two-passenger seats.

Territorial boundaries broke down under high densities (40+), however, with all seats being occupied and distances between passengers, both sitting and standing, being minimal. From their study Fried and DeFazio concluded that certain implicit byelaws exist with respect to territory which can be applied to other situations:

(1) Seated passengers may not be challenged or deprived of their territory except under very special circumstances. Such circumstances include very high-density or other extreme conditions when a person may be asked to 'move over'.

(2) There shall be little verbal interaction between passengers. This explains the success of the many territorial markers which are used: coats or bags on the adjacent seat and books on a desk all indicate temporary territorial control. Another person who wishes to sit at the seat needs either to ask for the marker to be moved (contravening rule 2) or move it, which breaks other accepted behavioural standards.

No matter how well the physical environment has been designed to match a person's behaviour, therefore, social constraints may intervene to reduce the system's efficiency. So the value of the perfect seat (in terms of comfort and reduced backache) may be reduced if it is placed so close to another that the two occupants' personal space requirements are infringed. A well-designed seminar or boardroom (in terms of noise level, temperature, ventilation, etc.) may be rendered ineffective if the seating arrangements are such that (a) the occupants are unable to mark their territories (for example, not enough desk space is provided to 'spread out' their paper) or (b) no account is taken of personal space requirements, with the result that the participants may tend to 'withdraw' into themselves to maintain 'distance'.

At this point it would be pertinent to ask how these social space requirements may be accommodated within the confines of a modern work environment. The obvious answer, clearly, would be to increase the space available to individuals in a potentially crowded condition. This would result in less density of people, and territorial and personal space requirements would be met.

In many cases, however, such propositions are not feasible. Indeed, sometimes the space available may not be able to be increased by a single inch. In such cases territorial requirements may be accommodated by providing fixed markers, for example, individual armrests to delineate seats, or small, individual tables. Structures such as armrests might help to segregate sitters enough to avoid actual physical contact.

Finally, although physical space may not be increased, it may be possible to increase apparent space using appropriate interior designs. Thus, it is well known that broad horizontal stripes make an object appear wider than is actually the case, whereas vertical stripes have the reverse effect. Interior designers know of other perceptual 'tricks' for altering the appearance of shape, depth, etc. For example, Wyburn, Pickford and Hirst (1964) suggest that colours and shadows may be used to produce apparent depth, distance and solidity.

Little (1965) has demonstrated that people take account of their background surroundings when considering their personal space requirements. Although the surroundings used in his study were the interior of a living-room, an office, and a street corner, his results suggests that a background which makes the distance between two people appear to be greater than it actually is would help to reduce perceived space infringement.

The Landscaped Offices Concept

A further practical solution to individuals' need for space is to allow them freedom to arrange their workplaces as they wish, thus allowing individual territories to be set up and ensuring that infringements do not occur unwittingly. The arrangement of both people and equipment in this freer way is embodied in the 'landscaped office' concept, said to have been proposed originally by West German furniture manufacturer, Ebehard and Wolfgang Schnelle, in the early 1960s (Brookes, 1972).

The important feature of the landscaped office lies in its lack of boundaries, so providing spatial flexibility to both the employees and to the employers. Whereas a conventional office system might take the form of one floor of a building which has been further divided into smaller offices by fixed walls and doors, a landscaped office will use the same floor space but the different work groups are scattered around without being restricted by walls. Spatial needs of privacy and territory are meant to be accommodated by providing low, movable screens and allowing users, within limits, to arrange desks (boundaries) as they feel fit. The geometry of the workgroups, therefore, is supposed to reflect the pattern of the work process and is arranged by the individuals rather than being superimposed as a rectilinear plan. Furthermore, it allows workgroups to adjust work areas to the changing needs of their business. Brookes and Kaplan (1972) also point out that the concept insists that all staff participate — not just clerical staff and a few supervisors. Among the many advantages which were claimed for this type of spatial organization were that group cohesiveness would be enhanced by the mixture of executives, management, supervisors and clerical staff and that productivity would be enhanced.

The few controlled studies which have been carried out to substantiate or refute these claims do not lead to any firm conclusions. Brookes (1972) has reviewed much of the literature which suggests that information flow between work-groups and a perception of group cohesiveness might increase in a landscaped office, and that employees prefer the brighter, more colourful and friendlier design that a landscaped office provides.

On the other hand, this type of office arrangement produces a greater loss of privacy, increased noise, distractions and interruptions and, paradoxically, a perceived loss of control of the space around workplaces (Nemecek and Grandjean, 1973). In terms of the loss of privacy, this occurs both at a visual and at an acoustic level. Thus, as Parsons (1976) points out,

In the open-plan office, even with head height partitions, everyone can see whether or not someone is at work, present or absent, writing a report or reading the newspaper, thinking, catching forty winks, typing or with feet on desk. Everyone can see who is talking (directly) with whom.

This last problem is interesting in so far as it suggests that allowing employees to have physical control over the size and arrangement of the immediate space is not enough to overcome territorial requirements — they must actually *feel* that they have control. Whereas the landscaped office concept allows some physical control, because of lack of privacy it does not allow users to have subjective control.

Brookes (1972), therefore, concludes that there is no strong body of evidence to support the claims of the landscapers. However, he also points out that evaluations so far carried out have been of a survey nature on existing designs rather than a systematic attempt to investigate variables which could be beneficial to the concept.

SUMMARY

When considering how the operator's workplace should be arranged, two factors need to be assessed. The first concerns communication requirements — communication with colleagues and machines (mobility, and visual and auditory needs). The second relates to feelings of ease and comfort with respect to the position of other people in the immediate environment. In this case concepts such as personal space and territoriality have been borrowed from analyses of animal behaviour to explain how these factors could help with performance.

CHAPTER 9

SEATING AND POSTURE

In Chapter 8 it was pointed out that an important feature that has to be decided early when designing the workplace is whether the operator should sit down to do the task. A seated posture has many advantages, indeed Grandjean (1973) describes sitting down as being 'a natural human posture'. For example, because sitting relieves an operator of the need to maintain an upright posture it reduces the overall static muscular workload required to 'lock' the joints of the foot, knee, hip and spine and so reduces energy consumption. Grandjean also points out that sitting is better than standing for the circulation. The blood and tissue fluids in a standing person tend to accumulate in the legs — a tendency which is reduced when seated; the relaxed musculature and lowered hydrostatic pressure in the veins of the legs offer less resistance to blood returning to the heart. Seating also helps the operator to adopt a more stable posture which might help when performing tasks that require fine or precise movements, and it produces a better posture for foot control operations.

Although seats offer these physiological advantages, seated operators are possibly disadvantaged in other respects — perhaps the most important being that mobility is severely restricted. As will be discussed later a 'good' seat is one which helps the sitter to stabilize the body joints to maintain a comfortable posture. A person who needs to move around the workplace will have to upset this stability to change from a sitting to a standing posture and, if this is repeated too frequently, fatigue will almost certainly occur.

A further aspect of sitting relates to the task to be performed. Because it aids stability a seated posture is often ideally suited for performing fine manipulative jobs. However, it is unlikely to be useful when hand controls have to be operated with large forces or torques. Under such circumstances the operator's normal behaviour will be to rise from the seat to adopt an appropriate posture — an activity which again is likely to induce fatigue if repeated too frequently.

A third disadvantage of being seated arises in a vibrating environment, particularly if it is vibrating sufficiently strongly for the vibrations to be transmitted through the seat. As will be discussed in Chapter 10 the seat backrest, armrests and even harness may cause vibrations to be transmitted to the controlling limb and often results in reduced manipulative performance.

Finally, although sitting is healthier in terms of spinal loads and short-term vascular circulation, prolonged sitting can cause health problems. For example,

Grandjean (1973) points out that a sitting posture causes abdominal muscles to slacken and curves the spine, in addition to impairing the function of some internal organs — particularly those of digestion and respiration. Furthermore, Pottier, Dubreuil and Mond (1969) have demonstrated that prolonged sitting (over 60 minutes) produces swelling in the lower legs of all sitters, which is caused by increased hydrostatic pressure in the veins and by compressing the thighs resulting in an obstruction in the returned blood flow.

Clearly, therefore, although a seated posture is generally less fatiguing and is likely to aid body stability when working, a number of factors need to be taken into account before a decision is made whether an operator needs to sit to perform a task.

This chapter considers three primary aspects of maintaining a seated posture. From each, guidelines may be derived relating to appropriate seat design. First, orthopaedic considerations relate to a possible damage to the sitter's health caused by poor design. Second, muscular aspects and third, features of the sitter's own behaviour who may be viewed as a 'comfort seeker' or as a 'discomfort avoider'. Finally, optimum seat dimensions which arise as a result of these considerations are discussed.

ORTHOPAEDIC ASPECTS OF SITTING

When seated, the body's main support structures are the spine, the pelvis and the legs and feet.

The spine consists of 33 vertebrae joined together by multiple ligaments and intervening cartilages, the functions of which were discussed in Chapter 3. For descriptive purposes the vertebrae are divided into four areas which correspond roughly to the areas in which the spine changes shape. These are the topmost seven cervical, then twelve thoracic and five lumbar vertebrae, followed by five fused sacral and four fused coccygeal vertebrae. From the viewpoint of seating design, the orientation of the lumbar and sacral vertebrae are important since it is these vertebrae and their respective discs and muscles which take most of the spinal load of a seated person.

Although when viewed from the front or back the normal, relaxed spine appears vertical, when viewed from the side its curved nature can be seen (Figure 9.1). The top, cervical, curve bends forwards leading into a convex backward bend throughout the thoracic region. The lumbar region bends forward again, ending in the sacrum which is positioned on the pelvis.

When standing, the natural curved shape of the spine enables the body's centre of gravity to pass through the trunk and the feet, so requiring only minimal muscular activity to maintain a posture. As Corlett and Eklund (1984) point out, only intermittent muscular activity is required when standing to restore momentary displacements of posture. Reduced trunk muscles activity is aided by the lumbar outward curve of the spine (lordosis) which brings the lumbar vertebrae close to or over the CG of the trunk, arms and head. Sitting,

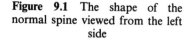

Figure 9.1 The shape of the normal spine viewed from the left side

however, upsets this vetebral arrangement. As pointed out by Grandjean (1973) sitting with a 90 degree angle between the trunk and thighs, for example, causes the pelvis to rotate backwards which reduces lumbar lordosis. This requires increased tension in the muscles and ligaments in the lumbar region to compensate for the movement of the CG towards the anterior of the body, leading to increased loads on the spine and the intervertebral discs. An appropriate chair design from the viewpoint of reducing spinal load, therefore, will be concerned greatly by the seat pan/backrest angle — i.e. with the amount of pelvic rotation.

Since the spine has evolved in this way it seems reasonable to suggest that this is a 'natural' shape and is also one which produces both the optimum pressure distribution over the cervical discs and static load on the intervertebral muscles. It follows, therefore, that a seat which causes a sitter to adopt a different posture will be likely to cause maldistributions in disc pressures and will result, over time, in lumbar complaints.

There have been a number of studies reported which have investigated the pressures between vertebrae when adopting various seat angles and postures. All arrive at similar conclusions and suggest that intradiscal pressure is gradually lowered when the angle is increased to above 110–120 degrees. Figure 9.2 illustrates data from Andersson (1980), which also demonstrates the importance of a backrest giving support to the lumbar region. Andersson and Örtengren (1974) have also shown that a slumped posture produces *less* intradiscal pressure than does one which is upright as adopted during typing, for example.

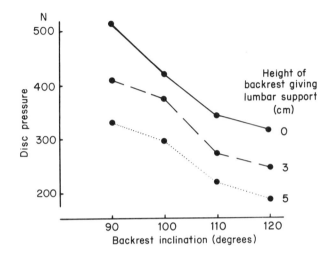

Figure 9.2 Relationship between disc pressure and backrest inclination with different levels of lumbar support. (*Reproduced with permission from Andersson, 1980. Copyright Academic Press Inc. (London) Ltd.*)

Regarding the actual spinal shape, Branton (1984) has collated data from anthropometric surveys which illustrates the general spinal shape of 114 people. Although very wide variability in measurements was reported, the shape finally produced does provide a starting point from which appropriate backrests may be designed. For example, in general the lumbar area extends to about 20 per cent of the full sitting height. This is the area which requires most support from the backrest since it receives the full weight of the rest of the body. The top of the thoracic curve, the area at which most 'back' pains are reported, extends to a position about 75 per cent of sitting height. It must be emphasized, however, that these are static measurements; sitting is very much a dynamic activity — as will be discussed later.

Using X-rays to study the spinal shape during different postures, Keegan and Radke (1964) suggest that the normal, relaxed spine shape is produced when a person is lying comfortably on his or her side with the thighs and legs moderately flexed. Comparing the lumbar curve produced in this position with those in ten other seated positions, wide variations in curve shapes can be seen (Figure 9.3). Keegan and Radke's data suggest that a sitting posture which produces the nearest approximation to the 'normal' lumbar shape is one in which the trunk-thigh angle is about 115 degrees and the lumbar position of the spine is supported. Their figures also suggest that a 'sitting-up-straight' position produces a great deal of spinal distortion. In this position the compressive weight from the upper part of the body is harmful to the lower lumbar vertebrae and this is the cause of discomfort and sometimes pain experienced when sitting in chairs which have this 90 degree backrest angle.

Figure 9.3   The degree of spine curvature produced in different postures. (*From Keegan and Radke, 1964, reprinted by permission © 1964 Society of Automotive Engineers Inc.*)

As may be seen from Figure 9.3 a forward posture causes the normally forwards-bent lumbar area to be straightened and, eventually, to bend backwards. Continuing up the spine this also affects the angles of the thoracic and cervical areas causing a 'hunchback' posture. If such a posture is maintained for long periods it increases the loads on the musculature supporting the head and produces both neck and back fatigue.

As the back moves from an upright to a hunched position, the pelvis makes a corresponding backward rotation because it is attached to the sacral area. Grandjean (1973) suggests, therefore, that seats should be designed so that in both the forward and backward sitting postures they provide support to the upper edge of the pelvis in an attempt to arrest this trend to rotate.

MUSCULAR ASPECTS OF SITTING

Because vertebrae are kept in positions by muscles and tendons, any alteration to a 'natural' spinal shape will produce corresponding stresses on the associated musculature. This increase in muscle activity can be demonstrated and measured by recording the electrical potentials (myoelectric activity) produced by the different muscles (a technique known as electromyography or EMG).

A study of this nature was carried out by Floyd and Ward (1969) who recorded the activity of four groups of muscles (in the neck, on the collarbone, on the back just below the shoulder blades, and in the lumbar region) when the sitter adopted various positions. Their results fully support the conclusions from orthopaedic studies. Thus, again, 'sitting-up-straight' without any backrest produced fair degree of activity in the lumbar region — presumably because this posture attempts to straighten the lumbar curve (see Figure 9.1). However, the activity ceased as soon as a backrest was provided. A forward, hunchback posture caused most activity to occur in the upper back and shoulder regions, again substantiating the orthopaedic observations. Finally, of interest to all who write for a living, Floyd and Ward's data indicate that providing a table support on which the author is able to rest the arms does not reduce muscle activity. Indeed, shoulder muscle activity on the side of the writer's preferred hand increased increased dramatically. Similar findings were obtained by Andersson et al. (1975) from both EMG recordings and from pressure recordings in the lumbar discs.

As was pointed out above, evidence from electromyographic studies have supported the orthopaedic studies in arguing for a backrest angle of at least 110–120 degrees. In fact, Andersson et al. (1975) found that backrest angle was the main seat feature that influences myoelectric activity. Again, however, such statements need to be tempered by the real-life situation. Thus Burton's (1984) EMG studies demonstrated that although backrest use is very important in reducing muscular activity, the technique adopted by the operator during a typing task had more effect on muscular activity than did the design of the chair.

An interesting use of muscle recording data was made by Mandal (1981) to suggest that working chairs should have their seat-pan tilted forwards rather than backwards. He measured the extent of sitters' muscle elongation in various chairs with both forwards and backwards tilting seat-pans, and demonstrated less muscle elongation and a more even pressure distribution over the seat using a forward-tilting (by 15 degrees) rather than a backwards-tilting seat. He supports these conclusions with observations of people actually sitting:

That this position really is one of the most frequently used can quite clearly be seen as only the front part of the seat covers of office chairs is worn; the rear part being almost untouched.

This suggestion of a forwards-tilting seat will be discussed in more detail later. In summary, therefore, both orthopaedic and muscular evidence suggest that:

(1) An upright and a forward leaning posture will cause fatigue.
(2) Providing a backrest will reduce some of the lumbar fatigue, as will
(3) an obtuse-angled backrest which helps to stabilize pelvic rotation.

BEHAVIOURAL ASPECTS OF SITTING

The Concept of Comfort

The discussion so far has concerned the effects of different seating positions on the body's structure but it will now turn to consider postural evidence gained from the person who is sitting. At this point, a subtle change in criterion occurs: previously the criteria for successful design have been discussed in terms of the operator's response speed, accuracy and ability to cope with the incoming information. Fatigue and poor anthropometric fit have been emphasized as contributing factors which help to reduce performance effectiveness. In seating, however, the criterion is in terms more of reduced fatigue and excessive postural strain on parts of the spinal column. Musuclar fatigue and spinal deformation reduces comfort and increases operator stress which, in turn, is likely to reduce performance. The emphasis, therefore, has shifted to consider the user's physical requirements rather than cognitive and motor performance abilities.

Since it is comfort, rather than ability, which is the main consideration with respect to sitting behaviour, it follows that the term needs to be defined. (An accurate measuring tool can only be developed when the properties of the subject-matter being measured are understood.) Unfortunately, however, it is extremely difficult to define comfort, primarily because it is such an entirely subjective concept; the features of a seat which one individual looks for in helping to adopt a comfortable posture may be different from those chosen by another. As Branton (1972) has suggested 'the problem is...to relate measurements of a physical nature to subjective and essentially private experiments of feeling'.

The problem is increased further by the possibility that one cannot define or measure comfort. Indeed, Hertzberg (1958) first operationally defined comfort as 'the absence of discomfort'. As an analogy Branton (1972) uses the definition of health: it is only possible to declare a person to be healthy when there is no evidence of illness. Branton further suggests that the absence of discomfort does not mean the presence of a positive feeling but merely the presence of no feeling at all.

> There appears to be no continuum of feelings, from maximum pleasure to maximum pain, along which any momentary state of feeling might be placed, but there appears to be a continuum from a point of indifference or absence of discomfort, to another point of intolerance or unbearable pain.

This argument suggests, therefore, that the ideal seat is one in which the sitter loses all awareness of the seat and the sitting posture. When in this state a person is able to give undivided attention to whatever activities may need to be pursued. This concept of comfort leads to another aspect which deserves consideration — the reason for sitting in the seat. In other words, the sitter's motivation to sit. If an ideal seat is one which allows the operator to pursue activities that need to be carried out it is reasonable to suggest that a soft, low, easy chair, for example, will be unsuitable for a task which requires fine, manipulative work at a console. Branton (1969), therefore, has suggested strongly that a seat may be 'inefficient' in terms of the extent to which it interferes with the primary activity. The assessment of 'comfort' therefore, does need sometimes to give way to consider the operator's 'efficiency' since it is unlikely that one can exist without the other.

A factor closely related to the motivation for sitting is the duration for which the sitter is sitting. If sitting comfort changes over time a chair which is designed for ease, comfort and long-term sitting would need to be assessed according to different criteria than one which is to be used for only a few minutes at a time.

The few data available on this point suggest that chair comfort is not affected significantly by the length of time for which the sitter is seated. Grandjean (1973), for example, cites an experiment in which 38 subjects were asked to assess the degree of discomfort in different parts of their body after both five and sixty minutes of sitting. No significant difference was observed between the responses. This is not the say, however, that the duration of sitting has no effects at all on sitting comfort — it is simply that for the durations studied it had no effect.

Behavioural Dynamics of Sitting

The discussion of seats and sitting so far has emphasized the fact that it is important always to consider the behaviours adopted by the sitter. For example, Mandal's (1976) observation that the front edge of a seat often assumes importance for seated workers illustrates the value of examining behaviour under natural settings. In addition, Grandjean et al. (1982) have demonstrated that people adopt different postures at computer workstations and that these can create different types of pain complaints. Individual behaviour, therefore, can interact with the environment to affect the efficiency of a design.

In addition to the spine, the main structures used by the sitter during sitting are the pelvis, legs and feet. These take the form of a simple mechanical lever system that helps to stabilize the body.

The hip portion of the sitting body — the pelvis — can be likened to an inverted pyramid. In fact, the main contact with the seat is made by only two rounded bones, the ischial tuberosities. Although this part of the buttocks is covered with very little flesh, because of the pressures placed on this area by the sitting person the blood supply to the buttocks can still be restricted. Indeed, Dempsey (1963) has pointed out that the human body supports approximately 75 per cent of the total body weight on 25 sq cm of the ischial tuberosities and the underlying flesh (this is illustrated in Figure 9.4). He also suggests that this load is sufficient to produce 'compression fatigue', which varies according to the compressive load of the body and the duration of loading. 'In physiological terms, compression fatigue is the reduction of blood circulation through the capillaries, which affects the local nerve endings and results in sensations of ache, numbness and pain.' Branton (1966) further adds that although the findings illustrated in Figure 9.4 relate to hard seats they are not altered drastically when sitting on a cushion:

> If the cushion is soft, it give as little support to the flabby muscle or fatty tissue; if it is compressed to the point of being solid, i.e. if 'bottoming' occurs, the cushion is no different from a hard seat.

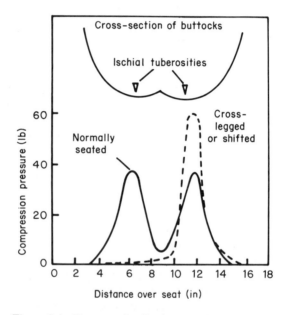

Figure 9.4 Pressure distributions produced over the seat during normal and cross-legged positions. (*From Dempsey, 1963, reproduced by permission of McGraw-Hill*)

The use of modern upholstery, however, may alter Branton's position slightly. Thus Diebschlag and Müller-Limroth (1980) recorded the pressure distributions of subjects sitting on either a hard seat or on one which was padded using polyurethane foam. As a result of the foam, the pressure values under the buttocks were reduced by nearly 400 per cent and the supportive area of contact between buttocks and seat were increased from approximately 900 to 1050 sq cm. Similar conclusions were arrived at when the backrest was also changed.

With the mass of the body suspended over what is essentially a two-point suspension system on the seat-pan, the system is mechanically unstable. This instability is increased as a result of the body's centre of gravity not being situated vertically over the tuberosities when sitting upright, but about $2\frac{1}{2}$ cm in front of the navel. This system is only made stable by the addition of levers provided by the legs and feet. Crossing the legs, for example, is a normal way of locking the system, as is resting the arms on a table or the head on the arms. The whole forms a most complex mechanical system which allows movement in both the horizontal and vertical planes.

Over long periods, blood circulation to the capillaries in the buttocks is also reduced if the body is unable to move at regular intervals. If the body is confined in a relatively fixed seating position for more than four hours the physiological functions that control the flow of body fluid slow down. This action, coupled with continuous pressure loading on the flesh, accelerates the rate of compression fatigue. Fatigue can be delayed, however, by periodic movements of all of the major body segments. This results in changes in the loading conditions and allows muscular expansion and contraction for adapting to new weight conditions.

For this reason, the sitter's behavioural repertoire is likely to include activities such as fidgeting which alter the pressure distribution on parts of the body caused by the compression fatigue. Indeed, the degree of fidgeting can act as an indicator of seat discomfort, as was demonstrated by Branton and Grayson (1967). They recorded the changes in sitting posture of 18 subjects during a five hour train journey while sitting in one of two types of seats. On the basis of the significant increase in the number of fidgets produced in one seat over the other the authors were able to recommend which seat should be adopted.

Any summary of these considerations (orthopaedic and muscular on the one hand, and behavioural on the other) must lead to antagonistic requirements for seat design. Thus, the orthopaedic and muscular considerations suggest strongly that the sitter should be supported as much as possible; that the intervertebral discs and muscles should be constrained so that pressures they experience should not be excessive. The behavioural evidence, however, suggests that the seat should allow the sitter to move body parts; that the sitter often needs to fidget to reduce compression fatigue. Unfortunately, a seat which allows movement is unlikely to be one which provides a great deal of support.

To accommodate these two requirements from the viewpoint of the sitter's behaviour, Branton (1966) has formulated a theory of postural homeostasis. Homeostasis is a concept which is widely understood in physiology and concerns the self-regulation of body functions. A common example is body temperature regulation: if the body temperature rises, sweat is produced which, when it evaporates, has a cooling effect. If the body becomes cold, however, blood is routed away from the skin to warmer, central parts of the body (thus giving cold skin its characteristic bluish appearance).

One of the characteristics of such homeostatic activities is that they are automatic; they are not under deliberate, conscious control. Awareness only comes with drastic changes of conditions and then only after the event has occurred. Branton argues that postural activity falls into the same category of autonomic regulation and that postural homeostasis is a process by which the sitter strikes a compromise between needs for both stability and variety. Sitting behaviour, therefore, is characterized by cycles of both inactivity and activity and so an efficient and comfortable chair needs to be able to accommodate these homeostatic requirements and allow both stability and flexibility.

SEAT DESIGN

A number of principles for seat design can be extracted from the above discussion. These include:

(1) The type and dimensions of the seat are related to the reason for sitting.
(2) The seat dimensions should fit appropriate anthropometric dimensions of the sitter.
(3) The chair should be designed to provide support and stability for the sitter.
(4) The chair should be designed to allow the sitter to vary posture, but the fabric needs to resist slipping when there is fidgeting.
(5) Backrests, particularly prominent in the lumbar region, will reduce the stresses on this part of the spinal column.
(6) The seat-pan needs sufficient padding and firmness to help distribute body-weight pressures from the ischial tuberosities.

Regarding the motivation for sitting, seats may be divided simply into three groups. First easy, comfortable chairs for relaxation. In these the criterion for an effective chair should be, in Branton's terms, lost awareness of the seat and minimal discomfort of any part of the body's supporting structure. The second group includes chairs which are used for work. In these cases stability is an important consideration, requiring adequate lumbar support and body-weight distribution over the seat-pan. The final group includes those chairs which Grandjean (1973) describes as 'multipurpose' chairs. These may be needed for a variety of different purposes, for example, they could be used at a table, occasionally for working, or as spare chairs and frequently need to be stacked.

Regardless of the seat function its linear dimensions must fit those of the likely user population. This by now is axiomatic and appropriate anthropometric data exist. Normally these figures all relate to an unclothed sitter so the presence of clothing and footwear will increase the dimensions by a proportional amount. The dimensions indicated below will take account of this factor.

Seat height: easy chair 38 to 45 cm; workchair 43 to 50 cm

The seat height is adjusted correctly when the sitter's thighs are horizontal, the lower legs vertical and the feet flat on the floor. This is because the soft undersides of the thighs are not suitable for sustained compression, and pressure from the front edge of the seat-pan can become uncomfortable. For this reason, the limiting case for the seat height is that of the short-legged person who would be prevented from resting his or her feet on the floor.

The reason for the differing recommended seat heights between easy and working or multipurpose chairs is the way in which they are likely to be used. The height of an easy chair should allow the legs to be stretched forward since this is one of the preferred relaxing postures, in addition to helping to stabilize the body. For a working chair, however, the sitter is likely to be in a more upright posture with feet flat on the floor.

Many authors recommend that working chairs should be made to allow the height to be adjusted to accommodate the wide range of workers who may have to use them. If the chair needs to be higher than the recommended dimensions (perhaps because of a tall machine or high workbench) an adjustable footrest is also recommended.

Finally, Grandjean (1973) argues that the optimal height for a work seat can only be decided in relation to the height of the working surface. This, he suggests, should be between 24 and 30 cm below the working surface.

Seat width: 40–43 cm

In this case the largest person needs to be accommodated. Since the appropriate dimension is the hip width, and since major sex differences are apparent in this dimension, the limiting case should be the upper range of the female sitter.

Seat depth: easy chair 43 to 45 cm; workchair 35 to 40 cm

An appropriate seat depth ensures that all potential sitters find support in the lumbar area from the backrest. Seats deeper than the thigh length of the shortest person will mean that the front edge of the seat will restrain the sitter, causing the lumbar area to curve to reach the backrest. In addition, pressure-sensitive areas at the back of the knee will become pressed against the seat. For a workchair which will be used by a larger proportion of the population, the recommendation is to make the seat depth accommodate even shorter people, since the only consequence of taller members sitting in such a seat will be that knees protrude slightly at the front. Providing the seat height is adequate and the feet are able to be placed flat on the floor, this is unlikely to induce compression fatigue in the thighs.

Seat angle: easy chair 19 to 20 degrees; workchair less than 3 degrees

This refers to the angle of the seat-pan to the horizontal. A seat-pan which is tilted backwards has two advantages: first, because of gravity the sitter is moved towards the backrest, so supporting the back and reducing static load on the back muscles. Secondly, the slight seat-pan inclination at the front helps to prevent the gradual slippage from the seat which was observed to occur over long periods in the sitting study by Branton and Grayson (1967). The 20 degree optimal inclination is supported by Andersson (1980) who measured the amount of EMG activity in the back muscles at different backrest angles. His results, shown in Figure 9.5, illustrate well the value of the sloping backrest.

218

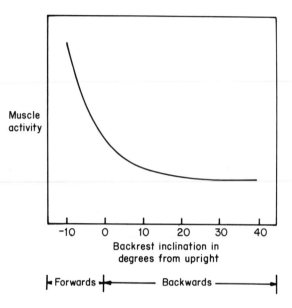

Figure 9.5 The relationship between back muscle activity and backrest inclination. (*Reproduced with permission from Andersson (1980), 'The load on the lumbar spine during sitting postures'. In D. J. Oborne and J. A. Levis (eds), Human Factors in Transport Research, Vol. II. Copyright by Academic Press Inc. (London) Ltd.)*

There seem, however, to be major divergences in the recommendations proposed for easy chairs and those suggested for workchairs. These relate to the chair's function and to the motivation for sitting. In an easy chair the sitter wishes to relax, the most relaxing position, of course, being horizontal. A backward sloping seat-pan helps to attain this. In a working chair, however, the requirements are to be positioned for easy access to a work area in front. A backward tilting seat would cause an operator to have to bend forward and would curve the spine unnecessarily.

Mandal (1976) has taken this further to argue that since most work is carried out in a forwards bent posture, a forward sloping seat is more appropriate. He suggests that a backward sloping seated work chair of even 5 degrees will cause straightening of the lumbar area and thus discomfort. For this reason, he suggests that a sitter will gradually tend to sit on the front edge of a seat, pivoted at the thighs. 'That this position really is one of the most frequently used can quite clearly be seen as only the front part of the seat covers of old office chairs is worn; the rear part being almost untouched.' (This is a good example of an unobtrusive investigation, as discussed in Chapter 14.)

As was discussed earlier, Mandal measured the extent of muscle elongation of sitters in various chairs with both forwards and backwards tilting seat-pans, and demonstrated less muscle elongation and a more even pressure distribution over the seat using a forwards-tilting (by 15 degrees) rather than a backwards-tilting seat. This suggestion of a forwards-tilting seat should be treated with some caution in the absence of information about appropriate seat coverings that might increase the sitter/seat friction. Otherwise, the tendency to slip forward out of the seat (Branton and Grayson, 1967) will be exacerbated and will have to be counteracted by increased muscular activity, particularly in the legs.

As well as reducing muscular activity, a forwards-tilting seat may have another advantage: helping the sitter when having to rise from the seat. Rising from a chair places quite extreme loads on both the spine and the knees. For example, Andersson, Örtengren and Nachemson (1982) demonstrated that intradiscal pressures doubled during the act of rising from a seat. The use of armrests reduced this effect. Similarly, Ellis *et al.* (1979) demonstrated knee joint forces almost seven times the body weight when rising. A motorized chair, in which the seat-pan lifts and tilts forwards to aid the person in rising, considerably reduced these forces. Mandal's forward tilting seat, therefore, could also help in this respect.

Backrest height and width: up to 48 to 63 cm high; 35 to 48 cm wide

Proposed backrest dimensions relate, quite simply, to the distance from the shoulder to the underside of the buttocks (height) and to the shoulder width (width). The height dimension, of course, extends from the compressed seat if padding is present.

As has become apparent, however, the linear dimensions of the backrest are only part of the question. Since its function is concerned as much with maintaining a relaxed (that is, non-fatiguing) spinal posture, the backrest shape and the angle are extremely important. In addition, since spinal curvature varies considerably from one person to another a complex relation between height and shape arises. In this respect, data concerning spinal shapes discussed in Chapter 3 and earlier in this chapter are important (e.g. Branton, 1984).

So that the sacrum and fleshy part of the buttocks which protrude behind a sitter can be accommodated, while at the same time allowing the lumbar region to fit firmly into the backrest, many authors suggest that the backrest should have an open area or should recede just above the seat-pan. A space of at least $12\frac{1}{2}$ to 20 cm is required to accommodate the buttocks in this way.

Finally, a high backrest might prevent full mobility of the arms and shoulders in certain tasks, for example, typing. In such cases, small backrests which support the lumbar region only are suggested by many authors.

Backrest angle: 103 to 112 degrees

Like an angled seat-pan, the angle of the backrest to the seat-pan serves two purposes. First, it prevents the occupant from slipping forwards and second, it helps the body to lean against the backrest with the lower (lumbar) part of the back and sacrum supported. From an orthopaedic viewpoint, the appropriate angle would be about 115 degrees which Keegan and Radke (1964), for example, demonstrated produced the nearest to a 'natural' lumbar shape. However, when sitting comfort responses have been elicited from seated laboratory subjects, a less obtuse angle has consistently been found to be more 'comfortable'.

Jones (1969) studied posture and feelings of comfort in a highly adjustable car seat in many different positions. Subjects were trained to recognize the sensations of 'no sensation', 'conscious of contact with the seat', 'numbness', 'ache' and 'pain' after varying intervals. From his data he suggested a backrest angle of 108 degrees.

Grandjean (1973) discusses work which he carried out with Burandt to determine the optimum backrest angle for easy chairs when used for different reasons. Their data suggests that an angle of 101 to 104 degrees is optimum when reading, whereas 105 to 108 degrees is an optimum relaxed angle.

Armrest height: easy chair 2s to 24 cm above the compressed seat.

The main function of armrests is to rest the arm and lock the body in a stable position. In an easy chair this is often accomplished by the arm being used to support the head. Armrests may also be useful in helping to change the sitting position or as an aid to getting up from the chair. However, it should be remembered that armrests may prove to be restrictive to the free movement of the arms and shoulders if they are incorporated in a working chair.

Cushioning and Upholstery

The importance of cushioning was demonstrated by Branton and Grayson (1967) in their observational study of sitters in two types of train seats. Although the dimsensions of the two seats were approximately similar, the type and strength of seat spring and padding differed. One gave a relatively 'soft' subjective feel whereas the other appeared subjectively 'firm'. After analysing the number of 'fidgets' observed in the sitters and the length of time for which stable postures were maintained, the authors were able to state that 'by almost all counts II (the firmer seat) is much better'. Furthermore, not only was the number of different postures greater in II, but they were more 'healthy'.

Cushioning performs two important functions. First, it helps to distribute pressures on the ischial tuberosities and buttocks caused by the sitter's weight; as was shown earlier, if not relieved this pressure will cause discomfort and fatigue. The second function is to allow the body to adopt a stable posture. To this end the body will be able to 'sink' into the cushioning which then supports it. However, in this respect, Branton (1966) raises a warning against the cushioning being too soft:

A state can easily be reached when cushioning, while relieving pressure, deprives the body structure of support altogether and greatly increases instability. The body then 'flounders about' in the soft mass of the easy chair and only the feet rest on firm ground. Too springy a seat would therefore not allow proper rest, but may indeed be tiring because increased internal work is needed to maintain posture.

Kroemer and Robinette (1968) agree with Branton's position and also caution that soft upholstery will allow the buttocks and thighs to sink deeply into the cushioning. If this occurs all areas of the body that come into contact with the seat will be fully compressed, offering little chance for the sitter to adjust position to gain relief from the pressure. In addition, the body often 'floats' on soft upholstery, again causing the posture to have to be stabilized by muscle contraction.

Regarding seat covering, the important aspects are its ability to dissipate the heat and moisture generated from the sitting body (which will, in turn, be related to the type of environment in which the sitter is sitting) and its ability to resist the natural forward slipping movement of the body over time. For both of these criteria adequate thermal and mechanical techniques exist to allow the designer to make appropriate measurements.

SUMMARY

Sitting is often considered to be a natural posture, relieving the sitter of the need to maintain an upright posture. However, as this chapter has demonstrated, a seated posture can sometimes cause more problems than are solved. A seat which requires the sitter to adopt certain postures can create at the least muscular fatigue due to the static loads placed on the spinal and other muscles. At worst, permanent orthopaedic damage can result from spinal pressure maldistributions. The second part of this chapter considered chair dimensions for alleviating some of these problems — particularly in relation to increased sitter comfort.

CHAPTER 10

THE PHYSICAL ENVIRONMENT

I   Vibration and Noise

Aspects such as controls and displays are 'visible' to the operator; they can be perceived and they affect working behaviour in so far as they restrict actions, judgement and immediate perceptions. The present and following chapter will consider the less tangible (perhaps the 'invisible') environmental aspects that arise both from the surroundings and from mechanical features of the workplace: environmental vibration, noise, temperature, and illumination. Of course, they are not the only aspects of the environment that may affect behaviour; atmospheric pressure, dangerous chemicals or radioactive materials, adverse climatic conditions, cigarette smoke, etc. are other examples of environmental features that could be encountered at work. However, only vibration, noise, temperature and illumination will be considered here.

The order in which the four factors are discussed in these two chapters is not intended to imply their relative importance to the operator. This depends entirely on the situation and the individual. Take, for example, two people standing on a small ship in cold, rough weather. One, being a 'poor' sailor will be concerned more about the ship's motion than any other factor; the other, a 'good' sailor, will probably worry more about the cold. The same environment, then, may affect people in different ways because of the importance each attaches to its effects.

Various environmental features can affect people in one or more of three ways: first health, second performance and third comfort. These, however, are not independent. For example, poor health can lead to poor performance and poor performance can lead to reduced work satisfaction; as was shown when discussing seating, reduced comfort may be a precursor to health hazards and can lead to poor performance; etc. Although these aspects will be considered independently, therefore, their affects are likely to be combined.

Purely physiological (health) effects of environmental stressors occur mainly at the extreme levels of the stressor's intensity. Even before such extremes are reached, however, the stressor (be it noise, vibration, temperature, illumination or any other aspects of the environment) can begin to affect the operator detrimentally, although this may not be apparent either to an observer or even to the person being affected. Although man is an extremely adaptable animal the

222

ideal range of any environmental factor for comfort or for performance is very narrow. As has been stressed throughout this book, having to adapt to conditions outside of this range can make the operator use more effort which can lead to reduced performance. The concept of a limited store of 'spare mental capacity', for example, was discussed in Chapter 1. In terms of the present discussion, performing a task under normal circumstances and within the narrow optimum range of environmental factors will take up a certain amount of this mental capacity. Having to adapt to more severe conditions (for example to hear in loud noise or to read under glaring conditions) will further reduce the amount available, until a point is reached when the 'spare mental capacity' is exhausted. When this happens, the argument suggests, performance begins to decrease.

VIBRATION

Vibration will be discussed first because it is the most fundamental environmental factor. It underlies the production and perception of noise and sounds in the environment and, depending on the theory to which one ascribes, the production and perception of light stimuli. Understanding the definitions and parameters of structure-borne vibration, therefore, will help the reader to understand the effects of many other environmental parameters.

Definitions

Vibration may be defined simply as any movement which a body makes about a fixed point. This movement can be regular, like the motion of a weight on the end of a spring, or it can be random. The vibration experienced from machinery is usually a very complex, but regular, motion. Using appropriate analysing techniques any complex motion can be analysed in terms of a number of simple components. This type of analysis — Fourier Analysis — is outside the bounds of this book but can be found in most texts dealing with vibration theory.

With vibration being defined in this simple way, it follows that a body can vibrate in a number of different directions, although the International Standards Organization (1974) suggests that any movement should be defined and measured in terms of three orthogonal components: 'x' — front to back; 'y' — side to side; and 'z' — up/down (Figure 10.1). Using these coordinates a person jumping up and down, for example, would be vibrating in the z direction. If the same person was rotating about an axis from shoulder to shoulder (for example, tumbling face-forwards from a roof) then the body would be vibrating in the x and z axes at the same time. Finally, a weightless astronaut in space may rotate uncontrollably and might be vibrating in all three axes together. For most experimental purposes, however, the effects of vibration are normally considered in one axis only — and this has generally been in the vertical (z) direction.

Once the direction of the motion has been determined, the *amount* of vibration is defined in terms of two parameters: its 'speed' and 'intensity' (Figure 10.2).

The 'speed' of a vibrating body is expressed in terms of its frequency of movement — simply the number of times the body, the weight on the end of a spring for example, completes one cycle of movement (i.e. from its fixed reference point to its highest point, to its lowest point and finally back to its reference point) within a specific time period (usually 1 second). The faster the body vibrates, therefore, the more cycles that occur per second. The normal unit of frequency is the Hertz (Hz), where 1 Hz = 1 cycle per seond.

Vibration intensity is normally expressed in terms of the maximum amount the body moves from the fixed point — usually its distance or amplitude (in cm or in mm). More recently acceleration units have been used to define vibration intensity. These are conventionally expressed in 'g' units (1 g being the amount of acceleration needed to lift a body off the earth's surface); although the convention has been changed slightly in recent years to use the metric units of metres per second^2 (1 g = 9.81 ms^{-2}).

Each of these parameters is related, thus:

$$\text{Acceleration in 'g' units} = \frac{4\pi^2 f^2 a}{981}$$

where f is the vibration frequency and a is the vibration amplitude.

Figure 10.1 The three vibration coordinates for a standing, seated and lying person

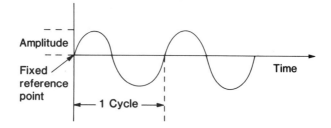

Figure 10.2 The frequency and amplitude of a body vibrating sinusoidally

THE BASES OF VIBRATION EFFECTS

Any simple structure: this book, a table, a door, a building, can be excited at a particular frequency which is known as its natural or resonant frequency. If vibration is applied to the structure at or near this frequency then it will vibrate at a higher intensity than that applied to it. This amplification is known as resonance. (Indeed this effect can also occur if the original vibration input is situated close to, but not actually touching, the structure — this is how sopranos can sometimes shatter glass.) At other frequencies the opposite of resonance can occur, so that the body structure absorbs and so reduces the input intensity. This process is known as damping or attenuation.

The human body is an extremely complex structure which is composed of different organs, bones, joints and muscles. Each of these parts, both individually and together, can be affected in the ways described above. At some frequencies, therefore, they might vibrate at higher intensities than the vibrations applied to them whereas at others they could absorb and attenuate the inputs. Because of resonance, then, body movements can sometimes become difficult for the operator to control whereas, at other frequencies, the vibration energy absorbed by the body during attenuation may be enough to cause structural damage.

The resonance effects of a particular system, for example the hand–arm complex, the head–neck complex, or the whole body itself, can be measured by comparing the vibration intensity of the system both at the point of stimulation and at the point of 'exit' for different frequencies. For example, to consider the resonance characteristics of the whole body, vibration measuring devices (accelerometers) could be placed at the feet (entry) and the top of the head (exit) of a standing person. The resonant frequencies, then, are those at which the 'exit' intensities exceed the 'input' intensities, i.e. when the exit:input intensity ratio is greater than 1. If the 'transmissibility' ratio is less than unity the system is absorbing (damping) the vibration.

A number of investigators have considered the biodynamic response of the whole body and there is general agreement that, for vertical vibration, the body has a whole-body resonance around 5 Hz (for example, Dieckmann, 1958; Guignard and Irving, 1960; Coermann, 1962; Lovesey, 1975). A seated operator, however, may be exposed to different vibration stimuli, particularly if the seat has a backrest which can help to transmit vibration to the operator. This was demonstrated well by Rowlands (1977).

As well as considering whole-body transmissibility Rowlands (1977) also investigated seat–shoulder transmissibility. In this case, two resonant peaks occurred — one at around 5 Hz and another at about 10–12 Hz.

Another important body system is the hand–arm complex: first, most control tasks use this system and second, there is a growing awareness of the possibility of damage to the hand from using high-speed vibrating tools. Until relatively recently, however, little work had been carried out to investigate the dynamic response of this system.

226

Abrahams and Suggs (1969) analysed the vibration characteristics of a cadaver hand and arm by mounting accelerometers on to the bones. Their results showed that as the vibration frequency applied to the hand increased, less vibration was transmitted up the arm. Similar conclusions were reached by Reynolds and Soedel (1972) and by Reynolds and Angevine (1977). Reynolds and Angevine (1977) placed accelerometers at seven points between the fingers and shoulders of five subjects who were asked to grip a vibrating handle. Their results are shown in Figure 10.3 (the graph co-ordinates are arranged logarithmically to cover the ranges measured) from which it is clear that less vibration is transmitted the further up the arm the test site is situated. Indeed vibration frequencies above about 100 to 150 Hz are almost totally absorbed in the hand itself. Reynolds and Soedel (1972) also demonstrated that changes in the position and stiffness of the arm had no significant effect on the vibration reponse of the hand–arm system. Not unexpectedly, however, grip tightness had a significant influence.

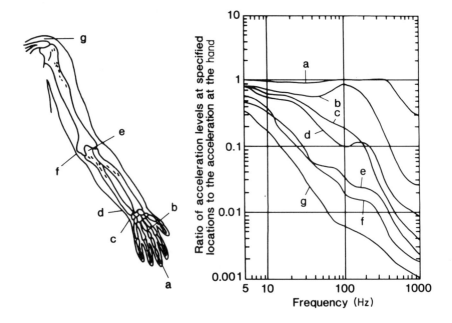

Figure 10.3 Hand–arm transmissibility obtained by Reynolds and Angevine (1977) at different test sites along the arm. (*Reproduced with permission. Copyright: Academic Press Inc. (London) Ltd.*)

Just as the dynamics of the hand–arm–shoulder systems have implications for understanding manual control difficulties under vibration, the behaviour of the eyes in their sockets can affect the operator's visual ability. In this case two aspects need to be considered: first, the movement of the head and eyes together, and second, the resonant characteristics of the eyes themselves.

The eyes are clearly not fixed inside the skull but are able to move by the action of muscles that attach them to the orbit in the skull. This means that the ways in which the eyes move during whole-body vibration are not necessarily the same as the head movements. Indeed, both Lee and King (1971) and Wells and Storey (1980) have demonstrated considerable damping effects in head-eye transmissibility. Although the authors appear to differ slightly in their assessment of the extent to which this damping occurs, both agree that the most damping occurs above 20 Hz.

At higher frequencies the eyeballs themselves are in danger of resonating — irrespective of the head movement. Stott (1980) was able to map the course of these resonance effects for five subjects by measuring the movement of a spot of light shone on to the cornea of the eye. His results demonstrate the start of eyeball resonance after about 30 Hz, with a maximum (vibrating approximately four times as much as the head alone) at 70 Hz.

HEALTH EFFECTS OF VIBRATION

The health effects of vibration lie basically in two areas. First, damage caused to body organs as a result of their being buffeted by high vibration levels at relatively low frequencies. These effects are basically intensity dependent. Second, the breakdown of body tissues due either to continued resonance or to their absorption of high energy vibration. These effects depend primarily on the frequency of stimulation.

Intensity-dependent Effects

For the majority of working environments the potential damage to large body organs or to the musculoskeletal system by high intensity buffeting is unlikely to be a problem. In vehicles which ride over rough terrain, however, the levels of vibration experienced for very short periods may, over time, cause structural damage.

Rosseger and Rosseger (1960) carried out a comprehensive survey of the health complaints of 371 tractor drivers (who frequently have to drive over rough, ploughed terrain) and recorded two forms of damage resulting from long periods of tractor operation: stomach complaints and spinal disorders (particularly in the lumbar and thoracic regions). Both the number and severity of such cases increased proportionately with the length of service as a tractor driver. Traces of blood in the urine have also been found in the drivers of these vehicles which is probably due to kidney damage (although this breakdown could be caused as much by resonating the kidneys as to damage from high intensity vibration *per se*).

The effects of these types of stimulation have been investigated at a descriptive level by Magid *et al.* (1962), who asked ten subjects to describe their feelings about different intense vertical stimuli in the frequency range 1–10 Hz. Many of their subjects reported 'chest pain' at between 4 and 8 Hz stimulation (at about 0.5 g) with all subjects reporting these symptoms at 7 Hz. Some reports of 'abdominal pain' were produced at lower frequencies (3–6 Hz) but the number of reports was fewer than for 'chest pain'. At 10 Hz (1.2 g) skeleto-muscular and abdominal pain was reported.

Frequency-dependent Effects

Injuries which are caused by the frequency aspects of vibration normally occur after prolonged exposure to the vibrating stimulus, and this mainly in the higher frequency ranges. In contemporary working environments the problem arises particularly from the use of powered hand-held machinery such as road drills, stone breakers and chain saws.

Intense vibration from hand-tools can be transmitted to the operator's fingers, hands and arms from the machines themselves and from hand-held objects. When this happens structural damage to the peripheral blood and nervous systems in the fingers can occur which, over time, produce 'intermittent numbness and clumsiness of the fingers, intermittent blanching of either all or part of the extremities, and a temporary loss of muscular control of the exposed parts of the body' (Agate, 1949). Because of the appearance of the affected limbs the condition is often referred to as 'white finger', although since the symptoms are similar to a disease first described by Raynaud in 1862 it is sometimes referred to as 'Raynaud's disease of occupational origin' (Taylor, 1974). In 1970, however, the Industrial Injuries Advisory Council rejected the various names in favour of the descriptive term 'Vibration Induced White Finger' (VWF) and described the complex of symptoms associated with vibrating tools as 'The Vibrating Syndrome'. These additional effects may include any or all of neuritis, damage to bones, joints or muscles (Taylor, 1974). Relief from all or some of these symptoms usually occurs after prolonged rest from exposure to the vibration stimulus, although they are likely to reappear promptly with renewed exposure.

It is difficult to estimate the extent of such damage in industry. Basing their assessment on studies of large groups of different types of workers using vibrating tools over periods of time, however, Guillemin and Wechsberg (1953) report that the incidence of neurovascular damage due to vibration exposure varied between 89.5 and 0.2 per cent in different groups. This wide range is probably due to differences between actual daily exposure times, types of vibration stimuli and materials, and to varying individual susceptibility to the vibration.

PERFORMANCE EFFECTS OF VIBRATION

Because body parts tend to vibrate in sympathy with vibrating machinery either nearby or on which they may rest, the effects of vibration on performance occur mainly in terms of reduced motor control. This might be the control of a limb (causing, for example, reduced hand steadiness) or of the eyeballs (causing fixation difficulties and blurring). Little evidence exists to suggest that vibration can affect central, intellectual processes.

Visual Performance Effects of Vibration

A clear perception of an object will only be perceived if a stable image falls on the retina. A moving figure stimulates different sets of receptors in the retina, producing a signal of overlapping and confused images. This is clearly likely to cause difficulty in detecting much of the object's detail, particularly if the retinal image oscillates with a relatively large amplitude.

Although a fair amount of work has been carried out to investigate visual vibration effects, it is difficult to draw too many conclusions about the types and levels of vibration that affect visual performance. This is because different investigators have used different tasks to measure visual performance (O'Briant and Ohlbaum, 1970). Because these different tasks require subjects to perform different activities it would be difficult to relate them to each other or to any standard performance criteria.

There are three combinations of observer and object vibration that can result in a moving image being perceived. First, if the object alone is vibrated; second when only the observer is vibrated; and third when both the oberserver and the object are vibrated. In this third case the degree of blurring will depend not only on the nature of the vibration experienced but on the phase relationship between the two moving bodies. The effect of these three aspects will be considered separately.

Vibrating the object alone

The effects on vision of vibrating the object alone appear to be due mainly to the vibration frequency and, to some extent, its intensity.

If the object is vibrating slowly enough (below about 1 Hz) the optical system is able to track it and so maintain a stable image on the retina. In doing so, however, the optic muscles need to work hard so muscular fatigue may occur quite quickly. This type of tracking task is known as pursuit eye movements. With frequencies above 1 Hz, however, the system effectiveness decreases considerably until by about 2–4 Hz and above the tracking ability is almost non-existent. Interestingly, studies have also demonstrated that at very low frequencies the tracking performance for unpredictable motions is almost as good as for predictable stimuli. With increasing frequency, however, this ability soon disappears, but at around 2–4 Hz and above (when pursuit eye movements are no longer effective) the system's inability to track unpredictable stimuli appears to be no worse than its inability to track predictable stimuli.

At higher object frequencies, when pursuit eye movements cannot usefully track a vibrating object, any performance reduction will be related directly to the degree of blurring on the retina. The quality of the image, then, will be inversely proportional to the number of extra retinal cells stimulated (i.e. the vibration amplitude), although at the same time it will be proportional to the length of time for which any one cell is stimulated. Since the time taken for an object to move through one cycle is inversely proportional to the frequency, it follows that the performance efficiency will be related to both the frequency and the amplitude of the vibrating image. Indeed O'Hanlon and Griffin (1971) have suggested that at frequencies above about 5 Hz an observer's error rate in perceiving fine detail in a moving object is proportional to the product of the frequency and the square root of the amplitude of the vibrating image. This relation appears to fit data produced by O'Hanlon and Griffin, and Meddick and Griffin (1976) state that the model was later confirmed by Alexander (1972).

In an attempt to map the relationships between vibration frequency and visual performance, Huddleston (1970) measured the proportion of time that subjects were able to maintain a stable image of an object vibrating at one or two different amplitudes. His results, shown in Figure 10.4, illustrate well the observer's problems involved in coping with vibrating material. Thus, for the smaller amplitude, the eye is able to track the moving object quite well at low frequencies. As the frequency is increased this ability is reduced in the manner described earlier. The attempt to track the object continues, although with decreasing efficiency, until at about 5 Hz the subject relinquishes the attempt and stabilizes on the object. At this point, then, the decrement is related more to the degree of image blurring. For the higher amplitude vibration, however, the relinquishing of pursuit tracking occurs at a lower frequency, with the result that the upturn in performance occurs earlier.

Figure 10.4 Tracking performance under vibration, showing how the main frequency effect is modified by an amplitude effect. (*From Huddleston, 1970. Copyright © 1970 by the American Psychological Association. Reprinted with permission.*)

Regarding the effect of the amplitude of the moving object, studies by Drazin (1962) and by Huddleston (1970) demonstrate that at frequencies below about 4 Hz (at which pursuit eye movements are possible), visual performance is reduced with increasing vibration amplitude. At higher frequencies, however, these deficiencies are not sustained. Indeed, Huddleston's data shown in Figure 10.4 suggest that at 5 Hz the higher amplitude was beneficial, and Drazin's results suggest that at 6 and 8 Hz the larger amplitudes produced lower error scores than did the smaller amplitudes. Griffin and Lewis (1978), however, argue that these results should not lead to a general conclusion that reading becomes easier with increased displacement. They suggest that the larger amplitudes were large enough to reduce the amount of confusion in the blurred image; more confusion is likely to result from smaller amplitudes and, when this occurs, the O'Hanlon and Griffin model of $E \propto f\sqrt{a}$ still holds true. No evidence is yet available to support or to refute this hypothesis. It must be remembered, however, that their model was proposed for performance reductions in a visual acuity task (perceiving the gap in a Landolt C). Griffin himself questions (1976a) whether it also holds true for other types of perceptual tasks. Indeed, data from Meddick and Griffin (1976), who used digits of the form recommended in British

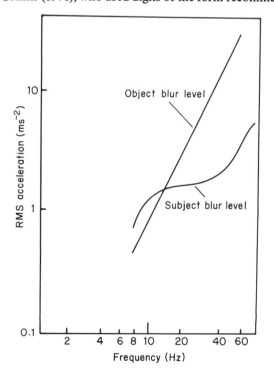

Figure 10.5 The average levels of vertical vibration needed to produce blur, compared with object blur levels. (*Reproduced with permission from Griffin, 1976a. Copyright: Academic Press* Inc. *(London) Ltd.*)

Standards 3693A, suggest that the error rate for this type of material is *not* proportional to $f\sqrt{a}$.

Finally, in an attempt to produce some simplified model of the effects of object vibration — at least above 5 Hz — Griffin (1975) argues that data relating to the threshold of visual blur could be used to predict the minimum levels of object vibration needed to affect visual acuity. This level, he suggests, is equal to a displacement of 1 minute of arc at the eye. However, since this would probably be over-restrictive in all but the most critical conditions, he later suggested (1976a) that displacements of greater than ± 2 minutes of arc may, depending on the task difficulty, start to affect reading ability. Figure 10.5 illustrates this boundary.

Vibrating the observer alone

The same problems appear when the observer is vibrated as when the object is vibrated — namely those concerning the optical system's tracking ability and the degree of blur experienced. These problems, however, are confounded by the dynamic characteristics of the body in which the eyes reside. These may be such as to produce head and eye motions that have different intensities to the input motion and, because the body is a flexible structure, the resultant eye motions may not even occur in the same axis as the input motion. (Indeed, Griffin (1976b) has demonstrated that in seated subjects vertical vibration is likely to cause some angular motions of the eyes.)

Because of these confounding problems, and because so much variability exists between individuals in their whole-body transmissibility, the only reasonable procedure for determining the effects of whole-body vibration on vision is to measure the level of vibration experienced at the head. During their study of seat to shoulder and head transmissibility, Guignard and Irving (1960) also asked subjects to scan blocks of typescript letters 'c' and to count randomly placed letters 'o'. The seated subject received vibration at five frequencies between 2.4 and 9.5 Hz, each at 0.25 g, measured at the seat/subject interface. Using the average time taken to complete the task as their measure of reading performance Guignard and Irving demonstrated very close similarity between the shape of the performance curve as a function of frequency and that of the velocity of the head motion. Unfortunately, only four subjects were tested which, given the levels of individual variability known to exist for these types of reading task (for example, Griffin, 1976b), is likely to limit the value of the results.

Considering the frequency of the vibration alone, the problems which occur when a vibrating observer views a stationary display are similar to those which occur when only the display is vibrated, that is, they operate in two frequency bands. First, low frequencies in which the moving observer's problem is to stabilize the eyes to maintain a stationary image and second, at higher frequencies in which eyeball resonance is involved.

Because the low-frequency task essentially involves stabilizing the eyes on a stationary display (rather than moving the eyes to keep up with a moving display) it is often referred to as compensatory (rather than pursuit) tracking. The difference between the two terms is more than simply semantic. For example, Guignard and Irving suggest that the upper frequency limit for compensatory eye movements is higher than that for pursuit movements.

At frequencies higher than those which allow compensatory tracking, the problem of eyeball resonance must clearly be taken into account. As discussed earlier Stott (1980) demonstrated the beginnings of resonance in the eye–orbit complex at about 30 Hz, with a maximum at 70 Hz.

Regarding the intensity aspects of the vibrating observer, the obvious problem relates to visual blur. In an experiment to map the frequency course of blurring when the observer alone is vibrated, Griffin (1975) vibrated subjects at frequencies between 7 and 75 Hz. At each frequency the subjects were required to adopt postures that resulted in the 'maximum sensation' at the head. They were then asked asked to adjust the vibration level to the minimum at which they observed any definite blurring of points of light. (Because subjects always adjusted down the intensity range, it is likely that this technique will produce 'conservative' estimates of the blur level.) Griffin's average 'minimum blur level' over the frequency range is also illustrated in Figure 10.5, along with the levels of vertical object vibration needed to produce blur. The divergence of these two curves at higher frequencies illustrates, once again, the effect of eye movement relative to head movement. From these curves, however, it is not possible to

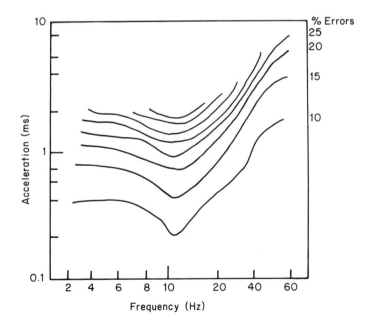

Figure 10.6 Levels of vibration needed to produce equal error rates for a reading task. (*Reproduced with permission from Lewis and Griffin, 1980a. Copyright: Academic Press* Inc. *(London) Ltd.*)

determine by how much the eyeball resonance affects visual performance. Furthermore, any interpretation of them must take account of Griffin's own cautions regarding the high levels of inter- and intra-subject variability which were obtained.

In an attempt to relate vibration levels to performance reductions, Lewis and Griffin (1980a, b) considered the effects of vibration frequency (2.8 to 63 Hz) on a number reading task. In addition, employing a model which assumed a linear relationship between error rate and vibration intensity experienced at the head at each frequency, the authors predicted performance contours outside the range of intensities which they investigated. Their results are shown in Figure 10.6.

With regard to the effect of the task on visual performance, the most obvious factor to consider is object size. Clearly larger objects are easier to see, and this is likely also to be true under vibrating conditions. This was illustrated by Lewis and Griffin (1979b) who used four character heights (1–2mm) while seated subjects were exposed to different vibration stimuli. Their results demonstrate significant increases in percentage reading errors with both increased vibration intensity and reduced character size.

Vibrating the object and the observer together

Although the previous two conditions have illustrated the many problems of viewing an object in a dynamic environment, they are quite simple compared with that in which both the observer and the object are vibrating. Unfortunately this is a common situation in real-life environments whenever the observer and objects are both attached to or are inside a piece of vibrating machinery, such as a vehicle passenger or driver.

When both the observer and the object are being vibrated, a number of conditions may occur — each of which is likely to affect the resultant visual performance in an individual manner. For example, the two may be vibrating at different frequencies or intensities, they may be moving in phase or out of phase, and they could even be moving in different axes. Because of these problems, very few well-controlled studies have been carried out to investigate combined object and subject vibration effects.

A specific situation which has been investigated, however, is when the display is in some way attached to an observer's head — usually in a helmet. These helmet-mounted displays allow information to be presented continuously to an operator such as a pilot — regardless of the head position.

Barnes, Benson and Prior (1978) investigated this form of the observer–object relationship for angular motion of the head (using both the 'yaw' and 'pitch' motions). Their results demonstrated a marked decrease in the ability to read the displayed digits with frequencies above about 1 Hz, with faster reductions for the smaller digit size. Some performance differences were apparent between axes, however: the overall number of digits read correctly was lower, and the reduction in reading efficiency higher, in pitch than in yaw.

A similar type of experiment was reported by Furness and Lewis (1978) although their subjects were vibrated in the vertical axis only (1.4 to 45 Hz). As with the Lewis and Griffin (1980a, b) studies, from the performance measures Furness and Lewis produced equal performance decrement contours over the frequency range studied.

In summary, the effects of vibration on visual performance are extremely complex. They depend on whether the observer or the object is vibrating, on the vibration frequency and intensity, and on the object size (and thus the distance from the observer). In general it would appear that the extent of performance reductions is determined largely by the vibration frequency. At low frequencies it is a function of the optical system's ability to track an object to maintain a stable retinal image. At higher frequencies it is a function simply of the degree of blur. The cut-off frequency of these two bands, however, is determined by whether it is the observer or the object which is being vibrated.

Motor Performance Effects of Vibration

Two types of tracking task are normally used by experimenters to investigate the effects of vibration on motor performance: pursuit and compensatory tracking.

In pursuit tracking the operator's function is to move the controls so that the object (usually a spot on an oscilloscope) follows a predetermined course (possibly following another moving spot). A 'real-life' example, in this case, could be a car driver's task of turning a steering wheel to keep the car on a winding road. The operator corrects errors by comparing the movement of the 'spot' (the car) with that of a standard (the road).

In the compensatory tracking task the operator 'sees' only errors. The task is to maintain an otherwise moving 'spot' in a particular position — to use the controls to compensate for the machine's movement. The spot only moves when the task is not performed correctly. The car driver's attempt to maintain a steady speed (i.e. to keep the speedometer needle in a particular place) is an example of such a task. Variations in the vehicle dynamics, the road incline, the weather or other environmental conditions may all act to influence the car speed and so make the driver have to compensate by using the accelerator and other pedals.

As Poulton (1974) argues, compensatory tracking is more difficult than pursuit tracking. An operator tracking in a compensatory manner cannot see what is being done nor predict what is meant to be done; the operator can only compensate when an error has occurred. Tracking in a pursuit manner, however, the operator can see both the movements produced by the track program and the results of control movements.

Although the two forms of tracking task differ in their difficulty, it would appear that they are not differentially affected by vibration. Thus Lewis (1980) asked subjects to perform, separately, both types of tracking task while being subjected to different vibration stimuli. His results suggest that irrespective of the measures used to record the subject's performance, and although different frequency stimuli affected the performance to different degrees, the performance curves for the two types of task were very similar in shape.

Whatever measure of motor performance is used, there appears to be general agreement that at low frequencies (less than about 15 Hz) performance reductions are related to the amount of vibration experienced at the controlling limb. In this case, therefore, the important variable to be considered is again the individual's seat or foot to arm (shoulder) transmissability. Thus Levison (1976) demonstrated that performance reductions in a vertical tracking task were linearly correlated with shoulder acceleration in the range 2–10 Hz. Furthermore, Buckhout (1964) showed tracking error to follow very closely a linear relationship with the intensity of vertical vibration measured at the sternum (at 6, 8 and 10 Hz).

Regarding the intensity domain, the results from a number of studies are extremely consistent and suggest that tracking performance decreases as the vibration intensity transmitted to the limb increases (for example, Catterson, Hoover and Asche, 1962; Lewis and Griffin, 1979b).

The lowest level of vibration required to affect performance appears to be very variable. Reviewing the field, for example, Lewis and Grififn (1978) point out that the levels of vibration at which some experimenters had failed to obtain an effect were higher than those at which other experimenters had obtained significant reductions in performance. They conclude, therefore, that

It seems reasonable to draw the general conclusion that increases in vibration level, above some threshold effect, will result in progressive degradation of performance. However, because of the great number of task variables which may affect the performance of specific systems during vibration ... it is not reasonable to expect to be able to discover an absolute threshold of effect, above which performance is affected by vibration and below which it is not.

Finally, Fraser, Hoover and Asche (1961) investigated the combined effects of vibration frequency and intensity on a tracking task. On the basis of their results they argued that the subjects' average tracking error (the number of subjects used was not reported) was proportional to the product of the vibration amplitude and the square root of the frequency (over the frequency range 2–12 Hz) (i.e. error prop $a\sqrt{f}$). This is interesting, particularly when the expression is compared with that reported earlier by O'Hanlon and Griffin in terms of visual acuity errors (error prop $f\sqrt{a}$). The two expressions clearly imply that visual performance degradation is mainly a function of the vibration frequency, whereas manual performance degradation is primarily intensity dependent.

With regard to the direction of the motion being applied to the operator, all of the studies conducted so far agree that the primary detrimental effect occurs in the axis in which the operator is being vibrated. For example, Fraser, Hoover and Asche (1961) demonstrated that horizontal tracking performance was affected more by y-axis vibration than by z-axis vibration of the same intensity. Vertical tracking was affected more by z-axis vibration than by y-axis vibration. Front–back (x)-axis vibration had no effect on either horizontal or vertical tracking. Similar conclusions were reached by Shoenberger (1970) who argues, not unreasonably, that the results suggest the primary mechanism responsible for decrements on tasks of this nature to be the interference with perceptual processes and hand control caused by the short duration whole-body vibration.

The studies by Fraser, Hoover and Asche and by Shoenberger were carried out using separate axes in different trials. Lovesey (1974), however, describes an experiment to investigate the effects of combined y and z axis vibration on a compensatory tracking task. He presented subjects with 2, 5 and 7 Hz vibration stimuli at 0.2g in the z-axis and 0.1g in the y-axis. These frequencies and levels were also combined at $2z+5y$, $2z+7y$, $5z+7y$, $7z+2y$ and $7z+5y$. His results are interesting since, in addition to illustrating decrements in tracking performance with all single-axis vibrations, when the axes were combined tracking performance tended to be degraded by an amount equal to the product of the tracking decrements produced by each single axis alone, i.e.

$$\text{combined error} = z\,\text{error} \times y\,\text{error}$$

Lovesey does add that this equation only holds true for cases when the task was difficult enough to be affected adversely by the single-axis vibrations. It does not hold if either the z or y error was zero or if the vibration actually helped to improve performance. (More will be said later regarding the possibility of performance increases under vibrating conditions.)

In addition to the vibration itself as a variable that could affect performance, the task to be performed by the operator must also be considered. In this respect its duration and the physical equipment provided could play important roles.

The variable of exposure duration (or 'time dependency') is one which is presently receiving much debate since it forms an important part in the levels set by the International Standards Organization (1974) for exposure to whole body vibration. Unfortunately, as will be discussed later, there is little evidence to support the contention that performance decreases the longer that the individual is exposed to the vibration stimulus (for example, Lewis and Griffin, 1979a, b; Guignard, Landrum and Reardon, 1976; Maslen, 1972; Hornick, 1962; Hornick and Lefritz, 1966). This is best exemplified by a very long-duration study carried out by Gray et al. (1976). They exposed their subjects for three hours to 5 Hz vertical vibration at 0.12g but, although tracking performance was worse under the vibration compared with the static conditions, the authors were unable to demonstrate any reduction in performance over the three hour period. Indeed, if anything, a slight improvement was observed.

Regarding the quality of the equipment provided for the operator, an obvious variable to consider is the type and degree of body restraint afforded during the task. Without such support the vibration will be likely to destabilize the body and make the manual control task more difficult. In this respect two restraint systems can be considered — harnesses and armrests.

Although at first it would appear sensible to argue that a restraining harness is likely to increase stability and thus improve performance, the effects of the harness on the amount of vibration transmitted through the body must be considered. Thus, as was noted earlier, Rowlands (1977) demonstrated significant increases in vibration transmitted to the shoulder when the back was against the backrest. Given the very strong relationship between the amount of vibration reaching the shoulder and performance decrement then, it could well be hypothesized that a restraining harness would have a detrimental effect on motor control. This was illustrated by Lovesey (1971) for tracking in both the y and z axes.

As far as armrests are concerned, Torle (1965) tested three subjects on a tracking task using a 'small', a 'large' or no armrest (unfortunately dimensions were not provided). His results demonstrated some improvement in tracking ability using the armrest although he observed no difference betweeen the types of armrest used. The armrest improvement increased with increasing vibration intensity. Whether the improvement was due to increased overall body stability created by the armrests, or simply to forearm or elbow stability is not, unfortunately, able to be deduced from the experimental report.

In summary, therefore, whole body vibration clearly degrades motor control, particularly when the task demands movement in the same plane as the vibration. Furthermore, the degree of degradation is primarily intensity dependent and is thus a strong function of the manner in which vibration is transmitted through the body.

THE EFFECTS OF VIBRATION ON REACTION TIME AND INFORMATION PROCESSING

For a number of years, particularly in the late 1950s and 1960s during the 'space race' era, a number of studies were carried out to investigate whether vibration affects operator response (reaction) times.

Fast reactions demand both central and peripheral abilities: a stimulus (for example a light) is perceived; the information is transmitted to the brain where a decision is made; and a motor action (for example pressing a button) is taken. Despite the fact that this type of task places minimal demands on the sensory and motor functions, they could be affected by vibration.

Much of the research in this area has demonstrated that reaction time is relatively unaffected by vibration (for example, Weisz, Goddard and Allen, 1967; Holland, 1965). For example, Hornick (1962) asked subjects to press a foot-pedal each time a particular sequence of coloured lights appeared under various vibration conditions. Under no condition was reaction time increased although, interestingly, he reported an increase during a post-vibration test in the y and z axes. In the light of information on similar responses after the cessation of other stressors (for example, Wohlwill et al., 1976), it could be argued that the vibration is acting in this case as a general stressor which causes the operator to have to work harder to maintain the same level of performance. When the stressor ends a 'let down' effect occurs which shows itself as reduced performance.

Despite experiments that show no effect of vibration, Shoenberger (1970) did demonstrate significant performance reductions using vibration, separately, in the x, y and z axes. The main effect was in the y (side-side) axis with highly significant decrements occurring at 1 Hz and 3 Hz. Very little reduction in reaction time occurred at either 11 Hz in the y-axis or in the other two axes at any frequency. It may be suggested, however, that Shoenberger's results simply reflect his apparatus arrangements: the stimulus lights and response buttons were arranged horizontally (i.e. along the y-axis) and so interference in the motor component of the reaction time task could have caused the increased reaction time.

An interesting validation of the hypothesis of peripheral, rather than central, interference, was produced by Shoenberger (1974). He used a memory reaction time task in which subjects were required first to memorize letters and then to react (verbally) to their presence or absence within a matrix on a screen. The motor component of the reaction time task, therefore, was reduced to one simply of controlling the diaphragm for speech. Using an analysis technique developed by Sternberg (1966) Shoenberger demonstrated that although the peripheral components of this task (perceiving the test letter and verbalizing the response) were susceptible to vibration, the central processing aspects (deciding to react) were relatively immune.

In terms of intellectual (cognitive) tasks, Shoenberger's conclusion of no vibration effects has been supported by some experimenters but not by others. For example, Schohan, Rawson and Soliday (1965) showed no appreciable effects of vibration on a navigation task, while Simons and Schmitz (1958) found no effects on mental arithmetic using 2.5 Hz and 3.5 Hz vibrations at up to 0.31 g. On the other hand Huddleston (1964), using a 'rolling arithmetic' task (which combined mental addition and recent memory), demonstrated that performance was significantly slower at 4.8, 6.7, 9.5 and 16 Hz at 0.5 g than during the static control condition. The wide frequency range demonstrates that the performance reductions were not frequency dependent, as are both visual and motor control decrements. In a subsequent experiment Huddleston (1965) used the same intensity at 4.8 and 6.7 Hz and confirmed these results.

The results of the effects of vibration on cognitive tasks, therefore, appear to be inconclusive. However, it must be remembered that with such tasks a number of possible variables can interfere to cause unpredictable results unless they are controlled. As will be discussed in more detail later in this chapter, an individual's level of arousal, for example, is known to have effects (both facilitative and detrimental) on subsequent performance. In this vein Poulton (1978) argues that vibration at 5 Hz can act as an alerting mechanism to increase performance. Furthermore, the arousal level is known to be related to the time of day as a result of the human body's cyclical (circadian) activities. Thus Sommer and Harris (1970) have demonstrated time of day effects on the relationship between a combined vibration and noise stressor and mental performance. Subjects were tested on a mental subtraction task at either 6 a.m. or 3 p.m. while exposed to either a 5 Hz, 0.25 g vibration and 110 dB noise stressor or to no stress. Whereas the stress condition produced poorer performance at 3 p.m., no difference in performance was observed at 6. a.m. Thus, the otherwise significant reduction in performance at 6 a.m. under the 'no stress' condition further supports the hypothesis that the degree of 'arousal' or 'alertness' plays a significant role in whether or not the stressor will affect performance.

COMFORT EFFECTS OF VIBRATION

The concept of comfort has already been discussed but two points should be re-emphasized: first, comfort is extremely difficult to define, and second, discomfort may both affect and be affected by performance decrements. These effects can be considered at two levels: firstly at a qualitative level, to ask how people feel vibration affects them; secondly at a quantitative level to relate vibration levels to comfort reduction.

Qualitative Effects of Vibration on Comfort

Oborne (1975) reports a series of questionnaire surveys carried out on fare-paying passengers using a number of different vehicles (trains, hovercraft, helicopters). His results suggest that vibration can affect comfort in one or more of three major ways. First, in the manner discussed earlier, it affects passengers' abilities to perform motor tasks. Large numbers of passengers complained that they were unable to read, write or eat under the conditions in which they were travelling. Since the majority of passengers are not merely passive beings while being transported from one place to another, and since many passengers use different activities to pass the journey time away, he argues that the reported

Figure 10.7   Levels of vehicle vibration and motion needed to produce varying levels of passenger comfort. (From Oborne, 1977.)

degradation in performance due to vibration and motion clearly has important implications.

The second effect of vibration on comfort is a positive one and relates to the information that the stimulus carries to the passenger. For example, one passenger travelling by helicopter reported that he found the vibration reassuring — it would certainly have affected his comfort had the machine suddenly stopped vibrating while in mid-air! Car drivers use the information from the noise and vibration of the car engine to know when to change gear or whether something is wrong. In such cases, then, it is the *implications* of the stimulus which is the important feature.

Third, and under conditions of extreme vibration, physiological effects were described. In such circumstances, reports of motion sickness and headaches predominated, although it is debatable whether the headaches arose from the buffeting action of the vibration or the noise caused by the vibrating structures. More will be mentioned about the problems of motion sickness later.

Quantitative Effects of Vibration on Comfort

Because of the many variables that impinge on passengers travelling in a vehicle, 'field' investigations of the quantitative relationship between vibration level and comfort are extremely difficult. For this reason most of the work in this area has been performed under more controlled, laboratory conditions, often using paid subjects. Much of this work has been criticized by Oborne (1976) on experimental grounds although, as will be seen later, many of their conclusions have appeared in the International Standard (International Organization for Standardization, ISO 2631, 1974) which is presently accepted for this area. Only one study (Oborne, 1977) has used actual fare-paying passengers and this was carried out on a hovercraft service between England and France; each journey took approximately 35 minutes. By comparing measured vibration levels with passengers' comfort ratings the function illustrated in Figure 10.7 was able to be derived (the figure illustrates vibration levels in two frequency bands shown to predominate in the vehicle).

The curves shown in Figure 10.7, then, illustrate how rated vehicle comfort varies with either the intensity of the vehicle vibration (8–16 Hz band — due to the engines) or the motion (0–4 Hz band — due to the vehicle motion over the water). Although the two curves have similar shapes they show that, at lower intensity levels, the higher frequency vibration is more important to comfort than is the lower frequency motion. As intensity levels increase, however, the importance of the motion increases until, after about 1.4 m^{-2}, it becomes more important to comfort than does the vibration. This was presumably because at the higher *motion* levels the motion was more likely to cause motion sickness and to affect the passengers' abilities to read, write or drink. Figure 10.7 also shows, of course, that this cross-over point is also related to the change from 'comfortable' to 'uncomfortable' experiences.

Motion Sickness

Motion sickness is one aspect of vibration which certainly causes discomfort and performance loss. This distressing effect is experienced by a large proportion of travellers and is caused by the low frequency (about 0.3–$0.5\,$Hz), high amplitude motion conditions prevailing in rough seas or air turbulence. The most commonly reported symptom is nausea, often leading to vomiting. For many the act of vomiting leads to a rapid recovery of well-being but in some the nausea exists even after vomiting — resulting in further bouts of vomiting and retching, and a continued decline in well-being. Nevertheless it is possible to become adapted to the stimulus. Prolonged exposure to the sickness-inducing motion is likely to lead to a diminution and eventual disappearance of the signs and symptoms in most people. This 'protective adaptation' can be affected by the type of activity in which the person engages, the abruptness with which the stimulus is presented (gradual presentation leads to better adaption), the victim's level of arousal, and the extent of the person's visual activity (Reason and Brand, 1975).

The part of the body which triggers the sensation of motion sickness very clearly lies in the vestibular system in the ear, since an intact aural system is needed before the symptoms can occur. However, Reason has suggested that its cause also lies in the fact that, in a moving environment, discrepant information is received by the brain from either the eyes and the vestibular apparatus (visual-inertial conflict) on the one hand, or from the semicircular-canals sensing rotational motion and the otoliths sensing vertical motion (canal–otolith conflict) on the other. Reason's suggestion, then, is that the sensations received from the body's position sensors are at variance not only with one another but also — and this is the crucial factor — with what is expected on the basis of previous dealings with environment (past experience). Reason (1978) makes various practical suggestions to alleviate such conflicts, all of which attempt to reduce the discrepancies of the incoming information. These include adopting a supine position, fixating on an otherwise stable object such as the horizon, closing the eyes, and wearing spectacles with thick, heavy frames.

Despite the plausible suggestion that motion sickness arises as a result of a sensory information mismatch it is difficult to understand why this should cause the body to try to expel the contents of the stomach rather than to take other, more useful, actions to avoid the mismatch. Money and Cheung (1983), however, have noted that the normal emetic reponse to certain poisons was impaired in dogs who had had their vestibular apparatus surgically removed. This led them to conclude that the inner ear is part of the normal mechanism for vomiting and this action could be stimulated by excessive motion. Because of the sensory mismatch that occurs, they argue that

> in a motion sickness situation the brain says, in effect 'This unusual requirement for callibration is such that my vestibular system must be sending me false information; therefore I have probably been poisoned by something that I ate, and I should vomit.

Whatever the behavioural cause of motion sickness, the fact that it is physiologically based means that it might be able to alleviated using the correct drugs. However, before an appropriate drug can be prescribed the true site of the cause of motion sickness needs to be determined. In this respect, controversy has raged for a number of years over whether the site of the important vestibular symptoms lie in the otoliths (the vertical motion receptors) or in the semicircular canals (which sense angular acceleration). A great deal of this controversy has been caused by the difficulty of delivering a stimulus to one part of the vestibular system (for example, the semicircular canals by rotation) without also stimulating the other part (for example, the otoliths by centrifugal force). Recent evidence using high amplitude lifts, however, tends to suggest that the otoliths represent the prime motion sickness centers. With information of this nature Reason (1978) suggests a number of drugs that can be used to combat the sickness symptoms, each having different qualities.

A VIBRATION STANDARD

Since 1964 attempts have been made to combine all of the information relating vibration to health, performance and comfort to compose an accepted standard for human exposure to whole-body vibration. Such a standard was finally produced in 1974 — ISO 2631 — *Guide for the Evaluation of Human Exposure to Whole Body Vibration.* The Committee which steered the standard through its various stages (Working Group No. 7 of the ISO Technical Committee 108 — i.e. ISO/TC 108/WG7) was initially composed of representatives from the USA, Germany, the Netherlands and Sweden, although representatives from other countries including Czechoslovakia, Japan and the UK joined later (Cowley, 1976).

The Guide deals with vibration in all three axes, but treats the two lateral axes (x, y) as being the same. It only considers vibrations in the strict range 1–80 Hz, thereby purposefully not including the problems of motion sickness (another standard is presently being drafted to account for frequencies lower than 1 Hz).

The Guide also lays down limits of exposure to both vertical and lateral vibration under three criteria: the preservation of health (exposure limit, EL), working efficiency (fatigue-decreased proficiency boundary, FDP) and comfort (reduced comfort boundary, RCB). As an innovation the levels for each criterion are defined in terms of the maximum time for which an operator should be exposed to the vibration (time dependency). These levels range from one minute to eight hours (i.e. a 'working day'). For any exposure time, $EL = 2 \times FDP$ and $RCB = FDP/3.15$. Figure 10.8 illustrates the levels ((FDP) produced for exposure to vertical and lateral vibration for 1–4 minutes and for one and eight hours. It should be noted that the *shape* of the response curve for either vertical or lateral vibration is assumed to be the same at whatever intensity (i.e. time dependency) level is being considered.

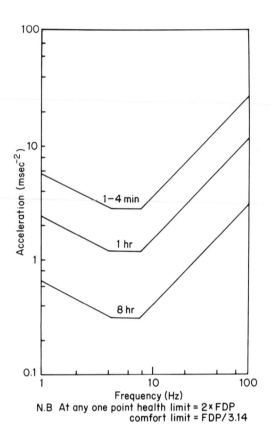

N.B At any one point health limit = 2×FDP
comfort limit = FDP/3.14

Figure 10.8 ISO fatigue decreased proficiency
boundaries for vertical vibration.

Despite its acceptance by so many countries, and despite its incorporation into electronic machines which are used to measure 'human response to vibration', the experimental evidence upon which the Committee based the Guide is sadly lacking both in quality and quantity. Thus Oborne (1976) has criticized many of the studies which are referred to in the Guide's reference list, primarily from the viewpoint of a lack of experimental design and/or reporting. Furthermore, Oborne (1983) has critically evaluated the Guide's empirical bases. He has demonstrated that many of the Guide's recommendations, including the shape of the weighting curves shown in Figure 10.8, the suggestion that response to vibration shape remains stable over the intensity range, the concept of time dependency, the response criteria, are not supported by empirical data.

The major innovation of the standard is to relate vibration to exposure time. Thus an operator who is likely to be working in an environment for eight hours in which, for example, 20 Hz vibration predominates, should only receive an average of 0.8 ms^{-2} vibration before performance deteriorates. The same person experiencing the same frequency vibration, however, but for a short, 16-minute period would be able to accept about 6.5 ms^{-2}.

Unfortunately, however, like the rest of the standard, the experimental evidence for this time dependency is sadly lacking. Indeed, Allen (1975) points to recent evidence that indicates that for casual exposures, any performance decrement which is due to vibration does not get worse with time — at least for exposures up to three hours (for example, Gray et al., 1976).

How much trust can be laid on many aspects of the Guide, therefore, is open to debate. As a guide the ISO document provides a useful starting point from which designers may begin to decide appropriate vibration levels, but these decisions will be more valid if its restrictions are understood. Thus the document refers, primarily, to whole-body vibration applied to seated or standing man. It provisionally applies to recumbent or reclining man but not to local (for example, hand–arm) vibration. Further, it covers only people in 'normal health', and most of the evidence for the limits appears to be based on averaged laboratory data obtained from fit young men. (Jones and Saunders (1972), for example, have demonstrated some significant differences between men and women's reactions to higher frequency (greater than 30 Hz) vibration stimuli.) Finally, and this restriction applies to all composite curves, different individuals react differently to vibration and curves such as the ISO standards which depict average reactions may mask these differences (see, for example, Oborne and Humphreys, 1976).

Despite such negative conclusions, however, Oborne (1983) does suggest that the Committee can claim a major success in having stimulated discussion and research in an area that has been poorly investigated prior to their work. Indeed, it might be postulated that the encouraging increase in controlled experimentation in this area, alluded to at the beginning of this chapter, arose largely because of the stimulation provided by ISO/TC 108/WG7. Furthermore, he points out that some revision of the standard is currently taking place although, given the slowness of committee decisions — particularly involving a number of different countries — it is likely that it will be a few years before the revised standards will emerge. In the meantime, however, the present standard is in operation as is being used to assess how the complex physical and behavioural structures known as humans are likely to respond to mechanical vibration.

NOISE

Noise is an aspect of the working environment which has received much attention for many decades. Indeed, audiometric surveys were being carried out before the effects of vibration on people began even to be considered. This is probably because the sites of the body which receive the noise stimuli (the ears) are obvious and are able to be stimulated directly, and the equipment used to produce acoustic stimuli is fairly easy to obtain.

Definitions

Noise is conveniently and frequently defined as 'unwanted sound', a definition which in its looseness enables a sound source to be considered as 'noise' or 'not noise' solely on the basis of the listener's reaction to it. Unlike the concept of noise in electronics, for example, no specific characteristic of the noise source (frequency, groups of frequencies or intensity) is involved. Acoustic noise is simply sound which is unwanted by the listener — presumably because it is unpleasant or bothersome, it interferes with the perception of wanted sound, or it is physiologically harmful. Furthermore, this definition implies that sounds which are labelled as being 'noise' by an individual on one occasion may not be so labelled on other occasions or in a different environment.

Because sound is vibration which is normally experienced through the air, the parameters of a single tone are the same as those of a single vibration stimulus — frequency and intensity.

In terms of the frequency, for the human listener sound is defined as acoustic energy between 2 and 20 000 Hz (20 KHz) (Kryter, 1970) which are the typical frequency limits of the ear. The ear is still able to separate the wave changes of the air below about 16 Hz but the sensations are perceived as 'beats'. Above about 16 Hz the beats begin to fuse and produce a tone-like quality.

Noise below about 16 Hz is normally described as infrasound. This is a stimulus which is gradually receiving more attention and can be produced by any pulsating or throbbing piece of equipment. Leventhall and Kyriakides (1976), for example, have measured significant levels of infrasound in transport, close to blast-furnaces and diesel engines in industry, and from ventilation systems in offices.

The effects of the levels of infrasound encountered in normal working conditions are not clear. At high intensities such as those produced near rockets and extremely large jet engines, detrimental performance effects have certainly been described. However, the infrasound levels measured in industry and transport, for example, do not reach these high intensities and the evidence of reduced performance caused by levels of infrasound less than about 120dB is very weak. This has led authors such as Harris, Sommer and Johnson (1976) to conclude

> Regardless of whether performance, nystagmus (loss of balance), or subjective measures are considered, it seems certain that the adverse effects of infrasound reported at low-intensity levels either do not exist or have been exaggerated.

Whereas the basic intensity measure of a vibration stimulus is its acceleration, the intensity of a pure tone is defined in terms of pressure changes associated with the compression and refraction in the air caused by the sound source. Sound intensity, therefore, is defined in terms of sound pressure level (SPL) and is measured in the logarithmic units of decibels (dB).

Because the decibel scale is logarithmic in nature a simple, linear relationship with sound intensity does not exist. Thus 100dB is not twice as intense as 50dB.

Being logarithmic a tenfold increase in power (intensity) occurs with each 10 dB increase. So 50 dB represents a 100 000 times intensity increase (10^5) and 100 dB represents 10 000 000 000 (10^{10}) increase (thus 100 dB is 100 000 times as intense as 50 dB). The starting point of the logarithmic scale (0 dB) is arbitrarily set to be at a sound pressure level of 0.0002 dynes/sq cm — the 'average hearing threshold' of the population at 1000 Hz. For this reason a negative decibel value indicates an extremely quiet sound with a SPL of less than 0.0002 dynes/sq cm. Examples of different sound sourcs on a decibel scale are shown in Table 10.1.

Table 10.1 Some commonly encountered noise levels

Sound 'power' increase	Noise level in dB A	
100 000 000 000 000	— 140	
		'Threshold' of pain
10 000 000 000 000	— 130	
		Pneumatic chipper
100 000 000 000	— 120	Loud automobile horn (from 1 m)
100 000 000 000	— 110	
10 000 000 000	— 100	
		Inside subway train
1000 000 000	— 90	
100 000 000	— 80	
		Average traffic on street corner
10 000 000	— 70	
		Conversational speech
1000 000	— 60	
		Typical business office
100 000	— 50	
		Living-room
10 000	— 40	
		Library
1000	— 30	
		Bedroom at night
100	— 20	
		Broadcasting studio
10	— 10	
1	— 0	Threshold of hearing

Just as the ear converts acoustic energy into nerve impulses to be decoded and 'measured' by the auditory cortex, electrical sound measuring machines (sound level meters) also convert the sound received from the microphone into electrical energy which is then measured. The ear, however, is more sensitive to some frequencies than to others whereas, unless modified, the microphone and amplifier would treat all frequencies in the same way. For this reason weighting networks are often included in sound level meters to make them operate in the same way as human ears. The three internationally recognized scales are the A, B and C scales.

As can be seen from Figure 10.9, the A scale tends to attenuate the lower frequencies more than do the B and C scales respectively. These weightings have been produced after measuring the response of the human ear under (A) normal (40 dB), (B) moderate (70 dB) and (C) intense noise conditions and thus would be used in these types of conditions. Because they affect any readings which are made, the scale used should always be quoted in any noise level report, the normal convention being to describe the sound pressure level in either dB (A), dB (B) or dB (C) terms.

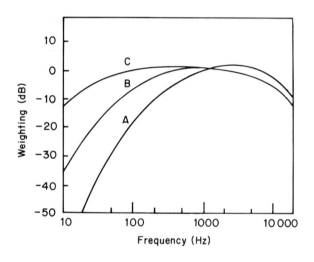

Figure 10.9   The A, B and C noise weightings

HEALTH EFFECTS OF NOISE

Noise can affect health in one or both of two ways: perhaps the most obvious being deafness from long-term exposure, but some types of noise have also been shown to affect personal and mental health.

Noise-induced Hearing Loss

A reduced ability to hear can have two causes. The first, conduction deafness, results from the airborne vibration being unable to make the eardrum vibrate adequately. It might be caused by such factors as wax in the ear canal, infection or a scarred eardrum. Although conduction deafness does not occur as a result of a noisy environment, it still has consequences for the individual's social life and safety.

The second type of deafness, nerve deafness, is caused by reduced sensitivity of the nerve cells in the inner ear. This is likely to result in the operator's hearing loss occurring at or near the frequency range of the environmental noise experienced. Dixon-Ward (1984) points out that temporary changes in the chochlear structure and in the chemical composition of the fluids in the inner ear are produced by even very moderate noises. As the severity of exposure increases such changes also increase, eventually being irreversible. Lim and Dunn (1979) have reviewed many of these physiological effects.

Kryter (1970) has suggested that noise-induced deafness is a significant health problem in most modern countries. It is an insidious complaint since an operator whose hearing is being damaged is unlikely to demonstrate reduced performance due to the deafness. Without continuous, objective audiometric testing the gradual hearing loss which may be caused by noise will not become apparent.

As will be discussed in more detail later, it is difficult to establish firm links between hearing loss and exposure to specific noises. This is because other environmental and natural sources can also lead to reduced hearing ability. For example, hearing loss can result from the combined effects of the normal noises and sounds that we encounter every day — loud vehicles, music, applause, etc. Hearing loss that occurs from these types of source is generally termed *sociacusis*. Such exposures, of course, vary from individual to individual. Secondly, infections, and drugs used to control them, can lead to hearing impairment, as can injuries such as a blow to the head. The net effect of these non-acoustic environmental factors on auditory sensitivity is called *nosoacusis*.

Finally, hearing loss can also occur as a result of the normal process of ageing: with changes occurring in the structure of the auditory apparatus (deposition of substances such as cholesterol, changes in the elasticity of parts of the inner ear, etc.). These have the effect of causing the normal threshold of noise detectability to decline more rapidly at higher frequencies. This ageing factor is termed *presbyacusis* and, because it does not occur consistently in all individuals, it also complicates the task of determining the extent to which long-term noise exposure contributes to deafness overall.

Noise-induced deafness can be temporary (up to 16 hours) or permanent, and these effects are commonly described as Temporary Threshold Shift (TTS) or Permanent Threshold Shift (PTS) respectively. Although TTS is not damaging to health, Kryter (1970) considers that the two types of deafness have so many factors in common that it is likely that the continued experience of TTS will lead eventually to PTS. Perhaps the most important of these similarities is that the same areas of the ear are affected in workers suffering from both TTS and PTS.

Variables which Affect Susceptibility to Hearing Loss

Exposure duration

Since becoming progressively deaf is a relatively long-term process, an operator who is continually exposed to a noise stimulus will also become older, and this

250

brings all of age's attendant problems of presbyacusis. Any assessment of the affects of long-term noise exposure, therefore, will be complicated by a need to account for the normal ageing effects.

As was discussed earlier, presbyacusis is symptomatized by a more rapid decline in the hearing threshold at high frequencies than at low. In addition it appears to occur more severely for men than for women. The variations in hearing threshold at different ages are illustrated in Figure 10.10 (from Spoor, 1967).

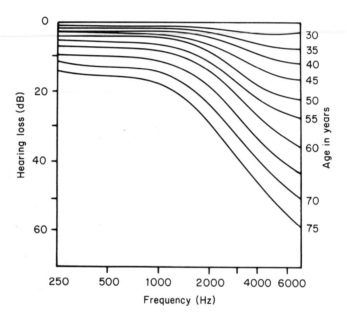

Figure 10.10   The amount of hearing loss due to presbyacusis with increasing age (male subjects). (*From Spoor, 1967, reproduced by permission of the International Society of Audiology.*)

Nixon and Glorig (1961) have considered in detail the relationship between presbyacusis and hearing loss. They were able to demonstrate that a significant increase in hearing loss with exposure was produced only in an industry in which the noise level exceeded 94dB(A). Furthermore, only workers with more than six years exposure to the noise in this industry had significant hearing losses at 2KHz. Other authors have also demonstrated similar effects in other industries (for example, Baughn, 1966).

Exposure intensity

In addition to duration, the noise intensity is an obvious variable to affect the extent to which an operator may become deaf (PTS). As Nixon and Glorig's results show, for example, workers in the industry which had an average noise level greater than 94dB(A) were liable to PTS whereas the incidence of hearing loss was less in the other industries with lower noise levels.

Figure 10.11 illustrates a relationship between sound level and hearing loss described by Dixon-Ward (1984) for different test tones (using an 8hour/day, 200 days/year criterion). This figure suggests that damage is likely to occur in exposure above 80dB(A), although losses for lower frequency tones occur only at higher intensities.

Figure 10.11 Estimated industrial noise-induced permanent threshold shift at 4kHz produced by ten years or more of exposure to noise. (After Dixon-Ward, 1984.)

Because high noise levels can damage hearing permanently, and lower levels can temporarily interfere with hearing, most modern industrialized countries have produced legally enforceable maximum noise levels for workers. Such levels are often derived from 'Damage Risk Contours' and Figure 10.12 illustrates one such set of contours produced by Kryter *et al.* (1966). Like the ISO standard for exposure to whole body vibration, the damage risk contours also relate exposure risk to exposure duration.

Type of noise

In addition to being defined in terms of the total length of time for which the operator is exposed to the noise, the duration of exposure can also be considered in terms of the intermittency of the stimulation, that is whether the noise is continuous or the continuity is broken either by bursts of louder noise or periods of quiet.

Although most of the investigations of hearing loss have been carried out using continuous noise, the effects of intermittent noise on hearing are gradually

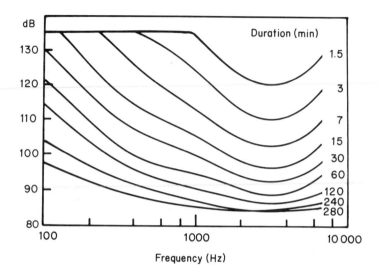

Figure 10.12 Damage risk contours for continuous noise. (*From Kryter* et al., *1966, reproduced by permission of the* Journal of the Acoustical Society of America.)

but slowly being documented. The few results available appear to suggest that the important stimulus characteristic, at least for recovery from TTS, is the average energy level of the noise to which the operator is exposed. Johnson, Nixon and Stephenson (1976), for example, exposed subjects to different types of noise for 24 hours as shown in Table 10.2 (Pink noise is a special type of random noise which is composed of frequencies within a specified bandwidth and with constant energy levels.) It is important to note that the levels of intermittent noises were set to produce equivalent energies to the 85 dB(A) continuous noise. The authors measured their subjects' hearing levels at different times during the 24-hour exposure period and for 24 hours after (recovery). Their results are shown in Figure 10.13, from which it is clear that although the continuous noise produced slightly more TTS than did the intermittent noises, the recovery trends for each type of noise were very similar. Kryter *et al.* (1966) discuss in more detail the damaging effects of interrupted noise, and have produced a series of damage risk contours for such noises (see Figure 10.14).

Table 10.2 Types of noise used by Johnson *et al.* (1976)

Condition	Noise	Time pattern	Exposure level (dB(A))
A	Pink	Continuous	85
B	Pink	3 min on/6 min off	90
C	Pink	20 sec on/40 sec off	90
D	Pink	3 min on/87 min off	100
E	Pink	20 sec on/580 sec off	100

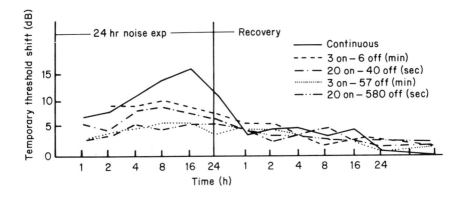

Figure 10.13 Growth and recovery from TTS using different types of noise. (*From Johnson, Nixon and Stephenson (1976), reproduced by permission of the Aerospace Medical Association.*)

Intermittent noise of another type can occur as sudden large 'bangs' or impulses arising from any percussion type of machine such as a gun, steam hammer or road hammer. Impulsive sound is characterized by an initial high

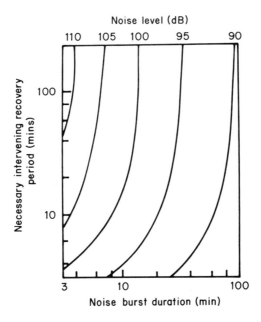

Figure 10.14 Damage risk contours for intermittent noise containing frequencies 1200–2400 Hz. (*From Kryter* et al. *(1966), reproduced by permission of the* Journal of the Acoustical Society of America)

energy surge which reaches its peak extremely quickly (a near instantaneous rise time), but which decays gradually over about 1 msec. The damaging effects of the stimulus are the intensity of the initial surge and the decay duration.

Coles *et al.* (1968) have reviewed many of the studies concerning the TTS and PTS resulting from such noise. On the basis of these studies they have produced a damage risk contour for impulsive sounds (shown in Figure 10.15) which relates the maximum sound pressure level acceptable to the ear (i.e. the noise from both the machine itself and reflected from the surroundings) to the impulse duration. They point out that such criteria will protect 75 per cent of the population at risk; to protect 90 per cent the contour should be reduced by 5 dB at each duration. They also emphasize that the criterion is based on repetition rates in the order of 6–30 impulses per minute, 'with the total number of impulses limited to around 100 per exposure'.

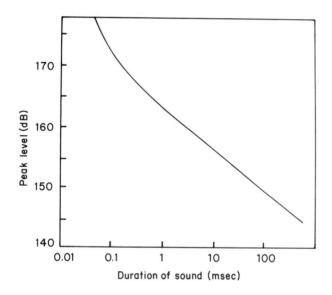

Figure 10.15 Damage risk contour for impulse sounds having near instantaneous rise times. (*From Coles* et al. *(1968)*, *reproduced by permission of the* Journal of the Acoustical Society of America)

PERFORMANCE EFFECTS OF NOISE

Communication

Effective verbal communication depends on both the speaker's ability to produce the correct speech sounds and on the listener's ability to receive and to decode these sounds. A noisy environment is likely to interfere with this last stage in the speech transmission due to an effect which is described as 'masking'.

The American Standards Association (1960) defines auditory masking as 'the process by which the threshold of audibility for one sound is raised by the presence of another sound'. Deatherage and Evans (1969), however, have redefined the concept as 'The process by which the detectability of one sound, the signal, is impaired by the presence of another sound, the masker'. This reformulation, then, recognizes that masking occurs at higher signal intensities than threshold (minimum audible) levels.

Since masking impairs the perception of a signal (in the present context the 'signal' is either speech or the output of an auditory display) it is important to realize under what conditions masking occurs so that its effects can be reduced. However, masking depends on almost any aspect of the signal and of the masker (noise) that could be considered: their respective intensities, frequencies, phases, durations, etc. The first three of these will now be considered in more detail.

Intensity relationships

The effects of the masker intensity on auditory masking have been investigated by a number of experimenters and the results are fairly consistent: more masking occurs as the masker (noise) intensity increases when the signal intensity remains constant; less masking occurs as the signal intensity increases if the masker intensity remains constant. Fletcher and Munson (1937) have shown that the level of masking increases in a nearly linear fashion with masker intensity (the relationship became less linear at lower masker intensities).

Frequency relationships

Masking also increases as the masker frequency approaches that of the signal. Fletcher (1940) took this observation further when he produced his concept of a 'critical band' (of masking). This arose from experimental results which indicated that a pure tone is really masked only by a certain narrow band of noises which are centred at the frequency of the tone. Frequency components outside of this critical band are relatively ineffective in their masking ability. Fletcher also demonstrated that the breadth of this critical band increases as the central frequency of the masker (noise) increases above 1000 Hz.

These data, therefore, have practical implications since they imply that it is important to know the frequency, as well as the intensity, characteristics of the ambient noise. If the noise is composed of frequencies outside of the critical band needed to mask, for example, a tone produced by an auditory display, then interference will not occur. If the noise frequencies lie inside the critical band, however, performance reductions due to masking will become increasingly important.

Although the notion of a critical band is adequate for most circumstances, if the noise intensity is 'sufficiently' high it can mask tones which lie outside its critical band. Bilger and Hirsh (1956) describe these effects as 'remote masking' and suggest that they occur as a result of the high noise intensity 'scattering' acoustic energy in the cochlea causing distortion, the products of which may act as masking stimuli.

Phase relationships

A pure tone is produced by the action of an earphone diaphragm vibrating sinusoidally. If a second diaphragm (B) is made to vibrate with the same frequency but A is at its peak position when B is at its lowest, then the two diaphragms are said to be out of phase. They are in phase when both move in the same direction at the same time. Different phase relationships occur between these two extremes of 0 degrees (in phase) to 180 degrees (out of phase).

During the Second World War workers at the Harvard psycho-acoustic laboratory conducted many experiments on masking — particularly masking speech by noise. It was discovered that when the noise and the signal (speech) are presented to both ears a substantial improvement in hearing could occur if either was reversed in phase at one ear relative to the other ear.

The initial research into these phase relations and their effect on masking was first described by Licklider in 1948, who considered three relationships. Thus Licklider describes the case where either the noise or the signal is reversed in phase between the two ears as *antiphasic*, the case where neither is reversed or where both are reversed as *homophasic*; and where the masker is random in nature as *heterophasic*. Using speech as his signal, Licklider showed that intelligibility was highest with the antiphasic relations and lowest with the homophasic arrangements — with the heterophasic conditions allowing intermediate intelligibility.

The reason for such differential phase effects probably lies in the fact that as tones vary in phase between the two ears the position of the resultant tone appears to 'rotate' around the head. If both the signal and masker are in phase, therefore, the two appear to be in the same position in space. As one moves out of phase between the ears, however, it appears to 'separate' from the other and thus becomes more discriminable. This is simply a further example of the general observation that masking decreases as the signal and masker become less 'similar'.

Implications for communication

All of this evidence has implications for speech communication in noise. For example, if the environmental noise has a similar bandwidth to that of normal speech, or if it is louder, then masking will occur.

Kryter (1970) indicates that speech (for both males and females) tends to predominate at around 400–500 Hz, but includes frequencies up to 5000 Hz. Clearly, therefore, significant environmental noise having these frequencies should be avoided. However, Licklider's data suggest that if the speech can be presented to the observer through earphones, adjusted so that one diaphragm is out of phase with the other, then masking may be reduced.

The normal behavioural response to increased ambient noise levels will be for the speaker's voice to be raised. Increases of 10 dB in the noise level, for example, have been shown to cause normal-hearing talkers to raise their voice levels by amounts varying between 3 dB (van Heusden, Plump and Pols, 1979) and 6–10 dB (Pearsons, Bennett and Fidell, 1977). However, as Kryter (1970) points out, the increase in effort is not sufficient to overcome the increases in noise level completely.

If the signal is masked by noise which is interrupted by periods of quiet then the degree of masking changes in quite a complex manner which is determined by the rate of interruption. Miller and Licklider (1950), for example, explain the relationship as follows:

> At interruptions of less than 2/sec, whole words or syllables within a word tend to be masked; at interruption rates of between 2 and 30/sec, noise detection is so brief that the listener is able to hear a portion of each syllable or phomeme of the speech signal, thereby tending to reduce the amount of masking; when the interruption rate is more frequent than 30/sec the spread of masking in time around the moment of occurrence of a burst of noise results in increased masking until by 100 interruptions per sec there is, effectively, continuous masking.
>
> (*Reprinted from the* Journal of the Acoustical Society of America *by permission of the publisher.*)

In conclusion it should be pointed out that most studies of this nature have been conducted using young (usually male), articulate subjects with normal hearing in situations where no face-to-face contact is permitted (which is analogous to using the telephone). Little attention has been paid to the social and non-verbal cues which also occur between people who are speaking. For example, Waltzman and Levitt (1978) reported that face-to-face encounters using visual cues improves the intelligibility of noisy messages quite considerably. Furthermore, Webster (1973) has shown that the speech intelligibility criteria that are used, which are based on speech without visual cues, overestimate the effect of noise for face-to-face communication by as much as 20 dB. Finally, as Jones, Chapman and Auburn (1981) point out, virtually nothing is known of the skills that we use to perceive speech in noisy conditions. This is despite the fact that there is ample anecdotal evidence to suggest that individuals who are practised at conversing in noisy settings are able to pick out speech more accurately than those who are not practised.

Cognitive Performance

There is presently much controversy over the question of whether environmental noise affects anything other than auditory-based performance. Basing his conclusions on work carried out at the Harvard Psycho-acoustic laboratory during the Second World War, for example, Stevens (1972) insisted that noise has no direct detrimental effects on man, apart from producing deafness and annoyance. After including masking as an effect, this suggestion has also been supported by Kryter (1970) and by Poulton (1977).

Other authors however, most notably Broadbent, claim that continuous broad band noise at levels greater than 100 dB (A) has a detrimental effect on work. This is distinct from the effects of the noise masking any auditory feedback cues which the operator is able to derive from the task.

The controversy was sparked off by experiments similar to those reported by Broadbent (1954). In his experiment (now known as the '20 dials test') subjects were asked to monitor 20 steam pressure gauges for $1\frac{1}{2}$ hours; if they saw any of the pointers reading above a danger mark they were required to turn a knob below the gauge to bring the pointer back to the mark. This was carried out under two conditions: 'noise' (100 dB) and 'quiet' (70 dB). His results indicated that the subject's performance was impaired in the noisy relative to the quiet condition.

Other experimenters have also indicated that high noise levels (above 100 dB) can effect monotonous vigilance performance over relatively long durations. Jerison (1959), for example, demonstrated that environmental noise at 114 dB produced significantly more errors on both a 'clock watching' and a 'complex mental counting' task after at least two hours work.

Poulton (1976), however, claims that many of these effects can be placed at the door of equipment deficiencies. For example, the equipment used by Broadbent contained microswitches mounted directly behind the knob which recorded the subject's response. He argues that these auditory feedback cues could have helped the subjects enough in the quiet condition to be able to produce a faster and a more accurate response than had they not been present. The 'noise' conditions, however, probably masked these cues. In his 1977 review, Poulton lists 32 experiments which have indicated a performance decrease in the presence of noise; in each case he suggests aspects of the equipment which could, if masked, have reduced the number or quality of cues given to the operator.

It is questionable, however, whether acoustic masking can account for all of the measured performance decrements. For example in his 'quiet' condition Jerison set the level of environmental noise to 'mask the sounds of equipment' and it ranged from 77.5 to 83 dB(A). These levels certainly should have overcome Poulton's (1977) objections to this experiment — that 'masking of the tap of the spring-loaded switch, which indicates that it has been depressed far enough, occurs in the "noisy" but not in the "quiet" condition'.

An extension of the 'masking' hypothesis has been proposed by Poulton (1976, 1977). He suggests that 'inner speech' is also masked by the noise: 'you can't hear yourself think in noise'. Many of the tasks which demonstrated a detrimental effect of noise had a large short-term memory component: subtracting a four-digit number from a memorized six-digit number; counting and holding in separate cumulative totals, the number of flashes from each of three sources; searching for a series of two-digit numbers; etc. In such tasks, Poulton argues that the noise masks the individual's internal verbal rehearsal loop, causing the person to work slower and to make more errors.

A separate hypothesis to account for some of the possibly observed detrimental effects due to noise has been advanced by Jerrison (1959). He suggests that the noise affects the operator's judgements of time. He asked his subjects to press a key at what they considered to be ten-minute intervals. Throughout the experimental period his subjects progressively contracted their internal time-scale when in the noisy condition but not in 'quiet'. Whereas in the first fifteen minutes of noise the key was pressed after an average period of $8\frac{3}{4}$ minutes (to signal the end of a ten-minute period), after $2\frac{3}{4}$ hours 'ten minutes' was contracted to about seven minutes. It is not entirely clear, however, how such distortions in time judgement can influence all cognitive or motor work performance.

Environmental noise can also affect memory, although it is not clear whether this occurs only at the input (memorizing) stage, at the output (retrieval) stage or both (for example, see Thomas, 1978). Furthermore, the direction of the effect (an improvement or reduction in memory) is equivocal. Some studies have suggested that noise improves immediate retention (for example, Archer and Margolin, 1970) while others have shown an impairment (McLean, 1969). Indeed, still others have suggested that noise has no effect on immediate retention (Sloboda and Smith, 1968).

The levels of noise used in experiments of this nature, however, have generally been very high (greater than about 80 dB A). Slightly lower noise intensities (65 dB(A)) generally *improves* immediate recall (for example, Berlyne *et al.*, 1965; Wesner, 1972). This is probably because of the inverted-U, arousal–performance relationship discussed in Chapter 1. Thus, moderate noise levels increase body arousal so that performance also increases. Too much noise, however, causes arousal to become too high with resultant *reductions* in performance. This suggests, therefore, that noise acts on cognitive behaviour as a general stressor, and that any performance increases or decreases in noise can be explained in these terms. This possibility will be considered later.

Finally, workers such as Broadbent and Gregory (1965) and Hockey (1970) suggest that noise may affect not so much the observer's ability to monitor a signal but both the criteria used to decide whether a signal is present and the search pattern employed. Thus, Broadbent and Gregory demonstrated that in 100 dB noise observers were more likely to report being 'sure yes' or 'sure no' of perceiving a signal than in quieter conditions. Hockey demonstrated that in noise the subject's search pattern changed to give more weight to areas of the panel which contained the highest proportion of signals. Results such as these, therefore, imply that observer's cognitive strategies change in noise to become more efficient and less wide ranging.

From laboratory based studies at least, therefore, a detrimental effect of noise on cognitive performance alone has not been shown to occur for all types of task. Noise clearly has an effect on overall performance, but this could be due as much to masking acoustic cues as to any deficiency in central cognitive processing.

In general, therefore, the conclusion must be that the relationship between noise and cognitive performance is similar to that between any environmental stressor and cognitive performance as discussed at the beginning of this chapter.

That is the stressor is unlikely to affect cognitive performance as long as it does not demand more mental capacity than the task leaves spare.

With stress, however, there is general agreement that it not only brings about quantitative changes in performance but also qualitative changes. Easterbrook (1959), for example, proposed that in over-aroused subjects attention tends to be concentrated on the dominant and obvious aspects of the situation. This suggests that some aspects of task performance might be relatively unaffected by stress but that performance on other, more difficult or less important, aspects may be impaired. For example, Boggs and Simon (1968) examined noise effects in relation to task complexity. They found a reliable noise/complexity interaction in which noise produced more errors in complex rather than simple tasks.

Views such as this have been extended recently to emphasize that stress also reduces the stability of attention and interferes with the capacity to discriminate relevant from irrelevant aspects of a task (for example, Kahneman, 1973). Since stress is also likely to narrow the span of attention in the way described above, Jones (1979) suggests that the qualitative results of stress are that it seems to produce strategic changes in behaviour rather than simply depressing performance.

The idea that coping with noise involves some cognitive intervention has also evolved in other areas of inquiry. Over the past decade or so there has been an increasing amount of interest in the notion of 'perceived control' as a means of alleviating the deleterious after-effects of noise. For example, Wohlwill et al. (1976) suggest that individuals are able to cope with noise through increased concentration and effort. They make the observation that subjects in such experiments sometimes experience considerable 'release of tension' after the experience — even to the extent of breaking down to cry. In a series of studies (Glass and Singer, 1972) subjects exposed to loud intermittent noise over which they had no control showed no detrimental effects in their performance *during* the noise (indeed physiological indices indicated that the subjects had adapted to the noise), but they performed badly when the noise had ceased and they moved to another room. These results contrasted with those from similar groups of subjects who were told that they could terminate the noise although they were encouraged not to do so. These subjects showed no detrimental effects after the noise.

Background Music and Productivity

In many respects this topic should not be considered in a section which discusses the effects of noise on performance. Noise, by definition, is unwanted sound whereas background music is often wanted and enjoyed by many workers. In cases in which it is not wanted (and thus becomes 'noise') the sound pressure levels produced are not high enough to cause the direct performance reductions discussed above. Then the effect is more likely to become one of annoyance as will be discussed later. The effects of background music on performance will be discussed in this section, however, since music is an acoustic stimulus which, it has been argued, may possibly affect performance. As with the effects of noise on cognitive performance the evidence regarding music and productivity is also controversial.

Fox (1983) distinguishes between two types of music at work — background music and industrial music. Although each might be said to be used in an attempt to increase commercial profitability they are quite different in their mode of operation. Background music is the type of music often heard in shops and supermarkets; it is an endless stream of light, quiet music designed to put shoppers at ease. Industrial music, on the other hand, generally varies and does not occur all of the time but only at selected periods during the day. Indeed, if it were to be played all of the time, it would defeat the basis for having the music.

The theoretical basis for suggesting that music might aid performance lies in alleviating the boredom and fatigue that often accompanies repetitive work. Again the inverted-U, performance/arousal relationship is invoked (Fox, 1971). Thus the normal stimulation which an operator receives from the task not only gives information about the job but provides stimulation for the part of the brain known as the reticular activating system (RAS) which determines how much attention, alertness or vigilance the operator will bring to the job. Repetitive work with little stimulation can lead to under-arousal and lost efficiency; so the basis of industrial music is that varying, secondary stimulation might provide the stimuli needed to 'reactivate' the RAS.

It is difficult to measure the effects of background music in actual organizational studies because other performance influencers are often also present. Thus music may influence not only attention and vigilance but feelings of well-being and job satisfaction, and these effects could be reflected by reductions in absenteeism, bad timekeeping and labour turnover which are likely to increase overall productivity.

Studies investigating the effects of industrial music on productivity have been reviewed by Fox (1971, 1983). Although many were poorly controlled he concluded, from both laboratory- and industrial-based studies, that under the right conditions music is beneficial. Thus subjects increased their performance in the laboratory, and the industry-based studies showed reduced errors, staff turnover and accidents, better timekeeping, and increased output and production quality.

When considering the music to be used for such purposes, two questions are important: 'When should the music be played?' and 'What type of music should be played?' Answers to these two questions can be found in the theoretical rationale for using industrial music — that of increasing arousal.

Regarding the times for music, then, the inverted-U arousal/performance hypothesis would suggest that it should be played at times during the day when arousal would otherwise be low. Daily variations in human performance and efficiency have long been recognized (Rutenfranz and Colquhoun, 1979) which are generally termed 'circadian rhythms'. For example, Blake (1971) demonstrated increases in performance between 08.00 and 10.30 hours, with a 'post-lunch' dip at about 14.00 hours. Unfortunately, precise times during the day for these peaks and troughs are not available (see Folkard and Monk, 1979) and so the appropriate times need to be determined empirically within each working situation.

Finally, with regard to the content of the music, a series of studies carried out by Fox and Embrey (1972) suggests that the workers themselves should be able to choose their music. In a laboratory experiment they tested six subjects on a detection task using four conditions:

(1) No music.
(2) Music played during the 15th to 20th minute of the test session using a programme of randomly selected music.
(3) As in (2) but using a commercially prepared, lively programme.
(4) As in (2) but allowing the subjects to select a programme from the tapes used in (3).

Their results demonstrated that average detection efficiency increased significantly from the 'no music' to the 'commercial music' conditions, with detection rate being higher when the subjects were able to choose their music ((4) rather than (3)).

ANNOYANCE EFFECTS OF NOISE

Annoyance is a common subjective response that we have all exhibited in the past when exposed to something which we do not want. Since, by definition, noise is unwanted sound, in whatever form is presents itself (speech, music or random acoustic energy) it can cause annoyance. The extent to which particular sounds are likely to cause annoyance will be determined not simply by their physical characteristics but by the extent to whch they are unwanted by the listener. This means that what is annoying to one person may not be so to another, and even what is annoying to someone on one occasion may not be so at another time. It is not possible, therefore, to define strictly the acoustic conditions likely to cause annoyance (as it is possible, for example, to define the conditions likely to lead to deafness or to reduced speech intelligibility). Nevertheless, there are some physical aspects of noise which are more likely to be annoying than others.

Physical Aspects of Noise Annoyance

Contrary to popular opinion the mere physical intensity of a noise is not the only feature which is likely to cause annoyance. Two noises can have the same intensity but cause different degrees of annoyance, perhaps due to the frequencies which they contain, their respective durations, or even their meanings to the listener.

Kryter (1970) suggests that five physical aspects of a noise stimulus can be identified as affecting its annoyance level: (a) the spectrum content and level; (b) the spectrum complexity; (c) the sound duration; (d) the sound rise time (that is, the length of time that it takes to reach its maximum level); and (e) the maximum level reached (for impulsive sounds such as a door bang).

The relationships between most of these parameters and annoyance are likely to be fairly obvious. For example, annoyance increases the louder the sound, the longer it remains, etc. With regard to the spectrum content, however, the relationship is not so straightforward. By asking subjects to adjust tones of different frequencies to make them equally 'noisy', Kryter and Pearsons (1966) were able to produce bands of equal 'noisiness' over a frequency range of 40 to 10000 Hz (a distinction was made between 'noisiness' and 'loudness'). These bands indicated that the higher frequencies (above about 2000 Hz) tend to contribute more to the sound noisiness (and thus are likely to be more annoying) than the lower frequencies — even though they were equally loud. This relationship can be seen in Figure 10.16: as the noise frequency increases above about 1000 Hz it appears to become more 'noisy' (or, interpreting the graph literally, with increasing frequency a lower intensity is needed to maintain the same noisiness level). Although the same relationship is apparent when the sounds are made to be equally 'loud', the increase in sensitivity for higher frequencies is not so marked.

Details of the procedures used to record and measure noise levels at a workplace are provided by Michael and Bienvenue (1983).

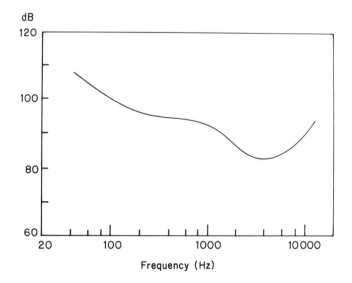

Figure 10.16 An equal noisiness contour. (*From Kryter and Pearsons (1966), reproduced by permission of the* Journal of the Acoustical Society of America.)

Subjective Aspects of Noise Annoyance

In many respects what is conveyed by the term 'annoyance' is not just 'noisiness'; annoyance implies something more. It commonly signifies one's reaction to sound that is based not only on physical characteristics of the stimulus but also on what it means; the emotional content and the novelty that the sound can have for the listener. As Wilson (1963) suggests,

> the annoyance may be ascribed to the 'information' which sounds may carry from the source to the recipient. The physical energy in the noise of a creaking door, a crying baby, or a distant party may be very small, and if distributed in the form of random noise probably would be quite unnoticed. But it may convey manifold suggestions of alarm, neglect, sadness, loneliness, and so in some people it has an emotional effect out of all proportion to its physical intensity.

Reviewing the many studies and surveys that have been carried out to investigate the types and levels of noise which cause disturbance, it is clear that annoyance generally occurs when the noise interferes with people's ability to carry out some activity that they wish to do.

Speech is a type of noise which carries with it a great deal of information and it is a significant source of noise in rooms such as offices. Thus, Nemecek and Grandjean (1973) surveyed the noise requirements of employees working in landscaped offices. Of the employees who considered that they were disturbed by noise, 46 per cent felt that the noise produced by conversations was most annoying; 25 per cent disliked office machinery noise and 19 per cent the telephones. Interestingly, further questioning revealed that the majority who indicated that conversation noise disturbed them most felt that it was the content of the conversation rather than its loudness which was most disturbing.

The problem of overhearing conversations was also advanced as a cause of annoyance by Cavanaugh et al. (1962) and by Waller (1969). Proposing the concept of 'speech privacy' these authors have argued that the disturbance might be caused by the worry that if one can hear other people talking then one can also be *heard by* other people. They also suggest that it is the degree to which the intruding speech can be understood, rather than its loudness, which destroys the feeling of office privacy.

Some studies have attempted to relate the noise sensitivity of individuals to individual traits. For example, Stephens (1970) examined the relationship between the judgement of loudness and annoyance in conjunction with various personality measures. He found that among tests measuring introversion, need-achievement, test anxiety, social desirability, and general annoyance, only the test anxiety scores correlated significantly with noise sensitivity. He ascribed this result to the tendency for anxious subjects to give extreme responses to very different stimulus levels. Interestingly, noise annoyance did not correlate at all well with noise sensitivity.

Noise sensitivity appears to be related to the extent to which individuals are actually disturbed by noise, however. On the basis of questionnaire responses obtained before students arrived on a University campus, Weinstein (1976) distinguished two groups of respondents — noise-sensitive and noise-insensitive. As would be expected, throughout the year at college the noise-sensitive students were bothered much more by dormitory noise and became increasingly disturbed during the year. The noise-insensitive students, however, showed no change in disturbance. In an extension to the study, sensitivity scores and scores from a range of personality tests were also examined. The results suggested that noise-sensitive subjects were generally lower in dominance, capacity for status, sociability and social presence. In addition, the results demonstrated that higher noise-sensitivity scores were related to increased intraversion scores. Commenting on these results Jones, Chapman and Auburn (1981) point out that since the sensitivity scales emphasized the importance of noises produced by other people, the question needs to be asked whether the association between sensitivity and sociability simply reflects a lack of social skills on the part of some of the respondents.

Despite valid experimental arguments such as these, evidence is available to suggest that continued noise does detrimentally affect social behaviour. For example, Mathews and Cannon (1975) investigated the influence of noise on the willingness to help an experimenter's confederate pick up materials that have been 'accidentally' dropped. Those subjects who were exposed to 85 dB(A) noise were less likely to help than those exposed to a maximum of 65 dB(A). Similar results were obtained in more naturalistic settings. In addition, a study by Crook and Langdon (1974) of classroom activity in schools around London Airport demonstrated the distracting effects of noise and the results that this can have on social interaction. As well as the aircraft noise interfering with lessons the authors also reported changes in the style of teaching on the noisier days (lessons abandoned and more pauses in the flow of the teacher), increased pupil fidgeting, and reduced teacher satisfaction with the class as a whole. Thus teachers often felt that the noise caused the whole atmosphere of the proceedings to deteriorate, that they and their pupils became irritable and tired, that they developed headaches and that the pupils became noisier and less inclined to work.

Finally, as well as directly interfering with tasks, the indirect consequences of noise can also be annoying. For example, Griffiths and Langdon (1968) investigated community responses to road traffic noise. In addition to causing problems such as headaches, noise was annoying because it made the respondents keep their windows shut during the summer months. In addition there were also complaints that living next to a noisy road resulted in house values being reduced. Similar points were also raised by Stockbridge and Lee (1973).

Annoyance, therefore, appears to be a subjective reaction to interference in the ability to carry out a preferred task (for example, talking or sleeping). It can also arise as a result of changes in the listener's physiological state, perhaps causing headaches and high blood pressure. In these cases, however, the effects of noise are due not to the specific attributes of the noise but to the (dis)stress which it causes.

Finally, one extreme response to noise as a stressor that has been documented slightly is reduced mental health. In this case, several lines of indirect evidence point to some increase in incidence of minor psychiatric disturbance as a result of exposure to noise. For example, Cohen, Glass and Singer (1973) have suggested that:

Existing evidence suggests that noise may indeed have some responsibility for the personal disorganization of those living or working in noisy environments. Industrial surveys, for example, report that noise exposure results in increased anxiety and stress responses. Workers habitually exposed to high intensity noise show increased incidence of nervous complaints, nausea, headaches, instability, argumentativeness, sexual impotency, changes in general mood and anxiety . . . . Jansen (1961) reports that workers in the noisiest places in a steel factory have a greater frequency of social conflicts both at home and in the plant.

Cohen, Glass and Singer do point out, however, that it is difficult to ascribe these effects solely to noise. There is a variety of other stresses associated with noisy work-places and a number of variables which are related to the types of people who are likely to work in them. At the very least, however, the evidence is suggestive of some distinctive social effects.

SUMMARY

This chapter has considered in detail the effects which two environmental parameters, vibration and noise, have on man. In both cases their effects can be threefold. At extreme intensities they can be dangerous, causing either a breakdown of body parts (in the case of vibration) or deafness (from noise). At lower intensities, however, they are more likely to affect performance, although these effects are more diverse. Thus vibration interferes primarily with the ability to control the affected body part (either a limb or the eyes). The performance effects of noise, however, are likely to occur in interference with hearing. Some evidence exists to suggest that both environmental parameters affect cognitive performance, although it is likely that they act in the manner of general stressors rather than affecting the brain directly. The final reaction to both vibration and noise is one of reduced comfort and increased annoyance. In both cases, however, although it is possible to relate the degree of annoyance or comfort reduction to physical aspects of the stimuli, the reaction is likely to be determined by the meaning of the stimulus to the individual and its effects on the ability to carry out a preferred task.

CHAPTER 11

THE PHYSICAL ENVIRONMENT
II Temperature and Illumination

The previous chapter looked at two aspects of the environment (vibration and noise) which could play a part in affecting health, performance and comfort. Each of these has a fairly clear relationship between its intensity and its importance: generally, the intensity effects fall on a single dimension which extends between no (or relatively little) effect to maximum interference. For example, if vibration could be eliminated it would not interfere with motor performance; when levels are high it interferes considerably. The position is slightly different, however, for both temperature and illumination. For both stimuli there is a narrow range of intensities under which someone can, and should, operate. Departure from this optimum, either by increasing or by reducing the intensity, is likely to affect performance, comfort and, in extreme cases, health. For example a person's ability to see fine detail is impaired when there is no light and when illumination levels are too high; the ability to perform complex mental operations is affected in conditions of both extreme cold and extreme heat.

In the same way that vibration and noise were treated separately in Chapter 10 so, too, will temperature and illumination in this chapter. Again, however, this is not to imply that they are independent factors or that one is more important than the other. As was stressed in Chapter 10 the importance of any environmental factor can change in different circumstances and their interactive effects can be unpredictable.

TEMPERATURE

Man's response to the thermal environment depends largely on a very complex balance between the levels of heat produced and heat lost. The heat resulting from the normal body metabolism, particularly during work, maintains the body at a temperature well above that of the usual surrounding environment. At the same time heat is constantly being lost from the body by radiation, convection and evaporation so that under ordinary resting conditions the body temperature is maintained within its normal narrow range of between 36.1 and 37.2°C

(97–99°F). These optimum temperatures refer to the conditions deep in the body and not simply to the surface temperature of the skin. Whereas the skin temperatures may fluctuate over quite a wide range without serious damage to performance or health, the deep body temperature must stay within this narrow range.

The body's thermal balance is maintained by a very complex self-regulating system situated in the hypothalamus in the brain: blood temperature is sensed and information is received from temperature receptors in the skin. Whenever the body needs to lose heat this area causes the blood vessels to dilate, the sweat glands to produce cooling sweat, the respiration rate to increase and the body's metabolic rate to be lowered. Under cold conditions, when the body needs to conserve and even generate heat, the hypothalamus causes the blood vessels to constrict and to route the blood away from the extremities (causing a 'blue' appearance), and increases the metabolic rate by inducing the often uncontrollable muscle activity described as shivering. By these processes the optimum body temperature is maintained through quite adverse external environmental conditions.

In some cases, however, this self-regulating system proves to be inadequate and the body either gains or loses too much heat. Depending on the amount of heat gain or loss, when this happens it can lead, progressively, to reduced performance, to damaged health and eventually to death. Any discussion of the effects of the thermal environments, therefore, is complicated by the need to assess the effects of heat and cold separately. Thus, the first part of this section will deal with health and performance effects of hot conditions. In the second part these aspects will be discussed in relation to cold conditions. The final part will deal with less extreme departures from optimal balance and their effects on comfort.

HOT ENVIRONMENTAL CONDITIONS

Health Effects (Hyperthermia)

The health of a worker exposed to high levels of radiant or convected heat may be damaged in one or both of two ways. First, the skin's elevated temperature can result in tissue damage from burning, particularly at skin temperatures of over 45 °C (113 °F). These effects, however, are immediately observable and under normal circumstances the pain will cause the operator to remove the exposed body part from danger.

The more insidious effects of an elevated body temperature occur if the deep body temperature increases to a level of about 42 °C (108 °F) (i.e. a core temperature increase of about 5 °C (10 °F)). When this occurs the onset of heat stroke (hyperthermia) can be very sudden with the collapse and (unless treated promptly with cooling agents) the imminent death of the individual. In some cases the loss of consciousness is preceded by a short period of general weakness or confusion and irrational behaviour.

There would appear to be three related reasons why the body may be unable to rid itself of the excess heat generated. First, exposure to environmental conditions which are so humid that the body is unable to reduce its heat by evaporating sweat. For example, inside protective clothing a small microclimate can be produced around the body which becomes supersaturated with water and thus impairs adequate evaporation. Secondly, heat stress can also be caused by the insulating effects of some protective clothing. In this case the stress occurs because of impaired evaporation due, perhaps, to the impermeability of the clothing and to its heat retaining properties. Finally hyperthermia can occur when the environmental conditions are too hot (although not dangerously so) and may interfere both with the body's ability to produce sweat and of sweat's ability to cool the body. In such conditions, of course, more and more sweat may be produced and dehydration from excessive sweating can, itself, lead to death.

Since heat stress is a function of the body's core temperature rather than the external conditions, it may still occur even if the surrounding temperature is less than the critical 42 °C. Thus strenuous physical exercise can, by itself, cause heat stroke if the metabolic heat released by the effort is greater than the body's ability to rid itself of the excess. Indeed, after reviewing many studies of the affliction, Shibolet, Lancaster and Danon (1976) argue that heat stroke is most likely to strike highly motivated young individuals who are engaged in hard work, military training and sport. Under other circumstances these individuals would rest when tired, take liquid when dry, or remain at home when ill. The authors suggest, therefore, that heat stroke prevention requires adequate rest and liquid consumption (to compensate for the increased liquid loss during sweating) before physical exertion, as well as periods of rest during work when the individual can cool off and drink adequately. When such seemingly obvious precautions were implemented in the South African mining industry, Wyndham (1966) demonstrated a significant fall in the incidence of heat stroke mortality among South African miners.

Another major factor in the likelihood of collapse from heat stroke is the duration for which the worker is exposed to the heat source. In this respect Bell, Crowder and Walters (1971) carried out an experiment using eight fit, unacclimatized young men (18–29 years) who were asked to perform a stool-stepping task under different thermal conditions. (The task was to step on and off a 22.9 cm high stool in time with a signal light flashing at a rate of 12 times per minute.) Each subject was encouraged to push himself to his individual limit of exhaustion, knowing that he would be protected from hazard by the presence of two competent and experienced observers in the hot chamber. From their data Bell *et al.* were able to produce a series of graphs of predicted safe exposure times for different combinations of dry and wet bulb temperature conditions. Two of these curves are shown in Figure 11.1. As can be seen, the figures match very closely similar limits produced by the American Society of Heating and Refrigeration Engineers (ASHRAE) (1965) based on physiological data (the average time taken to raise the pulse rate from 75 to 125 beats per minute, and the deep body temperature from 37 to 38.3°C (98–101°F)), although the ASHRAE guidelines are more conservative in their levels.

Figure 11.1 Tolerance to heat at different relative humidities, produced by Bell, Crowder, and Walters (1971) and the American Society of Heating and Refrigeration Engineers (ASHRAE) (1965)

Bell *et al.* do caution against the over-use of these figures, however. Thus they point out that the data were obtained from fit young men and it would be dangerous to extrapolate the findings to other populations of workers with different work rates, ages and physical fitnesses, etc. Secondly, the safe exposure times relate to subjects who were required to work continuously, whereas workers who normally carry out lighter or more intermittent work could be expected to endure longer exposures.

The third caution that needs to be raised is that their recommended limits apply to workers with very little heat acclimatization, whereas it has been shown that acclimatized men may be able to endure the heat for longer. For example, for durations of 400 minutes or longer Wyndham *et al.* (1970) have shown that resting, acclimatized men can tolerate nearly 2 °C more than can unacclimatized men. In a naturalistic study Clark and Edholm (1985) describe work carried out using acclimatized and unacclimatized soldiers in Eden. The platoon which had been acclimatized naturally by a prior period in Bahrain demonstrated higher sweat rates and lower deep body temperatures and heat rates than did their unacclimatized comrades. Although the differences between the two groups diminished over the twelve-day test period, significant differences still existed on the last day. Clark and Edholm note that the most dramatic differences between the two groups appeared in terms of heat collapse: three cases in the acclimatized group versus over thirty cases in the unacclimatized soldiers.

Performance effects of heat

Over the years many studies have been performed to investigate the effects of thermal conditions on performance — usually using some type of cognitive task such as memory or vigilance. Unfortunately, however, because of experimental limitations and wide differences between tasks, techniques and conditions, no firm conclusions can be drawn from the combined results. As Kobrick and Fine

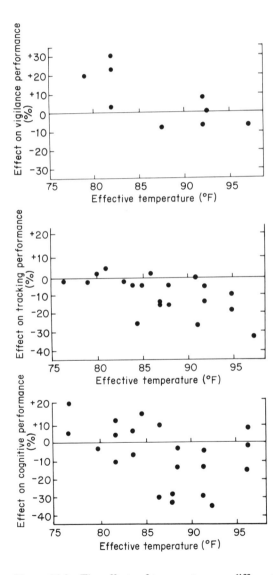

Figure 11.2 The effects of temperature on different forms of cognitive performance. (After Grether, 1973.)

(1983) point out following a comprehensive survey of the relevant literature, although numerous studies have demonstrated some performance impairment in heat, others have shown no differences, or even improvements, in performance.

Despite such negative conclusions, however, it can be said that studies which *do* suggest some performance impairment indicate that losses occur at around 29–30 °C (approximately 85 °F), although there appears to be a wide band above and below this level. Figure 11.2 (adapted from Grether, 1973) illustrates the extent to which varying the thermal conditions affects various types of cognitive performance.

Some of the earliest and most comprehensive experiments of the effects of various stressors (including temperature) on performance were carried out by Mackworth over a period of seven years at the Applied Psychology Unit at Cambridge. These were published in 1950 and his experiments on the performance effects of heat wave, perhaps, formed the basis for a number of subsequent investigations. Since this series also included physical performance tasks, it is useful to consider the studies in more detail.

Mackworth used five different performance tasks in his experiments. First, the 'clock test' tested vigilance. Subjects were asked to watch a clock face whose hand moved around the face with a jerk every second. Occasionally, however, after long and irregular intervals, the pointer moved through double the usual distance and the subject was asked to respond when this happened.

A second group of two tasks tested the subjects' cognitive abilities. In the first, the 'wireless telegraphy reception test', eleven experienced wireless operators were required to perform their normal job of rapidly writing down morse code messages heard over their headphones. In the second test, the 'coding test', twelve subjects were each presented with a set of small, flat, squared shapes and a form-board. Their work involved putting each shape into its corresponding hole on the board.

The final group of two tasks tested more physical work performance. First arm strength was measured in the 'pull test' in which the subject was asked to raise and lower a 15 lb weight attached to pulleys, by bending and straightening his arm in time with a metronome. This was continued until the men were unable to lift the weight again. In the second task, the 'heavy pursuit meter' task, the subject had to keep a pointer in a specific position on a display using both hands to operate a very heavy control. This experiment lasted for three hours.

Each test was carried out under different combinations of wet and dry bulb temperatures (see p. 279) and, as subsequent experimenters have demonstrated, performance on all tasks remained fairly constant until a dry/wet bulb temperature of about 30/24 to 32/27 °C (86/75 to 90/80 °F) was reached, after which the performance on all tasks decreased dramatically. The interesting observation, then, is that such performance reductions apply as much to physical tasks as to cognitive ones.

As well as considering the critical temperature levels for decreased performance, Mackworth also investigated the extent to which other, more individual, variables affected the heat/performance relationship.

As a possible moderator of the effects of the heat, Mackworth considered the subjects' experience during both the clock test and the wireless telegraphy test. In both tasks his results suggest that, over all conditions, the increased temperature did not affect the different skill-groups differently. Analysing the results in terms of the different hours of keeping watch on the task, however, the higher temperatures appeared to affect the unskilled operators in the final hour more than they did the skilled operators.

To test the effects of incentives, each subject who undertook the pull test completed the task twice. In one condition the subjects were given no idea of how they were performing, whereas in the second condition they knew their results and were urged and encouraged to perform on each trial 25 per cent better than previously.

As would be expected, Mackworth's results showed that the encouragement had an effect on overall performance so that the higher incentive group performed significantly better than when they did not know how they were doing. However, his data also demonstrated that the temperature conditions did not affect the two groups differently. Although the now predictable reduction in performance occurred after about 29 to 32 °C (85–90 °F), it occurred in both groups to the same extent.

Finally, the length of time for which subjects are exposed to the heat may be expected also to affect any heat/performance relationship. In this respect Wing (1965) has combined the data from many of the cognitive performance studies in an attempt to indicate, in terms of the duration of exposure, the temperature levels able to be endured before cognitive performance decrements become apparent. As can be seen from Figure 11.3, Wing's upper limit for impaired

Figure 11.3 Upper tolerance limit for impaired mental performance. (*From Wing 1965, reproduced by permission of the Aerospace Medical Association.*)

performance follows a very similar course to the predicted curves of the physiological limit illustrated in Figure 11.1.

COLD ENVIRONMENTAL CONDITIONS

Health Effects (Hypothermia)

In the same way that slight rises in deep body temperature can rapidly lead to hyperthermia, fairly small amounts of deep body cooling is likely to produce a severe risk to health. In this case the condition is known as hypothermia. Accidental hypothermia can result from exposure in bad weather; short-term immersion in very cold water or long-term exposure in slightly cold water; or, particularly in the elderly, it may be a consequence of illness or accident. Harnett, Pruitt and Sias (1983a, b) present a comprehensive review of problems and techniques relating to resuscitation from hypothermia.

Clinically, a state of hypothermia can be said to exist when the body's core temperature falls to about 35 °C (95 °F). Below this the risk of fatality increases, until at temperatures below 30 °C (86 °F) imminent death from cardiac arrest is likely. Again, therefore, it requires the deep body temperature to depart only slightly from its optimum (in this case 2–4°C) for fatalities to occur.

Following exposure to cold, the body's regulation system attempts to produce heat rapidly by increased muscular activity, manifested by an increase in muscle tone and shivering. Violent shivering appears not to begin until the deep body temperature begins to fall but, once started, its effect can be marked causing the falling trend to be reversed and the core temperature to rise. Shivering reaches a maximum at body temperatures around 34–35°C (93–95 °F). During the shivering stage the cardiovascular system responds to the cold by constricting the peripheral blood vessels and this increases the blood pressure. If the temperature falls further, however, the heart rate also falls due to a direct effect on the heart pacemaker. When the heat loss cannot be compensated further, the deep body temperature falls until at temperatures around 30–33°C (86–91°F) shivering gradually ceases and is replaced by muscular rigidity.

Tolerance to cold exposure, and thus susceptibility to hypothermia, varies greatly between individuals. For example, Timbal, Loncle and Boutelier (1976) immersed subjects in cold water at 30 °C for 15 minutes. After this time some subjects' temperatures had dropped by 2°C, whereas others had dropped by only 10 per cent of this amount. These differences in susceptibility are due, primarily, to morphological factors of which the amount of subcutaneous fat around the body is probably the most important. This acts as good insulating material, particularly when the blood vessels constrict in response to the cold and blood is routed away from the body surface. In addition, the individual's size and weight are important factors in cold susceptibility. This is because the degree of heat loss is proportional to the body's surface area, and the amount of heat which can be generated (perhaps by shivering) depends on the mass of active muscular tissue in the body.

Performance Effects of Cold

After reviewing much of the work of the effects of environmental cold on human performance, Fox (1967) concluded that cold can affect performance in five areas: (a) tactile sensitivity, (b) manual performance, (c) tracking, (d) reaction time, and (e) 'complex behaviours'. These five behaviours can be grouped into two main categories: motor performance and cognitive performance.

As far as motor performance is concerned, two factors appear to be important. First the temperature of the limb which is being used, and secondly the rate of cooling.

The limb temperature, rather than the overall body temperature, affects motor ability because of the effects which cold has on muscular control. It causes a loss of cutaneous sensitivity, changes in the characteristics of synovial fluid in the joints, and a loss of muscular strength. With respect to finger performance Morton and Provins (1960) have demonstrated a significant reduction in dexterity for skin temperatures below 20–25 °C (68–97 °F), although there was large individual variability. They suggest that the true relationship for any one person may be such that most of the change in performance is spread over only a few degrees. Thus skin sensitivity remains fairly normal for small falls in skin temperature, but deteriorates considerably after the individual's critical hand skin temperature has been reached.

Data from Clark (1961) tend to support this contention of a critical temperature. He showed that the longer his subjects were exposed to the cold the more their performance decreased as the skin temperature was lowered from 15 to 10.5 °C (51–59 °F). At a higher overall temperature (13–18 °C; 56–64 °F), however, this performance/exposure duration relationship was not apparent.

Effects of the rate of cooling were investigated by Clark and Cohen (1960) on a knot-tying task. They found that slow cooling to a 7.2 °C finger temperature (45 °F) resulted in more knot tying errors than did fast cooling to the same temperature. The authors suggested that this was because the slow cooling procedure allowed relatively lower subsurface temperatures to occur. Although the rate of cooling results have been unable to be replicated, their data do indicate significant performance reductions on a number of dexterity tasks when the temperature fell from 18 to 9°C (65–48°F).

To investigate the effects of long-term exposure to cold conditions on manual performance, Teichener and Kobrick (1955) asked their subjects to perform a tracking task for approximately five minutes each day over a 41-day period, during which time they lived in a constant temperature chamber. For the first 16 days the room temperature was maintained at 24 °C (65 °F); during the next, cold, period lasting 12 days the temperature was held at 13 °C (55 °F); and finally, during the 13-day recovery period, the temperature was again set to 24°C.

Teichener and Kobrick's results are shown in Figure 11.4, and a clear performance reduction in the cold conditions can be seen. Interestingly, the results also suggest that the subjects became adapted to the cold conditions fairly

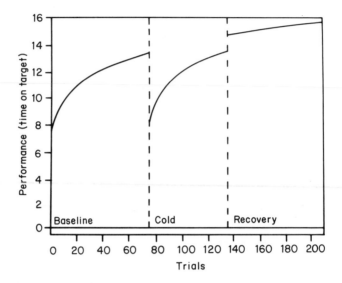

Figure 11.4 Performance changes in a cold environment. (From Teichener and Kobrick, 1955)

quickly. Whereas even at the end of the cold period the subject's performance was not as good as their performance the next day in the warm, within the cold period their performance increased by approximately 50 per cent.

Because the main factor affecting manual performance in the cold is related to the skin temperature of the affected limb, when gloves are unable to be worn it would appear sensible to attempt some local warming of the skin. Lockhart and Keiss (1971), for example, showed that for most tasks the impaired manual performance experienced during the cold conditions (when the average skin temperature of the little finger was 12 °C (54 °F)) was alleviated considerably by applying radiant heat to the hands only (raising the temperature of the little finger to 19.5 °C (67 °F)). Indeed, performance using the radiated heat in very cold conditions (−18 °C; 0 °F) was no worse than working in 15.5 °C (60 °F) conditions (when the average temperature of the little finger was 30 °C (80 °F)).

Artificially raising the temperature of the affected limb, however, cannot fully overcome the effects of the cold if the rest of the body is not similarly heated. For example, Lockhart (1968) maintained the temperature of his subject's hands at 'normal' temperature while cooling the body from 25.5 to 19 °C (78–66 °F). His results suggest that cooling the whole body affects the operator's ability to carry out some manual tasks even though the hands were kept 'warm'. The tasks affected involved fine dexterity and Lockhart suggests that part of the reason for the performance reduction could have been due to shivering. Support for this contention has been provided by Peacock (1956) who examined the effects of cold exposure on rifle aiming steadiness after vigorous exercise. Although steadiness was reduced, Peacock's results showed that if shivering is excluded as a cause of unsteadiness, rifle steadiness was not seriously affected in the standing position when compared with results taken during normal temperatures.

The effects of cold on manual performance, therefore, appear to be two-fold. First, if the cold is applied locally to the operating limb it can directly affect that limb's muscular control, reducing such abilities as dexterity and strength. This may be overcome somewhat by locally warming the limb. Cold applied to the whole body, however, can reduce performance due to shivering. If the body can be stabilized during this shivering, generalized cold would appear not to affect manual performance to any great extent.

As far as cognitive performance is concerned, the ability to think, to judge and to reason under conditions of low environmental temperatures have been investigated primarily from the point of view of the diver. It is frequently necessary for a diver to work in cold water and his life depends on an ability to think clearly and efficiently.

The experimental work in this area, however, does not lead to any firm conclusions — an argument supported by Kobrick and Fine (1983) after a detailed review of the available literature. Problems of interpreting the various results can best be exemplified by reference to two studies.

In an investigation of the effects of cold on various tasks Bowen (1968) required his subjects to carry out their tasks while immersed in cold water at 7 °C (45 °F) for up to 30 minutes. Both manual performance (for example tactile sensitivity, grip strength, dexterity) and cognitive aspects (for example, mental arithmetic, complex coding tasks) were tested. On all tasks Bowen's results indicated a performance impairment in the cold compared with the 'normal' temperature (22 °C; 72 °F) water. The problems involved in interpreting these results, however, stem from the fact that the cognitive tasks were scored not in terms of accuracy but in terms of the number of calculations attempted. Even Bowen himself realizes that the reduced performance in the cold could have been attributed to problems of writing in the cold water, in which the dexterity of gripping a grease pencil was reduced.

Although the cold appeared to have no effect on the mental arithmetic task, accuracy on the complex coding task did show a significant reduction. Subjects were given a set of symbols and colours which they were required to process in the following way: by entering the number and colour into a matrix a value for each colour was provided; the subject was then given a problem number which was used to read, from another array, four numbers; each of these numbers was paired with the previously ascertained number of the four colours; each pair was multiplied together and the products summed; the subject then marked the answer on the scoreboard using a grease pencil. This task, therefore, required accurate translation of symbols and colours into numbers, short-term storage of the different numbers, and mental arithmetic. Bowen concludes that his data indicate that 'mental performance is impaired providing the tasks are sufficiently demanding in terms of concentration and short-term memory requirements'. Hence the reason for an impairment in the cognitive task but not the mental arithmetic task.

Bowen's conclusions, however, have not been substantiated by other experimenters. For example, Baddeley *et al.* (1975) asked their divers to perform different cognitive tasks (vigilance, memory, reasoning) in colder water and for longer than usually accepted (4°C (40°F) for 50 minutes). However, a reduced performance was not demonstrated on either the reasoning test (judging a series of statements as being either 'true' or 'false') or the vigilance test (detecting the occasional onset of a dim light mounted in the helmet).

To test the divers' memory, the experimenters read to them part of a passage containing a number of 'facts'. The subjects were subsequently asked first to recall as many of the facts as possible, and were then given a list of features and asked to identify any which they recognized as being in the original list. No significant impairment in recall was obtained in the cold, although recognition was significantly affected.

On the basis of their experiments Baddeley *et al.* conclude that cognitive efficiency may be surprisingly resistant to the effects of cold, given good conditions and well motivated subjects.

The results of these different studies, therefore, are inconclusive. Both were well-controlled but each seems to lead to contrary conclusions. However, if the 'riders' introduced by both authors are noted, some conclusions may be drawn. Thus Bowen suggests that only the very complex tasks will be affected by the cold. Certainly the vigilance and reasoning tasks used by Baddeley *et al.* were not as complex as Bowen's complex reasoning task. Secondly, Baddeley *et al.* suggest that the cold will not affect the cognitive efficiency of well-motivated subjects since the cold 'tends to reduce his motivation by making him uncomfortable, and his discomfort may in turn distract him from the task in hand'. This is less likely to happen to a well motivated subject. Unfortunately, neither experimenter really considered the distracting effects of the cold on a complex task.

Some evidence is also available to suggest that cold interferes with an individual's ability to estimate time accurately. Baddeley (1966) asked 20 amateur scuba divers to count up to 60 at what they considered to be a one-second rate. His data indicate that after the divers had entered the 4°C (39°F) water their estimation of time increased, i.e. one second was judged to be a longer period than in fact it is. It may be remembered that a similar effect was obtained by Jerison (1959) from subjects working under noisy conditions (Chapter 10). The similarity of these results with those of noise suggests that the cold is acting in the way of a general stressor when dealing with cognitive efficiency, rather than on particular physiological functions such as muscle control or skin sensitivity.

In summary, therefore, it appears that the cold is likely to affect the efficiency of less-well motivated individuals carrying out complex cognitive tasks which contain an element of time estimation. The reason for this is likely to be due to distraction caused by the stressing effects of the cold.

THE EFFECTS OF TEMPERATURE ON COMFORT

From the foregoing discussion it is quite clear that the body's core temperature must be kept to within quite narrow limits. A temperature increase of about 5 °C (9 °F) is likely to lead to death, as is a reduction by only 3–4 °C (5.5–7 °F). Furthermore, small departures from this critical band can lead to reductions in both motor and cognitive performance, as can large changes in the general environmental conditions.

In addition to these effects, changes in the thermal environment can affect an individual's comfort. As with any interaction between man and the environment the resultant sensations of comfort experienced by an individual depend both on the environmental conditions and on the individual factors which the person brings to the situation. For most purposes the physical environmental factors can be distilled to a consideration of the air temperature, the air humidity and the amount of air movement. Each of these is likely to become stressful when it interferes with the body's ability to maintain an adequate thermal balance.

The effect of the air temperature, measured with any type of dry bulb thermometer, is likely to be to raise or lower the overall body temperature. This requires the balancing mechanisms to produce sweat in hot conditions or to constrict peripheral blood vessels when cold. However in very hot conditions, for example near a furnace, the amount of heat radiated from the hot source (the furnace) is also important in affecting the operator's feelings of 'comfort'. Radiation is emitted by the heat source as electromagnetic waves which are absorbed and converted back into heat when they fall on to solid objects. If the radiation is severe enough, the skin tissue can be burnt — as most people who lay for too long on a Mediterranean beach will know.

Radiant temperature is usually measured using a globe thermometer. This is a hollow, six-inch diameter, metal globe that is painted matt black (the original equipment used by Bedford and Warner in the early 1930s was a cistern ballcock) with a normal mercury thermometer placed in an opening in the bulb. In this apparatus, the thermometer receives radiant heat from all directions and an indication of the 'mean radiant temperature' can be obtained after noting also the air temperature and the air speed.

The humidity is an index of the amount of water vapour in the air and is normally measured using two mercury thermometers. On one, the 'wet bulb' thermometer, the bulb is kept damp and is thus cooled by the evaporating water. The other, the 'dry bulb' thermometer, indicates the 'normal temperature'. Since the amount of water that can evaporate from the wet bulb depends on the air humidity, and since the degree of evaporation is reflected by a lower wet bulb temperature, taken together the two temperatures (wet and dry bulb) indicate the amount of water vapour present in the air.

Excessive water vapour in the air, indicated by a high relative humidity, is likely to interfere with the efficiency by which sweat will evaporate from the skin for cooling purposes. At the other end of the scale, very low humidities are likely to cause discomfort by drying the normally moist membranes in the nose and throat, particularly if the air temperature is rather high.

Air that moves over the body has a cooling effect because it helps both to evaporate the sweat and dissipate heat from the body surface. Although this is likely to result in increased comfort, air movement that is too fast can lead to complaints of draughts. It should be remembered, however, that velocity is a relative term; in this case it applies to the relative motions of the air and the observer. If the observer is stationary the relative velocity is equal to the air speed. For a moving observer, however, the air velocity is a function of both the observer's speed and direction of movement with respect to that of the air.

The two important variables that the observer is likely to bring to the situation are activity (type and level) and clothing. Other variables such as age and physical condition are also likely to affect whether a particular thermal environment is perceived as being 'comfortable' or 'uncomfortable', but these act solely on the body's ability to maintain a thermal balance through sweating or vasoconstriction. Activity and clothing, on the other hand, act independently of the observer's physical capacities — unless there is evidence of any physiological deficiency.

The effects of activity level on body temperature have already been considered when discussing heat stress. Thus when the muscles do work heat is produced as a by-product of the oxidation process. This then has to be dissipated.

The transfer of dry heat between the skin and the outer surface of the clothed body is quite a complicated process and involves internal convection and radiation processes in the intervening air spaces, and conduction through the cloth itself. These variables are accounted for by the now internationally accepted, dimensionless unit of thermal resistance from the skin to the outer surface of the body — the 'clo' (Gagge, Stolwijk and Nishi, 1971).

It is extremely difficult to measure the clo value of any clothing system. As Fanger (1970) points out, to obtain reasonably accurate measurements it is necessary to use a life-sized heated manikin clothed in the clothing ensemble to be tested. As heated manikins which include the necessary electronic equipment are expensive to produce, few are available outside the large (usually military) laboratories. This means that data are available for relatively few clothing ensembles. The range of clothes investigated extends from nude (clo = 0) to heavy wool suits for Polar environments (clo = 3–4), but within these extremes Fanger is able to list the clo values of only twelve other clothing ensembles.

Apart from the conductive resistance of the textile itself, the air between textile layers also acts as an important insulator and so the quality of tailoring and fit will influence the clo value. With very loose and hanging clothing, such as that worn by inhabitants of very hot countries, the heat which rises from the bottom of the airspace can cause slight 'chimney' effects to occur which produce a forced ventilation over the skin.

A Combined Temperature Scale

Since each of the thermal variables, air temperature, air velocity, radiation and humidity can, separately and combined, affect thermal comfort, it is useful to attempt to combine them to produce a single temperature scale. The most used such scale is the Effective Temperature Scale first proposed by Houghton and Yaglou in 1923. Unfortunately, since the scale only took account of air temperature, humidity and velocity it is inapplicable for environments which contain high levels of thermal radiation.

Vernon and Warner (1932) applied a radiation correction factor to the ET scale by using the globe thermometer to measure thermal radiation rather than a

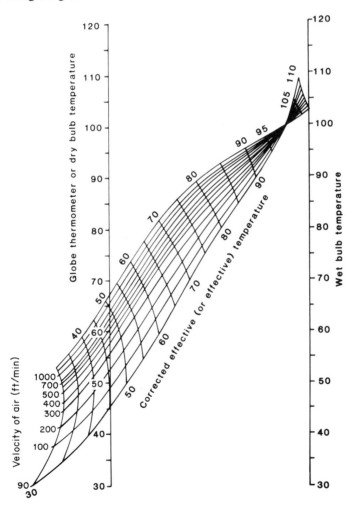

Figure 11.5 The corrected effective temperature scale (CET)

simple mercury thermometer to measure dry bulb temperature. Their resultant scale, the Corrected Effective Temperature Scale (CET), has been used extensively in many conditions and is shown in Figure 11.5. Under 'normal' conditions, however, the ET and the CET scales can be taken as being the same.

In more recent years attempts have been made to reassess the CET scale to bring it more up to date. For example, Nevins and Gagge (1972) suggest that there is now substantial evidence that the temperature criteria for thermal comfort have risen steadily from a range of 18–21 °C (65–70 °F) in 1900 to 24–26 °C (75–80 °F) in 1960. Although they do not support their contention with any written evidence they suggest that this shift has probably resulted from changes in clothing types and building construction.

A second reason for reassessing the scale has been the fear that both scales overemphasize the effects of humidity in cool conditions and underemphasize it in warm environments. Indeed 25 years after the introduction of his original scale, Yaglou (1947) himself recognized that the scale may perhaps have overemphasized the effects of humidity towards the lower temperatures. It was also felt that the old scales did not account sufficiently for the physiological processes which regulate the body's thermal response, including the 'insensible' heat lost from surfaces such as the lungs during breathing and vaporized water diffusing through the skin.

The American Society of Heating and Refrigeration Engineers, therefore, commissioned studies to produce a new comfort scale — the ASHRAE comfort scale (see Gagge, Stolwijk and Nishi, 1971). This New (Corrected) Effective Temperature Scale which was produced (designated the ET* scale to distinguish it from the old ET scale) is shown in Figure 11.6 and is compared with the old ET scale.

Figure 11.6 The old and new corrected effective temperature scales

Variables which Affect Thermal Sensations

A large number of variables contribute to the assessment of thermal comfort. Besides the obvious physical aspects of the environment discussed above, Rohles (1967) has listed such aspects as the room colour and size, the season of the year, the subject's age, activity, clothing and duration of exposure. To these Fanger (1970) adds national and geographical location, body build, the condition of a woman during her menstrual cycle, circadian rhythms and ethnic differences. Some of these will be discussed below.

Age

It would be reasonable to expect the elderly to prefer higher temperatures than younger people, since it is well known that metabolic rate decreases slightly with age. Furthermore, the elderly are less likely to lead the active life needed to help maintain a higher metabolic rate. Reduced body heat, then, should be compensated by increased need for warmth.

The research in this area, however, suggests that providing their physiological regulatory mechanisms remain effective the thermal preference of the elderly is no higher than for younger subjects. For example, Rohles (1969) asked 64 elderly subjects (mean age 75 years) to indicate whether they thought that each of 41 temperatures ranging from 32 to 110°F (0–43°C) would be 'too warm', 'too cold', or 'comfortable'. His results demonstrated that the distribution of responses for each category compared well with the distributions of more empirically derived responses from younger groups in other experiments.

Fanger (1970) conducted a more controlled series of experiments to investigate the same problem and found similar results. He ascribes the failure to show differences in preference to the body's bioregulation system. His measurements indicated that 'insensible' sweating (i.e. the evaporation of imperceptible amounts of sweat from the body which help to maintain thermal balance) in the elderly decreased in proportion to their reduced metabolic rate. Thus, although less heat is produced by the body less is lost.

Sex

In an experiment which measured the metabolic rate of subjects carrying out different levels of activity, McNall et al. (1968) demonstrated that males have higher metabolic rates than females. Again, therefore, the argument could be advanced that females might prefer warmer environments. Unlike for age, however, there is some *slight* evidence to suggest that this is the case. Thus, Beshir and Ramsey (1981) exposed subjects to different temperatures and asked them to rate their thermal sensation on a nine-point scale ranging from 'cold' to 'extremely hot'. Female subjects consistently rated lower (i.e. cooler) than males, although no statistical data are provided to assess the significance of the difference. Similar work (using a five-point scale) by Fanger (1970) resulted in similar conclusions although, in this case, the male–female difference was slight and non-significant for Danish subjects but just significant for American subjects. Even the American difference, however, was only very small: the females preferred, on average, temperatures 0.3 °C higher than the males.

Again, a reason for the lack of any significant difference between the thermal preferences of the two sexes could lie in the respective levels of insensible sweating. Thus, Fanger's data suggest that males sweated slightly more than females.

Circadian rhythm

The concept of the circadian rhythm will be discussed in more detail in the next chapter. However it is well known that the internal body temperature fluctuates on an hourly basis over a 24-hour period (see, for example, Folkard and Monk, 1985) and so some rhythm in thermal preferences may also be feasible. Nevins *et al.* (1966) found no difference in preferred temperature between experiments performed in the afternoon and those carried out in the evening, an observation which was confirmed by Fanger (1970). This is not to say, of course, that finer experimental analysis would not show a rhythm in thermal preferences. Both Nevins *et al.* and Fanger only divided the rhythm into two or three periods.

Colour

A considerable body of anecdotal evidence has been built up to suggest that the colour of the surroundings can influence man's thermal preferences. For example, an individual is presumed to feel warmer in a space having a colour scheme in which red predominates, compared with one in which blue is the prevailing colour.

Perhaps the first experimental study which bears on this question was conducted by Morgensen and English in 1926, who asked subjects to judge the temperature of heating coils wrapped in different colours. Apparently, the green ones were judged to be the hottest.

Unfortunately, however, experimental results relating to thermal preference show no such conclusive results. For example, Berry (1961) exposed each of 25 subjects to a temperature chamber illuminated by one of five colours: blue, green, white, yellow or amber. His subjects showed no change in the upper comfort limit in different coloured surroundings. Similar conclusions were reached by Fanger, Breum and Jerking (1977) who concluded that 'the effect of colour on man's comfort is so small that it hardly has any practical significance'.

In conclusion, however, Fanger (1970) rightly points out that any influence which colour has on the thermal sensation must be of a 'psychological nature'. The possibility cannot be denied, therefore, that an individual who is away from the oppressive, controlled laboratory environment may feel more at ease, more comfortable and, perhaps, experience more 'warmth' with different lighting conditions.

ILLUMINATION

Definitions

When discussing vibration and noise, the two defining characteristics of the stimulus were the signal's intensity and frequency. Although light can be considered to be fluctuating energy, the defining parameters of a light stimulus are its intensity and wavelength. The concept of wavelength is similar to that of frequency, except that it is related more to the distance between two peaks of a sinusoidal stimulus (rather like the distance between two waves on the sea) rather than the frequency with which the peaks occur. Wavelength, therefore, is measured in terms of distance but, because the distances between two energy 'peaks' are so small, the wavelength of light is normally described in terms of nanometers (1 nm = 10^{-9}, or one-billionth, of a metre). Visible light is simply a form of radiation with wavelengths between 380 and 780nm, and the eye discriminates between different wavelengths in this range by the sensation of colour. The violets are around 400nm, blending into the blues (around 450nm), the greens (around 500nm), the yellow-oranges (around 600nm), and the reds (around 700nm and above).

Illumination or illuminance

The intensity of a light source is expressed in terms of the amount of luminous flux (energy) which it generates. Just as the power of a car is described in relation to the power likely to be produced by a 'standard' horse (horsepower), the luminous flux produced by a light source is measured by comparing it with the flux produced by burning a standard candle of a specified material and weight. This candle is said to produce one candle power (or 1 candela, 1 cd) of energy.

Although flux so far has been used effectively as a synonym for energy, strictly speaking it refers to the rate at which the energy is produced and is measured in 'lumens'. Indeed, because a light source emits light in all directions, 1 candela is also defined as 1 lumen per steradian (i.e. the rate of flux produced per solid angle of the body).

As energy radiates from a source and travels through a dense medium such as air, water or glass it spreads out and loses its intensity. The amount of energy lost is inversely related to the square of the distance travelled (this is known as the inverse square law). Thus the level of illumination which falls on a surface will be lower than that which originated from the light source and, because of the diffusive nature of the medium through which it is travelling, will spread over the surface. Illumination, therefore, is defined in terms of the rate of flux (lumens) produced and the surface area over which it spreads (that is, lumens per square foot or lumens per square metre).

Unfortunately, the amount of flux being emitted from a source is not the only measure of the illumination of a surface. In addition to the inverse square law, there exists another law of illumination — the cosine law — which states that the surface illumination varies with the cosine of the angle between the surface and the light's direction. This is important for two reasons. First the efficiency of a light source can be varied by altering its angle of incidence to the surface — for example, by raising or lowering it. Second, the light that falls on a surface only rarely, and under specific conditions, arises *solely* from a single source. Most frequently it will arise both as direct illumination *and* as reflections from other surfaces — walls, ceilings, other objects, etc. These can be considered to be individual light sources and the efficiency of each will depend on the angle at which they reflect light onto the surface.

In any environment, therefore, the amount of light falling on a surface will depend on a number of factors. These are the luminous intensity of the light sources, the distances of the sources from the surface, the angles of the sources to the surface and the number of original and reflecting sources in the immediate environment.

Luminance

Although a particular light level may fall on a body, this is not to say that the observer will 'see' that level. Depending on their surface characteristics different bodies absorb and reflect different amounts and qualities of light. In this case the term used to define the amount of light reflected from the body's surface is its luminance and this is equal, simply, to the amount of light falling on the body multiplied by the proportion of light which the body reflects (its reflectance). Unfortunately for the novice illumination engineer, however, there are a multitude of terms to define luminance. It can be expressed either in terms of the luminous intensity per unit area (candelas per square metre), or in terms of the 'equivalent illumination' (equivalent lux), or apostilbs (asb), or in foot Lamberts (ft-L). The modern standard is to express it in terms of the candela per square metre, but a number of conversion tables exist to relate the various measures (see, for example, Megaw and Bellamy, 1983).

Brightness and retinal illuminance

The luminance qualities of an object will only be perceived by an observer after the light has stimulated the retinal cells and the information passed to the optic cortex in the brain. At this point the concept of the body's brightness is invoked, which is the subjective aspect of its luminance. When considering the response of the visual system to light, however, it is sometimes necessary to talk about the retinal illuminance. This is because the brightness of any image depends on the diameter of the limiting aperture of the image-forming device. In the eye this is set by the diameter of the pupil and retinal illuminance is measured in trolands (td). One troland is equal to the retinal illuminance obtained by looking through an artificial pupil having an area of 1 square mm at a matt surface whose luminance is 1cd per square metre.

The relationship between these definitions can perhaps be explained by reference to Figure 11.7. Thus a source (for example, a light bulb) illuminates a body. The level of illumination or illuminance is likely to be measured in units such as lux or lumens per square metre (lm m^{-2} (1 lux = 1 lm m^{-2}). This is unlikely to be the only source of light falling on the surface, however, and the total surface illuminance will depend also on the distance of the light sources and their angles to the surface. The surface of this body reflects light to the eye of the observer, the intensity being determined by the surface reflectance and being measured in many units such as candelas per square metre (cd m^{-2}). The observer then reports the body's brightness, the intensity of the report being determined by the amount of retinal illuminance allowed by the pupil and the experiences of the observer. These experiences, being subjective, are likely to depend on many factors including past experience and the brightness of other bodies in the visual field.

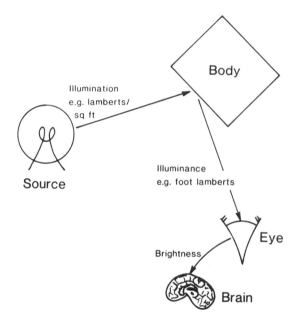

Figure 11.7 The relationship between illumination, luminance and brightness

LIGHTING AND BEHAVIOUR

Most of the important information regarding the relationship between illumination quality and performance has been discussed already when considering the way that the visual system operates. However, it is appropriate to recap some of the material here. Thus, for any one viewer performance is a function, primarily, of the overall illumination levels, the size of the object being viewed and the contrast between the object and its surround. This latter feature of the relationship between the object and its surround — comprising aspects such as contrast and location — is very important since it introduces the topic of glare and the effects that it can have both on comfort and on performance.

Illumination Level and Object Size

With regard to the relationship between overall illumination levels and performance, Gilbert and Hopkinson (1949) demonstrated that the potential for a particular type of performance (visual acuity) reduces after about 10 lumens/sq ft (107 lux). Subjects with visual deficiencies, however, required much higher illumination levels. A similar finding, that increased lighting will be of value only until a certain level has been reached, was demonstrated by Smith and Rea (1979). They asked subjects to check a list of 20 numbers for agreement with a comparison list, under different conditions of task luminance (i.e. the light reflected from the page). Performance increased with luminance up to 10 cd m^{-2}, but not above this level.

The relationship between overall illumination and more subjective factors such as comfort presents similar conclusions. For example, Saunders (1969) allowed subjects to adapt to windowless rooms lit only by ceiling lamps and then asked them to read from a book. Subsequent ratings of the illumination quality to which they had been exposed show that with increasing illuminance levels, subjects judged the lighting to increase in quality until, at about 800 lux there was no further value in increasing the levels (see Figure 11.8).

Figure 11.8 Quality of the lighting in a windowless office at different illuminations (Saunders, 1969). (*Reproduced by permission of the Chartered Institution of Building Services.*)

As far as the size of the object (i.e. the task) is concerned, Gilbert and Hopkinson's results demonstrated that as the objects (letters on the Snellen chart) became smaller, more light was required for them to be read accurately. In its code for interior lighting, the Illuminating Engineering Society (IES) suggest illumination levels for many different types of work interiors which are related to the type of work carried out. Overall, seven levels are suggested, as shown in Table 11.1. The code suggests, however, that before deciding on an appropriate illumination level for the task in hand, four important questions should be asked:

(1)   Are the reflectances or contrasts unusually low (for example, having to pick out dark objects from a dark, matt background)?
(2)   Will errors have serious consequences?
(3)   Is the task of short duration?
(4)   Is the area windowless?

On the basis of answers to these questions an appropriate illuminance level can be chosen as indicated in Table 11.1.

Contrast

An object's contrast refers simply to the relationship of its luminance to its surround. It is a measure, then, of how well the object 'stands out'. Without contrast an object cannot be seen and this applies equally to such stimuli as words on the printed page or on a visual display, to a large machine in a dimly lit room, to a well-camouflaged soldier, or to insects.

The normal way to express contrast is in terms of a ratio between the luminance difference of the object and its surround to the surround luminance. So, an object which is illuminated by 100 units of light placed on a background of 10 units will have a contrast ratio of $(100-10)/10 = 9$, as will a 10-unit object placed on a 1-unit background.

Unfortunately, however, as Hopkinson and Collins (1970) point out, the observer's visual behaviour also needs to be taken into account when determining contrast relationships. For example, whereas two light meters may register 100 and 10 units in one case and 10 and 1 units in another, and so 'deduce' that the contrast ratios in the two cases are the same, an observer's perceptual system is likely to treat the two sets of stimuli differently because of a phenomenon known as brightness constancy.

To explain this phenomenon, suppose an observer is looking at two different flat surfaces — one grey and one white — which are illuminated so as to ensure that the *luminances* arising from them are equal. Since the stimulus received by the retinal cells is related to the surface luminance, and since the two luminances are the same, it might be assumed that they would look the same. Unfortunately, they will not; the grey will still look greyer than the white *unless* they are not viewed together (say each is viewed through a tube in such a way that each surface covers the whole of the observer's field of view). Only under these very specific circumstances will the two appear to have similar luminances. Because

Table 11.1 A flow-chart for modifying standard service illuminances for unusual conditions. (After IES Code, 1977).

Task group and typical task or interior	Standard service illuminance (lx)	Are reflectances or contrasts unusually low?	Will errors have serious consequences?	Is task of short duration?	Is area windowless?	Final service illuminance (lx)
Storage areas and plant rooms with no continuous work	150					→ 150
Casual work	200				no / yes → 200	→ 200
Rough work Rough machining and assembly	300	no / yes → 300	no / yes → 300	yes → 300	no / yes → 300	→ 300
Routine work Offices, control rooms, medium machining and assembly	500	no / yes → 500	no / yes → 500	no → 500	no / yes → 500	→ 500

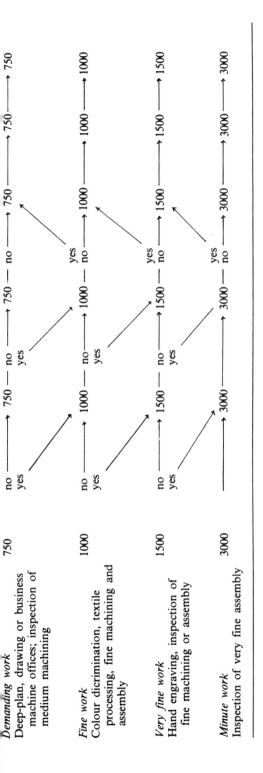

an object exists within a frame of reference which contains other objects and surfaces, well-defined textures, contours, contrasts and colours, the optic cortex interprets the stimuli in terms of past experiences and expectations to ensure that the visual 'world' remains 'constant'.

Because of this phenomenon Hopkinson and Collins suggest that contrast should be expressed not in terms of the actual luminance levels but of the difference between the 'apparent brightnesses' of the object and its surround. This rests on the assumption that everything that we see is evaluated, as far as brightness is concerned, in terms of some reference level which Hopkinson and Collins suggest is associated with the state of adaptation of the eye at the time. Light entering a large window, therefore, is likely to alter the eye's adaptive state and so affect vision by altering the apparent brightness of, say, characters on the page. Hopkinson, Waldram and Stevens (1941) have produced a set of curves from which one can read the apparent brightness of the object or surround given their respective brightnesses.

Although a high contrast is clearly important in ensuring that the object is perceived accurately, it is also important that the *direction* of the contrast effect is considered, for two reasons.

First, as has been discussed already, some evidence exists to suggest that dark characters on a brighter background (negative contrast) leads to slightly higher performance and 'preference' ratings than the reverse (Bauer and Cavonius, 1980; Radl, 1980). This is possibly because the printed page is normally also in negative contrast so that adaptation is maintained when the gaze has to move from the screen to paper and back again.

The second reason for concern about the contrast direction arises if the surround is *considerably* brighter than the object, perhaps because of reflected light falling on the screen. If this occurs then both the object's visibility and the observer's visual comfort are likely to be reduced due to glare. This will be discussed in more detail below.

As an example of the importance of contrast to efficient visual performance, in their illumination study Gilbert and Hopkinson (1949) asked their subjects to read the letters on a Snellen chart under different illumination levels, using different contrast ratios between the letters and the background. Their results indicated strongly that as the contrast was increased the subject's ability to read the letters accurately also increased. This effect was particularly marked at the lower levels of overall illumination, whereas the performance increase was not so marked when the overall illumination level was reasonably high.

GLARE

Glare occurs whenever one part of the visual field is brighter than the level to which the eye has become adapted. Excessive luminance levels can arise in one or both of two ways. First, direct glare occurs when the light appears directly from the source itself, such as a car headlight at night, the sun during the day, or perhaps a badly positioned light bulb. Second, and perhaps more insidious, reflected or specular glare is caused by very bright reflections from polished or glossy surfaces. VDUs, for example, often act as very good reflectors of specular light, as does glossy paper and even the keys on a keyboard. White walls and ceilings can also be a source of specular glare. The effects of these glare sources can often be unpredictable since they may occur under various circumstances — for example, when the object is placed at a certain angle to the light, when more than one light is brought together, or at certain times of the day when the sun is reflected off other surfaces.

Glare is commonly described as being of two types. If there is direct interference with visual performance the condition is referred to as disability glare. However, if performance is not directly affected but the bright stimulus still causes discomfort, annoyance, irritation or distraction, the condition is called discomfort glare. As Boyce (1981) points out, the distinction between these two terms if often blurred — the same lighting conditions can produce disability and discomfort simultaneously and, to confuse matters further, different lighting conditions can cause disability and create discomfort independently.

The effects of both types of glare, however, may eventually be to cause reduced performance, through distraction, through increased arousal or, because having to avoid the glare can constitute another task that the operator has to perform, through reduction in the available spare mental capacity. Furthermore, because the eye always tends to move to the brightest part of the visual field (the so-called phototropic effect), a consequence of glare can often be to draw the eyes away from the task in hand. For example, Hopkinson and Longmore (1959) have demonstrated that the eye makes more frequent, jerky darts towards the brighter area of the visual field.

Disability Glare

The reduced ability to see accurately due to interference from a bright light source has probably been experienced by all at some time or another, so the potential disabling effects of glare are well known.

At a descriptive level two of the earliest workers in the field, Lukiesh and Holladay (1925) considered disability glare to be of three types. Veiling glare, they felt, was due to light from the glare source being scattered in the fluids of the eye so reducing contrast and hence visibility. An effect is caused, therefore, which is similar to illuminated fog or mist. This was illustrated by Stiles and his colleagues (Stiles, 1929; Crawford and Stiles, 1937) who performed an experiment in which the glaring light source was presented on the blind spot of the retina. Although the light source itself was invisible, its veiling effect was still present.

The second type of disability glare, which Luckiesh and Holladay describe as 'dazzle glare', occurs as a short-term effect for the duration of the glare source. Finally 'blinding glare' lasts beyond the period of the glare stimulus due to the formation of 'blinding after-images'.

In a comprehensive series of experiments Holladay (1926) investigated many aspects of disability glare and he is perhaps best remembered for producing a glare formula which is still used today. His experiments indicated that the amount of glare (defined in terms of contrast reduction), is determined by both the position of the glaring source with respect to the observer and the amount of light entering the observer's eye. Thus:

Contrast reduction = $\dfrac{k \times \text{illumination produced by glaring source at eye}}{(\text{Angle at eye between source and object being viewed})^2}$.[4]

The value of k in this formula appears to depend on the age of the observer since age causes changes in the consistency of fluids in the eyeball (Christie and Fisher, 1966).

There are two important implication of Holladay's formula. First is its suggestion that the extent of the glare will decrease as the angle of the glare source to the observer increases. The other important factor concerns the amount of illumination produced by the glare source. As Hopkinson and Collins (1970) point out, the effect will be the same whether the glaring source is a small source of high illuminance or a large source of low illuminance — provided the illumination at the eye is the same. This means that a dark sky, for example, seen through a large window can cause as much disability glare as a small, more intense light bulb — even though its brightness may not be sufficiently high to cause any discomfort.

Discomfort Glare

Paradoxically, discomfort glare appears to have been studied more extensively than disability glare, and a number of formulae have been derived which relate various physical parameters of the glare source to levels of 'discomfort' (see, for example, Murrell, 1971 or Boyce, 1981 for a list and description of many of these formulae).

The discomfort produced by a glare source appears to have a different physiological origin than does disability glare. Thus Hopkinson (1956) has demonstrated a link between the level of discomfort and the activity of the eye musculature which controls the iris. This relationship, however, is not perfect and Hopkinson concludes that discomfort sensations were due only in part to the conflict which arises between the requirements for pupil control between the areas of the retina stimulated by the glaring source, and those receiving lower levels of illumination.

The most modern glare formula, which has become generally accepted, has been produced by the Illuminating Engineering Society based on empirical work developed by the Building Research Station in Great Britain. This work was carried out over a number of years by Hopkinson and his colleagues (see, for example, Hopkinson, 1940, 1972; Petherbridge and Hopkinson, 1950). The results of the various investigations produced the following glare formula:

$$\text{Glare constant } (G) = \frac{Bs^{1.6} \times w^{0.8}}{Bb \times \varnothing^2}$$

where Bs is the luminance of the source, w is the solid angle subtended by the source at the eye (i.e. this is related to its apparent size), Bb is the general background luminance and $\varnothing$ is the angle between the direction of viewing and the direction of the glare source.

The Glare Index, then, is computed by summing the glare constants from each source in the visual field, obtaining the logarithm of this sum, and multiplying this figure by a factor of 10. Thus:

Glare Index $= 10 \log_{10} (\text{sum } G)$

Using formulae of this nature, the glare constant obtained can be related to some criterion of discomfort. Thus a glare constant of 600 indicates the boundary of 'just intolerable'; 150 the boundary of 'just uncomfortable'; 35 the boundary of 'just acceptable' and 8 would be 'just perceptible'. A more useful criterion, however, might be to express the glare ratings in terms of the probability of producing 'visual comfort'. This the IES has done, which McCormick (1976) has adapted to form one, single graph as shown in Figure 11.9.

Figure 11.9 The relationship between discomfort glare ratings and the probability of retaining visual comfort. (*From McCormick (1976), reproduced by permission of the McGraw-Hill Book Co.*)

If more than one glaring source is present in the environment, Hopkinson (1940) showed that the simple arithmetical addition of the glare constants obtained from each source gave a glare value which corresponded closely to the sensation from the complete array of the sources. Later, however (1957), he modified his position slightly when he showed that the additive nature was a highly complex phenomenon, the exact function depending, among other things, on the luminance of the sources and their position in the field of view.

Finally, although the values of the exponents in the glare formula depend to some extent on the experimental conditions, it is possible to see that decreasing the size and luminance of the source (Bs) would increase glare, as would increasing the background luminance (Bb). In practice, however, increasing the source luminance is also likely to increase background luminance. Furthermore, as with disability glare, increasing the angle between the glare source and the observer also decreases glare. As a rough guide Hopkinson and Collins (1970) state that a Glare Index of less than 10 is rated as 'barely perceptible' glare while a value of over 28 is rated as 'intolerable'. Unfortunately, however, as Boyce (1981) has shown, there is wide individual variability in the extent to which glare (as measured by the Glare Index) causes discomfort.

Veiling Reflections

In addition to these two types of glare, a special case of glaring sources can occur when high levels of background illumination appear in the visual field and cover the objects of interest. For obvious reasons, these are called veiling reflections and their effect is to increase the overall levels of both the object and the background luminances. To measure the contrast between the object and surround, therefore, the basic formula discussed earlier needs to be modified slightly to include the luminance of the veiling source (Bv). Thus the new task contrast (C) will be:

$$C = \frac{(B_o + B_v) - (B_b + B_v)}{B_b + B_v}$$

In an attempt to discover how veiling reflections affect viewer satisfaction, De Boer (1977) asked subjects to read two journals; one printed on a moderately glossy paper the other on semi-matt paper, and also a piece of text written in pencil on matt paper. Figure 11.10 shows that there is a clear relationship between comfort and veiling reflections with the 'just disturbing' category having a contrast ratio of about 0.6.

Veiling reflections mainly present themselves at work as reflections from the working surface, and in modern office environments this is usually at computer screens. However, they can also occur over shiny keyboard keys and on glossy source document paper. As far as the screen is concerned, Cakir, Hart and Stewart (1980) point out that the smooth glass surface of a screen face typically reflects about 4 per cent of the light which falls on it, which is quite sufficient to produce clearly visible and sharply defined reflections. When the phosphor is bonded directly on to the inner surface of the screen glass, without any

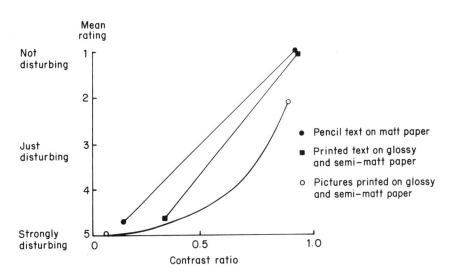

Figure 11.10 The effect of different contrast ratios, arising from veiling reflections from various surfaces, on perceived disturbance (De Boer, 1977). (*Reproduced by permission of the Chartered Institution of Building Services*)

intervening filter, this reflectance can rise to 22–27 per cent.

Cakir, Hart and Stewart also point out that veiling reflections can affect the eye's accommodation. Reflections on the face of a VDU screen, for example, represent an additional image which is interposed between the operator's eye and the plane on which the character images are displayed. Thus a 'double image' occurs which the optic cortex attempts to resolve (often unsuccessfully) by using the ciliary muscles to alter the lens curvature. In the long term this is likely to lead to visual fatigue.

Reducing Glare

From the above discussion, it is clear that glare arises mainly from two sources: specular glare reflected off material that is being used, and glare from large light sources such as windows or badly positioned lights.

Glare from screens

Perhaps the most obvious way to control reflected glare from VDU screens is to control the glaring source; to pull blinds, position the screen so that the window does not shine on it, arrange lights so that they are not reflected, etc. Often, however, this is not possible or convenient. For example, sun shining through a window at such an angle or intensity to be reflected on the screen may only occur for a relatively short time. Rearranging the workstation to take account of such possibilities may not be a feasible proposition. For these types of situation, screen filters are often used by manufacturers and individual operators to combat the problem of screen reflections.

Unfortunately, little work appears to have been reported which has investigated the efficiency of different types of screen filter. Nevertheless, Cakir, Hart and Stewart (1980) present a useful discussion of the different types of filter presently available and the advantages and disadvantages of each. As they point out, however, screen filters can have only limited value. It is not possible to place a filter between the eye and visual display and thereby improve all of the characteristics that contribute to the 'quality' of the display. While using an appropriate filter can be effective in reducing screen reflections, it is invariably accomplished at the expense of reduced character brightness and resolution.

Glare from windows

Consideration of the glare formula discussed earlier suggests two features of the illumination environment that can contribute to increased glare from large areas such as windows. Thus, glare is increased as the luminance of the glaring source (Bs) is increased and as its angle to the observer is decreased. This suggests that simply reducing the amount of light entering the room will go some way to reducing glare — but not the whole way. Hopkinson (1972), therefore, suggests that if the simple expedient of window blinds is not appropriate, architectural techniques can be employed such as using tinted glass, limiting the area of sky visible from any position in the room by using large, vertical fins on the window or fitting translucent blinds, by building an overhang above the window or, to increase the angle of the glaring source, by having windows higher up the wall. Furthermore, remembering that glare is a contrast effect, he suggests that it might be reduced if this contrast is also reduced, for example by painting the window surrounds a very light colour (possibly even white). Care needs to be taken, in this case, however, to ensure that the white surrounds do not, themselves, become glaring objects.

Windowless rooms

If glare from windows is a serious problem one obvious design possibility is to remove the windows and install lights, the intensity and angle of which are under the control of the operator. Research data suggests, however, that to do so can often create problems of a different form, possibly of reduced satisfaction with the workplace. Boyce (1981) presents a valuable review of such studies which have demonstrated mixed reactions to windowless rooms, often depending on the room function and the number of other occupants that it contains. For example, Ruys (1970) surveyed occupants in five different buildings in America, each containing a number of windowless offices. Whereas there appeared to be few complaints about the level of artificial lighting provided, nearly 90 per cent of the occupants expressed dissatisfaction with the lack of windows. Those office workers who often had to work alone complained that a lack of windows meant a lack of daylight, poor ventilation and an inability to know about the weather or to have a view. It also gave an impression of being cooped up and led to feelings of depression and tension.

On the other hand, studies performed in factories, which are often windowless but in which space is usually large and contains a number of other people, suggests few complaints (Pritchard, 1964). Boyce also reports similar findings from studies investigating the effects of windowless classrooms on school-children. Indeed, in some cases the children performed better in rooms without windows.

Contradictory data such as these lead Boyce to suggest that it is not the lack of windows *per se* which is a cause for discontent but the social setting of the environment and the size of the windowless space. In environments in which there was adequate scope for social interaction (factories and schools), with larger rooms, the complaints were rare. In smaller office-type environments, however, with reduced chances for social interaction, complaints were heard. Furthermore, Boyce argues that equality of circumstances is important in such cases. For example, Sommer (1974) found that the dislike of a windowless environment in the underground offices that he studied was amplified by the fact that the executives had offices above ground with windows overlooking fine views.

SUMMARY

As this chapter has demonstrated, small departures from the ideal levels of both illumination and temperature can lead to fairly large reductions in performance and, in the case of temperature, even to death. Both of these environmental parameters, however, are extremely complex in their composition and their effects on the operator, and this chapter has explained some of these actions.

CHAPTER 12

ERGONOMICS AND SAFETY

At first it might appear strange that safety is considered in a separate chapter in an ergonomics text which stresses throughout how various man–environment interactions can lead to unsafe acts. Safety, so the argument would go, was considered for example when discussing the maximum loads the operator should lift (Chapter 3), display design for accurate perception and performance (Chapter 5), designing and arranging controls for safe use (Chapters 6 and 7), and so on. What further information can a chapter on safety add?

Whereas it is true that safety and accidents have been examined in detail throughout this book, they were approached primarily from the viewpoint of the system and the operator's interaction with it (for example, loads able to be carried; displays, controls, machines; the noise, temperature; etc.). This chapter will examine some of the factors which the operator can introduce into an otherwise 'safe' situation which will be likely to make it 'unsafe'. Even if the system has been designed to take account of all ergonomic principles so far discussed, experience tells us that accidents still occur when a human operator is present. This chapter will consider some of the reasons why.

Although the main emphasis will be on characteristics of the operator's behaviour which lead to accidents, the man–machine systems concept is still valid and should not be forgotten. It is still argued that an accident occurs as a result of the environment (including machines) demanding more of the operator than is able to be given; when the environment demands more 'spare-mental capacity' from the operator than there is available.

At this point it is useful to ask the question 'What is an accident?', 'When does an accident become deliberate and hence blamable?' A number of definitions exist but all contain concepts which can be distilled to three main points (Suchman, 1961); the more of these points which are present, the more likely the event will be called an 'accident'. An accident, then, has a low degree of:

(a) expectedness,
(b) avoidability,
(c) intention to cause the accident.

Thus, accidents are unfortunate, unpredictable, unavoidable and unintentional interactions with the environment. This very unpredictability and rarity makes them extremely difficult to investigate directly and so most accident research has been carried out on either accident reports, or using the painstaking method of direct observation of minor 'incidents' or 'near misses' which do not result in reported accidents. Both of these techniques, however, have their drawbacks and can result in biases in interpretation as will be discussed in Chapter 14.

THE COST EFFECTIVENESS OF ACCIDENT PREVENTION

In many respects it could be argued that as far as accident prevention is concerned, to consider cost-effectiveness is both morally wrong and inherently difficult. How much value does one put on human life, grief, pain, etc.? This point is emphasized in Table 12.1 which compares the costs and benefits which were calculated for incorporating safety features in an automobile petrol tank said to have been produced by a major automobile company (reproduced from Biancardi, 1978).

Table 12.1   A cost/benefit analysis produced for the implementation of a new, safe, automobile petrol tank

---

Benefits
Savings: 180 burn deaths, 180 serious burn injuries, 2100 burned vehicles
Unit costs: $200000 per death, $67000 per injury, $700 per vehicle
Total benefit: 180 × ($200000) + 180 × ($67000) + 2100 × ($700) = $49.5 million

Costs
Sales: 11 million cars, 1.5 million light trucks
Unit costs: $11 per car, $11 per truck
Total cost: 11000000 × ($11) + 1500000 × ($11) = $137 million

---

Similar types of analyses have been proposed by other authors. For example Powell *et al.* (1971) initially consider the costs of over 2000 accidents which occurred during a study of four different types of shop-floor. They calculated that the number of man-hours lost through accidents was roughly equivalent to the permanent absence of four people. The total wages cost was in the region of £3500 per annum and, assuming the labour content of a factory product to be 20 per cent of the equivalent product, the sales loss was calculated to be £16500 per annum. As the authors point out, however, 'to a large factory this is peanuts and is no doubt one of the reasons why accidents are not regarded as a serious problem'.

The straightforward loss of productivity from injuries, however, cannot represent all of the costs in any cost/benefit analysis. As Powell *et al.* point out, the burden of an accident is not just a burden on the factory so much as on the community.

A factory may have a first-aid service included in its on-costs but the community has a hospital service, a national insurance scheme, and a legal service to pay for, thus relieving the factory of further responsibility for the people it maintains. The factory produces goods and injuries; the community at large pays for both.

Bearham (1976) takes this point a little further and divides accidents into three types:

(a) *Lost-time accident:* because of, for example, hospitalization, this causes a loss of time beyond the shift during which the accident occurred.
(b) *Non-lost time accident:* causes no loss of time beyond the shift during which the accident occurred.
(c) *Damage accident:* no injury is caused to people, but facilities, equipment or materials may be damaged.

He further suggests that these three types of accidents occur in the ratio of approximately 1:60:400, so that for every lost-time accident occurring in industry, there will be approximately 400 property damage/no injury accidents.

The costs of all three types of accidents, Bearham suggests, can be divided into direct and indirect costs (sometimes referred to as 'known' and 'hidden' costs). Direct costs are incurred through such aspects as settling claims for damages to equipment; compensation for loss of earnings, pain and suffering as a result of injury; legal liability under health and safety acts; and insurance premiums. This type of information is readily available since it is directly paid out. Because they do tend to be hidden, however, indirect costs are more difficult to evaluate. However, Bearham's list includes the following items:

(a) *Safety administration costs:* the time of the safety officer and committee dealing with the accident investigation and a proportion of time for any secretarial support.
(b) *Medical centre costs:* doctors' and nurses' time and the medical supplies used in the treatment of injuries. (Bearham does point out that these types of cost would still exist even if accidents were greatly reduced since they promote the well-being of employees. However, they are still costs which result from accidents.)
(c) *Welfare payments:* the proportion of the payment made by the company to the employee while off work.
(d) *Ambulance service costs:* running and depreciation of the ambulance and the ambulance driver's time.
(e) Cost of time of other employees: including (i) the time taken by other employees to help the injured person, (ii) the time taken by the foreman in aiding the injured person, (iii) the time taken by the witnesses in answering questions during the accident investigation, etc.
(f) *Replacement labour costs:* if the injured person is replaced.
(e) *Loss of production costs:* due to the unavailability of manpower and machines.
(f) *Damage to plant and machinery costs:* incurred when repairs are needed and replacements are ordered and fitted.
(g) *Other costs:* arising from the accident investigation — these include

stationery, and secretarial and clerical work performed in actually processing and recording the accident and corresponding with solicitors and insurance companies.

Clearly, when all of these costs are understood and are taken into account, the balance of the cost/benefit equation must tip towards the importance of increasing safety practices. The remainder of this chapter will consider some of the reasons (models) why accidents may occur.

MODELS OF ACCIDENT CAUSATION

Behavioural Models

As the name suggests behavioural models imply that an accident occurs due to some deficiencies in operator behaviour rather than in the machine itself.

Learning theories

The skills developed at work arise as a result of a complex series of behaviour patterns learned over long periods. In developing these skills feedback, both from the sense organs and in terms of a knowledge of results, plays an extremely important role. One of the basic requirements for learning an action or a skill rests in reinforcing, by feedback, the consequences of the response to a particular stimulus. For example, in attempting to knock a nail into a piece of wood a novice carpenter might sometimes miss the nail and hit some fingers (producing negative reinforcement) which would cause subsequent behaviour patterns to be altered (for example, moving the fingers or altering the hammer swing). Eventually a correct response (hit) to the stimulus (nail) is made and the resulting (positive) feedback (of a nail properly embedded in the wood without painful fingers) will reinforce the correct behaviour.

This type of learning is very similar to that described by Pavlov whose dog learned to salivate to the sound of a bell. It is known as conditioning. (To distinguish it from the 'passive' behaviour observed in Pavlov's dog — often called 'classical' conditioning— the form of conditioning in which a motor response is made is known as instrumental conditioning.) Two main principles apply in determining the strength of a conditioned response: First, positive reinforcement will tend to make an action more likely to be carried out, and secondly the more frequently the action is reinforced (either positively or negatively) the greater will be the learning effect.

Since skilled behaviour is composed of a collection of skilled responses it is possible to understand how inappropriate (dangerous) behaviour could be incorporated into the repertoire. First, in many respects safe behaviour is negatively reinforcing. It is often time consuming, it may involve using safety clothing and it sometimes attracts unwelcome comments from fellow workers. (Although this attitude is gradually being eroded, in many industries it is still considered 'unmanly' to take safety precautions.) Unsafe behaviour, on the other hand, is often quicker (one talks of 'cutting corners'), more comfortable and is often more socially acceptable. As an example of these effects Winsemius (1965) describes the operation of a machine used to punch the index letters on the sides of pages in address books:

> In order to start the machine a pedal was pushed down. As long as it was down the machine ran; as soon as the foot was lifted from the pedal the machine stopped almost instantaneously.
>
> The machines were operated by female workers. During their learning period they stopped the machine at every page so that the operator fixed the speed of work. Experienced workers however started the machine after having inserted a booklet and did not stop it again until the whole booklet had been punched. Experienced workers thus moved their fingers in the same rhythm as the machine. As the booklet approached completion, the index finger came nearer and nearer to the edge of the punching die, and was indeed very close to it during the punching of the last two or three leaves.
>
> (*Reprinted from* Ergonomics *by permission of the publisher.*)

The experienced operators, then, had learned to use unsafe behaviour patterns to unstick pages without stopping the machine. This behaviour was easier and less time consuming than the safe operation and so it was positively reinforced. The safe behaviour (stopping the machine before unsticking the pages), however, led to fatigue, lost time, and no obvious rewards. Only when the press descended on to the operator's fingers was the negative reinforcement stronger than that resulting from the safe behaviour.

The second principle, the number of times that the event is reinforced, is also important in applying learning theory to safety. Thus accidents are extremely rare occurrences, even when the behaviour is unsafe. For example, Winsemius calculated that accidents using the alphabet punch occurred less than 1 in 6 000 000 operations. The stronger negative reinforcement of a punched finger, therefore, is unlikely to be experienced.

Taken together, these two aspects (unsafe behaviour is positively reinforcing and its negative effects are extremely infrequent) suggest that training alone is unlikely to reduce unsafe behaviour. Unless the negatively reinforcing aspects have been sufficiently incorporated into the training repertoire, almost by a change in attitudes, the unsafe behaviour is likely to become positively reinforced as soon as the training period ends (as is often the case when learner drivers have recently passed their driving test).

Memory lapses

Many of the tasks commonly carried out at work involve large memory components. Operators have to remember sequences of operations, the meanings of different stimuli and reponses to make, etc. However, just as our capacity to process information is limited so is our ability to retain it. The more that needs to be remembered but which is not in the normal repertoire of behaviour, the more likely are particular aspects to be forgotten. Forgetting (the loss, permanent or temporary, of the ability to recall or to recognize something learned earlier), therefore, is a clear candidate for causing accidents.

The reasons why we forget are complex and are still not fully understood. In some cases it may be the result of repressing the action — blocking recall of the operation. Repression, however, a Freudian concept, is extremely difficult to investigate scientifically. More likely answers lie in the decay of the memory trace over time, interactions of the memory trace with other traces, or errors in storing and/or selecting the material to be remembered.

It is common experience that our ability to retain information decays from the time when the information was sorted in memory. Originally this was thought to be due to a physiological decay in the brain which loses the information (much like a leak in a cylinder). However, more modern thinking suggests that laying down the memory trace may be impaired by the presence of previously learned material (proactive interference) or that its retention is impaired by material which was learned subsequently (retroactive interference). For example, an operator's inability to remember a correct sequence of control actions could be due either to the fact that other, different, sequences had been learned which interfere with memory for the new ones, or that other tasks have subsequently to be learned and carried out, again, interfering with the memory trace.

In most cases a complete memory breakdown is unlikely to lead to accidents since performance will stop. Accidents are more likely to occur when an incorrect memory trace is recalled, that is when the wrong control sequence is carried out without the operator's awareness.

The causes of such 'absent-mindedness' have not been studied in such depth as have the causes of forgetting. However, Reason (1976, 1979) asked people to keep a diary of their 'non-planned actions' over a continuous two-week period. From his analysis of the 35 completed diaries (23 women and 12 men) he divided absent-minded acts into one of four types: storage errors, in which the original memory trace was incorrectly stored; test errors, in which the operator incorrectly checks the progress and outcomes of a sequence of actions; discrimination errors, in which the initial stimulus to carry out a sequence of activities is wrongly identified; and selection errors, in which the incorrect response is selected. Reason argues that absent-minded errors are a hazard for the skilled rather than for the unskilled operator.

They seem to be a feature of well-practised or habitual tasks which are carried out fairly automatically, with only intermittent conscious checking. As one's conscious mind is rarely still, it is likely to be engaged with something other than the present routine action most of the time.

Personality

Much of the work investigating the role of personality factors in accident causation has been carried out in the field of motor vehicle accidents. Two types of study can be seen: the accident prone personality, and the relationship between accidents and various measured personality variables such as intraversion and extraversion, curiosity, aggression, etc.

Accident proneness

The idea that an individual might have some personality trait which predisposes him or her to accidents was first suggested by three statisticians, Greenwood, Woods and Yule in 1919. Supported by the Industrial Fatigue Research Board, they published an account of accidents sustained by workers in a munitions factory during the First World War and showed that a small minority of workers had more accidents than they would have done if chance factors alone were operating.

The next major study in the area was carried out by Newbold in 1926. She described a similar analysis on nearly 9000 workers in factories manufacturing products of all sorts from motor-cars to optical instruments, chocolates and cardboard boxes, and her data substantiated many of Greenwood, Woods and Yule's findings.

Both sets of authors, however, were careful to emphasize that the statistical analysis of accident records is a study only of what happened — not of why or how it happened. In addition they record only the accident occurrences — not those of near accidents. Merely because an 'accident' was not sufficiently serious for it to be reported does not mean that the individual or the situation is not prone to causing accidents. Furthermore, Newbold pointed out that in her particular sample there were definite indications that youth, inexperience and possibly even poor health were associated with accident occurrence, and that it was not possible to rule out increased risk of exposure to dangerous situations as an important factor in the individual differences in 'proneness' to accidents.

The concept of accident proneness as a personal idiosyncrasy predisposing the individual to a relatively high accident rate was first suggested by Farmer and Chambers in 1939. They examined the accident records of a large group of drivers and found, again, that a few had a disproportionately large number of accidents. However, in their description of 'accident proneness' they went a stage further than their statistical data should have allowed. They argued that we can talk about an individual's personal proneness (regardless of the environmental circumstances) rather than the individual's and the environment's combined tendency to create a situation in which an accident is likely to occur.

If, as Farmer and Chambers suggest, accident proneness as a trait is 'no longer a theory but an established fact', using appropriate personality tests it should be possible to differentiate between the personalities of 'accident-free' people and 'accident repeaters'. This a number of investigators have tried to do but without much success. Many traits have been established — aggressiveness, inconsiderateness, hostility, timerity, etc. — but no single personality dimension has been found. For example, Tillman and Hobbs (1949) investigated the life-style of accident repeaters and showed that they had marked aggressive, antisocial tendencies, more frequent court appearances in both youth and adult life for non-traffic offences, a higher incidence of venereal disease, and a greater rate of attendance at social and welfare agencies. However, there was no indication of any particular group of traits consistently emerging to produce an 'accident prone' individual.

Such difficulties have led to a reformulation of the concept of an accident prone personality. Current thinking now suggests that if the trait of accident proneness does exist it is one which is not a permanent, unchangeable state of the individual. Rather it is an attribute influenced by both personal and environmental factors which vary from one period to another. Reason (1974), for example, suggests that

> examination of accident-repeaters over a lengthy period indicates that they are members of a club which is continuously changing its membership. New people are added, while long standing members cease to qualify. It is possible that in some people accident proneness is a passing phase, while in others it is more enduring.

Thus age, experience, hazard exposure, and a multitude of other factors may contribute to cause an individual at some times to be more liable to have an accident than at others. As Reason summarizes 'the whole business (of accident proneness) is a good deal more complicated than was first imagined any part of which may be safe or unsafe depending on the type of hazards to which he is exposed'. Accident proneness, therefore, if it exists, is likely to be a fault of the current man–machine system with all of its complexities, rather than only of the person.

Other Personality Traits

Because it is unlikely that a single dimension of 'accident proneness' exists it is not necessarily the case that personality traits or dimensions do not predispose an individual towards interacting with the environment in a dangerous manner. Using the Eysenck Personality Inventory, for example, Shaw and Sichel (1971) compared the personality profiles of a group of South African bus drivers with their accident records (categorized as 'good', 'fair', 'poor' and 'bad'). All but one of the 'good' drivers had personalities measured as being towards the 'stable introvert' type (thoughtful, peaceful, controlled, calm, etc.), while the 'bad' and 'poor' drivers tended towards the 'unstable extravert' ends of the dimensions (outgoing, anxious, touchy, active, etc.). Within this classification, their results indicated that the 'introversion–extraversion' personality dimension correlated more highly with their accident criterion than did the 'stability' dimension. Similar results have been found by other workers. For example Fine (1963) found that drivers scoring highly on the extraversion scale had more recorded accidents and driving violations than those who scored as introverts or intermediate between the two. Similarly, Mackay *et al.* (1969) have demonstrated that a sample of accident drivers showed a mean extraversion score higher than the norms for the general population.

Aggression is another trait which is likely to lead a person to cause or to be involved in an accident. For example, Wrogg (1961) have pointed to the evidence of a marked increase in aggression particularly just before an accident occurs. Similarly, Suchman (1965) has explained the greater severity rate of accidents among male drivers in terms of the role of the male in American Society as an aggressive risk taker. Unfortunately, however, very little statistical evidence has been advanced to link aggressiveness on its own with accidents.

Risk taking

Although there appears to be no single personality trait of 'accident proneness' an individual's predisposition to create an accident will be related to a willingness to 'cut corners' and to take risks.

Risk is the subjective probability which an operator assigns to an event occurring — to the degree of danger and hazard which the operator observes. In this respect, then, 'danger' represents the presence of a situation which could inflict injury or damage if an error is made; 'hazard' is the objective (i.e. measured) probability that a person will err in the presence of danger; and risk is the subjective probability (i.e. the individual's estimate) or error in the presence of known danger. Risk taking, therefore, is the extent to which an individual will perform an action which has previously been judged to be dangerous and has some degree of hazard.

The relationship between risk taking and the extent to which the operator feels able to perform the task has been demonstrated by a number of experimenters. For example, Cohen, Dearnaley and Hansel (1958) compared the anticipated abilities (risk) of bus drivers to drive through a progressively narrow gap with their actual performance. Their results indicated that a group of 15 experienced drivers took less risk (i.e. were more realistic in assessing their abilities) than did a group of inexperienced drivers. Furthermore, the one experienced driving instructor which they tested took no risk at all. Skill, therefore, is related to risk-taking, and a component of skilled behaviour is the ability to be able to predict accurately the outcome of ones' actions.

These suggestions lead, possibly, to a way of reducing the degree of risk-taking behaviour. First, the requirement for more appropriate training in avoiding the consequences of risky behaviour cannot be denied. However, designing the machine system so that 'short cuts' cannot be taken, and ensuring that the operator is aware that the risky act cannot be performed should also reduce the incidence of risk-taking behaviour. Guards and mechanical or electronic 'interfering' devices can help in this respect.

A number of authors, however (for example, Peltzman, 1975; O'Neill, 1977; Wilde, 1985), have argued that increased safety will be compensated for by individuals taking higher risks — a sort of 'danger compensation' or 'risk homeostasis'. The argument, then, is that individuals have within them some need for danger and thus some idealized level of risk. After safety measures have been introduced, therefore, individuals will increase their risky behaviours to bring their danger levels back to preceding amounts. The implications of such arguments, of course, are enormous: any safety improvements will be negated by the individual so that ergonomic measures may be useful in increasing operators speed, for example, but not in reducing accidents.

Because of the importance of such considerations some studies have been performed to test these assertions and have found, generally, that there is no substance to the theory. For example, Evans, Wasielewski and Buseck (1982) compared drivers' behaviour in a Canadian state which has mandatory seat belt laws with one that does not. They demonstrated no real differences in behaviour in the two regions.

Age and Experience

Age is one of the most frequently considered factors in accident research, but its effects are confounded by experience, the task and, indeed, by the accidents themselves causing individuals to leave the employment. For example, it is reasonable to assume that employees who have a high accident rate will tend to drop out either due to injury, separation or leaving voluntarily. Any simple fall in accident rate with age, therefore, might reflect this trend.

Despite these confounding variables the overall trend indicates that during the teens and early twenties the accident rate is high; it then drops sharply, levelling out in the mid-twenties. When such factors as employee turnover are taken into account some authors have then found a slight rise in accident rate towards ages in the mid-fifties.

The effects of experience and training cannot be excluded from these age effects — younger workers are likely to be less experienced and thus are more likely to make an error. However, even in studies which match different age groups for their experience (for example, Van Zelst, 1954), it appears that younger workers are still more likely to have accidents.

Many reasons have been advanced why younger workers are more likely to have accidents, although few are based on any empirical evidence. Reviewing the literature, for example, Hale and Hale (1972) suggest that factors such as inattention, indiscipline, impulsiveness, recklessness, misjudgement, over-estimation of capacity, pride, and lack of family responsibilities can be blamed. Although it is possible that all of these suggestions are valid in particular circumstances, as the authors point out they are based on very slim evidence and mainly on the subjective impressions of individual investigators.

Whereas younger workers labour under the handicap of the traits often ascribed to youth, such as impulsiveness, the problems of older workers lie in reduced and failing capacities which come with age. For example, Murrell (1962a) has suggested that tasks which have heavy perceptual demands, particularly when these are accompanied by speed, are not well tolerated by older people. This was supported by earlier studies which demonstrated that fewer older men were employed on jobs involving severe demands on attention to fine detail, or sustained care and attention. When older men are employed on such tasks the evidence appears to suggest that their accident rate rises.

Life Stress

Life stress is a concept which is becoming widely recognized as an influence on both health and behaviour. Significant stressful life experiences (such as a bereavement, divorce, taking out a house mortgage, etc.) have been shown to play a role in precipitating episodes of serious illnesses and, lately, even in the susceptibility to the common cold (Totman and Kiff, 1979).

The effects of life experiences on a worker's predisposition to accidents, however, have not been studied in any great detail. Verhaegen et al. (1976) quote a study which apparently demonstrated that the subjects they studied who had been responsible for an accident differed by their heavier 'psychological burden' from subjects who were the victims of an accident. 'Heavier psychological burden' was defined in terms of worries about children, housing, money, a marital partner, etc. However, when the authors attempted to replicate this study they obtained conflicting results. In one industrial plant that they investigated, no differences were obtained between the stress experiences of accident causers and victims. In another plant, however, they obtained differences in the expected direction for worries about children's health and satisfaction with the home, but not for the subject's own or spouse's health, their children's educational progress, or the repayment of mortgages.

Despite these conflicting conclusions some other authors have found a significant relationship between accidents and life stresses. For example, Whitlock, Stoll and Rekhdahl (1977) compared the life experiences of seventy-one 17–65-year-old orthopaedic patients who had sustained accidents, with a further 71 control subjects drawn from routine surgery wards who were matched for age, sex and marital status. Their results demonstrated that the accidentally injured patients had experienced more changes in their lives over the past six months. Unfortunately, however, a number of the accident victims had been taking various drugs for complaints such as hypertension, depression, diabetes, etc. The possibility that the life stresses had helped to cause these complaints, and therefore that the drugs had contributed to the accidents, cannot be ruled out.

In summary, it is difficult to decide on the importance of life stressors in accident causation. As has been demonstrated throughout it is certainly the case that distraction at an important point in the carrying out of a task can lead to an accident, and personal worries can be distracting. Whether life stresses *per se* (rather than specific worries) can make an individual liable to an accident, however, cannot be decided until more evidence is available.

Accidents as withdrawal behaviour

In 1953 Hill and Trist advanced the theory that people may be motivated to have an accident so that they can take time off work. Their withdrawal hypothesis was supported by comparing the uncertified absence rates of 200 men who had remained free from accidents with those of 89 men who had sustained one or more accidents. Their results indicated that those sustaining accidents had had significantly more other absences than those who had remained free of accidents. Unfortunately, since the authors only reported the number of accidents, it is not possible to determine whether the people who had had high accident rates had more accidents or merely reported more. Only the former would directly tend to support the theory. Hill and Trist's survey can also be criticized on the grounds that they did not match the jobs of their high and low accident groups. As Hale and Hale (1972) point out, it is plausible to suggest that those with higher accident rates came from dangerous jobs, which also tend to be heavier jobs and make greater physical demands on people. The workers, therefore, might feel incapable of doing the job when slightly 'under the weather' and so take more days off work, uncertified. This view is lent some support by the fact that Castle (1956) found no relation between accidents and uncertified absence in a photographic processing works where the work was much lighter. Powell *et al.* (1971), however, did show such a relationship in both men and women in a machine shop (heavier work), but not in an assembly shop.

It would appear, therefore, that there is very little evidence to support the hypothesis that workers either consciously or unconsciously cause an accident in order to escape from work.

Physiological Models

Physiological models suggest that accidents are caused as a result of the worker's body not being able to cope with the task requirements. In this respect, disabilities such as deafness, blindness (or at least poor eyesight), a lack of muscular strength, etc., might each be a cause of an accident occurring. Such factors have been discussed elsewhere. This section will discuss two aspects which might detrimentally influence the body's processing capacities — physiological rhythms and drugs (particularly alcohol).

Physiological rhythms

Our bodies contain a number of systems which regulate functions in a rhythmical fashion. Perhaps the most obvious is the heart which beats consistently throughout life, normally at between about 60 and 80 beats per minute. Less obvious are the rhythmical contractions of the intestinal muscles and the fairly high frequency voltage changes (about 13 Hz depending on one's alertness) generated by the brain (as measured by electroencephalography, EEG). Over slightly longer periods, but still within 24 hours, we have rhythms of waking and sleeping and of temperature regulation. These daily variations are known as circadian rhythms (from the Latin *circa* (around), *dies* (day)). Over even longer periods, up to a month, other bodily functions also cycle, for example the changes which occur in the lining of a women's uterus culminating each month in menstruation. In addition there are thought by some to be cycles of emotionality, and intellectual and physical performance. These longer-term variations are commonly known as biological and biorhythms.

Circadian rhythms and accidents

Daily variations in human performance and efficiency have long been recognized. Indeed, Rutenfranz and Colquhoun (1979) have traced these observations back to Kraepelin in 1893:

> With continued work the performance usually rises until noon. Soon after the meal it has decreased very significantly. Simultaneously a predominance of external associations and lower stability of imaginative combinations can be shown. These phenomena are no indication of work fatigue, since they disappear after 2–3 hours, even when work is continued. (After the noon meal) the performance again increases slowly. Sooner or later, however, without fail, fatigue gains the upper hand.

Rutenfranz and Colquhoun add to these the observation that much greater overall variation can be expected when the night hours are included.

Rhythmical variations in performance on a number of tasks have been shown to occur under laboratory conditions. For example, Folkard and Monk (1978) demonstrated that the amount of information able to be remembered is influenced by the time of day of presentation, although no such influence occurred for the ability to retrieve information from memory. Using a number of tasks (reaction time, calculations, card sorting, letter cancellation, etc.) Blake (1971) demonstrated performance increases between 08.00 and 10.30 hours with a 'post-lunch' dip at about 14.00 hours. However, on one task (digit span — i.e. the number of digits which can be remembered) the post-lunch performance dip did not occur until late evening. Rutenfranz and Colquhoun (1979) interpret these findings to imply that just as physiological processes show different circadian rhythms, so do different psychological functions.

There are fewer industrial studies relating circadian rhythms to performance, however, a fact which Folkard and Monk (1979) ascribe to factors such as union or management opposition and problems in finding appropriate measures. However, there appears to be agreement between the studies which have been carried out, primarily in relation to shiftwork. For example, Hildebrandt, Romert and Rutenfranz (1974) demonstrated a typical 24-hour circadian pattern of unintended brakings by train drivers (i.e. when the train came to a stop because the driver failed to respond to a signal in the cab). Other, similar, conclusions from different situations have been reviewed by Folkard and Monk (1979) and Figure 12.1 illustrates some of the rhythms that they observed.

The relationship between such rhythms and accidents, and the implications for shiftwork have been discussed by Colquhoun (1975b). Investigating sailors on a four-hour watchkeeping schedule he demonstrated a circadian variation in alertness (detecting a very faint auditory or visual signal) and in reaction time, implying that the potential for accident causation also varies rhythmically. Similar results were obtained using eight-hour shifts without any 'weekend break'. Furthermore, Folkard, Monk and Chobban (1978) demonstrated a highly significant rhythmical variation over the day in the frequency of 'minor accidents' occurring to patients during their stay in hospital. The changes in the

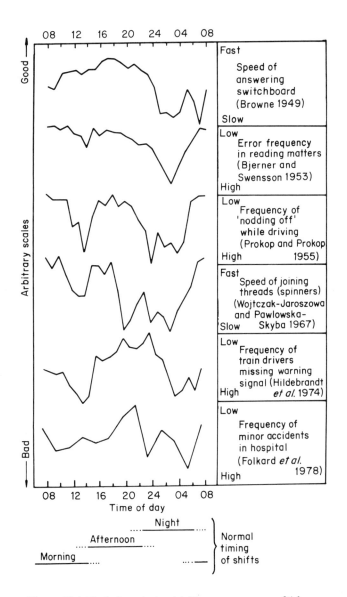

Figure 12.1 Variations in 'real job' measures over a 24-hour
period. (From Folkard and Monk, 1979.)

rhythm coincided well with the timings of the nurses' early day, late day and
night shifts. Although the authors point out that the relationship between the
two functions could be spurious (the tendency for accident peaks to occur in
early morning or late night could be attributed to the patient's need to 'pass
water' immediately before going to sleep or on awakening) they also suggest that
a causal relationship might exist.

Craig and Condon (1984) have also questioned the specific mechanism underlying the clear rhythmical variation in efficiency throughout the day. In their study, for example, they demonstrated a major variation in the performance being caused by a change in the operator's trade-off between speed and accuracy: operators became faster but less accurate at certain times of the day. They suggest that this shift may be the result of accumulating fatigue over a shift period, rather than to time of day *per se*. Nevertheless, irrespective of the effect's cause, their data and those of others do suggest that the potential for accidents could follow some sort of circadian rhythm.

Biorhythms and biological rhythms

Whereas circadian rhythms have been demonstrated and occur over a 24-hour period, the evidence for biorhythms is not so secure. If they exist they occur over periods of up to one month. The biorhythm theory suggests that there are cycles of 23, 28 and 33 day duration that govern physical, emotional and intellectual performance respectively. Each cycle is described by a sinusoidal curve having a positive and a negative phase, the cycle starting on a positive half-cycle at the moment of birth. (Why the theory should consider that the rhythm should begin at birth rather than from the time of conception is not clear.) The positive phase corresponds to periods when performance is best, the negative phase to periods of poorer performance, and the cross-over points are termed 'critical'. The length of this critical period is usually considered to be 24 hours. According to the theory accidents would be more likely to occur on critical days, that is on days when more than one cycle is in the critical phase and days when one cycle is in a critical phase and the other cycles are in a negative phase. In addition days when all cycles are in a negative phase are said to be critical because of the change from 'positive' to 'negative' behaviour — 'just as the most "dangerous" time for a light bulb to burn out is when power surges through it as it is switched on' (Gittelson, 1978).

Controversy continues in both the scientific and popular press concerning the existence of such cycles — whether they exist at all and, if so, whether they are fixed from birth. Certainly, it is not the purpose of this chapter to fuel the arguments. However, the theory does propose testable hypotheses with respect to accidents and a few investigators have attempted to correlate recorded accident data with that which would have been predicted according to the theory. After reviewing these studies, however, and after carrying out a study of their own on over 4000 pilot accidents, Wolcott *et al.* (1977a, b) concluded that there is no statistically significant correlation between the occurrence of an accident and biorhythmicity.

Support for these conclusions has also been provided by Khalil and Kurucz (1977). They investigated the relationship between the timing of 63 aircraft accidents in which 'pilot error' was said to be to blame, and the position of each pilot's biorhythm. Again their analyses indicated that 'biorhythm' had no significant influence on accident likelihood.

Alcohol

A great deal of work has been conducted on the effects of alcohol on judgement and on the performance of skilled tasks. In general the experimental work has shown that alcohol has a deleterious effect on performance because of its effects on vision, perceptual motor functions, judgement, reasoning and memory. For example, Jellinek and McFarland (1940), reporting on experiments of alcohol effects up to 1940, decided that the speed of reaction is 'lengthened' by alcohol, despite faulty techniques in almost every experiment. Similar conclusions were reached by Carpenter (1959) using alcohol levels as low as 40 mg/kg of body weight.

Many of the studies in this area have concerned driving tasks. For example, Bjerver and Goldberg (1950) used a special truck designed to measure the ability to operate a car within close limits. Such manoeuvres as parallel parking, driving out of a garage, and turning around in a narrow roadway were required. Their results showed that the time for skilled drivers to perform tests correctly was significantly lengthened when the subjects were at a blood-alcohol level of about 40 mg/100 ml of blood. Because of studies such as these which have consistently shown a positive relationship between alcohol level and performance decrement, most countries have fixed by law a blood level beyond which it is an offence to drive. These levels vary from 50mg/100ml of blood to 150mg/100ml.

The role of alcohol in industrial accidents has been less extensively studied. Some studies have certainly indicated, as did the Bjerver and Goldberg study, that the accident rate rises with the proportion of drinkers in the workforce. However, these are cases of alcohol consumed while at work — the question might well be posed as to the accident likelihood of the alcoholic worker who drinks heavily but not at work. As Trice and Roman (1972) point out, it is logical to expect a deviant drinker to have more accidents than other workers since steadiness would be impaired in addition to coordination, timing, motor responses and sense of danger. In addition, hangovers on the job could cause accidents.

Unfortunately the research data which have emerged over the years make generalizations about the relationships between alcohol and industrial accidents difficult. For example 'Observer' and Maxwell (1959) ('Observer' was a pseudonym) concluded that problem drinkers do have more accidents than other workers. They recorded three times as many accidents caused by problem drinkers than by members of their control group. Furthermore, in another study Brenner (1967), who considered the death rate due to fatal accidents in a sample of 1343 patients in four alcoholism rehabilitation clinics, concluded that the alcoholics were seven times as likely to become the victims of fatal accidents than were the non-alcoholic controls. Of the 35 fatal accidents, however, only one was reported as occurring while at work.

A direct comparison of alcoholism and accident rate, however, has many pitfalls. The first concerns the problem of accident statistics as a source of data, they give no indication of the situation leading to the accident, nor usually of the accident severity. Secondly the evidence appears to suggest that the risk of accidents from alcohol is related to the extent to which the alcoholic is able to cope with his or her 'disability'. When breaking down their accident data for different age groups, for example, Observer and Maxwell considered that while problem drinkers do account for more accidents than other workers of the same age during the early problem drinking years, by the time that the problem has developed fully problem drinkers are generally no more prone to on-the-job accidents than other employees.

These findings have been explained, by both Observer and Maxwell and by Trice and Roman, as being due to the improved coping behaviour of the committed alcoholics and their colleagues. Such factors include the routine nature of the job, extra caution, protection from accidents by fellow workers, absenteeism when incapacitated (e.g. from hangovers), and assignment by supervisors to less hazardous work. Apparently these factors — or at least some of them — do not play the same role during the early problem drinking period in protecting the individual from on the job accidents.

SUMMARY

Although one of the main themes of this book has been to illustrate ways in which the environment can be designed to promote safety, this chapter deals specifically with human accident behaviour. It has taken as its thesis the suggestion that accidents occur when the environmental demands surpass the operator's capabilities. Various behavioural and physiological models were proposed to account for why the operator's capacities may be reduced at the important point in time.

CHAPTER 13

INSPECTION AND MAINTENANCE

In many respects a chapter dealing with inspection and maintenance in a general ergonomics text could be considered to be out of place. Ergonomics is an applied discipline; an ergonomist applies knowledge and experience about how people interact with the environment to ensure that the environment fits the individual. This theme has been stressed throughout this book, and various routes to this goal have been illustrated. Both inspection and maintenance are areas of ergonomics application, in the same way that the ergonomics of space flight, of agriculture or of medicine are different areas of interest to different ergonomists. Why, then, should inspection and maintenance be singled out for special consideration?

Two answers can be given to this question. First, although it is true that inspection and maintenance are specific areas of interest, both exemplify the need to consider the total working system. They both provide ideal examples of how ergonomics can be implemented to help solve specific problems. Secondly both are important in their own right when designing a system; they need to be considered just as much as the design of individual displays, controls or workplaces. It is a fact of life that components in a system occasionally break down, and only if the system maintainability had been considered in the original design will the fault be able to be discovered and rectified quickly and easily.

In many ways, any distinction between inspection and maintenance would be a distinction without a difference. It is hard to draw a dividing line between the two processes since both involve detecting and eliminating faults. However, for the purposes of the present discussion inspection will be taken to be the process by which a faulty item is detected. Maintenance involves rectifying the fault, usually within the system.

INSPECTION

With the increasing efficiency and output of machines, the task of an industrial inspector has become more complex over the years. Faster, more productive, more accurate machinery is likely to produce goods at a pace which causes greater difficulties in detecting product defects. In addition, the consequences of missing a defect have also grown in importance. At one level reduced vigilance or bad inspection could cause dissatisfaction among customers, evidenced by the return of faulty goods and perhaps a loss of custom. Indeed, as Drury and Sinclair (1983) point out these days customers are demanding defect-free products, often in the courts. At another level poor inspection may raise production costs by causing unnecessary machine stoppages, by interrupting the production flow, or by wasting material.

It is possible, of course, to design machines to carry out some aspects of the inspector's job with almost 100 per cent efficiency. At present, however, this is feasible only if there is a limited number of specific faults that would occur within a product and if decisions are kept simple. For example, Drury and Sinclair (1983) compared human and machine inspectors and found that whereas the machine located more faults than did the humans it was unable to classify them as acceptable or rejectable with the same consistency. This ought to be expected when one remembers the list of functions best carried out by man and by machine that was discussed in Chapter 1. Thus, man is normally more efficient in complex, variable situations, particularly when fine form, depth or texture has to be perceived. It would be difficult to find a machine that could match human powers of examining for numbers of different faults at once over a wide range of products; that could assess a surface 'finish' or colour uniformity; or could take note of a rare, perhaps unspecified, fault. Man is as yet unsurpassed where discrimination is needed between a large number of faults, where classification and diagnosis are required, and where eliminating the fault involves liaison with other individuals or with other machines.

Regarding the types of task that would normally be carried out under the title of 'inspection' Czaja and Drury (1981) compared several taxonomies. From their review they distilled four task categories:

(1) *Monitoring* — observing a continuous process and reporting any deviations.
(2) *Examining* — searching items, or arrays of items, for defects. Judgements are made without numerical measurement.
(3) *Measurement* — using instruments and measuring tools to provide numerical measures on which decisions are based.
(4) *Patrolling* — checking and organizing the work of other inspectors.

Clearly, the first two of these groups require some subjective evaluation to be made; the third group depends entirely on an inspector's ability to measure accurately (and, thus, also on the ergonomic quality of the measuring instrument); whereas the fourth group may use any task covered in the first three groups. The following discussion will deal primarily with monitoring and examining.

A Simple Model of Industrial Inspection

Based on reports from inspectors a very simple model can be developed to explain the extremely complex inspection process. Generally, inspectors suggest that their task is to keep the idea of what constitutes a 'good' item in mind and then to look for faults in the object being inspected. In other words they appear to compare the object's 'external' appearance with an internal representation of the acceptable item. Any mismatch between the two perceptions would cause a decision to be made to reject the item. This model explains why an inspector who is asked to *identify* the fault will sometimes need to re-examine the item. Because the task is simply to identify a mismatch between the item and its internal model, time will not normally have been wasted in classifying the nature of the mismatch.

Thomas (1968) also points out than an inspector's job often does require the nature of the faults to be recognized — perhaps to send defective items for appropriate remedial treatment or to record the occurrence of various types of faults. To do this the inspector's model must contain sets of alternatives, similar to subroutines in a computer program, so that scanning can be continued beyond the stage of identifying a rejectable mismatch. The object's appearance, then, will have to be matched with detailed characteristics of a specific 'fault subsection' in the model.

Finally, the simple model recognizes one very important consequence of repetitive inspection — a possible drift in inspection standards. Since the task involves matching an external stimulus to an 'internal' representation it is quite possible that the internal representation may undergo small, subtle changes, perhaps because of past experience, social pressures, or a host of other factors. These changes will cause a corresponding change in the inspector's decision criteria to accept or to reject an item.

The ergonomist's task, therefore, is twofold: first to obtain the best possible stimulus of the object to be perceived; second, to assist in developing suitable internal models. Both of these aspects can be carried out by implementing many of the ergonomics principles discussed elsewhere in this book. As will become evident, however, this is an extremely complex task.

FACTORS AFFECTING INSPECTION ACCURACY

Megaw (1978) suggest four groups of factors that could influence inspection accuracy.

Into the first category fall all of the variables which the inspector brings to the task: visual ability and performance; age and experience at inspection; personality and intelligence; etc. There is little that the ergonomist can do to influence these variables alone although, having recognized their effects, other aspects of the work can be altered either to compensate for them or to accentuate them.

Some of these aspects fall into Megaw's second category — physical and environmental factors in which the inspection task is carried out. Thus aspects such as the lighting, the workplace layout, background noise and the presence or absence of visual aids are important.

Megaw's third category contains organizational factors and characteristics of the inspector's overall job. These include the number of inspectors who are available; the type of training and feedback received; rest pauses and shiftwork; social aspects of the job; etc.

Finally, Megaw collects together factors which pertain specifically to the inspector's task — whether the objects to be viewed are moving or stationary; the probability that any one piece is defective; the complexity of the object; the density of the items; etc.

Inspector Variables

Visual acuity

Since, in the majority of cases, inspection is often a visually based task, it is reasonable to expect that inspection performance will degrade as the inspector's visual ability decreases. On the other hand, it is not unreasonable to expect the reverse — that inspection performance increases with increasing visual ability.

For some time visual acuity has generally been the accepted criterion of visual ability for an inspection task. As an indication of the relationship between acuity and performance, McCormick (1950) measured the visual acuity of over 5000 employees doing different jobs (the sample included sewing machinists and close assembly workers in addition to visual inspectors). The relationship between visual acuity and performance that he obtained is shown in Figure 13.1. It would appear from the graph, for example, that approximately 55 per cent of the

Figure 13.1   The relationship between visual acuity and good
performance.
(From McCormick, 1950)

employees having fairly good near acuity (minimum visual angle of about 1 min of arc) were from the high criterion group, whereas all of the employees having poor acuity (for example, 10 min of arc) were from the low criterion group. Whereas McCormick's data suggest a trend of reduced performance with much reduced acuity the converse is by no means the case — about 45 per cent of the employees with good acuity fell into the low criterion category. As Megaw concludes 'the results demonstrate that the possession of good acuity does not ensure that person as a high criterion inspector, merely that the chances are relatively high'.

It is not altogether surprising that a perfect relationship between acuity and performance was not obtained. Being a laboratory based measure, the acuity task does not test the operator's performance within a work system: most acuity tasks use stationary stimuli whereas the objects in many inspection tasks are moving; most acuity tests are carried out under 'ideal' environmental conditions whereas this is not necessarily so at work; and most acuity tasks carry no reward or punishment for the testee. Again this is not necessarily the case at work.

Given these drawbacks it is unlikely that a simple relationship can, or will, be found. Nevertheless some attempts at more realism have been made. For example, Nelson and Barany (1969) developed a dynamic visual acuity test in which the test material and conditions incorporated many of the features of the inspection task for which the inspectors are being selected. As Megaw points out, however, such tests are difficult and expensive to develop if they are to be in any way predictive.

Another approach has been taken by some workers who feel that the size of the inspector's visual field (essentially a test of periphal acuity) should be related to inspection performance. For example, Johnston (1965) investigated the relationship between the size of observers' visual fields and the time required to locate targets on static displays. Her data suggested that people with large visual fields can find targets more rapidly than those with small fields.

Other studies have indicated that an important difference between best and poorest performance is the length of time taken by the observer between eye fixations during the search task. For example, Boynton, Elworth and Palmer (1958) found that their best subject averaged nearly twice the saccadic length of their 'worst' subject, and so they concluded that longer sweeps are an aid to efficient search. This is presumably because longer sweeps between fixations will result in fewer eyeball fixations. Thus it takes a shorter time to scan the material so that more scans can be made in the time available.

It still remains the case, however, that all of these are results obtained from subjects in the laboratory and have not been validated in the case of industrial tasks.

Age and experience

When considering features such as safety and accidents, difficulties involved in isolating age as a single variable were noted. Increasing age is often associated both with failing health (which can detrimentally affect performance) and increased experience (which can improve performance). It is not surprising, therefore, that few studies are available which have investigated the effects of ageing on inspectors.

Jamieson (1966) recorded the ages of his inspectors when carrying out two types of task: either inspecting switches for mechanical faults as they left the assembly line (which involved a minimum of 190 discriminations per switch) or checking telephone exchange racks for faulty soldered joints and connections. (Unfortunately no indication was given of the experience of his subjects.) In both types of task, inspection performance increased with increasing age, although the relationship was significant only in the telephone rack task. These results were confirmed with a further group of workers. Unfortunately, however, since it is likely that the sight of many of the older workers would have begun to fail, the study did not answer the question of whether experience and other variables such as conscientiousness outweighed the negative factors of ageing.

Although useful in illustrating the effects of age on inspector performance Jamieson's experiments, then, do not enable the positive effects of increased experience and the negative effects of reduced abilities to be tested. Nevertheless, recent work by Czaja and Drury (1981) suggests that any negative effects may be able to be overcome with appropriate training before the inspection task. In their study, pretraining took the form firstly of subjects organizing a list of words and then learning them and secondly sorting objects into different sized groups. Following this pretraining regime, subjects were required to inspect displayed characters and reject those which did not conform to particular sizes. Pretrained older subjects performed better on this task than did those who had no previous training.

Personality

Personality is a variable that has received considerable attention in the past, particularly in studies of its relationship with vigilance. In this case the evidence appears to suggest that, along an introversion–extraversion dimension at least, some differences may be apparent with introverts performing slightly better than extraverts (Weiner, 1975). Along another dimension — locus of control — Sanders et al. (1976) demonstrated that people scoring low (that is, they tend to internalize their view of the world) tend to make fewer errors on a vigilance task than do externals.

Unfortunately, there are fewer studies that have attempted to relate personality measures to quality control/inspection tasks (Weiner, 1975) although two reported by Wolke and DuCette (1974) could be placed under this heading. They used a proof-reading task and also measured their subjects' locus of control. As with the vigilance studies, internals were shown to produce better performance in both the paced and unpaced versions of the task. Eskew and Riche (1982) have since demonstrated that this superiority is because internals use more appropriate decision criteria and make fewer 'false alarms' (i.e. rejecting an otherwise perfect item).

Physical and Environmental Variables

Lighting

Because inspection is largely a visual task, it should be obvious that the inspector's main environmental needs are for adequate illumination. This implies providing enough light to be able to view the objects without undue fatigue, but not so much light that glare occurs. All of the factors discussed in the previous chapter which can affect visual performance need to be considered, therefore. However, two additional aspects ought to be emphasized: first the type of lighting and second its position.

Regarding the type of lighting Lion (Lion, 1964; Lion, Richardson and Browne, 1968) compared inspection and manipulation performance using two types of illumination: fluorescent and tungsten lights. In the first experiment she asked her subjects to carry out a variety of tasks (grading ballbearings, threading needles, reading numbers, and measuring the lengths of rods) using either an 80-watt 'warm' fluorescent tube or a 100-watt clear tungsten bulb. Both lights produced illumination of 14 lumens/sq foot at the work surface. Her subjects were significantly quicker completing the tasks using a fluorescent than a tungsten bulb (i.e. more units were performed in the time allotted), although the number of errors made in each case were not significantly affected. Since all tasks used stimuli which had a high degree of reflectivity, Lion argued that the performance difference was due to the filament (tungsten) light producing a concentrated light source and thus more glare. This was not enough to increase errors but it was enough to slow down the rate of work.

In a second series of experiments Lion and her colleagues used tasks more like those encountered in an inspection task, that is searching for defects in small objects moving on a conveyor belt. The defective objects were either buttons with off-centred holes or black plastic discs with a broken white design etched on to their surface. Again, tungsten and fluorescent room lighting was compared, this time producing equivalent illumination levels of 30 lumens/sq foot at the working level.

In this experiment the results were slightly less conclusive. Her subjects overlooked significantly fewer faulty broken designs on the disc sorting task under fluroescent than tungsten lighting, but there were no significant differences on the button sorting task. The authors explain the discrepancy by pointing to the type of task involved in each case. The 'faulty design' task required the operator to perceive a break in a line which is essentially simply an acuity task. The button sorting task, however, required a more 'global' perception of the object, since the rejection criterion was whether or not the four button-holes were central. The authors suggest that it is only the visual acuity task which is at a disadvantage under point-source illumination, possibly because of the glaring effects. However, more data would be required before the assertion could be substantiated.

With respect to the position of the light source, Fox (1977) describes an interesting series of experiments designed to investigate problems experienced in the quality control of coins produced at the Royal Mint. In one investigation he compared the error detection rate when a bank of five 40-watt fluorescent lights were placed immediately above the workplace in a horizontal arrangement, and when the bank was angled on its supports. This second condition purposefully produced specular glare from the coin surfaces. The interesting feature, however, was that the quality of the glare changed with the absence, presence and even type of coin defect. Thus, because the effect was to vary the contrast between the faulty part of the item and its background, to detect a damaged or misshapen coin the inspector's task becomes one of detecting the glare type (intensity) rather than comparing the coin with an internalized model. Although the fault detection rate did not differ using the two arangements, Fox argues that the angled position allowed a more 'standard' performance from the inspectors. Unfortunately, he provides no details of the angle used, and did not attempt to carry out any controlled study of this question. Nevertheless the use of glare to benefit the inspector is an interesting concept, although it should be pointed out that the prolonged use may well cause visual fatigue.

Visual aids

Although the level and type of illumination are extremely important aspects of the visual environment, as was pointed out in Chapter 1 the inspector's task can often be helped by using visual aids such as magnifiers or visual overlays.

Magnification is an obvious aid for the inspector — particularly if the task includes significant acuity components. Increasing the apparent size of the object will also increase the size of the defect to be detected. However, the term 'magnification' should not be limited solely to discussing 'size'. As Spencer (1968) points out, the term can be used in its broadest sense to denote a form of increase that enhances the perceived magnitude of the object or event being examined. Thus an inspection task which involves detecting small colour differences may be aided (i.e. the differences 'magnified') by using different coloured lights; a specific signal in an auditory discrimination task can be 'magnified' (i.e. the tone made more apparent) by modulation; etc.

If the apparent size of an object is magnified by a magnifying glass Spencer recommends using a jig or holder for the object being inspected. This has two advantages. First, because most optical magnifiers have a restricted depth of field, the jig will immediately place the object at the appropriate distance from the magnifying glass, ensuring a standard appearance of all the inspected objects. Second, although the natural hand tremor does not interfere with the normal perception of objects, behind a magnifying glass any movement caused by tremor is increased. This might affect visual acuity performance in the way discussed in Chapter 10 when considering the effects of vibration.

A note of caution must be sounded, however, against the 'unrestricted' use of linear, optical magnification. From the scanty data available it would appear that, as with most encounters with the physical world, there is an optimum level of magnification. Both higher and lower magnification levels tend to result in reduced performance. Early investigators to demonstrate this effect were Nayyar and Simon who, in 1963, asked subjects to perform a task which consisted of picking up, transporting, and assembling metal dots 0.01 in in diameter. Their subjects performed the task under three magnifications: 20×, 30×, and 40×, and the results indicated that the subjects took a shorter time to pick up the dots using the 30× magnification than either of the other two. In a subsequent study Simon (1964) demonstrated that this optimum magnification was strongly related to the size of the object to be manipulated. Again comparing 20× and 30× magnification, he demonstrated the advantage of the 30× magnification for a 0.01-in dot but, when a larger dot was used (0.015 in) the relative advantages of the two magnification sizes were reversed.

These results suggest, therefore, that it is the image size on the retina which is important rather than the magnification size. This contention is supported by Smith and Adams's (1971) results when they demonstrated that no matter what size object was used, the optimum magnification always produced an image which subtended an angle of about 8–9 min of arc at the eye. This factor remained constant even under different illumination levels.

Visual aids in the form of overlays have also been shown to benefit inspection performance. Using such aids it is often possible to help the inspector spot defects by making them stand out from the background. Like Fox's coin inspection, the inspection task thus becomes one of looking for things that are highlighted rather than looking at each and every individual item.

Noise

The effects of noise on performance have already been discussed in Chapter 10, and will not be discussed further here. However, it should be remembered that under some conditions noise may actually increase performance. Thus Poulton (1977) has suggested that noise may act as an arouser when dealing with boring, repetitive tasks, whilst Fox (1971) has demonstrated significant improvements in performance with background music.

Organizational Variables

In addition to the factors which the physical environment brings to the inspection task (in particular the illumination quality and the noise), the social and organizational environments should not be forgotten. These include the way in which the inspector interacts with colleagues and the organization, and the job arrangements as a whole.

Social factors

The inspection model described earlier relies heavily on the inspector's subjective judgement of whether or not the object perceived matches the ideal model in the 'mind'. However, it is well known that judgements of this type can be greatly influenced by social pressures on the observer to conform to the group norm. As a famous example Asch (1952) asked subjects to judge the length of a line. When exposed to various types of group pressures, individual's estimates conformed strongly to the group's estimates even when, by manipulating 'stooges' in the group, the group decision was widely in error.

As an example of the ways in which such pressures to conform may influence an inspector's judgement Belbin (1957) describes how, in a knitwear factory, inspectors reported very few 'seconds'; instead they classified nearly all defective work as 'mendable'. In this factory, then, although the knitters lost pay for defective work they lost more for 'seconds' than for 'menders'. It would appear, therefore, that lacking clear standards the inspectors were unable to resist the knitters' pressure to class most defects as 'menders' rather than as 'seconds'.

In addition to pressures from the workforce, an inspector often has to face similar types of coercion from the production management. As part of the production team the inspector's task includes maintaining a certain production flow. As Thomas and Seaborne (1961) point out, when the production department is in difficulties there will be considerable pressure to maintain a certain output by accepting some components which, in more favourable circumstances, might have been rejected. On the other hand, when output is high the criterion for acceptance could be made more stringent without an appreciable reduction in the productive flow.

McKenzie (1957) summarizes some of these aspects by pointing out that, particularly when objects are individually made, 'in the factory inspection is always, if implicitly, of people; inspection decisions about a man's work directly reflect on him'. Again, therefore, the implication is made that there are a number of social pressures placed on the inspector not to reject an item. These pressures may arise from the workplace (increased rejection might result in reduced bonuses; increased rejection implies reduced work quality) or even from the production management (increased rejection means reduced output schedules and higher cost).

Feedback

The benefit to performance of adequate feedback has been stressed throughout this book and its effects on inspection performance are no different. Since inspection involves comparing an external object with an 'internal' model it is essential that the inspector is given every opportunity to 'update' the model in the light of experience. Two separate rôles can be identified for feedback: first to maintain motivation and second to provide information about efficiency.

The value of feedback as a motivator is difficult to assess in any controlled way. However, Megaw (1978) considers that there is a 'general consensus of opinion' that feedback helps inspectors to appreciate the importance of their work and thus become more involved in their task.

As with most tasks, giving inspectors details of their performance is likely to improve accuracy: operators who realize that too many good items are being rejected, too many faulty items missed, or even that their performance is accurate can adjust their 'internal model' — the rejection criterion — accordingly. That feedback is effective in this rôle was demonstrated by Drury and Addison (1973) for inspecting complex glass items. During a specified period the inspectors' output was checked by a second group of inspectors who informed the first group immediately they had made an error. Introducing this undelayed feedback resulted in increased performance for the first group such that the probability of missing a fault was halved. However, the authors rightly caution that the improvement may not have occurred solely as a result of improved feedback since the new feedback arrangement was part of other procedural changes, including supervision methods.

Rest pauses

Inspection is normally a light, repetitive task, the speed of which is governed by the speed of the industrial process producing the objects to be inspected. It is also a task with a high vigilance component. Since most even highly motivated people require a short break after prolonged activity, it would be quite reasonable to suggest that the same principle holds for industrial inspectors. Murrell (1962b) has proposed the concept of an 'actile period', which he defines as 'a period during which there is a state of preparedness to respond optimally to stimulation either discretely or continuously' — in other words, the period during which a worker can maintain concentration on the task in hand. He further proposes that this period has finite duration depending on the individual involved and the task undertaken. At the end of the actile period, performance will start to deteriorate and, with continued activity, the deterioration will become serious and output will begin to fall. In addition to the projected fall in output, a further important consideration of an actile period concept is that, if no break is forthcoming, the operator will individually impose such a break of a few seconds at a time. Thus, Branton and Oborne (1979) have inferred the presence of 'mini-sleeps' among anaesthetists who had to monitor long and often boring operations.

The results of a number of studies are now available which have demonstrated the need for rest pauses throughout the working day (see, for example, Murrell, 1971). However, Colquohoun (1958) has demonstrated the need for such pauses at more frequent intervals during inspection work. In a laboratory study in which his subjects were required to spot faulty discs on a moving drum, his results indicated that when the work was performed uninterrupted for a period of an hour the efficiency, although initially high, declined after about 30 minutes. If a five-minute rest period was inserted at this point, however, the performance was maintained at a high level throughout the hour.

Task Variables

So far, consideration has been given to aspects of the inspection task which the inspector brings as an individual, and those which are added by the physical, social and organizational environments. Finally, factors supplied by the task itself need to be considered. In this respect, important considerations are the pace of the work, its complexity, and the likelihood of a fault being present.

Speed of working

Drury (1973) has pointed out that the rate at which an inspector can work is likely to be one of the most vital pieces of information required when designing industrial inspection systems. For a fixed production rate, knowing the time required to inspect an item determines the manning level and hence, to a large extent, the design of the physical facilities. Poor quality control is likely to occur if too slow or too fast a pace is imposed or too many inspectors are installed.

In his investigation of the quality control of coin production Fox (1977) varied the speed at which the coins passed the inspector's field of view, either in pairs or in triplets. Whereas no significant difference in inspection accuracy was obtained between the inspection speeds when only two coins appeared at any one time (inspection time/coin varied between 0.05s and 0.125s), when three coins were presented at a time a significant increase from 70.8 to 82.7 per cent correct detection occurred (inspection time/coin ranged between 0.033 and 0.83 sec).

The increase in detection efficiency with inspection time, however, is not linear. In fact, most of the studies reviewed by Drury (1973) demonstrate an exponential increase in fault detection as the time available for inspection is increased. The curve flattens out below perfect detection, with the critical inspection time unfortunately depending largely on the task complexity and on the conspicuity of the fault. No general guidelines can be given for appropriate times, therefore. In addition to this trend, however, there appear to be a very slight, although generally non-significant, increase in the probability of making the other type of inspection error (for instance, rejecting a good item rather than a bad one) with time. Although this trend is very slight, and in some studies completely absent, it does imply again that slight changes may occur in the inspector's criterion of a 'good' item.

Product complexity

The importance of the product's complexity as a variable that affects the time available to inspect each item has already been considered. However, even when inspectors are allowed long inspection periods the product's complexity can have a detrimental effect on performance. Thus, Harris (1966) demonstrated an almost linear reduction in detection performance with increasing item complexity (complexity was defined in two ways — either according to a rated complexity index, or in terms of the number of components — circuit boards, transistors, wires, etc. — in the equipment). Since the detection decrease could not be overcome simply by increasing inspector's time, Harris suggests using visual aids with complex equipment. As has already been seen, these can be useful in such circumstances.

The probability of a defect occurring

Since most of human behaviour is shaped by the probability of an event occurring or not occurring, it is not unreasonable for this also to be the case for inspection tasks. In a vigilance test, for example, Jenkins (1958) demonstrated that as the signals to be detected became more frequent, so the number of correct detections also increased. This view was later altered slightly, however, to suggest that it was not the frequency of 'wanted' signals *per se* which was the important criterion, but the ratio of wanted to the total number of signals (i.e. the probability of a wanted signal occurring) (for example, Jerison, 1966).

These assertions were tested in a factory environment by Fox and Haslegrave (1969) who varied the probability of a defect occurring in batches of screws and bolts. Their results indicated that detection efficiency increased almost linearly with an increase in the fault probability. However, a corresponding increase in false detections (i.e. rejecting a good item) also occurred. Again, therefore, it appears that the inspectors were altering their rejection criteria rather than simply becoming more efficient detectors. Increasing the probability of a defective item occurring, therefore, simply causes more items to be rejected rather than more items to be rejected correctly.

MAINTENANCE

From the discussion so far, it is clear that inspection is essentially a perceptual problem — the operator's task is to perceive faulty aspects of an object and to make judgements on the basis of these perceptions. Any part of the task, operator, environment, or organization which affects perceptual ability is also likely to affect inspection performance. Similarly, any way in which the ergonomist can increase the operator's perceptual acuity should help to increase inspection performance.

If this very crude analogy is extended, it could be argued that maintenance performance is largely composed of motor and control components. Thus, although the maintenance operator needs, perhaps, to scan 'faulty' equipment to isolate the fault, subsequent problems are likely to centre around the component's accessibility, the equipment controllability and/or an individual's ability to manipulate, lift or pull out the relevant machinery. In essence, therefore, this crude distinction could be explained in terms of the aspects of the body sensory nervous structure discussed in Chapter 2 (inspection) and its motor control structure considered in Chapter 3 (maintenance).

It is a fact of life that no machine or component is likely to survive the life of the total system and unless we accept the concept of a totally 'throw-away' society in which any machine which breaks down is discarded for a new model, faulty parts will continually have to be maintained or replaced. However, although great strides have been made in reducing the failure rate of various components (particularly in the electronics industry) such advances have not kept pace with system complexity or costs. As the system becomes more complex, maintaining parts of it is likely to become more difficult and costly. For example, it has been estimated that the US Department of Defense allocates one quarter of its total budget to maintenance costs (Smith, Westland and Crawford, 1970). There is no reason why this proportion should alter significantly in any large organization which uses large and complex man–machine systems. Maintenance, therefore, costs money, and it is in the interests of all who operate a system to reduce the costs by considering (or having others consider) at an early stage in the product or system design, the ease with which it can be maintained.

The remainder of this chapter will discuss some of the ways that this ideal state of affairs can be approached but, before doing so, it is well to consider the conditions under which equipment often has to be maintained.

First, extremes of environmental conditions. When having to locate faulty components or otherwise maintain systems under field conditions, the environmental considerations discussed in Chapters 10 and 11 may be far from optimum. In particular, illumination levels in the interiors of machines are often very low, usually requiring the maintenance engineer also to have to cope with some type of torch. At the other end of the illumination scale, bright sunlight or even unguarded lights in the machine mean that maintenance often has to be carried out under conditions of sometimes high disability glare. Other environmental conditions, for example temperature and weather, can also vary with the site of the equipment when it breaks down. A long-distance lorry driver, for example, may have to carry out vehicle repairs on an isolated, cold, windswept road in the Highlands of Scotland on one day, and then in the middle of a burning desert a few days later.

Secondly the workplace of the maintenance engineer is often very cramped, and this point becomes more salient with the continuing trend towards miniaturization. The problem applies not only to the engineer's difficulty in being able to climb into appropriate parts of the equipment as necessary, but to difficulties in being able to reach, grasp and manipulate components within the machine itself.

Finally it should be remembered that maintenance is often carried out under conditions of stress, and this can take many forms. Since a machine which is out of operation is costing money, the maintenance engineer is often under time stress both from the operator and 'management' to rectify the fault. There is also the possibility of danger from the immediate work environment. In armed combat this danger is clear and takes the form of enemy action, but other examples may be adduced from civilian maintenance, for example the presence of high-voltage electricity or perhaps toxic chemicals. Finally, stress can also take the form of some fear of failure to rectify the fault. When the machine breaks down it is the maintenance engineer's profession which is called upon to make an unworkable machine workable. 'Professional pride' and worry about an inability to carry out the task as the job progresses may itself create a stressful environment.

Clearly, therefore, it is important to consider maintainability when designing equipment. The length of time for which a machine is out of operation is wasted time for that machine. The more difficult the maintenance task, the longer the engineer is likely to take, and this increases call-out costs and reduces the machine's value.

DESIGNING FOR MAINTAINABILITY

Although it is so important to consider ease of maintenance at an early stage in the design process, in many respects the techniques for doing so have evolved through common sense rather than through scientific investigation. Unfortunately it can be argued that even today designing for maintainability is more an art than a science, and that good maintenance design is more a state of mind than an established procedure.

However, various suggestions can be made to help the designer produce equipment which is easily maintainable, and all tend to follow very closely the various suggestions made throughout this book. For example, considerations of display and control design and arrangement; appropriate workplace and workspace design; the effect of various environmental parameters, etc. Many of these suggestions are described by Morgan *et al.* (1963) but it is useful to reiterate the importance of some of these aspects with respect to maintenance design.

Anthropometric Considerations

As was discussed earlier, with the increasing trend towards miniaturization the problem of the maintenance worker's accessibility to the machine or to the component in question becomes paramount. This applies equally well to large pieces of machinery that the operator might need to climb into or crouch behind, as to small machines (usually electronic machines in the present era) into which the operator may need to be able to manipulate fingers or hands. At both extremes, and in all cases between, efficiency is likely to be reduced if insufficient consideration is given to the anthropometric dimensions of the appropriate body or limb, plus its associated (protective) clothing.

Communication: Maintenance Manuals, Labelling and Symbols

Since a maintenance engineer is likely to have to service a number of different machines it is not unreasonable to expect to be provided with detailed information about the machine to be mended — its performance characteristics, mode of construction, possible faults, details and values of its components, etc. This is likely to be obtained from the mainenance manual. As Sinaiko and Brislin (1973) demonstrated, however (p. 96), a poorly designed manual is likely to lead to reduced performance in terms of increased errors and maintenance time. Thus much of the information provided in Chapter 4 (Man–man communication) is important in this context.

Being provided with a good maintenance manual, however, is only half of the battle for the maintenance operator. Having located a possible fault using, perhaps, a diagram the appropriate image from the diagram needs to be 'translated' to the machine so that the relevant component can be found. Labels, numbers, symbols, etc. can greatly expedite matters in this respect.

Information Displays

As well as being a means of communication between the operator and the machine, displays can also be used to inform the maintenance engineer whether the system, or parts of it, are performing normally. In this respect the principles important in display design were considered in detail in Chapter 5.

Controls

Again, most of the controls which are likely to be used by maintenance engineers will also be used by the normal operator, and the important principles in control design were considered in both Chapters 3 and 6.

One type of 'control' which is likely to be used more by the maintenance operator, however, is the connector or fastener. In the strict sense of the word, of course, connectors are not controls since they perform no controlling function between 'man' and machine. However, they have to be operated in much the same ways as controls (using the limbs) and their design involves many of the same principles (for example, ensuring that the connector size is appropriate to fit the limb (fingers) operating it; ensuring that the forces required to connect two connectors together are within the abilities of the operator, etc.).

Each of the principles which have been suggested for the appropriate design and location of connectors and fasteners follow two main themes:

First, ease of connection and disconnection. For easy maintenance, plug-in electrical connectors are likely to be better than screw terminals, and screw terminals better than solder connections. Similarly U-shaped lugs at the end of cables which can be connected without removing the securing screw are likely to be easier to maintain that O-shaped lugs containing a hole through which the screw is inserted. For connectors which fasten equipment together, wing-nuts are easier to remove than bolts, whilst a bolt which can be unscrewed using either a spanner or a screwdriver (i.e. has both hexagonal sides and a screwdriver slot) is likely to be more easily operated than a bolt which has only one such feature.

Second, ensuring that the connectors are not easily connected either the 'wrong way round' or to the wrong socket. Various techniques are available to ensure that the appropriate connections are made. These include using connectors and sockets of different sizes and colour; cutting and shaping cables so that a connector cannot reach a wrong socket; and using lugs or other aligning pins inside the connector and socket. If lugs are used, however, it is sensible to ensure that they are arranged a symmetrically so that the plug cannot be inserted 180 degrees from the correct position.

Arranging the Workspace and Workplace

Whereas the normal operator has to contend with a number of groups of men and machines in the environment, the nature of the maintenance operator's problems with respect to the workspace and workplace are much the same, although often scaled down in size since they concern only the particular machine being mended. Thus the problems involve access to the appropriate part of the machine (primarily anthropometric problems) and the layout of components inside the machine. Each of these have been considered in Chapters 8 and 9.

Finally, with regard to the layout of components within the machine, McKendry, Corso and Grant (1960) have demonstrated that an appropriate arrangement can considerably reduce the time required to locate a fault. In their experiment the components in either a simple radio receiver or a complex radar simulator were arranged according to one of four principles:

(1) Component packaging, in which all similar components, for example all tubes, all transistors, were grouped together in one place on the equipment. Using this procedure, once the area of a fault is determined, for cheap components at least, a whole plug-in section could be replaced.
(2) Circuit packaging, in which components relating to the various circuits (for example amplification, tuning, trimming, etc.) were placed together.
(3) Logical flow, which represents a combination of two approaches: first the use of modules and sub-assemblies so that only a single, simple input and output check is necessary to isolate trouble to that unit, and secondly the modules are arranged in a clear sequence representing the 'flow' through the circuitry, for example tuning–amplification–speaker.
(4) The 'standard' packaging method, which did not employ any grouping or modules nor did it attempt to suggest a logical flow in components. The parts of the equipment on top of the chassis were appropriately spaced to distribute weight and heat.

In all conditions the subject's task was to isolate a fault to a given component. The results demonstrated that the subjects found the faulty component significantly faster when using the logical flow method than the standard arrangement. The 'circuit' and 'component' arrangements produced intermediate times. Clearly, therefore, simply varying the arrangement of the components to be maintained can have significant effects on maintenance time.

SUMMARY

Both of the topics discussed in this chapter, inspection and maintenance, provide fitting summaries for many of the topics discussed elsewhere in this book. In their own right, both represent problems in the design of man–machine systems. However, the solution of these problems involves considering all aspects of the man–machine system — communication, displays, controls, workspace and workplace design, and the physical and social environment — and ensuring that they interact to the benefit of the operator.

CHAPTER 14

ERGONOMICS INVESTIGATIONS: SOME PROBLEMS AND TECHNIQUES

The purpose of this final chapter is *not* to present the reader with a list of different techniques and methods available for investigating the multitude of problems and questions that may occur when interactions between 'man' and the environment are considered. These are covered well enough by a number of specific books in this area, such as Chapanis (1959) or Oppenheim (1966). Rather, the chapter's aim is to illustrate and to emphasize pitfalls and problems about which the unsuspecting investigator may be unaware — particularly when studying the behaviour of *human* operators at work.

When faced with a problem, there are normally two avenues available to the intelligent inquisitor. First, attempts can be made to discover how other people have solved similar problems: by reading accounts of their investigations or attempting to apply their results to the particular situation. It is hoped that this book will have some value for these sorts of activities. The other, not necessarily mutually exclusive, approach is for the inquisitor to solve the problem by independent study. This has the major advantage that the investigation concerns problems experienced in a specific workplace and the results and conclusions obtained will be applicable to that particular problem. If only one message has been extracted from the book so far, it should have been that ergonomics is a discipline which attempts to fit together the person and the environment within a system, and that the results and conclusions from one system are not always applicable to another.

By deciding to investigate a particular man–machine relationship in the system, however, the potential investigator immediately encounters a multitude of further problems — all of which are caused by the human part of the system. There are a number of ways in which an individual's complex nature can bias or distort the outcome of experiments designed to investigate human behaviour within particular settings. Indeed, there are a number of ways in which subjects can make the investigator's task so difficult that it becomes impossible.

Perhaps the first bias, about which any aspiring psychologist is taught, is that of respondent bias (sometimes called volunteer error).

For obvious reasons, any experiment normally has to be carried out on a sample of subjects which has been selected from the population being studied.

For example, if the investigation is concerned with the response speed of women workers on a shop floor, it would be sensible only to use those particular workers in the experiment and not to draw subjects from any other population. However, it may not be feasible to measure the speed of response of all women workers in the factory, and so a sensible solution might be to select randomly a dozen or so individuals as being a representative sample. But how does the investigator go about the selection?

Since it is the normal expectation in a democratic society to be asked to participate, rather than to be commanded, the random sample is likely to be drawn from those individuals who were actually asked and who agreed to participate. Unfortunately, however, although observing such democratic principles meets the ethical requirements for research, it leaves open the question of whether the 'representative' sample was truly representative or whether it could have been biased: the sample contains only those subjects who agreed to be studied (the volunteers). But why were *they* chosen and why did *they* volunteer? Do they have characteristics that make them different from individuals who refused, or were not asked (perhaps because of personality, fears, age, intellectual level, etc.)? Why were some not asked? Answers to any of these questions could raise serious doubts regarding the impartiality of the sample selected.

Although some degree of volunteer bias normally has to be accepted, other biases can also easily be introduced into the investigation. These can occur simply *because* the investigation is being carried out; because of the interest which is being shown towards the person who is in the system.

Perhaps the most appropriate example of this bias is illustrated by a series of studies conducted at the Hawthorne plant of the Western Electric Company, under the direction of Elton Mayo, in the 1920s. The studies began by examining ways in which changes in the worker's physical environment would affect production, and the first feature to be investigated was the factory's illumination level. The results obtained, however, proved to be rather surprising: they indicated that illumination changes resulted in productivity increases — whatever the direction of the changes. Indeed, in one experiment the illumination level was reduced considerably, almost to moonlight levels, yet productivity still increased.

These paradoxical results have since been explained by suggesting that the individuals increased their output *because* they were in an experimental situation. Perhaps they acted in this way because they felt that the experimenters were taking an interest in them. Whatever the reason, this 'Hawthorne Effect' — that subject's performance may vary solely as a result of the experimental situation — has now become a recognized pitfall in psychological investigations.

If these biases were constant and always acted in one direction (for example, always caused the subject to perform better or worse), the problems that they cause would not be too great. Unfortunately they are neither constant nor consistent. For a number of reasons the same pressures which produce the 'Hawthorne Effect' can act in the reverse direction — to cause subjects to perform at a slower, less accurate rate than normal.

One reason for this effect may be due to attitudes which the workforce, the unions and/or the management may have towards the investigation. In some respects, for example, ergonomics has many features in common with Work Study and with Time and Motion Study. Unfortunately, however, both of these disciplines enjoy considerable popular notoriety which could interfere with the investigation. If the interference is extreme enough to be symptomatized by a complete withdrawal of cooperation and work then this is bad enough. From the point of view of the investigator, however, a worse situation would be if the subjects are apparently cooperative but are, nevertheless, antagonistic to the aims of the study. In such cases the investigator has no idea of the effect of these antagonistic attitudes on the subject's behaviour — particularly if the subject appears to cooperate.

Another negative 'Hawthorne Effect' can arise in studies carried out in industrial premises, when measures of workers' productivity are recorded — particularly if the operators feel that the investigation's results might affect future productivity and payment norms (again the memory of time and motion study is difficult to erase). In this case productivity may be depressed purposefully during the investigation period so that, once the norms have been set and after the investigation has ended, 'normal' production will appear as increased productivity.

The message to be gained concerning each of these biases, then, suggests that as far as possible the subjects' confidence (whether they be subjects in the laboratory or operators at work) should be sought. For many reasons it may not be possible to explain all of the reasons for the experiment (for example, telling subjects that an experiment will investigate the effects of different noise levels on behaviour may cause them to react differently to the noise than they otherwise might have done). However, in many cases it should be possible to allay fears, to discuss the aims of the investigation, and to ensure the subjects that their results are likely to be of benefit (if, indeed, they are).

At this stage it is well to consider where the study can be carried out — in the laboratory or, in situ, in the field. Both environments have their advantages and their disadvantages.

If the research is to be carried out in the laboratory, precise questions can be asked and controlled stimuli can be presented to the subject, ensuring that all subjects receive the same stimulus. In the field, however, the investigator is not so well acquainted with the nature of the stimulus which the operator is receiving. Different operators might be receiving (either subjectively or physically) different stimuli due to factors outside of the investigator's control, such as variations in seating positions or even the operators' states of health at the time.

In contrast, however, field investigations have one major advantage over laboratory studies. This concerns the validity of the results which are obtained finally, and have to be related back to the working situation. In this respect it is well to notice that in the preceding paragraph 'subjects' were discussed as receiving stimuli in the laboratory, whereas 'operators' were said to receive the simulus in the field. This simple semantic distinction highlights the advantage of the field over the laboratory investigation — namely that if the investigation is to benefit any particular section of the community, then members of that group should be used in the investigation.

The advantage of field studies, therefore, relates to the fact that a laboratory experiment cannot take account of all of the extraneous variables which may influence the operator at work. For example, laboratory subjects do not have to earn a living at that particular point in time; they may not fully understand the various consequences of their actions; they are not likely to be at ease — in fact, they may enter the laboratory fearing the worst; and they are not being subjected to all of the extraneous stimuli that occur in normal work, for example noise, temperature and even pressures from management and colleagues.

It is possible, of course, to combine the two research environments of 'laboratory' and 'field' to produce a third arrangement. In this case subjects' responses are measured under field conditions, that is personnel are 'employed' specifically to carry out an experiment (they then become 'subjects'), but the investigation is carried under field conditions. This field (subject) approach has been used quite extensively in the past (see Oborne, 1978) and has much to recommend it. At least the experiment is carried out in the appropriate environment with all of the relevant extraneous stimuli. However, it still suffers from the drawback that 'subjects' rather than 'operators' are used.

Before discussing some of the techniques suitable for an ergonomics investigation it is well to pose one further problem — whether it is possible to investigate behaviour at all, without affecting the behaviour being investigated.

The question is perhaps better understood by nuclear physicists following the proposition of the 'Uncertainty Principle' by Heisenberg in the 1930s. Heisenberg was concerned with measuring the behaviour of atoms but concluded that it is not possible to measure their behaviour without affecting them: 'Every subsequent observation ... will alter the momentum (of the atom) by an unknown and undeterminable amount such that after carrying out the experiment our knowledge of the electronic motion is restricted by the uncertainty relation'. The same is also true, unfortunately, for human behaviour. As soon as the investigator enters the system and inserts measuring equipment (whether the equipment is in the form of 'hardware' such as meters or probes, or 'software' such as questions or observation) the subsequent behaviour of that system (including the human operator) is likely to be affected in an uncertain manner. Unfortunately, this cannot be totally overcome, although it can be reduced by using unobtrusive techniques such as observation.

OBSERVATION AND OTHER UNOBTRUSIVE MEASURES

Whatever technique is chosen to investigate the human operator's performance within the system, Heisenberg's Uncertainty Principle still operates. However, some techniques produce less interference than others and, providing it is carried out properly, perhaps the least intrusive in this respect is simply to observe behaviour or its concomitants.

Direct Observation

Directly observing what the operator does when interactions take place with the environment is possibly one of the most commonly used techniques. At a basic level it is simple, requires little equipment and often produces data which can be easily interpreted. However, direct observation can be misused and produce misleading results — particularly if the observer intrudes into the system. Then any of the biases and hindrances discussed earlier can occur.

The most important principle of direct observation, therefore, is that the observer (and any equipment used) should be unobtrusive. This is not to say that the observer should be invisible — merely that the system being observed should not be interfered with in any way. In many cases, of course, an invisible observer (for example, one who is behind a screen) is also likely to be unobtrusive. However, situations can arise in which the absence of an observer who otherwise would have been expected could lead to mistrust or worry. A subject could be upset more by knowing (or feeling) that he or she is being observed, for example, through a one-way screen, than if the observer was visible.

The second important principle of direct observation is that a permanent record of the behaviour should be made for future, detailed analysis. This is normally done in one of two ways: either by recording all of the activities using cine film or videotape, or by sampling the operator's activities and recording aspects of the behaviour on either precoded paper sheets or directly into a computer.

The advantages of using cine or video-films should be obvious: all of the operator's activities are recorded and the film can subsequently be played back many times during the analysis. As long as the camera has been positioned appropriately, therefore, the investigator is ensured of obtaining a complete, permanent record of the operator's behaviour. Furthermore, when analysing the record the film can be played back at a slower speed than normal (again ensuring that no activity, however slight, is missed), or at a speed which is faster than normal.

The ability to play the record back at a faster speed than that recorded has two advantages. First, it speeds up the analysing time. By the time it has been stopped, started and re-run a few times, a two-hour record, for example, is likely to take at least three or four times as long (6–8 hours) to analyse at normal speed. Playing it back at a faster rate should reduce this time. Secondly fast playback allows the observer to 'see' motions which might otherwise be too slow to observe at normal speeds. For example, Branton and Grayson (1967) used cine-film to record the sitting behaviour of passengers in two types of train seats throughout a five-hour journey. When the films were played back at a faster speed than normal it became apparent that one type of seat caused the sitter to slip forward gradually and out of the seat, requiring the seating position to be adjusted constantly. This 'slipping' action, however, was too slow to be observed in 'real' time. As a further example Branton and Oborne (1979) recorded the behaviour of anaesthetists during various operations. When the video-film was speeded up (20× normal speed) a head 'nodding' behaviour was able to be observed which the authors suggest could be related to the onset and continuation of fatigue and monotony.

One disadvantage of cine or video records has already been discussed — namely the mass of data which is obtained and which needs to be analysed. For example, Lovesey (1975) used a cine-film to record pilot activity during different types of helicopter flying. Just over two hours of flying was recorded, which then needed to be analysed on a frame-by-frame basis. Since the film speed was eight frames per second, Lovesey needed to analyse the head and hand positions of his pilots in each of 63 370 frames.

Another, perhaps less obvious, disadvantage of visual recording lies in the (often) fixed positions needed to set up the cameras. To be unobtrusive they should not be too visible and the presence of a camera operator is likely to make them apparent. Unfortunately, however, environmental conditions do not remain constant to those which prevailed at the time of setting up the equipment. For example, during Branton and Oborne's anaesthetist study mentioned above some operations were filmed which required the theatre lights so be extinguished while the surgeon used particular light sources. During these periods, of course, the video camera was unable to record the anaesthetist's activities. Rennie and Wilson (1980) discuss similar problems using video-films to record pedestrian behaviour. Movements of the sun (or at least of the earth in relation to the sun) and clouds can cause illumination levels that are too high or too low for the camera.

Analysing the behaviour as it is carried out obviates these problems. This is the one advantage of sampling behaviour and recording the operator's activities, say, every minute on a precoded sheet or directly into a computer. Unless the observer is fully conversant with the activities which are likely to have to be recorded, however, and unless the sampling time periods are sufficiently long, this method can place the observer under considerable time stress. As an example of this approach, Christensen (1950) recorded the activities of navigators and radar operators during 15-hour flights. The observer used a metronome to produce a tone once a minute and recorded his subject's activities when he heard the tone.

Indirect Observation

No matter how well the observer is integrated in the system, Webb et al. (1966) argue that there is still the potential to bias the results in many of the ways discussed above. For this reason, they suggest techniques by which the activities of the subject(s) can be observed indirectly.

Physical traces

If an activity is carried out frequently, over time the equipment, or the part of it which is operated, is likely to become well used. To an observant individual, this is useful data. As an example, Webb *et al.* cite the wear on library books: less popular books remain in a newer condition than do books which are borrowed frequently, and the page corners and edges of the popular parts of the book are likely to be dirtier and more dog-eared than the less popular parts. As a further example, the wear and tear on various parts of a floor can indicate the extent to which various machines are used.

The same type of approach can be used to determine the nature of the activity which is carried out. For example, dial settings which an operator leaves on the machine, say at night, may indicate the way in which the machine has been used; as may the positions in which movable machines and components are left after use.

Statistical records

In many respects by using statistical records the investigator is merely observing what has happened in the past rather than what is happening at present. As was discussed in Chapter 12, records are most frequently used to study accident trends, their types, places and personnel involvement. They can be very useful in locating areas of potential danger — either in the person or in the environment. As long as a large enough pool of accidents is sampled useful statistical analyses can be computed and, of course, an investigator who is never at the scene of the accident, cannot be intrusive.

Statistical records, however, have limited value. As Chapanis (1959) points out, accidents or near accidents are infrequent events and it may take years to collect enough instances to form any sort of reasonable classification of the kinds of troubles that can occur. Secondly, it is virtually impossible to compare or contrast different accident situations because of the difficulty of assessing exposure risks. This point was emphasized, for example, when considering the concept of accident proneness — 'accident prone' individuals may simply be in riskier situations. Thirdly, the statistics tell us simply that an event (accident) had occurred. It is difficult, if not impossible, to reconstruct what happened or why. For these reasons, statistical evidence is only useful as 'back-up' information or for helping to generate hypotheses which can later be tested by more controlled observation or experimentation.

SUMMARY

This chapter has not attempted to equip the reader with the practical or statistical skills required to carry out an ergonomic investigation. The techniques available are so numerous and so diverse that to be able to do so one would need to produce a separate book. Instead this chapter has provided the reader with a background to the problems involved with human experimentation, the interpersonal problems which can occur but about which the investigator may be unaware. It has also suggested simple, unobtrusive measures which can be used. Armed with an understanding of these problems, the potential ergonomist will be equipped to investigate further the multitude of ways in which people and their environments interact.

REFERENCES

Abrahams, C. F. Jr. and Suggs, C. W. (1969). *Chain Saw Vibration: Isolation and Transmission Through the Human Arm.* Paper presented to Annual Meeting of the American Society of Agricultural Engineers, Indiana, June.

Agate, J. N. (1949). An outbreak of cases of Raynaud's phenomenon of occupational origin. *British Journal of Industrial Medicine,* **6,** 144–63.

Alden, D. G., Daniels, R. W. and Kanarick, A. F. (1972). Keyboard design and operation: A review of the major issues. *Human Factors,* **14,** 275–293.

Alexander, C. (1972). *Performance Changes Due to the Single and Dual Frequency Vibration of Reading Material.* PhD Thesis, University of Southampton.

Allgeier, A. R. and Byrne, D. (1973). Attraction towards the opposite sex as a determinant of physical proximity, *Journal of Social Psychology,* **90,** 213–19.

Allen, G. R. (1975). *Ride Quality and International Standard 2631.* Paper presented to Ride Quality Symposium, Williamsburg, August. NASA TM X-3295.

American Society of Heating and Refrigeration Engineers (1965). *ASHRAE Guide and Data Book: Fundamentals and Equipment.* (ASHRAE).

American Standards Association. (1960). *American Standards Acoustical Terminology S1.* New York: ASA.

Anderson, J.R. (1980). *Cognitive Psychology.* San Francisco: W.H. Freeman

Andersson, G. B. J. (1980). The load on the lumbar spine in sitting postures. In D. J. Oborne and J. A. Levis (eds) *Human Factors in Transport Research Volume II.* London: Academic Press.

Andersson, G. B. J. and Örtengren, R. (1974). Lumbar disc pressure and myoelectric back muscle activity during sitting. Studies on an office chair, *Scandinavian Journal of Rehabilitation Medicine,* **3,** 104–14; 122–7; 128–35.

Andersson, G. B. J., Örtengren, R., and Nachemson, A. (1982). Disc pressure measurements when rising and sitting down on a chair, *Engineering in Medicine,* **11,** 189–90.

Andersson, G. B. J., Örtengren, R., Nachemson, A. L., Elfstrom, G. and Broman, H. (1975). The sitting posture: an electromyographic and discometric study, *Orthopaedic Clinics of North America,* **6,** 105–20.

Andrew, I. and Manoy, R. (1972). Anthropometric survey of British Rail footplate staff, *Applied Ergonomics,* **3,** 132–5.

Anglin, J. M. and Miller, G. A. (1968). The role of phrase structure in the recall of meaningful verbal material, *Psychonomic Science,* **10,** 340–4.

Anon. (1966). *Lifting in Industry.* Pamphlet prepared by the posture subcommittee. London: Chartered Society of Physiotherapy.

Archer, B. U. and Margolin, R. R. (1970). Arousal effects in intentional recall and forgetting, *Journal of Experimental Psychology,* **86,** 8–12.

Argyle, M. and Cook, M. (1976). *Gaze and Mutual Gaze.* Cambridge: Cambridge University Press.

Arroyo, F. V. (1982). Negatives in context, *Journal of Verbal Learning and Verbal Behaviour,* **21,** 118–26.

344

Asch, S. E. (1952). *Social Psychology.* N.J.: Prentice-Hall.

Baddeley, A. D. (1966). Time estimation at reduced body temperature, *American Journal of Psychology,* **79,** 475-9.

Baddeley, A. D., Cuccaro, W. J., Egstrom, G. H., Weltman, G. and Willis, M. A. (1975). Cognitive efficiency of divers working in cold water, *Human Factors,* **17,** 446-54.

Bahrick, H. P. (1957). An analysis of stimulus variables influencing the proprioceptive control of movements, *Psychological Review,* **64,** 324-8.

Ball, R. G., Newton, R. S. and Whitfield, D. (1980). Development of an off-display, high resolution, input device: the RSRE Touchpad, *Displays,* **1,** 203-7.

Barkala, D. (1961). The estimation of body measurements of British population in relation to seat design, *Ergonomics,* **4,** 123-32.

Barnard, P. and Wright, P. (1977). A preliminary investigation of factors influencing the interpretation of pictorial instructions for the use of apparatus, *Proceedings of the 8th International Symposium on Human Factors in Telecommunications,* Cambridge, September, pp. 379-92.

Barnard, P. and Marcel. A. (1976). The effects of spaced character formats on the production and legibility of handwritten names, *Ergonomics,* **19,** 81-92.

Barnard, P. and Marcel, A. (1983). Representation and understanding in the use of symbols and pictograms. In R. Easterby and H. Zwaga (eds) *Information Design.* Chichester: John Wiley & Sons.

Barnard, P., Wright, P. and Wilcox, P. (1979). Effects of response instructions and question style on the ease of completing forms, *Journal of Occupational Psychology,* **52,** 209-26.

Barnard, P. J., Hammond, N. V., Morton, J., Long, J. B. and Clarke, I.A. (1981). Consistency and compatibility in human-computer dialogue, *International Journal of Man-Machine Systems,* **15,** 87-134.

Barnard, P. J., Hammond, N.V., MacLean, A., and Morton, J. (1982). *Learning and Remembering Interactive Commands.* IBM Research Report HF 055. Hants: IBM.

Barnes, G. R., Benson, A. J. and Prior, A. R. J. (1978). Visual-vestibular interaction in the control of eye-movement, *Aviation, Space and Environmental Medicine,* **49,** 557-64.

Bartlett, F. C. (1959). Programme for experiments of thinking, *Quarterly Journal of Experimental Psychology,* **2,** 145-52.

Bauer, D. and Cavonius, C.R. (1980). Improving the legibility of visual display units through contrast reversal. In E. Grandjean and E. Vigliani (eds) *Ergonomic Aspects of Visual Display Terminals.* London: Taylor and Francis.

Baughn, W. L. (1966). Noise control — percent of population protected, *International Audiology,* **5,** 331-8.

Bearham, J. (1976). *The Cost of Accidents Within the Port Industry.* London: Manpower Services Commission.

Beevis, D. and Slade, I. M. (1970). Ergonomics — costs and benefits, *Applied Ergonomics,* **1,** 79-85.

Begg, I. and Paivio, A. (1969). Concreteness and imagery in sentence meaning, *Journal of Verbal Learning and Verbal Behaviour,* **8,** 821-7.

Belbin, R. M. (1957). New fields for quality control, *British Management Review,* **15,** 79-89.

Beldie, L. P., Pastorr, S. and Schwarz, E. (1983). Fixed versus variable letter width for televised text, *Human Factors,* **25,** 273-7.

Bell, C. R., Crowder, M. J. and Walters, J. D. (1971). Durations of safe exposure for men at work in high temperature environments, *Ergonomics,* **14,** 121-8.

Bendix, T. and Eid, S. F. (1983). The distance between the load and the body with three bi-manual lifting techniques, *Applied Ergonomics,* **14,** 185-92.

Benn, R. T. and Wood, P. H. N. (1975). Pain in the back: an attempt to estimate the size of the problem, *Rheumatology and Rehabilitation,* **14,** 733-57.

Benson, A. J., Huddleston, J. H. F. and Rolfe, J. M. (1965). A psychophysiological study of compensatory tracking on a digital display, *Human Factors*, **7**, 457–72.

Bergenthal, J. (1971). Preferred pushbutton switch operating forces, *IEEE Transactions — Man and Cybernetics*, **1**, 385–7.

Berlyne, D. E., Borsa, D. M., Craw, M. A., Gelman, R. S. and Mandell, E. E. (1965). Effects of stimulus complexity and induced arousal on paired-associate learning, *Journal of Verbal Behaviour and Verbal Learning*, **4**, 291–9.

Berry, P. C. (1961). The effect of coloured illumination upon perceived temperature, *Journal of Applied Psychology*, **45**, 248–50.

Beshir, M. Y. and Ramsey, J. D. (1981). Comparison between male and female subjective estimates of thermal effects and sensations, *Applied Ergonomics*, **12**, 29–33.

Bever, T. G., Garrett, M. F. and Hartig, R. (1973). The interaction of perceptual processes and ambiguous sentences, *Memory and Cognition*, **1**, 277–86.

Biancardi, M. (1978). The cost/benefit factor in safety decisions, *Professional Safety*, **November**, 17–22.

Biegel, R. A. (1934). An improved typewriter keyboard, *The Human Factor*, **8**, 280–5.

Bilger, R. C. and Hirsh, I. J. (1956). Masking of tones by bands of noise, *Journal of the Acoustical Society of America*, **28**, 623–30.

Bird, P. F. (1977). 'Digilux' touch sensitive panel. In *Displays for Man-machine Systems*. IEE Conference publication No. 150. London: IEE.

Bjerner, B., Holm, A. and Swensson, A. (1948) Om natt och skiftarbete. *Statens Offentliga Utredningar (Stockholm)*, **51**, 87–159.

Bjerver, K. and Goldberg, L. (1950). Effects of alcohol ingestion on driving ability, *Quarterly Journal on the Study of Alcohol*, **11**, 1–30.

Blackwell, O. M. and Blackwell, H. R. (1971). Visual performance data for 156 normal observers of various ages, *Illuminating Engineering Society Journal*, **1**, 3–13.

Blake, M. J. F. (1971). Temperament and time of day. In W. P. Colquohoun (ed.) *Biological Rhythms and Human Performance*. London: Academic Press.

Bodmann, H. W. (1962). Illumination levels and visual performance, *International Lighting Review*, **13**, 41–7.

Boggs, D. H. and Simon, J. R. (1968). Differential effect of noise on tasks of varying complexity, *Journal of Applied Psychology*, **52**, 148–53.

Booher, H. R. (1975). Relative comprehensibility of pictorial information and printed words in proceduralized instructions, *Human Factors*, **17**, 266–77.

Bouma, H. (1973). Visual interference in the parafoveal recognition of initial and final letters of words, *Vision Research*, **13**, 767–82.

Bouma, H. (1980). Visual reading processes and the quality of text displays. In E. Grandjean and E. Vigliani (eds) *Ergonomic Aspects of Visual Display Terminals*. London: Taylor & Francis.

Bowen, H. M. (1968). Diver performance and the effects of cold, *Human Factors*, **10**, 445–64.

Bowen, H. M. and Guiness, G. V. (1965). Preliminary experiments on keyboard design for semi-automatic mail sorting, *Journal of Applied Psychology*, **49**, 194–8.

Boyce, P. R. (1981). *Human Factors in Lighting*. London: Applied Science Publishers.

Boynton, R. M. (1960). Summary and Discussion. In A. Morris and E. P. Horne (eds) *Visual Search*. Washington, DC: National Academy of Science.

Boynton, R. M., Elworth, C. and Palmer, R. M. (1958). *Laboratory Studies Pertaining to Visual Air Reconnaisance*. USAF, WADC TR 55–304.

Bradley, J. W. (1967). Tactual coding of cylindrical knobs, *Human Factors*, **9**, 483–96.

Bradley, J. W. (1969a). Glove characteristics influencing control manipulability, *Human Factors*, **11**, 21–36.

Bradley, J.W. (1969b). Optimum knob diameter, *Human Factors*, **11**, 353–60.

Bradley, J. W. (1969c). Desirable dimensions for concentric controls, *Human Factors*, **11**, 213–26.

Bradley, J. W. (1969d). Optimum knob crowding, *Human Factors*, **11**, 227–38.

Branton, P. (1966). *The Comfort of Easy Chairs.* Furniture Industry Research Report No. 22.

Branton, P. (1969). Behaviour, body mechanics and discomfort, *Ergonomics,* **12,** 316–27.

Branton, P. (1972). Ergonomic Research Contributions to the Design of the Passenger Environment. Paper presented to the Institute of Mechanical Engineers Symposium on Passenger Comfort, London.

Branton, P. (1984). Backshapes of seated persons — how close can the interface be designed? *Applied Ergonomics,* **15,** 105–7.

Branton, P. and Grayson, G. (1967). An evaluation of train seats by an observation of sitting behaviour, *Ergonomics,* **10,** 35–41.

Branton, P. and Oborne, D. J. (1979). A behavioural study of anaesthetists at work. In D. J. Oborne, M. M. Gruneberg and J. R. Eiser (eds) *Research in Psychology and Medicine Volume I.* London: Academic Press.

Brebner, J. and Sandow, B. (1976). The effect of scale side on population stereotype, *Ergonomics,* **19,** 571–80.

Brenner, B. (1967). Alcoholism and fatal accidents, *Quarterly Journal on Studies of Alcohol,* **28,** 517–28.

Brinkmann, P. (1985). Pathology of the vertebral column, *Ergonomics,* **28,** 77–80.

British Standards Institute (1964). *Recommendations for the Design of Scales and Indexes. Part I Instruments of Bold Presentation and for Rapid Reading.* BS 3693. London: BSI

British Standards Institute (1969). *Recommendations for the Design of Scales and Indexes. Part II Indicating Instruments to be Read to 0.33–1.25% Resolution.* BS 3693. London: BSI

Broadbent, D. E. (1954). Some effects of noise on visual performance, *Quarterly Journal of Experimental Psychology,* **6,** 1–5.

Broadbent, D. E. (1977). Language and ergonomics, *Applied Ergonomics,* **8,** 15–18.

Broadbent, D. E. and Gregory, M. (1965). Effects of noise and of signal rate upon vigilance analysed by means of decision theory, *Human Factors,* **7,** 155–62.

Brookes, M. J. (1972). Office landscape: does it work? *Applied Ergonomics,* **3,** 224–36.

Brookes, M. J. and Kaplan, A. (1972). The office environment: space planning and effective behaviour, *Human Factors,* **14,** 373–91.

Brown, I. D. (1965). A comparison of two subsidiary tasks used to measure fatigue in car drivers, *Ergonomics,* **8,** 467–73.

Brown, I. D. and Poulton, E. C. (1961). Measuring the 'spare mental capacity' of car drivers by a subsidiary task, *Ergonomics,* **5,** 35–40.

Brown, C. R. (1974). Human factors problems in the design and evaluation of key-entry devices for the Japanese language. In A. Chapanis (ed) *Ethnic Variables in Human Factors Engineering.* (Baltimore: The Johns Hopkins University Press).

Brown, J. L. (1965). Flicker and intermittent stimulation. In C. H. Graham (ed) *Vision and Visual Perception.* New York: John Wiley & Sons.

Browne, R. C. (1949) The day and night performance of teleprinter switch board operators *Occupational Psychology,* **23,** 121–126.

Buck, P. C. and Coleman, V. P. (1985). Slipping, tripping and falling accidents at work: a national picture, *Ergonomics,* **28,** 949–58.

Buckhout, R. (1964). Effect of whole body vibration on human performance, *Human Factors,* **6,** 157–63.

Buckler, A. T. (1977). *A Review on the Legibility of Alphanumerics on Electronic Displays.* May 1977. AD-A040-625.

Burrows, A. A. (1965). Control feel and the dependent variable, *Human Factors,* **7,** 413–21.

Burt, C. (1959). *A Psychological Study of Typography.* Cambridge: Cambridge University Press.

Burton, A. K. (1984). Electromyography and office-chair design: a pilot study. *Behaviour and Information Technology,* **3,** 353–7.

Buswell, G. T. (1935). *How People Look at Pictures.* Chicago: University of Chicago Press.

Byrne, D., Baskett, G. D. and Hodges, L. (1971). Behavioural indicators of interpersonal attraction, *Journal of Applied Social Psychology*, **1**, 137–49.

Cakir, A., Hart, D. J. and Stewart, T. F. M. (1980). *Visual Display Terminals*. Chichester: John Wiley & Sons.

Caldwell, L. S. (1963). Relative muscle loading and endurance, *Journal of Engineering Psychology*, **2**, 155–61.

Caldwell, L. S. (1964). Measurement of static muscle endurance, *Journal of Engineering Psychology*, **3**, 16–22.

Card, S. K., English, W. K. and Burr, B. J. (1978). Evaluation of mouse, rate-controlled isometric joystick, step keys, and text keys for text selection on a CRT, *Ergonomics*, **21**, 601–13.

Carlson, B. R. (1969). Level of maximum isometric strength and relative load isometric endurance, *Ergonomics*, **12**, 429–35.

Carlsoo, S. (1972). *How Man Moves*. London: Heinemann.

Carpenter, J. A. (1959). The effect of caffeine and alcohol on simple visual reaction time, *Journal of Comparative and Physiological Psychology*, **52**, 491–6.

Carroll, J. M. (1982). Learning, using and designing command paradigms, *Human Learning*, **1**, 31–62.

Cashen, V. M. and Leicht, K. L. (1970). Role of the isolation effect in a formal education setting, *Journal of Educational Psychology*, **61**, 484–6.

Castle, P. F. C. (1956). Accidents, absence, and withdrawal from the work situation, *Human Relations*, **9**, 223–33.

Catterson, A. D., Hoover, G. N. and Asche, W. F. (1962). Human psychomotor performance during prolonged vertical vibration, *Aerospace Medicine*, **33**, 598–602.

Cavanaugh, W. J., Farrell, W. R., Hirtle, P. W. and Walters, B. G. (1962). Speech privacy in buildings, *Journal of the Acoustical Society of America*, **34**, 475–92.

Chambers, J. B. and Stockbridge, H. C. W. (1970). Comparison of indicator components and push-button recommendations, *Ergonomics*, **13**, 401–20.

Chaney, F. B. and Teel, K. S. (1967). Improving inspector performance through training and visual aids, *Journal of Applied Psychology*, **51**, 311–15.

Chapanis, A. (1951). Studies of manual rotary positioning movements. II: The accuracy of estimating the position of an indicator knob, *Journal of Psychology*, **31**, 65.

Chapanis, A. (1959). *Research Techniques in Human Engineering*. Baltimore: The Johns Hopkins University Press.

Chapanis, A. (1960). Human Engineering. In C. D. Flagle, W. H. Higgins and R. N. Roy (eds) *Operations Research and Systems Engineering*. Baltimore: The Johns Hopkins University Press.

Chapanis, A. (1965a). On the allocation of functions between men and machines, *Occupational Psychology*, **39**, 1–11.

Chapanis, A. (1965b). Words, words, words, *Human Factors*, **7**, 1–17.

Chapanis, A. (1974). National and cultural variables in ergonomics, *Ergonomics*, **17**, 153–75.

Chapanis, A. (1976). Engineering Psychology. In M. D. Dunnette (ed.) *Handbook of Industrial Psychology*. Chicago: Rand McNally Corp.

Chapanis, A. and Lindenbaum, L. E. (1959). A reaction time study of four control-display linkages, *Human Factors*, **1**, 1–7.

Chapanis, A. and Lockhead, G. R. (1965). A test of the effectiveness of sensor lines showing linkages between displays and controls, *Human Factors*, **7**, 219–29.

Chapanis, A. and Mankin, D. A. (1967). Tests of ten control-display linkages, *Human Factors*, **9**, 119–26.

Chorley, R. A. (1973). Human factors, *Aviation Review*, **March**, 12–15.

Christ, R. E. (1975). Review and analysis of colour coding research for visual displays, *Human Factors*, **17**, 542–70.

Christensen, J. M. (1950). A sampling technique for use in activity analysis. *Personnel Psychology*, **3**, 361–8.

348

Christie, A. W. and Fisher, A. J. (1966). The effect of glare from street lighting lanterns on the vision of drivers at different ages, *Transactions of the Illuminating Engineering Society,* **31,** 93–108.

Christie, B. (1981). *Face-to-File Communication: A Psychological Approach to Information Systems.* Chichester: John Wiley & Sons.

Cirello, V. M. and Snook, S. H. (1983). A study of size, distance, height and frequency effects on manual handling tasks, *Human Factors,* **25,** 473–83.

Clark, R. E. (1961). The limiting hand skin temperature for unaffected manual performance in the cold. *Journal of Applied Psychology,* **45,** 193–4.

Clark, R. E. and Cohen, A. (1960). Manual performance as a function of rate of change in hand skin temperature, *Journal of Applied Psychology,* **44,** 496–8.

Clark, R. P. and Edholm, O. G. (1985). *Man and His Thermal Environment.* London: Edward Arnold.

Coe, J. B., Cuttle, K., McClellon, W. C., Warden, N. J. and Turner, P. J. (1980). *Visual Display Units.* Report W/1/80. Wellington: New Zealand Department of Health.

Coermann, R. R. (1962). The mechanical impedance of the human body in sitting and standing position at low frequencies, *Human Factors,* **4,** 227–53.

Cohen, E. and Follert, R. L. (1970). Accuracy of interpolation between scale gradations, *Human Factors,* **12,** 481–3.

Cohen, J., Dearnaley, E. J. and Hansel, C. E. M. (1958). The risk taken in driving under the influence of alcohol, *British Medical Journal,* **1,** 1438–42.

Cohen, S., Glass, D. C. and Singer, J. E. (1973). Apartment noise, auditory discrimination and reading ability in children, *Journal of Experimental Social Psychology,* **9,** 40–7.

Coles, A. R. A., Garinther, G. R., Hodge, D. C. and Rice, C. G. (1968). Hazardous exposure to impulse noise, *Journal of the Acoustical Society of America,* **43,** 336–43.

Colquhoun, W. P. (1958). The effect of short rest pause on inspection accuracy, *Ergonomics,* **2,** 367–72.

Colquhoun, W. P. (1975a). Evaluation of auditory, visual and dual mode displays for prolonged monitoring in repeated sessions, *Human Factors,* **17,** 425–37.

Colquhoun, W. P. (1975b). *Accidents, Injuries and Shiftwork.* Paper presented to NIOSH Symposium on 'Shiftwork and Health'; Cincinnati.

Connell, S. C. (1948). *Psychological Factors in Check Reading Single Instruments.* USAF Air Material Command Memo Report No MCREXD–694–17A.

Conrad, R. and Hull, A. J. (1968). The preferred layout for data-entry keysets, *Ergonomics,* **11,** 165–73.

Conrad, R. and Longman, D. J. A. (1965). Standard typewriter versus chord keyboard — An experimental comparison, *Ergonomics,* **8,** 77–88.

Cooper, M. B. (1976). The effect of keypad angle of a table telephone on keying performance, *Applied Ergonomics,* **7,** 205–11.

Corlett, E. N. and Bishop, R. P. (1975). Foot pedal forces for seated operators, *Ergonomics,* **18,** 687–92.

Corlett, E. N. and Parsons, A. T. (1978). Measurement of changes: what criteria do we adopt? *International Journal of Management Sciences,* **6,** 399–406.

Corlett, E. N. and Eklund, J. A. E. (1984). How does a backrest work? *Applied Ergonomics,* **15,** 111–14.

Corlett, E. N., Morcombe, V. J. and Chanda, B. (1970). Shielding factory noise by work-in-progress storage, *Applied Ergonomics,* **1,** 73–8.

Corlett, E. N., Hutcheson, C., DeLugan, M. A. and Rogozenski, J. (1972). Ramps or stairs: the choice using physiological and biomechanical criteria, *Applied Ergonomics,* **3,** 195–201.

Courtney, A. J. (1984). Hand anthropometry of Hong Kong Chinese females compared to other groups, *Ergonomics,* **27,** 1169–80.

Cowley, D. M. (1976). International Standards in the Vibration Field. In Tempest, W.

349

(ed.) *Infrasound and Low Frequency Vibration.* London: Academic Press.

Craig, A. and Condon, R. (1984). Operational efficiency and time of day, *Human Factors,* **26,** 197–205.

Crawford, B. H. and Stiles, W. S. (1937). The effect of a glaring light source on extra-foveal vision, *Proceedings of the Royal Society (Series B),* **122,** 255–80

Creamer, L. R. and Trumbo, D. A. (1960). Multifinger tapping performance as a function of the direction of tapping movements, *Journal of Applied Psychology,* **44,** 376–80.

Cromer, W. (1960). The difference model: a new explanation for some reading difficulties, *Journal of Educational Psychology,* **61,** 471–83.

Crook, M. A. and Langdon, F. J. (1974). The effects of aircraft noise in schools around London airport, *Journal of Sound and Vibration,* **12,** 221–32.

Crossman, E. R. F. W. The information capacity of the human operator in symbolic and nonsymbolic control processes. In *Information Theory and the Human Operator.* Ministry of Supply Publication WR/D2/56, 1956.

Crouse, J. H. and Idstein, P. (1972). Effects of encoding cues on prose learning, *Journal of Educational Psychology,* **61,** 484–6.

Cushman, W. H. (1980). Selection of filters for dark adaptation goggles in the photographic industry, *Applied Ergonomics,* **11,** 93–9.

Czaja, S. J. and Drury, C. G. (1981). Training programs for inspection, *Human Factors,* **23,** 473–84.

Dainoff, M. J. (1982). Occupational stress factors in visual display terminal (VDT) operation: a review of empirical research, *Behaviour and Information Technology,* **1,** 141–76.

Dainoff, M. J., Happ, A. and Crane, P. (1981). Visual fatigue and occupational stress in VDT operators, *Human Factors,* **23,** 421–38.

Damon, A. and Stoudt, H. W. (1963). The functional anthropometry of old men, *Human Factors,* **5,** 485–91.

Damon, A., Stoudt, H. W. and McFarland, R. A. (1971). *The Human Body in Equipment Design.* Massachusetts: Harvard University Press.

Daniels, G. S. (1952). *The 'Average Man'?* Wright Patterson Airforce Base Technical Note WCRD 53–7. Ohio.

Dashevsky, S. G. (1964). Check reading accuracy as a function of pointer alignment, patterning and viewing angle, *Journal of Applied Psychology,* **48,** 344–7.

David, G. C. (1985a). U.K. National statistics on handling accidents and lumbar injuries at work, *Ergonomics,* **28,** 9–16.

David, G. C. (1985b). Intra-abdominal pressure measurements and load capacities for females, *Ergonomics,* **28,** 345–58.

Davies, B. T. (1972). Moving loads manually, *Applied Ergonomics,* **3,** 190–4.

Davies, B. T., Abada, A., Benson, K., Courtney, A. and Minto, I. (1980). Female hand dimensions and guarding of machines, *Ergonomics,* **23,** 79–84.

Davis, P. R. (1983a). Slipping, tripping and falling accidents: an introduction, *Ergonomics,* **26,** 1–2.

Davis, P. R. (1983b). Human factors contributing to slips, trips and falls, *Ergonomics,* **26,** 51–60.

Davis, P. R. and Stubbs, D. A. (1977a). Safe levels of manual forces for young males (1), *Applied Ergonomics,* **8,** 141–50.

Davis, P. R. and Stubbs, D. A. (1977b). Safe levels of manual forces for young males (2), *Applied Ergonomics,* **8,** 219–28.

Davis, P. R. and Stubbs, D. A. (1978). Safe levels of manual forces for young males (3), *Applied Ergonomics,* **9,** 33–7.

Davis, P. R. and Troup, J. D. G. (1964). Pressures in the trunk cavities when pulling, pushing and lifting, *Ergonomics,* **7,** 465–74.

Davis, P. R., Ridd, J. E. and Stubbs, D. A. (1980). Acceptable Loading Levels for British Workers. Paper presented at the Annual Conference of the Ergonomics Society. Nottingham.

De Boer, J. B. (1977). Performance and comfort in the presence of veiling reflections, *Lighting Research and Technology*, **9**, 169.

Deatherage, B. H. and Evans, T. R. (1969). Binaural masking: backward, forward and simultaneous effects, *Journal of the Acoustical Society of America*, **46**, 362–71.

Deininger, R. L. (1960). Human factors engineering studies of the design and use of pushbutton telephone sets, *The Bell System Technical Journal*, **39**, 995–1012.

Dempsey, C. A. (1963). The design of body support and restraint systems. In E. Bennett, J. Degan and J. Spiegel (eds) *Human Factors in Technology*. New York: McGraw-Hill.

Dempster, W. T. (1955). *Space Requirements of the Seated Operator: Geometrical, Kinematic, and Mechanical Aspects of the Body with Special Reference to the Limbs.* WADC Technical Report 55–159. Ohio: WPAFB.

Dewar, M. E. (1977). Body movements in climbing a ladder, *Ergonomics*, **20**, 67–86.

Dickinson, J. (1974). *Proprioceptive Control of Human Movement*. London: Lepus Books.

Diebschlag, W. and Müller-Limroth, W. (1980). Physiological requirements on car seats: some results of experimental studies. In D. J. Oborne and J. A. Levis (eds) *Human Factors in Transport Research, Volume II*. London: Academic Press.

Dieckmann, D. (1958). A study of the influence of vibration on man, *Ergonomics*, **1**, 347–55.

Diffrient, N., Tilley, A. R. and Bargady, J. C. (1974). *Humanscale 1/2/3*. Mass: MIT Press.

Dixon-Ward, W. (1984). Noise-induced hearing loss. In D. Jones and A. Chapman (eds) *Noise in Society*. Chichester: John Wiley & Sons.

Dooling, D. J. and Lachman, R. (1971). Effects of comprehension on the retention of prose, *Journal of Experimental Psychology*, **88**, 216–22.

Drazin, D. H. (1962). Factors affecting vision during vibration, *Research*, **15**, 275–80.

Droege, R. C. and Hill, B. M. (1961). Comparison of performance on manual and electric typewriters, *Journal of Applied Psychology*, **45**, 268–70.

Drury, C. G. (1973). The effect of speed of working on industrial inspection accuracy, *Applied Ergonomics*, **4**, 2–7.

Drury, C. G. (1985). The role of the hand in manual materials handling. *Ergonomics*, **28**, 213–27.

Drury, C. G. and Addison, J. L. (1973). An industrial study of the effects of feedback and fault density on inspection performance, *Ergonomics*, **16**, 159–69.

Drury, C. G., Law, C. H. and Paivenshi, C. S. (1982). A survey of industrial box handling, *Human Factors*, **24**, 553–65.

Drury, C. G. and Pitzella, T. (1983). Hand placement in manual materials handling, *Human Factors*, **25**, 551–62.

Drury, C. G., Roberts, D. P., Hansgen, R. and Bayman, J. R. (1983). Evaluation of a palletising aid, *Applied Ergonomics*, **14**, 242–6.

Drury, C. G. and Sinclair, M. A. (1983). Human and machine performance in an inspection task, *Human Factors*, **25**, 391–9.

Drury, C. G., Begbie, K., Ulate, C. and Deeb, J. M. (1985). Experiments on wrist deviation in manual materials handling, *Ergonomics*, **28**, 577–89.

Dunn, A. G. (1971). Engineering the keyboard from the human factors viewpoint. *Computers and Automation*, **February**, 32–3.

Dwyer, F. M. (1967). Adapting visual illustrations for effective learning, *Harvard Educational Review*, **37**, 250–63.

Earl, W. K. and Goff, J. D. (1965). Comparison of two data entry methods, *Perceptual and Motor Skills*, **20**, 369–84.

Easterbrook, J. A. (1959). The effect of emotion on cue utilization and the organization of behaviour, *Psychological Review*, **66**, 183–201.

Easterby, R. S. (1970). The perception of symbols for machine displays, *Ergonomics*, **13**, 149–58.

Easterby, R. S. and Hakiel, S. R. (1981). Field testing of consumer safety signs: the

comprehension of pictorially presented messages, *Applied Ergonomics,* **12,** 143–52.
Easterby, R., Kroemer, K. H. E. and Chaffin, D. B. (1982). *Anthropometry and Biomechanics: Theory and Application.* New York: Plenum Press.
Eckstrand, G. A. and Morgan, R. L. (1956). *The Influence of Training on the Tactual Discriminability of Knob Shapes.* WADC Technical Report 56–8.
Eddy, J. K. and Glass, A. L. (1981). Reading and listening to high and low imagery sentences. *Journal of Verbal Learning and Verbal Behaviour,* **20,** 333–45.
Edholm, O. G. and Murrell, K. F. H. (1973). *The Ergonomics Society: A History 1949–1970.* London: Ergonomics Research Society.
Ekholm, J., Arborelius, U.P. and Németh, G. (1982). The load on the lumbo-sacral joint and trunk muscle activity during lifting, *Ergonomics,* **25,** 145–62.
Elias, M. F., Snadowski, A. M. and Rizy, E. F. (1965). Identification of televised symbols as a function of symbol resolution, *Perceptual and Motor Skills,* **21,** 91–99.
Ellis, N. C. and Hill, S. E. (1978). A comparative study of seven segment numerics, *Human Factors,* **20,** 655–660.
Ellis, M. I., Seedhom, B. B., Amis, A. A., Dowson, D. and Wright, V. (1979). Forces in the knee joint whilst rising from normal and motorized chairs, *Engineering in Medicine,* **8,** 33–40.
Ellis, J. G. and Dewar, R. E. (1979). Rapid comprehension of verbal and symbolic traffic sign messages, *Human Factors,* **21,** 161–8.
Engel, F. L. (1980). Information selection from visual display units. In E. Grandjean and E. Vigliani (eds) *Ergonomic Aspects of Visual Display Terminals.* London: Taylor & Francis.
Ernest, C. H. (1979). Visual imagery ability and the recognition of verbal and non verbal stimuli, *Acta Psychologica,* **43,** 253–69.
Eskew, R. T. and Riche, C. V. (1982). Pacing and locus of control in quality control inspection, *Human Factors,* **24,** 411–15.
Estes, W. K. and Wolford, G. L. (1971). Effects of spaces on report from tachistoscopically presented letter strings, *Psychonomic Science,* **75,** 77–80.
Evans, G. W. and Howard, R. B. (1973). Personal Space, *Psychological Bulletin,* **80,** 334–44.
Evans, L., Wasielewski, P. and Buseck, C. R. (1982). Compulsory seat belt usage and driver risk taking behaviour, *Human Factors,* **24,** 41–8.
Fanger, P. O. (1970). *Thermal Comfort.* New York: McGraw-Hill.
Fanger, P. O., Breum, N. O. and Jerking, E. (1977). Can colour and noise influence man's thermal comfort? *Ergonomics,* **20,** 11–18.
Farmer, E. and Chambers, E. G. (1939). *A Study of Accident Proneness Amongst Motor Drivers.* Industrial Health Research Board Report No 84. London: IHRB.
Fellmann, Th., Bräuninger, U., Giere, R. and Grandjean, E. (1982). An ergonomic evaluation of VDT's, *Behaviour and Information Technology,* **1,** 69–80.
Ferguson, D. and Duncan, J. (1974). Keyboard design and operating posture, *Ergonomics,* **17,** 731–44.
Fidell, S. (1978). Effectiveness of audible warning signals for emergency vehicles. *Human Factors,* **20,** 19–26.
Fine, B. J. (1963). Introversion, extraversion and motor driver behaviour, *Perceptual and Motor Skills,* **16,** 95.
Fisher, B. A. (1978). *Perspectives on Human Communication.* London: Collier Macmillan.
Fitch, J. M., Templer, J. and Corcoran, P. (1974). The dimensions of stairs, *Scientific American,* **231,** 82–90.
Fitts, P. M. (1954). The information capacity of the human motor system in controlling the amplitude of movement, *Journal of Experimental Psychology,* **47,** 381–91.
Fitts, P. M. (1962). Functions of man in complex systems, *Aerospace Engineering,* **21,** 34–9.
Fitts, P. M. and Jones, R. E. (1947a). Psychological aspects of instrument display. I

Analysis of 270 'pilot error' experiences in reading and interpreting aircraft instruments. Aeromedical Laboratory Report AMRL–TSEAA–694–12A, July. In W. Sinaiko (ed.) *Selected Papers in the Design and Use of Control Systems.* 1961. New York: Dover.

Fitts, P. M. and Jones, R. E. (1947b). Analysis of factors contributing to 460 'pilot error' experiences in operating aircraft controls. Aeromedical Laboratory Report AMRL–TSEAA–694–12, July. In W. Sinaiko (ed.) *Selected Papers in the Design and Use of Control Systems.* 1961. New York: Dover.

Fitts, P. M. and Seeger, C. M. (1953). S-R Compatibility: Spatial characteristics of stimulus and response codes, *Journal of Applied Psychology,* **46**, 199–200.

Fleishman, E. A. (1966). Human abilities and the acquisition of skill. In E. A. Bilodeau (ed.) *Acquisition of Skill.* New York: Academic Press.

Flesch, R. (1948). A new readability yardstick, *Journal of Applied Psychology,* **32**, 221–33.

Fletcher, H. (1940). Auditory patterns, *Review of Modern Physics,* **12**, 47–65.

Fletcher, H. and Munson, W. A. (1937). Relation between loudness and masking, *Journal of the Acoustical Society of America,* **9**, 1–10.

Floyd, W. F. and Ward, J. S. (1969). Anthropometric and physiological considerations in school, office and factory seating, *Ergonomics,* **12**, 132–9.

Folkard, S. and Monk, T. H. (1978). Time of day effects in immediate and delayed memory. In M. M. Gruneberg, P. E. Morris and R. N. Sykes (eds) *Practical Aspects of Memory.* London: Academic Press.

Folklard, S. and Monk, T. H. (1979). Shiftwork and performance, *Human Factors,* **21**, 483–92.

Folkard, S. and Monk, T. H. (1985). *Hours of Work: Temporal Factors in Work-scheduling.* Chichester: John Wiley & Sons.

Folkard, S., Monk, T. H. and Chobban, M. C. (1978). Short and long term adjustment of circadian rhythms in 'permanent' night nurses, *Ergonomics,* **21**, 785–99.

Fortuin, G. J. (1963). Age and lighting needs, *Ergonomics,* **6**, 239–45.

Foster, J. J. and Bruce, M. (1982). Reading upper and lower case on viewdata, *Applied Ergonomics,* **13**, 145–9.

Foster, J. and Coles, P. (1977). An experimental study of typographic cueing in printed text, *Ergonomics,* **20**, 57–66.

Fowler, R. L., Williams, W. E., Fowler, M. G. and Young, D. D. (1968). *An Investigation of the Relationship Between Operator Performance and Operator Panel Layout for Continuous Tasks.* USAF AMRL-TR-68-170.

Fowler, R. L. and Barker, A. S. (1974). Effectiveness of highlighting for retention of text material, *Journal of Applied Psychology,* **63**, 309–13.

Fox, J. G. (1963). A comparison of gothic elite and standard elite typefaces, *Ergonomics,* **6**, 193–8.

Fox, J. G. (1971). Background music and industrial productivity — a review, *Applied Ergonomics,* **2**, 70–3.

Fox, J. G. (1977). Quality control of coins. In J. S. Weiner and H. G Maule (eds) *Human Factors in Work, Design and Production.* London: Taylor & Francis.

Fox, J. G. (1983). Industrial music. In D. J. Oborne and M. M. Gruneberg (eds) *The Physical Environment at Work.* Chichester: John Wiley & Sons.

Fox, J. G. and Haslegrave, C. M. (1969). Industrial inspection efficiency and the probability of a defect occurring, *Ergonomics,* **12**, 713–21.

Fox, J. G. and Embrey, E. D. (1972). Music — an aid to productivity, *Applied Ergonomics,* **3**, 202–5.

Fox, W. F. (1967). Human performance in the cold, *Human Factors,* **9**, 203–20.

Fraser, T. M., Hoover, G. N. and Asche, W. F. (1961). Tracking performance during low frequency vibration, *Aerospace Medicine,* **31**, 829–35.

Fried, M. L. and DeFazio, V. J. (1974). Territoriality and boundary conflicts in the subway, *Psychiatry,* **37**, 47–59.

Furness, T. H. and Lewis, C. H. (1978). *Helmet Mounted Display Reading Performance under Whole-body Vibration.* Paper presented to Human Response to Vibration Meeting, Silsoe, Beds.

Gagge, A. P., Stolwijk, J. A. J. and Nishi, Y. (1971). An effective temperature scale based on a simple model of human physiological regulatory response *ASRAE Transactions,* **77,** 247–62

Galitz, W. O. (1965). CRT keyboard human factors evaluation. UNIVAC, Systems Application Engineering, Roseville DPD. **March.**

Gane, C. P., Horabin, I. S. and Lewis, B. N. (1966). The simplification and avoidance of instruction, *Industrial Training,* **1,** 160–6.

Garg, A., Sharma, D., Chaffin, D. B. and Schmidler, J. M. (1983). Biomechanical stresses as related to motion trajectory of lifting, *Human Factors,* **25,** 527–39.

Garrett, J. W. (1971). The adult human hand: some anthropometric and biomechanical considerations, *Human Factors,* **13,** 117–31.

Geldard, F. A. (1972). *The Human Senses.* New York: John Wiley & Sons.

Ghiringhelli, L. (1980). Collection of subjective opinons on use of VDUs. In E. Grandjean and E. Vigliani (eds) *Ergonomic Aspects of Visual Display Terminals.* London: Taylor & Francis.

Gibbs, C. B. (1970). Servo-control systems in organisms and the transfer of skill. In D. Legge (ed.) *skills.* Harmondsworth: Penguin.

Gibson, J. J. (1950). The perception of visual surfaces. *American Journal of Psychology,* **63,** 367–84.

Giddings, B. J. (1972). Alpha-numerics for raster displays, *Ergonomics,* **15,** 65–72.

Gilbert, M. and Hopkinson, R. G. (1949). The illumination of the Snellen chart, *British Journal of Ophthalmology,* **33,** 305–10.

Gilchrest, B. and Shenkin, A. (1979). The impact of scanners on employment in supermarkets, *Computers and Society,* **10,** 4–8.

Gilchrest, B. and Shenkin, A. (1981). The impact of scanners on employment in supermarkets — an update, *Computers and Society,* **11,** 31–3.

Gittelson, B. (1978). *Biorhythm: A Personal Science* (2nd Edition). New York: Arco Publishing Co.

Glass, D. C. and Singer, J. E. (1972). *Urban Stress.* London: Academic Press.

Goodwin, N. C. (1975). Cursor positioning on an electronic display using lightpen, lightgun, or keyboard for three basic tasks, *Human Factors,* **17,** 289–95.

Gough, P. B. (1965). Grammatical transformations and speed of understanding, *Journal of Verbal Learning and Verbal Behaviour,* **4,** 107–11.

Gould, J. G. (1968). Visual factors in the design of computer-controlled CRT displays, *Human Factors,* **10,** 359–76.

Gould, J. D. (1976). Looking at pictures. In R. A. Monty and J. W. Senders (eds) *Eye Movements and Psychological Processes.* Hillsdale, New Jersey: Lawrence Erlbaum Associates.

Graf, R. and Torrey, J. W. (1966). Perception of phrase structure in written language, *American Psychological Association Convention Proceedings,* 83–8.

Grandjean, E. (1973). *Ergonomics in the Home.* London: Taylor & Francis.

Grandjean, E. (1980a). Ergonomics of VDUs: review of present knowledge. In E. Grandjean and E. Vigliani (eds) *Ergonomic Aspects of Visual Display Terminals.* London: Taylor & Francis.

Grandjean, E. (1980b). *Fitting the Task to the Man: An Ergonomic Approach.* London: Taylor & Francis.

Grandjean, E., Nishiyama, K., Hünting, W. and Piedermann, M. (1982). A laboratory study on preferred and imposed settings of a VDT workstation, *Behaviour and Information Technology,* **1,** 289–304.

Grandjean, E., Hünting, W. and Piedermann, M. (1983). VDT workstations design: preferred settings and their effects, *Human Factors,* **25,** 161–75.

Gray, R., Wilkinson, R. T., Maslen, K. R. and Rowlands, G. F. (1976). *The Effects of 3hrs of Vertical Vibration at 5Hz on the Performance of some Tasks.* Royal Aircraft Establishment Technical Report 76011.

Green, H. F. and Anderson, L. K. (1956). Color coding in a visual search task, *Journal of Experimental Psychology,* **51,** 19–24.

Greene, J. M. (1970). The semantic function of negatives and passives, *British Journal of Psychology,* **61,** 17–22.

Greenwood, M., Woods, H. M. and Yule, G. U. (1919). A report on the incidence of industrial accidents upon individuals with special reference to multiple accidents. Report No 4. Industrial Health Research Board. In W. Haddon, E. A. Suchmann and D. Flein (eds) *Accident Research.* (1964). New York: Harper.

Gregory, M. and Poulton, E. C. (1970). Even versus uneven right-hand margins and the rate of comprehension in reading, *Ergonomics,* **13,** 427–34.

Grether, W. F. (1949). Instrument Reading I. The design of long-scale indicators for speed and accuracy of quantitative readings, *Journal of Applied Psychology,* **33,** 363–72.

Grether, W. F. (1973). Human performance at elevated environmental temperatures, *Aerospace Medicine,* **44,** 747–55.

Grieve, D. W. and Pheasant, S. T. (1981). Biomechanics. In *The Body at work – Biological Ergonomics* (ed. W. T. Singleton). London: Cambridge University Press.

Griffin, M. J. (1975). Levels of whole-body vibration affecting human vision, *Aviation, Space and Environmental Medicine,* **46,** 1033–40.

Griffin, M. J. (1976a). Vibration and visual acuity. In W. Tempest (ed.), *Infrasound and Low Frequency Vibration.* London: Academic Press.

Griffin, M. J. (1976b). Eye motion during whole-body vibration, *Human Factors,* **18,** 601–6.

Griffin, M. J. and Lewis, C. H. (1978). A review of the effects of vibration on visual acuity and continuous manual control: Part I Visual acuity, *Journal of Sound and Vibration,* **56,** 383–413.

Griffiths, I. D. and Langdon, F. J. (1968). Subjective response to road traffic noise, *Journal of Sound and Vibration,* **8,** 16–32.

Guignard, J. C. and Irving, A. (1960). Effects of low frequency vibration on man, *Engineering,* 9 September, 364–7.

Guignard, J. C., Landrum, C. J. and Reardon, R. E. (1976). *Experimental Evaluation of International Standard (ISO 2631) for Whole-body vibration exposures.* University of Dayton Research Institute. UDRI–TR–76–79.

Guillemin, V. and Wechsberg, P. (1953). Physiological effects of long term repetitive exposure to mechanical vibration, *Journal of Aviation Medicine,* **24,** 208–21.

Guillien, J. and Rebiffé, R. (1980). Anthropometric models of a population of bus drivers. In D. J. Oborne and J. A. Levis (eds). *Human Factors in Transport Research Volume I.* London: Academic Press.

Gunnarsson, E. and Österberg, O. (1977). *Physical and Mental Working Environment in a Terminal-based Data System.* Research Report No. 35. Stockholm: Industrial Welfare Council.

Gunnarsson, E. and Soderberg, I. (1979). *Work with Visual Display Terminals in Newspaper Offices.* Stockholm: National Board of Occupational Safety and Health.

Haaland, J., Wingert, J. and Olsen, B. A. (1963). Force required to actuate switches, maximum finger pushing force, and coefficient of friction of Mercury gloves, *Honeywell Memo.* **February 1963** (cited in Alden *et al.,* 1972).

Hackmeister, R. (1979). Focus on keyboards, *Electronic Design,* **11,** 169–75.

Hall, E. T. (1976). The anthropology of space: an organising model. In H. M. Proshansky, W. H. Ittleson and L. G. Rivlin (eds) *Environment Psychology* (2nd Edition). New York: Holt, Rinehart & Winston.

Haines, R. F. and Gilliland, K. (1973). Response time in the full visual field, *Journal of Applied Psychology,* **58,** 289–95.

Hale, A. R. and Hale, M. (1972). *A Review of the Industrial Accident Research Literature.* Committee on Safety and Health at Work Paper. London: HMSO.

Hall, E. T. (1959). *The Silent Language.* New York: Doubleday & Co.

Hall, E. T. (1976). The anthropology of space: An organising model. In H. M. Proshansky, W. H. Ittleson and L. G. Rivlin (eds) *Environmental Psychology* (2nd edn). New York: Holt, Rinehart and Winston.

Hammond, N. V., Long, J. B., Morton, J., Barnard, P. J. and Clark, A. (1981). Documenting human-computer mismatch at the individual and organizational levels, *IBM Research Report HF 040* Hampshire: IBM.

Harding, G. F. A. (1979). Photosensitive epilepsy. In D. J. Oborne, M. M. Gruneberg and J. R. Eiser (eds) *Research in Psychology and Medicine, Volume I.* London: Academic Press.

Hardyck, C. and Petrinovich, L. F. (1977). Left-handedness, *Psychological Bulletin,* **84,** 385–404.

Harnett, R. M., Pruitt, J. R. and Sias, F. R. (1983a). A review of the literature concerning resuscitation from hypothermia: Part I — The problem and general approaches, *Aviation, Space and Environmental Medicine,* **54,** 425–34.

Harnett, R. M., Pruitt, J. R. and Sias, F. R. (1983b). A review of the literature concerning resuscitation from hypothermia: Part II — selected rewarming protocols, *Aviation, Space and Environmental Medicine,* **54,** 487–95.

Harris, C. S., Sommer, H. C. and Johnson, D. L. (1976). Review of the effects of infrasound on man, *Aviation, Space and Environmental Medicine,* **47,** 430–4.

Harris, D. (1966). Effect of equipment complexity on inspection performance, *Journal of Applied Psychology,* **50,** 236–7.

Hartley, J. and Burnhill, P. (1976). *Textbook Design: A Practical Guide.* Paris: UNESCO.

Hartley, J., Young, M. and Burnhill, P. (1975). On the typing of tables, *Applied Ergonomics,* **6,** 39–42.

Haslegrave, C. M. (1979). An anthropometric survey of British drivers, *Ergonomics,* **22,** 145–53.

Hemingway, J. C. and Erickson, R. A. (1969). Relative effects of raster scan lines and image subtense on symbol legibility on television, *Human Factors,* **11,** 331–8.

Hepburn, H. A. (1958). Portable ladders. I: The quarter-length rule, *British Journal of Industrial Safety,* **4,** 155–8.

Hertzberg, H. T. E. (1958). Annotated Bibliography of Applied Physical Anthropometry in Human Engineering. Report No WADC–TR–56–30. Wright Patterson Airforce Base, Ohio.

Hertzberg, H. T. E. and Burke, F. E. (1971). Foot forces exerted at various aircraft brake-pedal angles, *Human Factors,* **13,** 445–56.

Hettinger, T. (1961). *Physiology of Strength.* Springfield, Ill: Charles C. Thomas.

van Heusden, E., Plomp, R. and Pols, L. C. W. (1979). Effect of ambient noise on the vocal output and the preferred listening level of conversational speech, *Applied Acoustics,* **12,** 31–43.

Hildebrandt, G., Rohmert, W. and Rutenfranz, J. (1974). Twelve and twenty four hour rhythms in error frequency of locomotive drivers and the influence of tiredness. *International Journal of Chronobiology,* **2,** 175–180.

Hill, J. M. M. and Trist, E. L. (1953). A consideration of industrial accidents as a means of withdrawal from work situation, *Human Relations,* **6,** 357–80.

Hirsch, R. S. (1970). Effects of standard versus alphabetical keyboard formats on typing performance, *Journal of Applied Psychology,* **54,** 484–90.

Hitt, W. D. (1961). An evaluation of five different abstract coding methods, *Human Factors,* **3,** 120–30.

Hochberg, J. (1957). Effects of the Gestalt revolution: the Cornell symposium on perception, *Psychological Review,* **64,** 78–84.

Hochberg, J. and McAlister, E. (1953). A quantitative approach to figural 'goodness',

Journal of Experimental Psychology, **46,** 361–4.

Hochberg, J. and Silverstein, A. (1956). A quantitative index of stimulus-similarity: proximity vs differences in brightness, *American Journal of Psychology,* **69,** 456–8.

Hockey, G. R. J. (1970). Signal probability and signal location as possible bases for increasd selectivity in noise, *Quarterly Journal of Experimental Psychology,* **22,** 37–42.

Hoffman, M. S. and Cramer, M. L. (1981). Workstation design optimization through a stimulation model, *Proceedings of 25th Annual Meeting of the Human Factors Society.* Baltimore: HFS.

Hoffman, M. A. and Heimstra, N. W. (1972). Tracking performance with visual, auditory or electrocutaneous displays, *Human Factors,* **14,** 131–8.

Holladay, L. L. (1926). The fundamentals of glare and visibility, *Journal of the Optical Society of America,* **12,** 271–319.

Holland, C. L. (1965). Performance effects of long term random vertical vibration, *Human Factors,* **9,** 93–104.

Holmes, V. M. and Langford, J. (1976). Comprehension and recall of abstract and concrete sentences, *Journal of Verbal Learning and Verbal Behaviour,* **15,** 559–66.

Hopkin, V. D. (1971). The evaluation of touch displays for air traffic control tasks, *IEE Conference on Displays: Publication No. 80.*

Hopkinson, R. G. (1940). Discomfort glare in lighted streets, *Transactions of the Illuminating Engineering Society,* **15,** 1–30.

Hopkinson, R. G. (1956). Glare discomfort and pupil diameter, *Journal of the Optical Society of America,* **46,** 594–656.

Hopkinson, R. G. (1957). Evaluation of glare, *Illumination Engineering (NY),* **15,** 305–16.

Hopkinson, R. G. (1972). Glare from daylight in buildings, *Applied Ergonomics,* **3,** 206–15.

Hopkinson, R. G. and Collins, J. B. (1970). *The Ergonomics of Lighting.* London: McDonald Technical and Scientific.

Hopkinson, R. G. and Longmore, J. (1959). Attention and distraction in the lighting of workplaces, *Ergonomics,* **2,** 321–33.

Hopkinson, R. G., Waldram, J. M. and Stevens, W. R. (1941). Brightness and contrast in illuminating engineering, *Transactions of the Illuminating Engineering Society,* **6,** 37–47.

Hornick, R. J. (1962). The effects of whole body vibration in three directions upon human performance, *Journal of Engineering Psychology,* **1,** 93–101.

Hornick, R. J. and Lefritz, N. M. (1966). A study and review of human reaction to prolonged random vibration, *Human Factors,* **8,** 481–91.

Houghton, F. C. and Yaglou, C. P. (1923). Determining lines of equal comfort. *ASHRAE Transactions,* **29,** 163–76.

Huddleston, J. H. F. (1964). *Human Performance and Behaviour in Vertical Sinusoidal Vibration.* Institute of Aviation Medicine Report 303.

Huddleston, J. H. F. (1965). *Effects of 4.8 and 6.7 c.p.s. Vertical Vibration on Handwriting and a Complex Mental Task, With and Without Abdominal Restraint.* Institute of Aviation Medicine Memo 60.

Huddleston, J. H. F. (1970). Tracking performance on a visual display apparently vibrating at 1–10Hz, *Journal of Applied Psychology,* **54,** 401–8.

Huddleston, J. H. F.. (1974). A comparison of two 7×9 matrix alphanumeric designs for TV displays, *Applied Ergonomics,* **5,** 81–3.

Hultgren, G. V. and Knave, B. (1974). Discomfort glare and disurbances from light reflections in an office landscape with CRT display terminals, *Applied Ergonomics,* **5,** 2–8.

Hunt, D. P. (1953). *The Coding of Aircraft Controls.* USAF, WADC Technical Report 53–331.

Illuminating Engineering Society (1977). *IES Code for Interior Lighting.* (London: IES).

International Organization for Standardization (1974). *Guide for the Evaluation of Human Exposure to Whole-body Vibration.* ISO 2631 — 1974.

Jackson, A. (1982). Some Problems in the Specification of Rolling Ball Operating

Characteristics. Paper presented to IEE 'Man–Machine systems' conference. London: IEE.

James, D. I. (1983). Rubbers and plastics in shoes and flooring: the importance of kinetic friction, *Ergonomics*, **26**, 83–100.

Jamieson, G. H. (1966). Inspection in the telecommunications industry: a field study of age and other performance variables, *Ergonomics*, **9**, 297–303.

Jansen, G. (1961). Adversive effects of noise in iron and steel workers, *Stahl und Eisen*, **81**, 217–20.

Jeavons, P. M. and Harding, G. F. A. (1975). *Photosensitive Epilepsy*. London: Heinemann.

Jellinek, E. M. and McFarland, R. A. (1940). Analysis of psychological experiments on the effects of alcohol, *Quarterly Journal on the Study of Alcohol*, **1**, 272–371.

Jenkins, H. M. (1958). The effect of signal rate on performance in visual monitoring, *American Journal of Psychology*, **71**, 647–61.

Jenkins, W. L. and Connor, M. B. (1949). Some design factors in making settings on a linear scale, *Journal of Applied Psychology*, **33**, 395–409.

Jenkins, W. O. (1947). The tactual discrimination of shapes for coding aircraft-type controls. In P. M. Fitts (ed.) *Psychological Research on Equipment Design*. USAF Research Report No. 19.

Jerison, H. J. (1959). Effects of noise on human performance. *Journal of Applied Psychology*, **43**, 96–101.

Jerison, H. J. (1966). Remarks on Colquhoun's 'effect of unwanted signals on performance in a vigilance task', *Ergonomics*, **9**, 413–16.

Johnsgard, K. W. (1953). Check reading as a function of pointer symmetry and uniform alignment, *Journal of Applied Psychology*, **37**, 407–11.

Johnson, E. A. (1967). Touch displays: a programmed man-machine interface, *Ergonomics*, **10**, 271–7.

Johnson, D. L., Nixon, C. W. Stephenson, M. R. R. (1976). Long-duration exposure to intermittent noises, *Aviation, Space and Environmental Medicine*, **47**, 987–90.

Johnson, S. L. and Roscoe, S. N. (1972). What moves, the airplane or the world? *Human Factors*, **14**, 107–29.

Johnston, D. M. (1965). Search performance as a function of peripheral activity, *Human Factors*, **7**, 527–35.

Jones, A. J. and Saunders, D. J. (1972). Equal comfort contours for whole-body, vertical, pulsed sinusoidal vibration, *Journal of Sound and Vibration*, **23**, 1–4.

Jones, D. M. (1979). Stress and memory. In M. M. Gruneberg and P. E. Morris (eds) *Applied Problems in Memory*. London: Academic Press.

Jones, D. M., Chapman, A. J. and Auburn, T. I. (1981). Noise in the environment: a social perspective, *Journal of Environmental Psychology*, **1**, 43–59.

Jones, I. (1976). The technology of visual display units. In D. Grover (ed.) *Visual Display Units*. Guildford: IPC Science and Technology Press Ltd.

Jones, J. C. (1969). Methods and results of seating research, *Ergonomics*, **12**, 171–81.

Jones, M. R. (1962). Colour coding, *Human Factor*, **4**, 355–65.

Jones, S. (1968). *Design of Instruction*. Training Information Paper Paper 1. London: HMSO.

Jorgensen, K. and Poulsen, E. (1974). Physiological problems in repetitive lifting with special reference to tolerance limits to the maximum lifting frequency. *Ergonomics*, **17**, 31–39.

Kahneman, D. (1973). *Attention and Effort*. London: Prentice-Hall.

Kak, A. V. and Knight, J. L. (1980). Text formatting effects in speed reading, *Proceedings of the 24th Human Factors Society Meeting, Baltimore*, Baltimore: HFS.

Kamman, R. (1975). The comprehensibility of printed instructions and the flowchart alternative, *Human Factors*, **17**, 183–91.

Keegan, J. J. and Radke, A. O. (1964). Designing vehicle seats for greater comfort. *SAE Journal*, September, **72**, 50–55,

Kelly, D. H. (1961). Visual responses to time-dependent stimuli. I Amplitude sensitivity measurements, *Journal of the Optical Society of America*, **51**, 422–9.

Kemsley, W. F. F. (1960). Weight and height of a population in 1943, *Annals of Eugenics*, **15**, 161–83.

Kennedy, K. W. (1975). International anthropometric variability and its effects on aircraft cockpit design. In A. Chapanis (ed.) *Ethnic Variables in Human Factors Engineering*. Baltimore: Johns Hopkins University Press.

Khalil, T. M. and Kurucz, C. N. (1977). The influence of 'biorhythm' on accident occurrence and performance, *Ergonomics*, **20**, 389–98.

Kimura, D. and Durnford, M. (1974). Normal studies of the function of the right hemisphere in vision. In S. J. Dimond and J. G. Beaumont (eds) *Hemisphere Function in the Human Brain*. London: Elek Science.

Kimura, D. and Vanderwolf, C. H. (1970). The relation between hand preference and the performance of individual finger movements by left and right hands, *Brain*, **93**, 767–74.

King, L. E. (1971). A laboratory comparison of symbol and ward roadway signs, *Traffic Engineering and Control*, **12**, 518–20.

Kinkead, R. (1975). Typing speed, keying rates and optimal keyboard layouts. In *Proceedings of 1975 Human Factors Society Annual Meeting*. Baltimore: HFS.

Klare, G. R. (1963). *The Measurement of Readability*. Des Moines, Iowa: Iowa State University Press.

Klemmer, E. T. (1971). Keyboard entry, *Applied Ergonomics*, **2**, 2–6.

Kobrick, J. L. and Fine, B. J. (1983). Climate and human performance. In D. J. Oborne and M. M. Gruneberg (eds) *The Physical Environment at Work*. Chichester: John Wiley.

Kolers, P. A. (1976). Buswell's discoveries. In R. A. Monty and J. W. Senders (eds) *Eye Movements and Psychological Processes*. Hillsdale, New Jersey: Lawrence Erlbaum Assoicates.

Kroemer, K. H. E. (1965). Comparison of a keyboard of a normal typewriter with a "K"-keyboard, *Internat. Zeitschchrift angewandt Physiologie*, **20**, 453–64.

Kroemer, K. H. E. (1970). Human strength: terminology, measurement, and interpretation of data, *Human Factors*, **12**, 297–313.

Kroemer, K. H. E. (1972). Human engineering the keyboard, *Human Factors*, **14**, 51–63.

Kroemer, K. H. E. (1974). Horizontal push and pull forces, *Applied Ergonomics*, **5**, 94–102.

Kroemer, K. H. E. (1983). Work space and equipment to fit the user. In D. J. Oborne and M. M. Gruneberg (eds) *The Physical Environment at Work*. Chichester: John Wiley.

Kroemer, K. H. E. and Robinette, J. C. (1968). *Ergonomics in the Design of Office Furniture: A Review of European Literature*. AMRL–TR–68–80.

Krohn, G. S. (1983). Flowcharts used for procedural instructions, *Human Factors*, **25**, 573–81.

Kryter, K. D. (1970). *The Effects of Noise on Man*. New York: Academic Press.

Kryter, K. D. and Pearsons, K. S. (1966). Some effects of spectrum content and duration on perceived noise level, *Journal of the Acoustical Society of America*, **39**, 451–64.

Kryter, K. D., Ward, W. D., Miller, J. D. and Eldredge, D. H. E. (1966). Hazardous exposure to intermittent and steady-state noise, *Journal of the Acoustical Society of America*, **39**, 451–64.

Kurke, M. I. (1956). Evaluation of a display incorporating quantitative and check-reading characteristics, *Journal of Applied Psychology*, **40**, 233–6.

Lauback, L. L. (1976). Comparative muscular strength of men and women: a review of the literature, *Aviation, Space and Environmental Medicine*, **47**, 534–42.

Läubli, Th., Hünting, W. and Grandjean, E. (1981). Postural and visual loads of VDT workplaces. II Lighting conditions and visual impairment, *Ergonomics*, **24**, 933–44.

Lee, R. A. and King, A. I. (1971). Visual vibration response, *Journal of Applied Physiology*, **30**, 281–6.

Leskinen, T. P. J., Stalhammar, H. R., Kuorinka, I. A. A. and Troup, J. D. G. (1983). A dynamic analysis of spinal compression with different lifting techniques, *Ergonomics*, **26**, 595–604.

Leventhall, H. G. and Kyriakides, K. (1976). Environmental infrasound: its occurrence and measurement. In W. Tempest (ed.) *Infrasound and Low Frequency Vibration*. London: Academic Press.

Levison, W. H. (1976). *Biomechanical Response and Manual Tracking Performance in Sinusoidal, Sum of Sines and Random Vibration Environments*. Army Medical Research Laboratories Report: AMRL–TR–75–94.

Lewin, T. (1969). Anthropometric studies on Swedish industrial workers when standing and sitting, *Ergonomics*, **12**, 883–902.

Lewis, C. H. (1980). *The Interaction of Control Dynamics and Display Type with the Effect of Vibration Frequency on Manual Tracking Performance*. Paper presented to Human Response to Vibration Meeting, Swansea.

Lewis, C. H. and Griffin, M. J. (1978). A review of the effects of vibration on visual acuity and manual control. Part II. Continuous manual control, *Journal of Sound and Vibration*, **56**, 415–57.

Lewis, C. H. and Griffin, M. J. (1979a). The effect of character size on the legibility of numeric displays during vertical whole-body vibration, *Journal of Sound and Vibration*, **67**, 562–5.

Lewis, C. H. and Griffin, M. J. (1979b). Mechanisms of the effects of vibration frequency, level and duration on continuous manual control performance, *Ergonomics*, **22**, 855–89.

Lewis, C. H. and Griffin, M. J. (1980a). Predicting the effects of vertical vibration frequency, combinations of frequencies and visual distance on the reading of numeric displays, *Journal of Sound and Vibration*, **70**, 355–77.

Lewis, C. H. and Griffin, M. J. (1980b). Predicting the effects of vibration frequency and axis, and seating conditions on the reading of numeric displays, *Ergonomics*, **23**, 485–501.

Licklider, J. C. (1948). The influence of interaural phase relations upon the masking of speech by white noise, *Journal of the Acoustical Society of America*, **20**, 150–9.

Liebman, M. (1970). The effects of sex and race norms on personal space, *Environmental Behaviour*, **2**, 208–46.

Lim, D. J. and Dunn, D. E. (1979). Anatomic correlates of noise-induced hearing loss. In *Symposium on Noise — Its Effects and Control*. Otolaryngologic Clinics of North America, **12**, No. 3. Philadelphia.

Lion, J. S. (1964). The performance of manipulative and inspection tasks under tungsten and flurorescent lighting, *Ergonomics*, **7**, 51–61.

Lion, J. S., Richardson, E. and Browne, R. C. (1968). A study of the performance of industrial inspectors under two kinds of lighting, *Ergonomics*, **11**, 23–34.

Litterick, I. (1981). QWERTYUIOP — dinosaur in a computer age. *New Scientist*, **89**, 66–8.

Little, K. B. (1965). Personal space, *Journal of Experimental Social Psychology*, **1**, 237–47.

Lockhart, J. M. (1968). Extreme body cooling and psychomotor performance, *Ergonomics*, **11**, 249–60.

Lockhart, J. M. and Keiss, H. O. (1971). Auxiliary heating of the hands during cold exposure and manual performance, *Human Factors*, **13**, 457–65.

Loftus, G. R. (1972). Eye fixations and recognition memory for pictures, *Cognitive Psychology*, **3**, 325–51.

Loveless, N. E. (1962). Direction-of-motion stereotypes: a review, *Ergonomics*, **5**, 357–83.

Lovesey, E. J. (1971). *An Investigation into the Effects of Dual Axis Vibration, Restraining Harness, Visual Feedback and Control Force on a Manual Positioning Task*. Royal

360

Aircraft Establishment Technical Report 71213.

Lovesey, E. J. (1974). The occurrence and effects upon performance of low frequency vibration. In Tempest, W. (ed.) *Infrasound and Low Frequency Vibration*. London: Academic Press.

Lovesey, E. J. (1975). The helicopter — some ergonomic factors, *Applied Ergonomics*, **6**, 139–46.

Lukiesh, M. and Holladay, L. L. (1925). Glare and visibility, *Transactions of the Illuminating Engineering Society*, **20**, 221–52.

Lundberg, U. (1976). Urban commuting: crowdedness and catecholamine excretion, *Journal of Human Stress*, **2**, 36–32.

Mackay, G. M., DeFoneka, C. P., Blair, I. and Clayton, A. B. (1969). *Causes and Effects of Road Accidents*. Department of Transportation, University of Birmingham.

Mackworth, N. H. and Morandi, A. J. (1967). The gaze selects informative details within pictures, *Perception and Psychophysics*, **2**, 547–52.

Macki, B. E., Bartlett, S. A. and Fernie, G. R. (1984). Influence of stairway handrail height on the ability to generate stabilizing forces and moments, *Human Factors*, **26**, 705–14.

Maddox, M. E., Burnette, J. T. and Gutman, J. C. (1977). Font comparisons for 5×7 dot matrix characters, *Human Factors*, **19**, 89–93.

Magid, E. B., Coermann, R. R., Lowry, R. D. and Bosley, W. J. (1962). *Physiological and Mechanical Response of the Human to Longitudinal Whole-body Vibration as Determined by Subjective Response*. Biomedical Research Laboratory's Technical Document. MRL–TDR–62–66.

Magora, A. (1972). Investigation of the relation between low back pain and occupation. Three physical requirements: sitting, standing and weight lifting, *Industrial Medicine*, **41**, 5–9.

Mahoney, E. R. (1974). Compensatory reactions to spatial immediacy, *Sociometry*, **37**, 423–31.

Maki, B. E. E., Bartlett, S. A. and Fernie, G. R. (1985). Effect of stairway pitch on optimal handrail height, *Human Factors*, **27**, 355–9.

Mandal, A. C. (1976). Work chair with tilting seat, *Ergonomics*, **19**, 157–64.

Mandal, A. C. (1981). The seated man. (Homo Sedens), *Applied Ergonomics*, **12**, 19–26.

Manning, D. P. (1983). Deaths and injuries caused by slipping, tripping and falling, *Ergonomics*, **26**, 3–10.

Marschark, M. and Paivio, A. (1977). Integrative processing of concrete and abstract sentences, *Journal of Verbal Learning and Verbal Behaviour*, **16**, 217–31.

Martin, A. (1972). A new keyboard layout, *Applied Ergonomics*, **3**, 48–51.

Maslen, K. R. (1972). *Efficiency Under Prolonged Vibration and the ISO 'Guide'*. Royal Aircraft Establishment Technical Memo EP 512.

Mathews, K. and Cannon, L. (1975). Environmental noise level as a determinant of helping behaviour, *Journal of Personality and Social Psychology*, **32**, 571–7.

Matin, E. (1974). Saccadic suppression: a review and analysis, *Psychological Bulletin*, **81**, 899–917.

McBride, G., King, M. G. and James, J. W. (1965). Social proximity effects on GSR in adult humans, *Journal of Psychology*, **61**, 153–7.

McClelland, I. and Ward, J. S. (1976). Ergonomics in relation to sanitary ware design, *Ergonomics*, **4**, 465–78.

McCormick, E. J. (1950). An analysis of visual requirements in industry, *Journal of Applied Psychology*, **34**, 54–61.

McCormick, E. J. (1976). *Human Factors in Engineering and Design*. New Jersey: McGraw-Hill.

McEwing, R. W. (1977). Touch displays in industrial computer systems. In *Displays for Man-machine Systems*. London: IEEE.

McIntyre, D. R. and Bates, B. T. (1982). Effects of rung spacing on the mechanics of ladder ascent, *Journal of Human Movement Studies*, **8**, 55–72.

McKendry, J. M., Corso, J. F. and Grant, G. (1960). The design and evolution of maintainable packaging methods for electronic equipment, *Ergonomics*, **3**, 255–72.

McKenzie, R. M. (1957). On the accuracy of inspectors, *Erognomics*, **1**, 258–72.

McLaughlin, G. H. (1966). Comparing styles of presenting technical information, *Ergonomics*, **9**, 257–9.

McLean, P. D. (1969). Induced arousal and time of recall as determinants of paired-associate recall, *British Journal of Psychology*, **60**, 57–62.

McLean, N. V. (1965). Brightness contrast, colour contrast and legibility, *Human Factors*, **7**, 521–6.

McNall, P. E., Ryan, P. W., Rholes, F. H., Nevins, R. G. and Springer, W. E. (1968). Metabolic rates at four activity levels and their relationship to thermal comfort, *ASHRAE Transactions*, **74**, Part I, VI.3.1. to IV.3.20.

Mead, P. G. and Sampson, P. B. (1972). Hand steadiness during unrestricted linear arm movements, *Human Factors*, **14**, 45–50.

Meddick, R. D. L. and Griffin, M. J. (1976). The effect of two-axis vibration on the legibility of reading material, *Ergonomics*, **19**, 21–33.

Megaw, E. D. (1978). Some Factors Affecting Inspection Accuracy. Paper presented to Symposium on Ergonomics and Visual Inspection, Birmingham.

Megaw, E. D. and Bellamy, L. J. (1983). Illumination at work. In D. J. Oborne and M. M. Gruneberg (eds) *The Physical Environment at Work*. Chichester: John Wiley & Sons.

Mehrabian, A. and Diamond, S. G. (1971). Effects of furniture arrangements, props, and personality on social interaction, *Journal of Personality and Social Psychology*, **20**, 18–30.

Meisels, M. and Canter, F. M. (1970). Personal space and personality characteristics: a non-confirmation, *Psychological Reports*, **27**, 287–90.

Michael, P. R. and Bienvenue, G. R. (1983). Industrial noise and man. In D. J. Oborne and M. M. Gruneberg (eds) *The Physical Environment at Work*. Chichester: John Wiley & Sons.

Michaels, S. E. (1971). QWERTY versus alphabetic keyboards as a function of typing skill, *Human Factors*, **13**, 419–26.

Middlemist, R. D., Knowles, E. S. and Matter, C. F. (1976). Personal space invasions in the lavatory: Suggestive evidence for arousal. *Journal of Personality and Social Psychology*, **33**, 541–6.

Miller, G. A. (1956). The magical number seven plus or minus two: some limits on our capacity to process information, *Psychological Review*, **63**, 81–97.

Miller, G. A. and Licklider, J. C. R. (1950). The intelligibility of interrupted speech. *Journal of the Acoustical Society of America*, **22**, 167–73.

Miller, G. R. (1972). *An Introduction to Speech Communication* (2nd Ed.). Indianapolis: The Bobbs-Merrill Co. Inc.

Miller, R. B. (1983). Transaction structures and format in form design. In R. Easterby and H. Zwaga (eds) *Information Design*. Chichester: John Wiley & Sons.

Milroy, R. and Poulton, E. C. (1978). Labelling graphs for improved reading speed, *Ergonomics*, **25**, 55–61.

Minor, F. J. and Revesman, S. L. (19627. Evaluation of input devices for a data setting task, *Journal of Applied Psychology*, **46**, 332–6.

Mital, A. and Manivasagan, I. (1983). Maximum acceptable weight of lift as a function of material density, center of gravity location, hand preference, and frequency. *Human Factors*, **25**, 33–42.

Money, K. E. and Cheung, B. S. (1983). Another function of the inner ear: facilitation of the emetic response to poisons, *Aviation, Space and Environmental Medicine*, **54**, 208–11.

Monod, H. (1985). Contractility of muscle during prolonged static and repetitive dynamic activity, *Ergonomics*, **28**, 81–9.

Moore, T. G. (1974). Tactile and kinaesthetic aspects of push-buttons, *Applied Ergonomics*, **5**, 66–71.

Moore, T. G. (1975). Industrial push-buttons, *Applied Ergonomics*, **6**, 33–8.

Moore, T. G. (1976). Controls and tactile displays. In K. F. Kraiss and J. Moral (eds.) *Introduction to Human Engineering*. Koln: TUV Rhineland.

Morgan, C. T. (1965). *Physiological Psychology*, 3rd Edition. New York: McGraw-Hill.

Morgan, C. T., Cook, J. S., Chapanis, A. and Lund, M. (1963). *Human Engineering Guide to Equipment Design*. New York: McGraw-Hill.

Morgensen, M. F. and English, H. B. (1926). The apparent warmth of colours, *American Journal of Psychology*, **37**, 427–8.

Morril, C. S., Goodwin, N. C. and Smith, S. L. (1968). User input mode and computer aided instruction, *Human Factors*, **10**, 225–32.

Morris, D. (1977). *Manwatching: A Field Guide to Human Behaivour*. London: Jonathan Cape.

Morton, J., Barnard, P., Hammond, N. and Long, J. B. (1979). Interacting with the computer: a framework. In E. Boutmy and A. Danthine (eds) *Teleinformatics '79*. Amsterdam: North-Holland.

Morton, R. and Provins, K. A. (1960). Finger numbness after acute local exposure to cold, *Journal of Applied Psychology*, **15**, 149–54.

Mortimer, R. G. (1974). Foot brake pedal force capability of drivers, *Ergonomics*, **17**, 509–13.

Mourant, R., Lakshmanan, R. and Chantadisai, R. (1981). Visual fatigue and cathode ray tube terminals, *Human Factors*, **23**, 529–40.

Müller, E. A. (1965). Physiological methods of increasing human physical work capacity, *Ergonomics*, **8**, 409–24.

Munsell Colour Co. (1929). *The Munsell Book of Colour*.

Murrell, K. F. H. (1958). The relationship between dial size, reading distance and reading accuracy, *Ergonomics*, **1**, 182–90.

Murrell, K. F. H. (1962a). Industrial aspects of ageing, *Ergonomics*, **5**, 147–53.

Murrell, K. F. H. (1962b). Operator variability and its industrial consequence, *International Journal of Production Research*, **1**, 39.

Murrell, K. F. H. (1969). Beyond the panel, *Ergonomics*, **12**, 691–700.

Murrell, K. F. H. (1971). *Ergonomics: Man in His Working Environment*. London: Chapman & Hall.

Murrell, K. F. H. (1980). Occupational psychology through autobiography: Hywel Murrell, *Journal of Occupational Psychology*, **53**, 281–90.

Murrell, K. F. H. and Kingston, P. M. (1966). Experimental comparison of scalar and digital micrometers, *Ergonomics*, **9**, 39–47.

Musatti, C. L. (1931). Forme e assimilazione, *Archivo Italiano di Psichologia*, **9**, 61–156.

Nakaseko, M., Grandjean, E., Hünting, W. and Grierer, R. (1985). Studies on ergonomically designed alphanumeric keyboards, *Human Factors*, **27**, 175–88.

Nayyar, R. M. and Simon, J. R. (1963). Effects of magnification on a subminiature assembly operation, *Journal of Applied Psychology*, **47**, 190–5.

Nelson, J. D. and Barany, J. W. (1969). A dynamic visual recognition test for paced industrial inspection, *AIIE Transactions*, **1**, 327–32.

Nemecek, J. and Grandjean, E. (1973). Noise in landscaped offices, *Applied Ergonomics*, **4**, 19–22.

Nevins, R. G. and Gagge, A. P. (1972). The new ASHRAE comfort chart, *ASHRAE Journal*, **14**, 19–22.

Nevins, R. G., Rholes, F. H., Springer, W. and Feyerherm, A. M. (1966). A temperature-humidity chart for thermal comfort of seated persons, *ASHRAE Transactions*, **72**, 283–91.

Newbold, E. M. (1926). *A Contribution to the Study of the Human Factor in the Causation of Accidents*. Report 34 Industrial Health Research Board. London: IHRB.

Nicholson, A. S. (1983). *CEC Workshop: Prevention of Low Back Pain*. Luxembourg: CEC.

Nixon, J. C. and Glorig, A. (1961). Noise-induced permanent threshold shift at 2000 cps and 4000 cps, *Journal of the Acoustical Society of America,* **33,** 904–8.

Norman, D. A. and Fisher, D. (1982). Why alphabetic keyboards are not easy to use: keyboard layout doesn't much matter, *Human Factors,* **24,** 509–19.

Noyes, J. (1983a). The QWERTY keyboard: a review, *International Journal of Man-machine Studies,* **18,** 265–81.

Noyes, J. (1983b). Chord keyboards, *Applied Ergonomics,* **14,** 55–9.

Oborne, D. J. (1975). *An Investigation of Passenger Comfort with Particular Reference to the Effects of Vibration.* PhD Thesis. University of Wales.

Oborne, D. J. (1976). A critical assessment of studies relating whole-body vibration to passenger comfort, *Ergonomics,* **19,** 751–74.

Oborne, D. J. (1977). Vibration and passenger comfort, *Applied Ergonomics,* **8,** 97–101.

Oborne, D. J. (1978). Techniques for the assessment of passenger comfort, *Applied Ergonomics,* **9,** 45–9.

Oborne, D. J. (1983). Whole-body vibration and ISO 2631: A critique. *Human Factors,* **25,** 55–70.

Oborne, D. J. (1985). *Computers at Work: A Behavioural Approach,* Chichester: John Wiley & Sons.

Oborne, D. J. and Humphreys, D. A. (1976). Individual variability in human response to whole-body vibration, *Ergonomics,* **19,** 719–26.

O'Briant, C. R. and Ohlbaum, M. K. (1970). Visual acuity decrements associated with whole-body Gz vibration stress, *Aerospace Medicine,* **41,** 79–82.

O'Brien, M. (1985). Women in sport, *Applied Ergonomics,* **16,** 25–39.

'Observer' and Maxwell, M. A. (1959). A study of absenteeism, accidents and sickness payments in problem drinkers in one industry, *Quarterly Journal of Studies on Alcohol,* **20,** 302–12.

Office of Population Censuses and Surveys (1981). *Adult Heights and Weights Survey.* OPCS Monitor Ref SS81/1. London: OPCS.

O'Hanlon, J. G. and Griffin, M. J. (1971). *Some Effects of the Vibration of Reading Material Upon Visual Performance.* ISVR Technical Report 49; University of Southampton.

Ogden, G. D., Levine, J. M. and Eisner, E. J. (1979). Measurement of workload by secondary tasks, *Human Factors,* **21,** 529–48.

Ohlsson, K., Nilsson, L-G. and Rönnberg, J. (1981). Speed and accuracy in scanning as a function of combinations of text and background colours, *International Journal of Man-Machine Studies,* **14,** 215–22.

Olsen, D. R. and Filby, N. (1972). On the comprehension of active and passive sentences, *Cognitive Psychology,* **3,** 361–81.

O'Neill, B. (1977). A decision-theory model of danger compensation, *Accident Analysis and Prevention,* **9,** 157–65.

Oppenheim, A. N. (1966). *Questionnaire Design and Attitude Measurement.* London: Heinemann.

Orth, B., Weckerle, H. and Wendt, D. (1976). Legibility of numerals displayed in a 4×7 dot matrix and seven-segment digits, *Visible Language,* **10,** 145–55.

Paivio, A. (1971). *Imagery and Verbal Processes.* New York: Holt, Rinehart & Winston.

Paivio, A., Yuille, J. C. and Madigan, S. A. (1968). Concreteness, imagery and meaningfulness values for 925 nouns, *Journal of Experimental Psychology Monograph Supplement,* **76,** No. 1, Part 2.

Paivio, A. and Begg, I. (1981). *Psychology of Language.* New Jersey: Prentice-Hall.

Parsons, H. M. (1976). Work environments. In I. Altman and J. F. Wohlwill (eds) *Human Behavior and Environment* Volume I. New York: Plenum Publishing.

Pastoor, S, Schwarz, E. and Beldie, I. P. (1983). The relative suitability of four dot-matrix sizes for text presentation on colour television screens, *Human Factors,* **25,** 265–72.

Paterson, D. G. and Tinker, M. A. (1946). Readability of newspaper headlines printed in capitals and lower case, *Journal of Applied Psychology*, **30**, 161–8.

Patterson, M. L. and Sechrest, L. B. (1970). Interpersonal distance and impression formation. *Journal of Personality*, **38**, 161–6.

Patterson, M. L., Mullens, S. and Romano, J. (1971). Compensatory reactions to spatial intrusion, *Sociometry*, **34**, 121–44.

Peacock, L. J. (1956). *A Field Study of Rifle Aiming Steadiness and Serial Reaction Performance as Affected by Thermal Stress and Activity*, US AMRL Report 231.

Pearsons, K. S., Bennett, R. L. and Fidell, S. (1977). *Speech Levels in Various Noise Environments*. US Environmental Protection Agency Report EPA-600/1-77-025. Washington, DC.

Pëizer, E. and Wright, D. W. (1974). Human locomotion. In Institute of Mechanical Engineers (ed.) *Human Locomotion Engineering*. London: I. Mech. E.

Peltzman, S. (1975). The effects of automobile safety regulation, *Journal of Political Economy*, **83**, 677–725.

Perry, D. K. (1952). Speed and accuracy of reading Arabic and Roman numerals, *Journal of Applied Psychology*, **36**, 346–7.

Petherbridge, P. and Hopkinson, R. G. (1950). Discomfort glare and the lighting of buildings, *Transactions of the Illuminating Engineering Society*, **15**, 39–79.

Petropoulos, H. and Brebner, J. (1981). Stereotypes for direction-of-movement of rotary controls associated with linear displays: the effects of scale presence and position, of pointer direction, and distances between the control and the display, *Ergonomics*, **24**, 143–51.

Pfauth, M. and Priest, J. (1981). Person-computer interface using touch screen devices, *Proceedings of the 25th Annual Meeting of the Human Factors Society*. Baltimore: HFS.

Pheasant, S. T. (1982a). A technique for estimating anthropometric data from the parameters of the distributions of stature, *Ergonomics*, **25**, 981–92.

Pheasant, S. T. (1982b). Anthropometric estimates for British civilian adults, *Ergonomics*, **25**, 993–1001.

Pheasant, S. T. (1983). Sex differences in strength — some observations on their variability. *Applied Ergonomics*, **14**, 205–11.

Pheasant, S. T. (1984). *Anthropometrics – An Introduction for Schools and Colleges*. London: British Standards Institute.

Pheasant, S. T. and O'Neill, D. (1975). Performance in gripping and turning — a study in hand/handle effectiveness, *Applied Ergonomics*, **6**, 205–8.

Phillips, R. J. (1979). Why is lower case better? *Applied Ergonomics*, **10**, 211–14.

Plath, D. W. (1970). The readability of segmented and conventional numerals, *Human Factors*, **12**, 493–7.

Pollack, I. and Ficks, L. (1954). Information of elementary multi-dimensional auditory displays, *Journal of the Acoustical Society of America*, **26**, 155–8.

Pook, G. K. (1969). Colour coding effects in compatible and noncompatible display control arrangements, *Journal of Applied Psychology*, **53**, 301–3.

Postman, L. (1975). Verbal learning and memory. *Annual Review of Psychology*, **26**, 291–350.

Pottier, M., Dubreuil, A. and Mond, H. (1969). The effects of sitting posture on the volume of the foot, *Ergonomics*, **12**, 753–8.

Poulsen, E. and Jorgensen, K. (1971). Back muscle strength, lifting, and stooped working postures, *Applied Ergonomics*, **2**, 133–7.

Poulton, E. C. (1967). Searching for newspaper headlines printed in capitals or lower-case letters, *Journal of Applied Psychology*, **51**, 417–25.

Poulton, E. C. (1969a). Searching lists of food ingredients printed in different sizes, *Journal of Applied Psychology*, **53**, 55–8.

Poulton, E. C. (1969b). How efficient is print? *New Society*, **5 June**, 869–71.

Poulton, E. C. (1974). *Tracking Skills and Manual Control*. New York: Academic Press.

Poulton, E. C. (1975). Colours for sizes: a recommended ergonomic colour code, *Applied Ergonomics*, **6**, 231–5.

365

Poulton, E. C. (1976). Continuous noise interferes with work by masking auditory feedback and inner speech, *Applied Ergonomics,* 7, 79–84.

Poulton, E. C. (1977). Continous intense noise masks auditory feedback and inner speech. *Psychological Bulletin,* 84, 977–1001.

Poulton, E. C. (1978). Increased vigilance with vertical vibration at 5 Hz: an alerting mechanism, *Applied Ergonomics,* 9, 73–6.

Poulton, E. C. and Brown, C. H. (1968). Rate of comprehension of an existing teleprinter output and of possible alternatives, *Journal of Applied Psychology,* 52, 16–21.

Powell, P. I., Hale, M., Martin, J. and Simon, M. (1971). *2000 Accidents.* London: Nat Inst Ind Psych.

Price, H. E. (1985). The allocation of functions in systems, *Human Factors,* 27, 33–45.

Prince, J. H. (1967). Printing for the visually handicapped, *Journal of Typographic Research,* 1, , 31–47.

Pritchard, D. (1964). Industrial lighting in windowless factories, *Lighting and Lighting Research,* 57, 265.

Radl, G. W. (1980). Experimental investigations for optimal presentation-mode and colours of symbols on the CRT screen. In E. Grandjean and E. Vigliani (eds) *Ergonomic Aspects of Visual Display Terminals.* London: Taylor & Francis.

Rasch, P. J. and Pierson, W. P. (1963). Some relationships of isometric, isotonic strength, and anthropometric measures, *Ergonomics,* 6, 211–15.

Ratz, H. C. and Ritchie, D. K. (1961). Operator performance on a chord keyboard. *Journal of Applied Psychology,* 45, 303–8.

Rayner, K. (1977). Visual attention in reading: eye movements reflect cognitive processes, *Memory and Cognition,* 5, 443–8.

Rayner, K. (1978). Eye movements in reading and information processing, *Psychological Bulletin,* 85, 618–60

Reason, J. (1974). *Man in Motion: The Psychology of Travel.* London: Weidenfeld and Nicolson.

Reason, J. (1974). Absent minds. *New Society,* 4 November, 244–5.

Reason, J. T. (1978). Motion sickness — some theoretical and practical considerations, *Applied Ergonomics,* 9, 163–7.

Reason, J. (1979). Actions not as planned: the price of automization. In G. Underwood (ed.) *Aspects of Consciousness. I Psychological Issues.* London: Academic Press.

Reason, J. T. and Brand, J. J. (1975). *Motion Sickness.* London: Academic Press.

Redgrove, J. (1979). Fitting the job to the woman: a critical review, *Applied Ergonomics,* 10, 215–23.

Rennie, A. M. and Wilson, J. R. (1980). The observation of behaviour at road crossing facilities. In D. J. Oborne and J. A. Levis (eds) *Human Factors in Transport Research, Vol 2.* London: Academic Press.

Rey, R. P. and Meyer, J. J. (1980). Visual impairments and their objective correlates. In E. Grandjean and E. Vigliani (eds) *Ergonomic Aspects of Visual Display Terminals.* London: Taylor & Francis.

Reynolds, D. D. and Angevine, E. N. (1977). Hand-arm vibration, Part II: Vibration transmission characteristics of the hand and arm, *Journal of Sound and Vibration,* 51, 255–65.

Reynolds, D. D. and Soedel, W. S. (1972). Dynamic response of the hand-arm system to a sinusoidal input, *Journal of Sound and Vibration,* 21, 339–53.

Reynolds, L. (1983). The legibility of printed scientific information and technical information. In R. Easterby and H. Zwaga (eds) *Information Design,* Chichester: John Wiley & Sons.

Ridd, J. E. (1985). Spatial restraints and intra-abdominal pressure, *Ergonomics,* 28, 149–66.

Riggs, L. A. (1972). Vision. In J. W. Kling, and L. A. Riggs (eds) *Experimental Psychology.* New York: Methuen.

Ritchie, G. J. and Turner, J. A. (19757. Input devices for interactive graphics,

International Journal of Man-Machine Studies, **7**, 639–60.

Roberts, D. F. (1960). Functional anthropometry of elderly women, *Ergonomics,* **3**, 321–7.

Roberts, D. F. (1975). Population dimensions, their genetic basis and their relevance to practical problems of design. In A. Chapanis (ed.) *Ethnic Variables in Human Factors Engineering.* Baltimore: The Johns Hopkins University Press.

Robinette, K. M. and McConville, J. T. (1981). *An Alternative to Percentile Models.* SAE Technical Paper 810217. Warrendale, PA: Society of Automotive Engineers.

Rodger, A. and Cavanagh, P. (1962). Training occupational psychologists, *Occupational Psychology,* **36**, 82–8.

Roebuck, J. A., Kroemer, K. H. E. and Thompson, W. G. (1975). *Engineering Anthropometry Methods.* New York: John Wiley & Co.

Rogers, J. G. (1963). The effects of target distance and direction on maximum velocity of the rolling ball control, *Human Factors,* **5**, 379–83.

Rohles, F. H. (1967). Environmental psychology. *Psychology Today,* **June**, 54–63.

Rohles, F. H. (1969). Preference for the thermal environment by the elderly, *Human Factors,* **11**, 37–41.

Rolfe, J. M. (1969a). Human factors and the display of height information, *Applied Ergonomics,* **1**, 16–24.

Rolfe, J. M. (1969b). *Some Investigations Into the Effectiveness of Numerical Displays for the Presentation of Dynamic Information.* IAM Technical Report R470.

Rolfe, J. M. and Allnutt, M. F. (1967). Putting the man in the picture, *New Scientist,* **16 February**, 401–6.

Ronnholm, J. (1962). Physiological studies on the optimum rhythm of lifting work. *Ergonomics,* **5**, 51–2.

Rosegger, R. and Rosegger, S. (1960). Health effects of tractor driving, *Journal of Agricultural Engineering Research,* **5**, 241–75.

Ross, S., Katchmar, L. T. and Bell, H. (1955). Multiple-dial check reading: Pointer symmetry compared with uniform alignment, *Journal of Applied Psychology,* **39**, 215–18.

Rowlands, G. F. (1977). *The Transmission of Vertical Vibration to the Heads and Shoulders of Seated Men.* Royal Aircraft Establishment Technical Report TR77068.

Royal Society for the Prevention of Accidents (1977). *Factory Accidents.* London: ROSPA.

Rutenfranz, J. and Colquhoun, W. P. (1979). Circadian rhythms in human performance, *Scandinavian Journal of Work, Environment and Health,* **5**, 167–77.

Ruys, T. (1970). *Windowless Offices.* MA Thesis; University of Washington.

Sanders, M. G., Halcomb, C. G., Fray, J. M. and Owens, J. M. (1976). Internal-external locus of control and performance on a vigilance task, *Perceptual and Motor Skills,* **42**, 939–43.

Saunders, J. E. (1969). The role of the level and diversity of horizontal illumination in an appraisal of a simple office task, *Lighting Research and Technology,* **1**, 37.

Savinar, J. (1975). The effect of ceiling height on personal space, *Man-environment Systems,* **5**, 321–4.

Scales, E. M. and Chapanis, A. (1954). The effect on performance of tilting the toll-operator's keyset, *Journal of Applied Psychology,* **38**, 452–6.

Schiepers, C. W. J. (1980). Response latency and accuracy in visual word recognition, *Perception and Psychophysics,* **27**, 71–81.

Schmidtke, H. (1980). Ergonomic design principles of alphanumeric displays. In E. Grandjean and E. Vigliani (eds) *Ergonomic Aspects of Visual Display Terminals.* London: Taylor & Francis.

Schohan, B., Rawson, H. E. and Soliday, S. M. (1965). Pilot and observer performance in simulated low altitude high speed flight, *Human Factors,* **7**, 257–65.

Seibel, R. (1962). Performance on a five-finger chord keyboard. *Journal of Applied Psychology,* **46**, 165–9.

Seibel, R. (1964). Data entry through chord, parallel entry devices, *Human Factors*, **6**, 189–92.

Sell, R. G. (1977). Ergonomics as applied to crane cabs. In J. S. Weiner and H. G. Maule (eds) *Human Factors in Work, Design and Production*. London: Taylor & Francis.

Seminara, J. L. (1979). A survey of ergonomics in Poland, *Ergonomics*, **22**, 479–505.

Schackel, B. (1962). Ergonomics in the design of a large digital computer console, *Ergonomics*, **5**, 229–41.

Sharp, E. D. and Hornseth, J. P. (1965). *The Effect of Control Location Upon Performance Time for Knob, Toggle Switch and Push Button*. AMRL Technical Report TR–65–41.

Shaw, L. and Sichel, H. S. (1971). *Accident Proneness: Research in the Occurrence, Causation, and Prevention of Road Accidents*. Oxford: Pergamon.

Shibolet, S., Lancaster, M. C. and Danon, Y. (1976). Heat stroke: a review, *Aviation, Space and Environmental Medicine*, **47**, 280–301.

Shinar, D. and Acton, M. B. (1978). Control-display relationships on the four-burner range: population stereotypes versus standards, *Human Factors*, **20**, 13–17.

Shipley, L. J., Gentry, J. and Clarke, J. W. (1980). *VDT vs. Pencil: A Comparison of speed and Accuracy*. Columbia: University of Missouri Department of Journalism.

Shoenberger, R. W. (1970). *Human Performance as a Function of Direction and Frequency of Whole-body Vibration*. Army Medical Research Laboratories Report: AMRL–TR–70–7.

Shoenberger, R. W. (1974). An investigation of human information processing during whole-body vibration, *Aerospace Medicine*, **45**, 143–53.

Shurmer, C. R. (1967). *A Review of the Effects of Low Frequency Vibration on Man and His Tracking Performance*. BAC (Bristol) Guided Weapons Div Report R41A/20/RES/415.

Siegel, A. I. and Brown, F. R. (1958). An experimental study of control console design, *Ergonomics*, **1**, 251–7.

Simon, C. W. and Roscoe, S. N. (1956). *Altimeter Studies Part II. A Comparison of Integrated versus Separated Displays*. Hughes Aircraft Co., Culver City, California. Technical Memo. No 435.

Simon, J. R. (1964). Magnification as a variable in subminiature work, *Journal of Applied Psychology*, **48**, 20–4.

Simon, J. R. and Rudell, A. P. (1967). Auditory S-R compatibility: the effect of an irrelevant cue on information processing, *Journal of Applied Psychology*, **51**, 300–4.

Simons, A. K. and Schmitz, M. A. (1958). *The Effect of Low Frequency, High Amplitude Whole Body Vibration on Human Performance*. Washington DC: Office of the Surgeon General, Research and Development Div.

Sinaiko, H. W. and Brislin, R. W. (1973). Evaluating language translations: experiments on 3 assessment methods, *Journal of Applied Psychology*, **57**, 328–34.

Slobin, D. I. (1966). Grammatical transformations and sentence comprehension in childhood and adulthood, *Journal of Verbal Learning and Verbal Behaviour*, **5**, 219–27.

Sloboda, W. and Smith, E. E. (1968). Disruption effects in human short-term memory: some negative findings, *Perceptual and Motor Skills*, **27**, 575–82.

Smith, G. L. and Adams, S. K. (1971). Magnification and microminiature inspection, *Human Factors*, **13**, 247–54.

Smith, M. J., Cohen, B. G., Stammerjohn, L. W. and Happ, A. (1981). An investigation of health complaints and job stress in video display operations, *Human Factors*, **23**, 387–400.

Smith, M. M. and Marriott, A. M. (1982). Vision and proprioception in simple catching, *Journal of Motor Behaviour*, **14**, 143–52.

Smith, R. L., Westland, R. A. and Crawford, B. M. (1970). The status of maintainability models: a critical review, *Human Factors*, **12**, 271–83.

Smith, S. L. (1978). The limited readability of Lansell numerals, *Human Factors*, **20**, 57–64.

Smith, S. L. (1979). Letter size and legibility, *Human Factors*, **21**, 661–70.

Smith, S. L. and Thomas, D. W. (1964). Colour versus shape coding in information displays, *Journal of Applied Psychology*, **48**, 137–46.

Smith, S. W. and Rea, M. S. (1979). Relationships between office task performance and ratings of feelings and task evaluation under different light sources and levels, *Proceedings of the CIE 19th Session*, Kyoto.

Smith, M. J., Stammerjohn, L. W., Cohen, B. G. F. and Lalich, N. R. (1980). Job stress in video display operations. In E. Grandjean and E. Vigliani (eds) *Ergonomic Aspects of Visual Display Terminals*. London: Taylor & Francis.

Smith, M. J., Cohen, B. G. F., Stammerjohn, L. W. and Happ, A. (1981). An investigation of health complaints and job stress in video display operations, *Human Factors*, **23**, 387–400.

Sommer, H. C. and Harris, C. S. (1970). *Combined Effects of Noise and Vibration on Mental Performance as a Function of Time of Day*. Army Medical Research Laboratories Report: AMRL–TR–70–36.

Sommer, R. (1968). Intimacy ratings in five countries, *International Journal of Man–Machine Studies*, **3**, 109–14.

Sommer, R. (1969). *Personal Space: The Behavioural Basis of Design*. New York: Prentice-Hall Inc.

Sommer, R. (1974). *Tight Spaces: Hard Architecture and How to Humanize It*. New Jersey: Prentice-Hall Inc.

Spencer, J. (1963). Pointers for general purpose indicators, *Ergonomics*, **6**, 35–49.

Spencer, J. (1968). Inspection and human factors. In *Human Factors in the Management of Industrial Inspection*. Paper presented to the Industrial Section of the Ergonomics Research Society and the Institute of Mechanical Engineers.

Spoor, A. (1967). Presbyacusis values in relation to noise-induced hearing loss, *International Audiology*, **6**, 48–57.

Sprent, N., Crawshaw, M. and Bartram, D. (1983). Structuring timetable information, *Ergonomics*, **26**, 505–16.

Stammerjohn, L., Smith, M. J. and Cohen, B. (1981). Evaluation of workstation design factors in VDT operations, *Human Factors*, **23**, 401–12.

Starr, S. J., Thompson, C. R. and Shute, S. J. (1982). Effects of video display terminals on telephone operators, *Human Factors*, **24**, 699–712.

Stephens, S. D. G. (1970). Studies on the uncomfortable loudness level, *Sound*, **4**, 20–3.

Sternberg, S. (1966). High-speed scanning in human memory, *Science*, **153**, 652–4.

Stevens, S. S. (1972). Stability of human performance under intense noise, *Journal of Sound and Vibration*, **21**, 35–56.

Stiles, W. S. (1929). The scattering theory of glare, *Proceedings of the Royal Society (Series B).*, **105**, 131–46.

Stockbridge, H. C. W. and Lee, M. (1973). The psycho-social consequences of aircraft noise, *Applied Ergonomics*, **4**, 44–5.

Stott, J. R. R. (1980). *Mechanical Resonance of the Eyeball*. Paper presented to Human Response to Vibration Meeting, Swansea.

Stoudt, H. W. (1978). *Are People Still Getting Bigger – Who, Where and How Much?* SAE Technical Paper No. 780280. Warrendale, P.A.: Society of Automotive Engineers.

Stoudt, H. W. (1981). The anthropology of the elderly. *Human Factors*, **23**, 29–37.

Stoudt, H. W., Damon, A., McFarland, R. A. and Roberts, J. (1965). *Weight, Height and Selected Body Dimensions of Adults US 1960–1962*. Report No 8; Natonal Center for Health Statistics, Public Health Service Publication No 1000, Washington, DC.

Strandberg, L. (1983). On accident analysis and slip-resistance measurement, *Ergonomics*, **26**, 11–32.

Stubbs, D. A. (1985). Human constraints on manual working capacity: effects of age on intratruncal pressure, *Ergonomics*, **28**, 107–14.

Stubbs, D.A., Buckle, P. W., Hudson, M. P., Rivers, R. M. and Worrington, R. M. (1983). Back pain in the nursing profession: Part I, Epidemiology and pilot methodology, *Ergonomics*, **26**, 755–65.

Suchman, E.A. (1961). A conceptual analysis of the accident phenomenon. *Social Problems*, **8**, 241.

Suchman, E. A. (1965). Cultural and social factors in accident occurrence and control, *Journal of Occupational Medicine*, **7**, 487.

Szlichcinski, K. P. (1977). Symbols and pictograms: a review of their usefulness and the methodology of their design, *Proceedings of the 8th International Symposium on Human Factors in Telecommunications*. Harlow: STL Ltd.

Szlichcinski, K. P. (1977a). Diagrams and illustrations as aids to problem solving, *Instructional Science*, **8**, 253–74.

Szlichcinski, K. P. (1977b). Telling people how things work, *Applied Ergonomics*, **10**, 2–8.

Tanner, J. (1962). *Growth at Adolescence*. Oxford: Blackwell Scientific.

Tanner, J. (1978). *Foetus into Man – Physical Grown from Conception to Maturity*. London: Opus Books.

Taylor, F. V. and Garvey, W. D. (1966). The limitations of a 'Procrustean' approach to the optimisation of man-machine systems, *Ergonomics*, **9**, 187–94.

Taylor, W. (1974). The vibration syndrome: introduction. In Taylor, W. (ed.) *The Vibration Syndrome*. (London: Academic Press).

Teel, K. S. (1971). Is human factors engineering worth the investment? *Human Factors*, **13**, 17–21.

Teichener, W. H. and Kobrick, J. L. (1955). Effects of prolonged exposure to low temperature on visual-motor performance, *Journal of Experimental Psychology*, **49**, 122–6.

Teichner, W. H. and Krebs, M. J. (1974). Visual search for simple targets, *Psychological Bulletin*, **81**, 15–28.

Terrana, T., Merluzzi, F. and Guidici, E. (1980). Electromagnetic radiation emitted by visual display units. In E. Grandjean and E. Vigliani (eds) *Ergonomic Aspects of Visual Display Terminals*. London: Taylor & Francis.

Thomas, J. R. (1978). Noise and memory. In M. M. Gruneberg, P. E. Morris, and R. N. Sykes (eds) *Practical Aspects of Memory*. London: Academic Press.

Thomas, L. F. (1968). Setting subjective and objective standards and making judgements. In *Human Factors in the Management of Industrial Inspection*. Papers presented to the Industrial Section of the Ergonomics Research Society and the Institute of Mechanical Engineering.

Thomas, L. F. and Seaborne, A. E. M. (1961). The socio-technical context of industrial inspection. *Journal of Occupational Psychology*, **35**, 36–43.

Tichauer, E. R. (1978). *The Biomechanical Basis of Ergonomics*. New York: John Wiley.

Tillman, W. A. and Hobbs, G. E. (1949). The accident-prone automobile driver, *American Journal of Psychiatry*, **106**, 321–31.

Timbal, J., Loncle, M. and Boutelier, C. (1976). Mathematical model of man's tolerance to cold using morphological factors, *Aviation, Space and Environmental Medicine*, **47**, 958–64.

Tinker, M. A. (1939). The effect of illumination intensities upon speed of perception and upon fatigue in reading, *Journal of Educational Psychology*, **30**, 561–71.

Tinker, M. A. (1960). Legibility of mathematical tables, *Journal of Applied Psychology*, **44**, 83–7.

Tinker, M. A. (1965a). *Legibility of Print*, Iowa: Iowa State University Press.

Tinker, M. A. (1965b). *Bases for Effective Reading*. Iowa: Iowa State University Press.

Torle, G. (1965). Tracking performance under random acceleration: effects of control dynamics, *Ergonomics*, **8**, 481–6.

Totman, R. G. and Kiff, J. (1979). Life stress and the susceptibility to colds. In D. J. Oborne, M. M. Gruneberg and J. R. Eiser (eds) *Research in Psychology and Medicine Volume I*. London: Academic Press.

Trice, H. M. and Roman, P. M. (1972). *Spirits and Demons at Work: Alcohol and Other*

Drugs on the Job. New York: New York School of Industrial and Labor Relations, Cornell University.

Trotter, M. and Gleser, G. (1951). The effect of aging on stature, *American Journal of Physical Anthropology,* **9,** 311-24.

Usher, D. M. (1982). A Touch Sensitive VDU Compared with a Computer-aided Keypad for Controlling Power Generating Plant. Paper presented to IEE Conference on Man/machine Systems.

Van Nes, F. L. and Bouma, H. (1979). Legibility of Segmented Numerals. Paper presented to 30th Annual Conference of the Ergonomics Society, Oxford.

Van Nes, F. L. and Bouma, H. (1980). On the legibility of segmented numerals, *Human Factors,* **22,** 463-74.

Van Zelst, R. H. (1954). The effects of age and experience upon accident rate, *Journal of Applied Psychology,* **38,** 313-17.

Vartabedian, R. H. (1971). Legibility of symbols on CRT displays, *Applied Ergonomics,* **2,** 130-2.

Vartabedian, A. G. (1973). Developing a graphic set for cathode ray tube display using a 7 × 9 dot pattern, *Applied Ergonomics,* **4,** 11-16.

Verhaegen, P., Vanhalst, B., Derycke, H. and VanHoeke, M. (1976). The value of some psychological theories of industrial accidents, *Journal of Occupational Psychology,* **1,** 39-45.

Vernon, H. M. and Warner, C. G. (1932). The influence of the humidity of the air on capacity for work at high temperatures, *Journal of Hygiene (Cambridge),* **32,** 431.

Vernon, M. D. (1953). Presenting information on diagrams, *Audio-visual Communication Review,* **1,** 147-58.

Vickers, D. (1979). *Decision Processes in Visual Perception.* New York: Academic Press.

Waller, R. A. (1969). Office acoustics — effect of background noise, *Applied Acoustics,* **2,** 121-30.

Waltzman, S. B. and Levitt, H. (1978). Speech interference level as a predictor of face-to-face communication in noise, *Journal of the Acoustical Society of America,* **63,** 581-90.

Ward, J. S. (1984). Women at work — ergonomic considerations, *Ergonomics,* **27,** 475-80.

Ward, J. S. and Bealding, W. (1970). Optimum dimensions for domestic staircases, *Architects Journal,* **152,** 513-20.

Ward, J. S. and Fleming, P. (1964). Changes in body weight and body composition in African mine recruits, *Ergonomics,* **7,** 83-90.

Ward, J. S. and Kirk, N. S. (1967). Anthropometry of elderly women, *Ergonomics,* **10,** 17-24.

Warner, H. D. and Mace, K. C. (1974). Effects of platform fashion shoes on brake response time, *Applied Ergonomics,* **5,** 143-6.

Warrick, M. J. (1947). Direction of movement in the use of control knobs to position visual indicators. In P. M. Fitts (ed.) *Psychological Research on Equipment Design.* US Army Air Force, Aviation Program Research Department Report No 19.

Wason, P. C. (1965). The contexts of plausible denials, *Journal of Verbal Learning and Verbal Behaviour,* **4,** 7-11.

Weale, R. A. (1963). *The Ageing Eye.* London: H. K. Lewis.

Webb, E. J., Campbell, D. T., Schwarz, R. D. and Sechrest, L. (1966). *Unobtrusive Measures: Nonreactive Research in the Social Sciences.* Chicago: Rand McNally.

Webster, J. C. (1973). S. I. L. — past, present and future, *Journal of Sound and Vibration,* **3,** 22-6.

Weiner, E. L. (1975). Individual and group differences in inspection . In C. G. Drury and J. G. Fox (eds) *Human Reliability in Quality Control.* London: Taylor & Francis.

Weinstein, N. D. (1976). Human evaluations of environmental noise. In K. Craik and E. H. Zube (eds) *Perceiving Environmental Quality.* New York: Plenum Press.

Weisz, A. Z., Goddard, C. and Allen, R. W. (1965). *Human Performance under Random and Sinusoidal Vibration.* Aerospace Medical Research Laboratories, Ohio, Report AMRL-TR-65-209.

Welford, A. T. (1976). *Skilled Performance: Perceptual and Motor Skills.* Illinois: Scott, Foresman & Co.

Welford, A. T. (1984). Theory and application in visual displays. In R. Easterby and H. Zwaga (eds) *Information Design.* Chichester: John Wiley & Sons.

Wells, J. and Storey, N. (1980). *Investigations of Vibration-induced Eye Movements Under Whole-body Vibration.* Paper presented to Human Response to Vibration Meeting, Swansea.

Wertheimer, M. (1958). Principles of perceptual organization. In D. C. Beardslee and M. Wertheimer (eds) *Readings in Perception.* Princeton: Van Nostrand.

Wesner, C. E. (1972). Induced arousal and word-recognition learning by mongoloids and normals, *Perceptual and Motor Skills,* **35,** 586.

Wetherall, A. (1981). The efficacy of some auditory-vocal subsidiary tasks as measures of the mental load on male and female drivers, *Ergonomics,* **24,** 197–214.

White, R. M. (1975). Anthropometric measures of selected populations of the world. In A. Chapanis (ed.) *Ethnic Variables in Human Factors Engineering.* Baltimore: The Johns Hopkins University Press.

White, W. J., Warrick, M. J. and Grether, W. F. (1953). Instrument reading II: check reading of instrument groups, *Journal of Applied Psychology,* **37,** 302–7.

Whitfield, D., Ball, R. G. and Bird, J. M. (1983). Some comparisons of on-display and off-display touch input devices for interaction with computer generated displays, *Ergonomics,* **26,** 1033–53.

Whitlock, F. A., Stoll, J. R. and Rekhdahl, R. J. (1977). Crisis, life events and accidents, *Australian and New Zealand Journal of Psychiatry,* **11,** 127–32.

Wickens, C. D., Vidulich, M. and Sandry-Garza, D. (1984). Principles of S-C-R compatibility with spatial and verbal tasks: the role of display-control location and voice interactive display-control interfacing, *Human Factors,* **26,** 533–43.

Wilde, G. J. S. (1985). Assumptions necessary and unnecessary to risk homeostasis, *Ergonomics,* **28,** 1531–8.

Wilkins, A. J. (1978). *Epileptogenic Attributes of TV and VDUs.* Paper presented to Ergonomics Society Conference on Eyestrain and VDUs. Loughborough.

Wilkins, A. J., Darby, C. E. and Binnie, C. D. (1979). On the triggering of photosensitive epilepsy. In D. J. Oborne, M. M. Gruneberg and J. R. Eiser (eds) *Research in Psychology and Medicine, Volume I.* London: Academic Press.

Willis, F. N. (1966). Initial speaking distance as a function of the speaker's relationship, *Psychonomic Science,* **5,** 221–2.

Wilson, A. (1963). *Noise-Final Report.* (London: HMSO)

Wilson, J. R. (1983). Pressures and procedures for the design of safer consumer products, *Applied Ergonomics,* **14,** 109–16.

Wilson, J. R. and Grey, S. M. (1984). Reach requirements and job attitudes at laser-scanner checkout systems, *Ergonomics,* **27,** 1247–66.

Wilmore, J. H. (1975). Inferiority of female athletes: myth or reality? *Journal of Sports Medicine,* **3,** 1–6.

Wing, A. (1965). Upper tolerance limits for unimpaired mental peformance. *Aerospace Medicine,* **36,** 960–4.

Wing, A. (1979). The slowing of handwritten responses made in spaced character formats, *Ergonomics,* **22,** 465–8.

Winsemius, W. (1965). Some ergonomic aspects of safety, *Ergonomics,* **8,** 151–62.

Wohlwill, J. F., Nasar, J. L., De Joy, D. M. and Foruzami, H. H. (1976). Behavioural effects of a noisy environment: Task involvement versus passive exposure. *Journal of Applied Psychology,* **61,** 67–74.

Wojtczak-Jaroszowa, J. and Pawlowska-Skyba, K. (1967) Night and shift work I: Circadian variations in work. *Medycyna Pracy,* **18,** 1

372

Wolcott, J. H., McMeekin, R. R., Burgin, R. E. and Yanowitch, R. E. (1977a). Correlation of occurrence of aircraft accidents with biorhythmic criticality and cycle phase in US Air Force, US Army and civilian aviation pilots, *Aviation, Space and Environmental Medicine,* **48,** 976–83.

Wolcott, J. H., McMeekin, R. R., Burgin, R. E. and Yanowitch, R. E. (1977b). Correlation of general aviation accidents with biorhythm theory, *Human Factors,* **19,** 382–93.

Wolford, G. and Hollingsworth, S. (1974a). Retinal location and string position as important variables in visual information processing, *Perception and Psychophysics,* **16,** 437–42.

Wolford, G. and Hollingsworth, S. (1974b). Lateral masking in visual information processing. *Perception and Psychophysics,* **16,** 315–20.

Wolke, S. and DuCette, J. (1974). Intentional performance and incidental learning as a function of personality and task dimensions, *Journal of Personality and Social Psychology,* **29,** 90–101.

Wright, P. (1977a). Presenting technical information: a survey of research findings, *Instructional Science,* **6,** 93–134.

Wright, P. (1977b). Decision making as a factor in the ease of using numerical tables, *Ergonomics,* **20,** 91–6.

Wright, P. (1978). Feeding the information eaters: suggestions for integrating pure and applied research on language comprehension, *Instructional Science,* **7,** 249–312.

Wright, P. (1980). The comprehension of tabulated information: some similarities between reading prose and reading tables, *National Society for Performance and Instruction Journal,* **19,** 25–9.

Wright, P. (1983). Informed design for forms. In R. Easterby and H. Zwaga (eds) *Information Design.* Chichester: John Wiley & Sons.

Wright, P. and Barnard, P. (1978). Asking multiple questions about several items: the design of matrix structures on application forms, *Applied Ergonomics,* **9,** 7–14.

Wright, P. and Fox, K. (1970). Presenting information in tables, *Applied Ergonomics,* **1,** 234–42.

Wright, P. and Fox, K. (1972). Explicit and implicit tabulation formats, *Ergonomics,* **15,** 175–87.

Wright, P. and Reid, F. (1973). Written information: Some alternatives to prose for expressing the outcomes of complex contingencies. *Journal of Applied Psychology,* **57,** 160–6.

Wrogg, S. G. (1961). The role of emotions in industrial accidents. *Archives of Environmental Health,* **3,** 519.

Wyburn, G. M., Pickford, R. W. and Hirst, R. J. (1964). *Human Senses and Perception.* London: Oliver Boyd.

Wyndham, C. H. (1966). A survey of the causal factors in heat stroke and of their prevention in the gold mining industry, *Journal of the South African Industry of Mining and Metallurgy,* **1,** 245–58.

Wyndham, C. H., Strydom, N. B., Benade, A. J. S. and Van Rensburg, A. J. (1970). Tolerance times of high wet bulb temperatures by acclimatized and unacclimatized men, *Environmental Research,* **3,** 339–52.

Yaglou, C. P. (1947). A method for improving the effective temperature index, *ASHVE Transactions,* **53,** 307–26.

Yarbus, A. L. (1967). *Eye Movements and Vision.* New York: Plenum.

Young, L. R. and Sheena, D. (1975). Survey of eye movement recording techniques, *Behavior Research Methods and Instrumentation,* **7,** 397–429.

Zeff, C. (1965). Comparison of conventional and digital time displays, *Ergonomics,* **8,** 339–45.

Zwaga, H. and Easterby, R. (1983). Developing effective symbols for public information. In R. Easterby and H. Zwaga (eds) *Information Design.* Chichester: John Wiley & Sons.

AUTHOR INDEX

SUBJECT INDEX